# THE DEVELOPMENT OF
# PEIRCE'S PHILOSOPHY

# THE DEVELOPMENT OF
# PEIRCE'S PHILOSOPHY

*By*

MURRAY G. MURPHEY

HARVARD UNIVERSITY PRESS

*Cambridge, Massachusetts*

1961

DISTRIBUTED IN GREAT BRITAIN BY OXFORD UNIVERSITY PRESS, LONDON

PUBLICATION OF THIS VOLUME HAS BEEN AIDED BY A
GRANT FROM THE FORD FOUNDATION

LIBRARY OF CONGRESS CATALOG CARD NUMBER 61–13739

PRINTED IN THE UNITED STATES OF AMERICA

FOR

BRADFORD JAMES MURPHEY

AND

MARGARET GRIFFIN MURPHEY

# *Preface*

THE chief published collection of Peirce's writings is the *Collected Papers of Charles Sanders Peirce*,[1] and in referring to these volumes, I have adopted the method of numerical reference used by all Peirce scholars. Thus, 5.446 means volume 5, paragraph 446 of the *Collected Papers*. References to the bibliography of Peirce's writings in volume 8 of the *Collected Papers* have been given in the form 8.G. 1893, where 8 stands for the volume, G for the general bibliography, and 1893 for the year.

The chief collection of unpublished Peirce manuscripts is in the Houghton Library at Harvard University. In my text I have made extensive use of these manuscripts, and have quoted rather freely from them. In all cases I have preserved Peirce's paragraphing, grammar, and spelling, including the errors, for since most of these manuscripts will probably never be published again I have felt it best to reproduce the virgin text exactly. Four manuscripts have been reproduced in entirety, complete with the original pagination, as an appendix. These manuscripts are early drafts of the paper "On a New List of Categories," and are cited in the text as D1, D2, D3, and D4. Whenever the date of composition of a manuscript is known I have given it. There are, however, many undated manuscripts and, where it was important to my argument to do so, I have endeavored to estimate the time of composition. Where the date cited is my estimate, it is preceded by "c." In citing the Peirce manuscripts I have followed the method of cataloguing used by the Harvard Library. Thus IB2 Box 8 refers to a specific box of those manuscripts in Houghton Library.

To the many people who have generously helped me with my work I owe more than I can say. I am indebted to the Harvard Department of Philosophy for permission to use the Peirce manuscripts in the Harvard libraries, and particularly to Professor Morton G. White, who made it possible for me to see some materials which had hitherto been

---

[1] Vols. 1–6, ed. Charles Hartshorne and Paul Weiss (Cambridge, Mass., 1931–1935), and vols. 7–8, ed. Arthur Burks (Cambridge, Mass., 1958).

restricted. Dr. C. K. Shipton, Mr. K. C. Elkins, Miss Mary Meehan, and Mrs. Trehub of the Harvard University Archives gave me invaluable assistance. To Mr. Homer Halverson of the Johns Hopkins University Library I am indebted for permission to use the Peirce and Gilman papers there, and to Miss Frieda Thies for her assistance in their use. Mr. White of St. John's College, Cambridge, kindly consented to let me use the Sylvester manuscripts and to make copies of some of them. Through the kindness of Victor Lenzen and Professor Max Fisch I was able to consult Peirce's copy of Russell's *Principles of Mathematics*. Professor John Myhill gave me invaluable help on several important technical problems, and Professor John Smith gave me useful advice on several matters. To Professor R. B. Braithwaite of King's College, Cambridge, I am much indebted for his help and advice on several portions of my manuscript. Professor Carolyn Eisele of Hunter College has read part of my work and has given me constant help and encouragement. Mr. Eric Lenneberg and my brother, Dr. Bradford G. Murphey, helped me with translations of German and Greek respectively, and Mr. Jackson I. Cope kindly permitted me to copy some of his transcripts of Peirce letters in the National Archives. To Mrs. Marshall Miner I am indebted for assistance in ways too numerous to mention. Miss Ann Goolsby has read and corrected the entire manuscript, and assisted me with some of the research. To Professor Smbat Abian I am deeply indebted for many corrections and suggestions concerning the mathematical portions of the text. And most of all I am indebted to Professor Rulon Wells, under whose direction this book was first begun as a dissertation, who has patiently suffered through draft after draft, providing always penetrating criticisms and suggestions and indispensable encouragement.

The following acknowledgments of permission to quote are made: Justus Buchler, *Charles Peirce's Empiricism*, Harcourt, Brace and Company and Routledge & Kegan Paul Ltd.; Georg Cantor, *Contributions to the Founding of the Theory of Transfinite Numbers*, Dover Publications, Inc., New York 14, New York; *The Collected Papers of Charles Sanders Peirce*, vols. 1–6, eds. Charles Hartshorne and Paul Weiss, The Belknap Press of Harvard University Press, vols. 7–8, ed. Arthur Burks, Harvard University Press; David Hume, *A Treatise of Human Nature*, Oxford University Press; C. I. Lewis, *A Survey of*

*Symbolic Logic*, University of California Press; Alexander Macfarlane, *Lectures on Ten British Mathematicians of the Nineteenth Century*, 1916, John Wiley & Sons, Inc.; Ralph Barton Perry, *The Thought and Character of William James*, 2 vols., Little, Brown & Company, Ralph Barton Perry estate; Bertrand Russell, *Introduction to Mathematical Philosophy*, The Macmillan Company and George Allen and Unwin Ltd.; *Immanuel Kant's Critique of Pure Reason*, trans. Norman Kemp Smith, Macmillan & Company Ltd. and St Martin's Press, Inc.

M.G.M

# CONTENTS

# Introduction

IT is generally agreed that Charles Sanders Peirce was one of America's greatest philosophers, yet even today there is little agreement as to the nature of his philosophy. I have therefore set myself the task of discovering the underlying principles upon which his work was based and of showing that those principles bring order to the mass of fragmentary manuscripts which remains to us. This undertaking is ambitious, but it is also necessary if a just assessment of Peirce's worth as a philosopher is to be reached.

It is obvious from the character of his writings that Peirce regarded himself as a systematic philosopher,[1] and the first question which must therefore be asked is, what kind of system did he attempt to build? The answer to this question becomes clear very early in Peirce's work.

[1] It is unfortunate that Hartshorne and Weiss should have prefaced Volume II of the *Collected Papers* with the following statement by Peirce: "All that you can find in print of my work on logic are simply scattered out-croppings here and there of a rich vein which remains unpublished. Most of it I suppose has been written down; but no human being could ever put together the fragments. I could not myself do so." This statement, so prominently placed, suggests that Peirce was not systematic and therefore that the attempt to treat him systematically is ill advised. But the passage quoted is not the whole passage, and when it is put back into context its meaning appears in a different light. The complete paragraph is as follows: "But I must tell you that all that you can find in print of my work on logic are simply scattered out-croppings here and there of a rich vein which remains unpublished. Most of it I suppose has been written down; but no human being could ever put together the fragments. I could not myself do so. All I could do would be to make an entirely new presentation and this I could only do in five or six years of hard work devoted to that alone. Since I am now sixty three years old and since all this is matter calculated to make a difference in man's future intellectual development, I can only say that if the *genus homo* is so foolish as not to set me at the task, I shall lean back in my chair and take my ease. I have done a great work wholly without any kind of aid, and now I am willing to undergo the last great effort which must finish me up in order to give men the benefit of that which I have done. But if I am not in a situation to do so but have to earn my living, why that will be infinitely the more comfortable way of completing the number of my days; and if anybody supposes that I shall regret missing the fame that might attach to the name of C. S. Peirce, — a name that won't be mine much longer, — I shall only say that he can indulge that fancy without my taking the trouble to contradict him. I have reached the age when I think of my home as being on the other side rather than on this uninteresting planet." (Lowell Lectures, 1903, Lecture 2, IIa, p. 11, IB1 Box 2.) When it is recalled that this statement occurs in a draft of one of the Lowell Lectures, I think it is obvious that this is an appeal for money, not a considered judgment of his own work.

I

Peirce believed in the architectonic theory of philosophy, and his commitment to this view constitutes his most enduring debt to Kant from whom he derived it. It will be recalled that Kant defined "architectonic" as follows:

By an architectonic I understand the art of constructing systems. As systematic unity is what first raises ordinary knowledge to the rank of science, that is, makes a system out of a mere aggregate of knowledge, architectonic is the doctrine of the scientific in our knowledge, and therefore necessarily forms part of the doctrine of method.

. . . By a system I understand the unity of the manifold modes of knowledge under one idea. This idea is the concept provided by reason — of the form of a whole — in so far as the concept determines a priori not only the scope of its manifold content, but also the positions which the parts occupy relatively to one another. The scientific concept of reason contains, therefore, the end and the form of that whole which is congruent with this requirement. The unity of the end to which all the parts relate and in the idea of which they all stand in relation to one another, makes it possible for us to determine from our knowledge of the other parts whether any part be missing, and to prevent any arbitrary addition, or in respect of its completeness any indeterminateness that does not conform to the limits which are thus determined a priori. The whole is thus an organized unity (articulatio), and not an aggregate (coacervatio). It may grow from within (per intussusceptionem), but not by external addition (per appositionem). It is thus like an animal body, the growth of which is not by the addition of a new member, but by the rendering of each member, without change of proportion, stronger and more effective for its purposes. [A832f B860f][2]

Moreover, Kant held that the basis of the architectonic structure was to be found in formal logic. Peirce adopted from his master both this concept of system and this view of the role of logic in that system, and his entire philosophic development must be seen as governed by these beliefs.

Because he believed in the architectonic theory, Peirce was always a system builder, and in each stage of his career he had in mind a definite concept of an over-all philosophic system. In general, his method was first to formulate his position as systematically and completely as possible, and then, having found certain difficulties in it, to solve these

---

[2] In referring to the *Critique of Pure Reason*, I will employ the method of numerical reference usual among Kant scholars. Thus A832 B860 means page 832 of the first edition and page 860 of the second. All references are to *Immanuel Kant's Critique of Pure Reason*, trans. Norman Kemp Smith (London, 1956).

difficulties piecemeal. During the time he was occupied with these specific problems, he paid little attention to the remainder of the system, returning to it only when the specific difficulties had been eliminated. He would then revise the whole system to incorporate his new results. Thus the fact that Peirce worked on different problems at different times does not mean that he had made a radical shift in position: it rather indicates that the chief problems confronting the system were different at different times.

But it also follows from this interpretation that since logic is the basis of the architectonic order, the creative or dynamic agent in the development of Peirce's philosophy should have been his logic. And it further follows that each major discovery in logic should have led to a major reformulation of his philosophy. This is in fact the case. Peirce's philosophy went through four major phases. The first extended from the earliest of his papers which we have, dated 1857, until 1865 or 1866, and was very much a Kantian phase based on Kantian logic. The second began with the discovery of the irreducibility of the three syllogistic figures in 1866 and extended until 1869 or 1870. The third was inaugurated by the discovery of the logic of relations and continued until 1884. And the last stemmed from the discovery of quantification and of set theory and continued until his death.

It is essential to recognize, however, that Peirce himself did not regard these different phases as constituting distinct systems: rather he regarded them as different revisions of a single over-all architectonic system. As a result, in each revision Peirce preserves as much of the preceding system as possible, only altering those doctrines which conflict with the conclusions he drew from the new logical discoveries or which proved unsatisfactory on other grounds. In particular, Peirce preserves the terminology and over-all formal outline, even in cases where the content of the doctrines has been radically changed. What Peirce meant by the terms "First," "Second," and "Third" in the early 1860's has little or nothing in common with their meaning in 1890, but Peirce never states explicitly that he has altered their meaning. Thus Peirce's philosophy is like a house which is being continually rebuilt from within. Peirce works now in one wing, now in another, yet the house stands throughout, and in fact the order of the work depends upon the house itself since modification of one part necessitates the modification of another. And although entire rooms are altered, walls moved, doors cut or blocked, yet from the outside the appearance is ever the same.

If my interpretation of Peirce's method of doing philosophy is correct, there are several consequences which ought to follow. In the first place, most of the flagrant contradictions with which Peirce's philosophy is supposed to abound should turn out to be the results of combining passages belonging to different phases of his development. And where this is not the case and the contradictions are real, it should be possible to show why they exist — that is, to trace them to basic problems which it is reasonable to believe Peirce could not solve. I cannot claim to have been wholly successful in my attempts to do this, but I think I have at least clarified some of these difficulties. Secondly, the order in which Peirce worked ought to be fairly predictable. Given his system at a particular time, it should be possible to say what changes will be required by a given innovation in logic, or by a new solution to a problem, and to show that his writings follow the order so determined. This I believe is generally the case. Thirdly, the creative factors in Peirce's development should be logical — i.e., the major philosophic changes should follow and be based upon logical discoveries. I wish to make it very clear exactly what I mean by this statement. I do not believe that either logic or mathematics "requires" the adoption of any particular philosophic position. So far as I can see these disciplines are philosophically neutral, and any number of alternative philosophical interpretations of a given logical or mathematical doctrine are possible. But Peirce thought otherwise: like Kant, he believed that logic "requires" a specific philosophic position. This belief was for him a premiss upon which he acted. It does not follow that Peirce was right, or that the revisions which he made in his philosophy following a new logical discovery were actually required by that discovery; but it does follow that he believed they were so required, and from that belief, together with a knowledge of his system, it is, I believe, possible to see what changes he thought had to be made.

The book which follows is divided into four parts. Part One covers Peirce's work from the beginning through the "New List." Part Two covers the period from 1867 to 1884. Part Three breaks the chronological development: it is concerned solely with his work in mathematics and particularly in geometry and set theory. Since most of this work falls within the period after 1885, I have not thought it necessary to treat the development of his technical work chronologically. The final part covers the period from 1885 to Peirce's death. I have not attempted in this book to treat Peirce's biography in any detail, but since some knowledge of his activities is relevant to my study I have given brief biographical introductions to the first, second, and fourth parts. So summary a treatment of so important an aspect of my topic would scarcely be justifiable were it not for the fact that we shall soon have a definitive biography of Peirce from the hand of Max Fisch, and the reader is referred to that work for all further biographical information.

PART ONE

# I

# *The Early Years*

CHARLES SANDERS PEIRCE was born September 10, 1839, in Cambridge, Massachusetts, the second son of Benjamin and Sarah Hunt Mills Peirce. The household of which he became a part was one of those peculiar products of Puritan stock, Harvard, and China tea which helped to make Boston the cultural center of nineteenth-century America. By 1839 the Puritanism had faded into Unitarianism and the riches of the East had passed into other hands, but Harvard, family connections, and the brilliance of Benjamin Peirce guaranteed the social and academic position of the family.[1] Charles Peirce did not inherit the wealth that smoothed the path of William and Henry James, nor did he inherit the tradition of unmatchable family achievement that so oppressed Henry Adams; yet he was always to see himself as a member of that aristocracy of culture — "the caste of trained 'college men' who were to preside over the arts and the professions"[2] — which was so much a part of the meaning of the Harvard and Cambridge of his day. The influence of his family, and particularly of his gifted father, was deep and lasting — and in a sense, fatal.

Benjamin Peirce was born in Salem, Massachusetts, on April 4, 1809, and was, his biographer Archibald tells us, "of the purest Puritan stock," being descended from one John Pers, a weaver, who had settled at Watertown in 1637. His mother was Lydia Nichols, a sister of a renowned minister — the Reverend Ichabod Nichols — and a mem-

---

[1] The family name is pronounced "Pers" or "Purse." Further biographical information may be found in Paul Weiss, "Charles Sanders Peirce," *Dictionary of American Biography*, vol. XIV (New York: Scribners, 1934); Raymond Clare Archibald, "Benjamin Peirce," *ibid.*; Moses King, *Benjamin Peirce, A Memorial Collection* (Cambridge, Mass., 1881); Robert S. Rantoul, "Memoir of Benjamin Peirce" (Salem, 1881), in *Historical Collections of the Essex Institute*, XVIII, 4f. See also C. S. Peirce, "First Rough Draft of Substance of a Logical Examination of the Christian Creed in Brief Summary," January 23, 1911, p. 5, IB3.

[2] Edmund Wilson, *The Triple Thinkers* (New York, 1948), p. 162.

ber of a family famous in the China trade. His father, also named Benjamin, was for a time engaged in the tea trade and served several years in the Massachusetts legislature, but he failed in business in 1825 or 1826, and from 1826 until his death in 1831 was librarian of Harvard College.

One of young Benjamin's classmates at the Salem Private Grammar School was Henry Bowditch, whose father was Nathaniel Bowditch. Through the son Peirce came to know the father, and the association so begun was apparently the decisive factor which led him to dedicate himself to mathematics. Bowditch was then the most outstanding American mathematician and he became a personal hero to the young man. One of Peirce's earliest mathematical tasks was the correction and revision of Bowditch's translation of Laplace's *Traité de Mécanique Céleste*, and years later Peirce dedicated his own work on analytic mechanics "to the cherished and revered memory of my master in science, Nathaniel Bowditch, the father of American Geometry." [3]

Benjamin Peirce entered Harvard in 1825 and graduated in 1829. For the next two years he taught at George Bancroft's Round Hill School in Northampton. Then in 1831 he returned to Harvard where he was to remain for forty-nine years. By 1833, when he was only twenty-four years old, his ability won him the position of University Professor of Astronomy and Mathematics, and from 1842 until his death in 1880 he was Perkins Professor of Mathematics and Astronomy.

The impression which Benjamin Peirce made upon his contemporaries is well illustrated by a comment of Abbott Lawrence Lowell. "Looking back over the space of fifty years since I entered Harvard College, Benjamin Peirce still impresses me as having the most massive intellect with which I have ever come into close contact, and as being the most profoundly inspiring teacher that I ever had." [4] Of nineteenth-century American scientists, Benjamin Peirce was one of the most eminent. As an astronomer, he won international recognition for his computation of the perturbations of Uranus and of the orbit of Neptune, and for his

[3] Archibald, "Benjamin Peirce," p. 394.

[4] Raymond Clare Archibald, *Benjamin Peirce, 1809–1880. Biographical Sketch and Bibliography* (Oberlin, 1925), p. 4.

work in celestial mechanics.[5] In mathematics, he was unrivaled in his own time.[6] Although his greatest work — his *Linear Associative Algebra* — was not published until 1870, his reputation was so great by 1849 that when in that year Congress established the *American Nautical Almanac*, its head office was placed at Cambridge, where it could benefit by the technical knowledge of experts, "especially of Professor Benjamin Peirce, who was recognized as the leading mathematician of America."[7] Peirce was the second American — Bowditch having been the first — to be elected to the Royal Society of London, and by the time of his death he had been elected to half a dozen of the leading European learned societies.

The influence which Benjamin Peirce exerted upon American science was profound and extended far beyond the classroom. He was one of the founders of the Harvard Observatory, and as professor of astronomy exerted great influence over its development. Through his connections with the *Nautical Almanac,* his close friendship with Alexander Dallas Bache, Superintendent of the United States Coast and Geodetic Survey, and his brother-in-law, Admiral Charles Henry Davis,[8] Peirce was able to play an important part in the scientific activities of the government. From 1852 to 1867 he was director of longitude determinations for the Coast Survey, and in 1867 he succeeded Bache as superintendent — a post which he held until 1874. Peirce was also president of the American Association for the Advancement of Science, one of the organizers of the Smithsonian Institution, one of the fifty incorporators of the National Academy of Sciences, and the chairman of the mathematics and physics class of the Academy, associate editor of the *American Journal of Mathematics*, and a leading member of the Scientific Lazzaroni — a private society which included many of the leaders of American science and which played an important part in the history of government science. His position was thus a commanding one in almost every field of physical science in America.

Benjamin Peirce's greatest influence however was as a scholar and

[5] Sven Peterson, "Benjamin Peirce: Mathematician and Philosopher," *Journal of the History of Ideas,* XVI, 92 (January 1955) and Dirk Struik, *A Concise History of Mathematics* (New York, 1948), p. 266.

[6] Peterson, p. 89.

[7] Simon Newcomb, quoted by Archibald, "Benjamin Peirce," p. 395.

[8] A. Hunter Dupree, *Science in the Federal Government* (Cambridge, Mass., 1957), p. 107.

teacher. His early mathematical work dealt chiefly with geometry and with analysis, particularly as applied to questions of mechanics. When Hamilton's quaternion theory appeared in 1853, its close connection with these topics recommended it strongly to Peirce, and it became almost at once his favorite subject. The *Linear Associative Algebra*, to which Peirce devoted his later years and which was his most impressive achievement, was a direct extension of the ideas introduced by Hamilton. More than any one else, Peirce was responsible for the vogue which quaternions enjoyed in America,[9] and he thus prepared the way for rule of algebraic invariants which was to be inaugurated at Johns Hopkins in the 1880's.

As a teacher Peirce was exceptional among his contemporaries in two important respects. First, he kept abreast of the latest mathematical work in Europe, particularly in England, and used this material as the basis of much of his teaching. Second, he encouraged his students to do original research work, and as one historian has remarked, "Mathematical research in American Universities began with Benjamin Peirce." [10] Among his students were Simon Newcomb, Thomas Craig, Charles William Eliot, A. Lawrence Lowell, Asaph Hall, G. W. Hill, Chauncey Wright, and many others who were to play an important part in the history of American science.[11]

Benjamin Peirce's position in the world of science, together with his personal charm and warmth, made his home in Cambridge a meeting place for scientists from all parts of the country, and from abroad as well. Charles Peirce has left the following description of the house in Quincy Street:

My father was universally acknowledged to be by far the strongest mathematician in the country, and was a man of great intellect and weight of character. All the leading men of science, particularly astronomers and physicists, resorted to our house; so that I was brought up in an atmosphere of science. But my father was a broad man and we were intimate with literary people too. William Story the sculptor, Longfellow, James Lowell, Charles Norton,

[9] Eric Temple Bell, *Men of Mathematics* (New York, 1937), p. 354.
[10] Archibald, *Benjamin Peirce, 1809–1880*, p. 8.
[11] Thomas Craig to Daniel Coit Gilman, March 23, 1876, Gilman Papers, the Johns Hopkins University Library. Newcomb became a famous astronomer. Craig became an outstanding mathematician and was one of the men who got his start on the Coast Survey. Eliot and Lowell became presidents of Harvard. Hall made his name at the Harvard Observatory and Hill and Wright with the *Nautical Almanac*.

Wendell Holmes, and occasionally Emerson, are among the figures of my earliest memories . . . The Quincy's we also knew very well, but not the Adams's . . . Bancroft had been very intimate with my mother's family, as in his old age he was a great friend of my wife here. I used occasionally to see him; and Lothrop Motley was one of our friends. . . . Among the lawyers I remember Rufus Choate, Judge Story, etc. Another figure of my childhood was Emerson's friend Margaret Fuller (Countess d'Oesoli).[12]

To the list could be added many more, including Webster, James Freeman Clarke, W. H. Channing, J. J. Sylvester, C. A. Bartol, and especially Louis Agassiz, who was probably Benjamin Peirce's closest friend. The Peirce children thus grew up in an atmosphere which was at once scientific and cultured — in the best Boston sense. Their father "alone of the Cambridge professors was consulted in advance concerning (the Concord School of Philosophy); and perhaps he was the only one among them who could have foreseen, as he did, its mission and its probable success, or who would have lent his name and voice to the undertaking." [13] His wide interest in philosophy and in the religious implications of science influenced all his children.

Because Charles Peirce idolized his father and was greatly influenced by his father's beliefs, it is important to know something of what those beliefs were. The elder Peirce was a deeply religious man of the Unitarian school. He regarded nature as the exemplar of the wisdom of the "Divine Geometer," and science as a means to the understanding of that wisdom. "There is but one God, and science is the knowledge of Him." [14] In his early years, Peirce was strongly opposed to the theory of evolution in any form, but he was too good a scientist to ignore the evidence. Thus in 1851 he wrote to Dana that despite his early opposition to the nebular hypothesis "I am free to admit that the farther I extend my researches into the physical universe, the stronger appears to me the evidence that the process of creation was conducted by the divine Geometer in a modified form of that very hypothesis, which was contrived by a shallow and wicked philosophy for the direct purpose of excluding the Deity from his own works." [15] The contradic-

[12] *Charles S. Peirce's Letters to Lady Welby*, ed. Irwin Lieb (New Haven, 1953), p. 37.
[13] King, *Benjamin Peirce*, p. 27.
[14] *Ibid.*, p. 20.
[15] Benjamin Peirce to James D. Dana, 1851, Scientific Correspondence of James D. Dana, Yale University Library.

tion between evolution and Scripture was thus raised for Peirce well before the advent of Darwin. Although at first he refused to compromise the authority of the Bible, by 1853 he had adopted the strategy later used by many others — that of granting science and the Bible equal authority in separate areas. "We acknowledge . . . that science has no authority to interfere with the Scriptures and perplex the Holy Writ with forced and impossible constructions of language. This admission does not derogate from the dignity of science; and we claim that the sanctity of the Bible is equally undisturbed by the denial that it was endowed with authority over the truths of physical science." [16] When the Darwinian theory appeared in 1859, therefore, Peirce had already made his peace with evolution, and he was prepared to accept the general doctrine.

As one might expect, Peirce's theory of the evolution of the material universe was modeled upon the nebular hypothesis. He posited a primal chaos with a perfectly homogeneous distribution of matter and energy. The exertion of any force by the Creator would then be sufficient to upset the equilibrium of forces and begin the process of nebular evolution from which star and earth must result. The entire theory lies wholly within the Newtonian framework and assumes that the evolutionary process is governed by mechanical laws from the beginning. In this sense, it is actually very similar to the Spencerian theory.

But where Peirce differed from Spencer and the materialists was in his denial that mind could be reduced to matter. In contradiction to them, he asserts a radical dualism: mind and matter are fundamentally different in kind. Mind or spirit he held to be indestructible, not only in general, but in its individuality as well. Each soul must therefore continue after death in some other form. Peirce carried the doctrine of evolution so far as to suggest that spirits too evolve to higher and higher orders, and that the individual soul may in some after life — perhaps on a different planet or in a different solar system — attain to powers far beyond its present ones.

The assertion of such a dualism left Peirce with the problem of explaining how mind and matter can be related. His solution was to assert a pre-established harmony — a solution which presumably was meant to leave the mind independent of mechanical causation while guaran-

[16] Peterson, "Benjamin Peirce," p. 99.

teeing the correspondence between its ideas and reality. Thus Peirce believed that every theorem of mathematics is realized somewhere in nature, and that all nature is but the realization of our mathematical ideas.

The discovery of the true structure of reality through science was therefore more than a possibility: it was a religious duty. Since the harmony of mind and matter was preordained, all investigators, given adequate time, must come to the same conclusion. "The conclusion in every department of science is essentially the same. Whatever may have been the play of fancy, or the delusion of superstition, or the allurement of profit, at the outset, the end has ever been a congregation of facts, organized under law, and disciplined by geometry." [17] Thus knowledge also evolves: from the facts collected by observation, generalizations are derived, which then must be tested and corrected against further facts. But eventually this process must lead us to one determinate truth, and this truth is a copy of an order implanted by the "Divine Geometer."

Charles Peirce followed his father in many things, but he did not become a Unitarian. Looking back in later years, he wrote:

I abominate the unitarians myself, because all through my boyhood I heard in our unitarian family nothing but angry squabbles between Calvinists and Unitarians, and though the latter were less absurd than the former, I thought their church was based on mere denial and when I grew up I joined the Episcopal church, without believing anything but the general essence and spirit of it. *That* I did and do profoundly believe . . .[18]

Nevertheless, in his early years, Charles Peirce did adopt many of his father's views concerning religion and the relation between religion and science. Speaking before the Cambridge High School Association in 1863, he thus described the religious functions of science:

When the conclusion of our age comes, and skepticism and materialism have done their perfect work, we shall have a far greater faith than ever before. For then man will see God's wisdom and mercy, not only in every event of his own life, but in that of the gorilla, the lion, the fish, the polyp, the tree, the crystal, the grain of dust, the atom. He will see that each one of these has an inward existence of its own, for which God loves it, and that He

[17] *Ibid.*, p. 105.
[18] C. S. Peirce to Smith, July 25, 1908, Scientific Correspondence.

has given to it a nature of endless perfectibility. He will see the folly of saying that nature was created for his use. He will see that God has no other creation than his children. So the poet in our days — and the true poet is the true prophet — personifies everything, not rhetorically, but in his own feeling. He tells us that he feels an affinity for nature, and loves the stone or the drop of water. But the time is coming when there shall be no more poetry, for that which was poetically divined shall be scientifically known. It is true that the progress of science may die away, but then its essence will have been extracted. This cessation itself will give us time to see that cosmos, that esthetic view of science which Humboldt prematurely conceived. Physics will have made us familiar with the body of all things, and the unity of the body of all; natural history will have shown us the soul of all things in their infinite and amiable idiosyncrasies. Philosophy will have taught us that it is this *all* which constitutes the church. Ah! what a heavenly harmony will be that when all the sciences, one as viol, another as flute, another as trumpet, shall peal forth in that majestic symphony of which the noble organ of astronomy forever sounds the theme.[19]

One sees here the same belief that nature is a symbol of spiritual truth which inspired Louis Agassiz's "Essay on Classification," and the same conviction that the practice of science is the study of a divine text to which his father, and the scientists of his father's generation, were so devoted. This religious spirit was always present in Peirce's work, whether overtly expressed or not, and was an important factor in determining the nature of his philosophy.

Although Charles was five years younger than his brother James, he seems to have been his father's favorite almost from birth. He was evidently a most precocious child, learning to read and write without the usual instruction, and showing from the first an intense interest in puzzles, mathematical card tricks, codes, and chess problems. At the age of eight, he records, he "began to be most seriously and hopelessly in love. Sought to drown my care by taking up the subject of Chemistry — an antidote which long experience enables me to recommend as Sovereign." [20] By the time he was twelve he had set up his own laboratory and was experimenting with Liebig bottles and quantitative analysis. Concerning the following year, Peirce later recalled: "It was when

[19] "The Place of Our Age in the History of Civilization," Oration Delivered before the Cambridge High School Association, November 12, 1863, in *Values in a Universe of Chance*, ed. P. Wiener (New York, 1958), pp. 13f. © 1958 by Philip P. Wiener; reprinted by permission of Doubleday and Company, Inc.
[20] Thomas A. Goudge, *The Thought of C. S. Peirce* (Toronto, 1950), p. 348.

my brother, James Mills Peirce, was entering his Junior year in College, which would be in the autumn of 1852, when I was just thirteen years old, that I remember entering his room, picking up Whateley's 'Logic,' and asking him, " 'What is Logic?' " [21] Peirce tells us that he threw himself on the rug and read the book straight through.

Benjamin Peirce supervised the education of his children personally, and particularly that of Charles. To teach the boy concentration, "they would play rapid games of double dummy together, from ten in the evening until sunrise, the father sharply criticizing every error." [22] Particular pains were taken to make the boys proficient in mathematics, and they were required to work out theorems from examples. But like the elder James, the elder Peirce did not neglect the sensuous side of their educations, and the children were later to show considerable breadth in their tastes. James Peirce was secretary of the Harvard Shelley Society,[23] and Charles prided himself on his ability at sensuous discrimination, even going to the extent of paying a sommelier to make him a connoisseur of wines.

Despite the strictness of the intellectual discipline to which Charles was subjected, he seems to have received no discipline at all in other respects. As his wife later remarked, "All his life from boyhood it seems as though everything had conspired to spoil him with indulgence." [24] And Peirce himself admitted that "I was brought up with far too loose a rein . . . " [25] As a schoolboy he played hookey successfully, and unsuccessfully, and managed to be expelled from the Cambridge High School on several occasions. Nevertheless, he did graduate in 1854, and after a brief course at E. S. Dixwell's preparatory school, he entered Harvard in 1855.

Peirce's college career was notable chiefly for its utter lack of distinction. He followed the prescribed courses closely, studied mathematics under his father, and brother James, who was already teaching mathematics there. He took the minimum of religious instruction —

[21] "First Introduction," 1911, p. 1, IB2 Box 11.

[22] Weiss, "Peirce," p. 399.

[23] James Mills Peirce to T. R. Lounsbury, January 26, 1888, Lounsbury Papers, Sterling Memorial Library, Yale University.

[24] Melusina Fay Peirce to Captain Patterson, December 15, 1875, Private Correspondence 1874–1877, Records of the United States Coast and Geodetic Survey, National Archives, Washington, D.C.

[25] *Letters to Lady Welby*, p. 37.

one term in his first year — and as much philosophy and science as he could. The philosophy was chiefly Scotch common sense, particularly Reid and Jouffroy, which he studied under Walker and Bowen. (5.111) The only logic course he took was on Mill's *Logic* and Thompson's *Laws of Thought* and was taught by Bowen. He graduated seventy-first in a class of ninety-one for the four years, and ranked seventy-ninth in his last year.

But while Peirce's college career was not distinguished, it was apparently because he would not allow his course work to interfere with his education. His mathematical ability was becoming increasingly apparent and was encouraged by his father. "About that time, [Charles and his father] began to have frequent discussions together, in which, pacing up and down the room, they would deal with problems in mathematics beyond even the purview of the elder brother, himself destined to become a mathematician" and already an instructor at the college.[26] Furthermore, in 1855 — the year in which he entered college — Charles had read Schiller's *Aesthetische Briefe* and had begun his intensive study of Kant's *Critique of Pure Reason*. The interest in philosophy deepened into a passion, and Peirce became a "devotee of Kant, at least as regards the Transcendental Analytic . . . . " (4.2) Such views did not make him sympathetic to the Scotch realism of his courses, and his lack of academic distinction is probably due in part to this fact.

Peirce graduated from Harvard in 1859 at the age of twenty. The following year was spent surveying in Louisiana,[27] presumably on business connected with the Coast Survey. He returned from Louisiana in 1860 and the following year he became a paid assistant of the Survey — a position which he held until 1891. Since the Survey was a government agency, his position protected him from military service.[28]

In 1860 Peirce entered the Lawrence Scientific School at Harvard as a student in chemistry. His abilities now began to show themselves in his work. He took an M.A. degree in 1862, and in 1863 he became the

[26] Weiss, "Peirce," p. 399.
[27] Philip Wiener, *Evolution and the Founders of Pragmatism* (Cambridge, Mass., 1949), p. 71.
[28] C. S. Peirce to A. D. Bache, August 11, 1862 and A. D. Bache to C. S. Peirce, Letter, August 16, 1862, Civil Assistants G–Z, vol. III, 1862, Records of the United States Coast and Geodetic Survey, National Archives, Washington, D.C.

first man in the history of Harvard to take an Sc.B. degree in chemistry *summa cum laude*. Meanwhile two other events of importance occurred in his life. On October 16, 1862, he married Harriet Melusina Fay — a granddaughter of Bishop John Henry Hopkins. A woman of considerable ability and great insight, she was respected in Cambridge circles and later distinguished herself as a feminist writer and organizer. And at about this time Peirce met a young man named William James [29] who was later to become his closest friend.

For the first six months after his graduation, Peirce studied classification under Louis Agassiz. As a zoologist he was not a success; he later recalled that Agassiz "set me to sorting fossil brachiopods without knowing anything about them, and I understand that my work was preserved at the museum, as a most amazing monument of incapacity, to the high delectation for all who entered as students for many years." [30] During the next four years, Peirce continued as a graduate student and also began to teach. In 1864–65 he lectured at Harvard on the philosophy of science, and in 1866–67 he was given the honor of delivering the Lowell Lectures on "The Logic of Science and Induction."

By 1867, Charles Peirce had established himself as one of Harvard's most promising young men. His father believed him destined for a career as a great mathematician, and Harvard had recognized his talents by the lectureships it had given him. For a young man of twenty-eight, this was indeed an achievement, but in certain respects Peirce was still untried: he had yet to set foot beyond the magic circle of his father's influence. At Harvard and on the Coast Survey, he was still Benjamin Peirce's son. No one ever questioned Charles Peirce's brilliance — he earned his recognition by his own ability: but because he was his father's son he was not held to account as others were. The indulgence was to bear bitter fruit.

[29] Ralph Barton Perry, *The Thought and Character of William James* (Boston, 1935), I, 209–211.

[30] C. S. Peirce, "The Author's Response to the Anticipated Suspicion that he attaches a Superstitious or Fanciful Importance to the Number Three," September 16, 1910, pp. R15f., IB1 Box 2.

# II

# *The First System, 1859–1861*

In 1898 Peirce wrote concerning his early studies in philosophy:

I came to the study of philosophy not for its teaching about God, Freedom, and Immortality, but intensely curious about Cosmology and Psychology. In the early sixties I was a passionate devotee of Kant, at least as regards the Transcendental Analytic in the *Critic of the Pure Reason*. I believed more implicitly in the two tables of the Functions of Judgment and the Categories than if they had been brought down from Sinai. [4.2]

In view of this explicit statement of his debt to Kant, it is well to bear in mind the meanings which Kant gave to the key terms in this passage. In the *Critique* Kant wrote: "These unavoidable problems set by pure reason itself are *god*, *freedom*, and *immortality*. The science which, with all its preparations, is in its final intention directed solely to their solution is metaphysics." (B7) Peirce's declaration of 1898 would therefore seem to be as clear-cut a statement as one could wish of his early indifference toward metaphysics and his preference for less speculative subjects.

A second reading of this passage, however, recalls to mind the fact that the terms "psychology" and "cosmology" also occur in the *Critique* where, together with "theology," they are used as names for the three classes of ideas of reason. (A334 B391) If Peirce believed that these subjects were nonmetaphysical, this belief must have come upon him late in life, for in 1859 he wrote that "Theology, Cosmology, Psychology are eminently metaphysical sciences, but they are not pure metaphysics but applied metaphysics." [1] And accordingly we find that when Peirce set out to systemize his early thought, it was a system of metaphysics which he undertook to build.

---

[1] "Proper Domain of Metaphysics," May 21, 1859, IB2 Box 8.

Peirce formally defined metaphysics both as "the philosophy of primal truths"[2] (Pr. 4) and as the logical "analysis of conceptions." (Pr. 14) Since it is not obvious that these two phrases are synonymous, some clarification is in order, and it will therefore be necessary to examine, first, what is meant by saying that a statement is "primal," second, whether "primal" statements are true, and third, what is meant by a "logical analysis" of such truths. And for these purposes we must look closely at certain aspects of Peirce's theory of knowledge.

One of the most important principles concerning knowledge which Peirce derived from Kant is the doctrine that every cognition involves an inference. The reasoning behind this principle is as follows. In the Kantian theory there is no cognition until the manifold of sense has been reduced to unity. This reduction can only be accomplished by introducing a concept which is not itself a sensuous intuition. Hence every cognition requires some operation upon the manifold to bring it to unity, and "an operation upon data resulting in cognition is an inference." (Pr. 35) This argument Peirce elaborates in his theory of perceptual judgment.

Every judgement consists in referring a predicate to a subject. The predicate is thought, and the subject is only thought-of. The elements of the predicate are experiences or representations of experience. The subject is never experienced but only assumed. Every judgement, therefore, being a reference of the experienced or known to the assumed or unknown, is an explanation of a phenomenon by a hypothesis, and is in fact an inference. Hence there is a major premiss behind every judgement, and the first principles are logically antecedent to all science, which I call *a priori*.[3]

If all cognition involves inference, it becomes important to determine what sort of inference is involved. Peirce's position in these early papers is that all forms of inference, including hypothesis, may be reduced to Barbara. Thus in 1860 he wrote, "It is clear that we can draw no other inference from a thing's being in a class other than what is directly expressed by Barbara namely *that whatever is true of an entire*

---

[2] Untitled manuscript, August 21, 1861, IB2 Box 8. This manuscript consists of an introduction and Book I, entitled "Principles." Reference to this work will be given hereafter as "Pr.," followed by the page number.

[3] "A Treatise of the Major Premises of Natural Science," fragment, c. July 1859, IB2 Box 8.

*class is true of every member of the class* (Aristotle's Dictum); hence all other syllogisms may be reduced to Barbara." [4]

From this position it follows that every cognition is derived from a major and a minor premiss, and the question at once arises, what is the origin of these premisses?

All proveable propositions have for their ancestors a major premiss and a minor premiss, a major premiss and a minor premiss, a major premiss and a minor premiss until we come to their very progenitors which are primal truths. Where do these primal truths come from. Some, perhaps, from experience; but the original major premiss cannot come to us so, for a major premiss distributes the middle term, and must therefore be either universal or negative. Now experience *unreasoned upon* (which has no ancestry) cannot be universal. Neither can it be negative; for instance, the proposition This is not Green cannot be an experience, for it is a thought of Green and that thought Green experience by the very statement, did not give. It is only minor premisses, then, that nature affords us; for all Universal, Negative, Unconditional, and Necessary Truths exist and *have their truth* in the mind. They, being true without proof, can have but one basis and must be independent of nature. [Pr. 15f]

If every cognition is the conclusion of a syllogism in Barbara, some cognition is derived from premisses which are not themselves cognitions, or we have an infinite regress. Hence there is some premiss not itself a cognition, and since Barbara requires a universal premiss, this "primal" statement must be universal. But Kant had demonstrated to Peirce's satisfaction that universal propositions cannot be derived from experience alone. Thus Peirce found himself confronted by the conclusion that there must exist in the mind major premisses not derived from experience without which cognition would be impossible.

Two quite different problems are involved in the theory sketched above — the question of the logical structure of our knowledge, and the question of whether or not our knowledge is true. The argument which Peirce presents above suffices to answer the first but not the second. Indeed, if Peirce's theory of cognition and inference is correct, it is clear that our knowledge forms an axiomatized system such that every idea is either an axiom or is derived from the axioms and theorems by the syllogism in Barbara.

But is this system true? It must be borne in mind that Peirce was

[4] "The Rules of Logic Logically Deduced," June 23, 1860, p. 6, IB2 Box 8.

writing before the modern work upon axiomatic systems and confirmation had fairly begun. He was still wedded to the older view that the verification of such a system depends upon the verification of the premisses. Since he held all inference to be in Barbara, he had not yet recognized induction as an autonomous form of reasoning and therefore had no clear comprehension of the possibility of the inductive confirmation of an axiomatic system.

The problem of truth in this early system thus becomes that of proving that the axioms, or "primal truths," are true. Such "primal truths" are clearly synthetic a priori statements, and the problem confronting Peirce is accordingly the same as that which Kant attempted to solve in the *Critique of Pure Reason*. In view of Peirce's debt to Kant, one would expect him to adopt Kant's proof, but this he did not do. Not only does Peirce reject the Kantian argument but he declares that the truth of the "primal truths" cannot be demonstrated — they must be accepted on faith.

This extraordinary claim would appear to rest upon two rather crucial misinterpretations of Kant. In the first place, Peirce believed that the theory of the transcendental object was Kant's true teaching concerning the object of knowledge and that those passages in the *Critique* which are inconsistent with this theory must be rejected. (5.213) [5] Thus, in the passage quoted above, when Peirce writes that "the subject is never experienced but only assumed" it is clear that he is thinking of the subject as the transcendental object rather than the empirical object. Again, in criticizing Kant's theory of the relation between knower and known, he assumes that our thoughts do refer to the transcendental object.

The common, and as I think, erroneous view of the relation of the Thing known to the Person knowing is as follows: — First, there is the Subject, the *Ego*. The Thing Known, is known by an *affection* of the consciousness, consequently only by its effect. Therefore, a distinction is drawn between (2) the *Neumenon* or thing as it exists — which is entirely unknown (except, according to some philosophies, by reason) and (3) the Object or *thing as thought*. (4) There is the affection of the consciousness or Phenomenon and (5) There is the relation of Causality between the Object and the Phenom-

---

[5] Compare Norman Kemp Smith, *A Commentary to Kant's "Critique of Pure Reason,"* 2nd ed. (New York, 1950), pp. 204ff. This work will be cited hereafter in the text as "KS," followed by the page number.

enon. . . . If the *neumenon* is thought of it is known. If it is not thought of, it has no relation to the consciousness. But it is represented as both totally unknown, yet the *ground* of knowledge.

"Thing as thought" contains mental elements, but the mind does not really affect the things that it knows. Hence the word *object* like neumenon is a mere logical form, incapable of comprehension. I represent the relationship as follows: — (1) There is the soul (2) There is the field of consciousness in which we know the soul (3) There is the thing *thought of* (4) There is the power it exerts on the soul (5) There is the Idea or impression it makes on the soul (6) There is the *thought* or the idea as it appears in consciousness. [Pr. 7f]

To be thought-of, in Peirce's terminology of this period, is to be the object of a representation, and the problem here posed — that if representations apply to the noumenon then we have knowledge of things-in-themselves — is precisely the problem which ultimately led Kant to repudiate the doctrine of the transcendental object. (KS 204ff) But Peirce's solution was just the opposite of Kant's: he identified the empirical object with the transcendental object and thus concluded that noumena are apprehended because they are thought-of.

The second misinterpretation is the result of a confusion over the meaning of the term "a priori." The basis of this confusion is illustrated in the following passage.

If there is any positive science of psychology — that is the science of the mind itself — it must be that the mind is more than a *unit*. It must have parts, and these will be faculties. Each of these faculties will have special functions and these functions will be simple conceptions. We can only know faculties, however, through their functions; accordingly the knowledge of simple conceptions will be the knowledge of the mind itself and the analysis of conceptions will be psychology. Moreover, if the mind has these faculties, every thought will be an action of the faculties by whatever means excited, and there must always be an occasion for such excitation. Hence, in one view all thoughts are *a priori*, in another all are *a posteriori*. This abolishes, *as real*, the distinction upon which all philosophy is based and makes metaphysics the whole of reasoning; and, indeed, it is obvious that the logical examination of truths is the same as the practise of Logic. [Pr. 15]

The psychological theory here expounded is the faculty theory which both Peirce and Kant held. According to this theory, the data of psychology are our concepts and the task of the science is to explain how these concepts are produced. Some of our concepts may be explained as

191.9 P353m
c.1

combinations of other concepts, but obviously this cannot be done for all of them and so some must be regarded as ultimate and simple. In order to explain the production of these ultimate concepts, both Kant and Peirce hypothesize the existence of "faculties" or "powers" of the mind, whose special function it is to produce these concepts. Since the sole justification for the hypothesis that the faculty exists is the necessity of explaining the existence of the concept, what faculties there are depends upon what concepts are simple, and this only can be learned through the logical analysis of concepts. Thus Peirce holds that the analysis of concepts is the whole of psychology, since only by this means are the faculties discoverable. (KS 235ff, 270–284)

The second half of the paragraph is devoted to an attack on the distinction between the a priori and the a posteriori. Peirce's argument here rests upon Kant's ambiguous use of these terms to distinguish, on the one hand, between judgments which are universal and necessary as opposed to those which are particular and contingent, and, on the other, between judgments derived from the nature of our faculties and those derived from experience. (KS xxxiiiff) The former is a logical, the latter a psychological, distinction. In the above passage, Peirce is using "a priori" and "a posteriori" solely in the psychological sense. Thus he argues that since concepts cannot be given in sensation, all are derived from the nature of the mind and so all are a priori; but since concepts are only known as they appear actualized in experience, all are equally a posteriori. The distinction between a priori and a posteriori is thus made to coincide with that between actualized and unactualized innate ideas: "Each element of thought is a motion of the mind. Therefore each of thought is Innate. It is innate in its possibility. It is true in its actuality." (Pr. 46)

Kant's ambiguous use of these terms is partially justified by the equivalence which holds between the two sets of meanings in his system. Whatever is universal and necessary is derived from the nature of the mind, and whatever is derived from the nature of the mind is universal and necessary. In Peirce's system, however, this biconditional fails. Peirce can still show that universal propositions must be derived from the nature of the mind, and, conversely, that propositions derived solely from the nature of the mind must be universal. But it is one of the most serious consequences of retaining the doctrine of the transcendental object that the necessity of such propositions cannot be demonstrated. For although these propositions would remain true of our phenomenal experience, they need not be true of things-in-themselves and it is truth to things-in-themselves which the theory of the transcendental object requires.

Interpreted from this noncritical perspective, Kant's aim in the *Critique* must appear as the attempt to demonstrate that Innate Ideas are true to things-in-themselves, and his method as purely psychological. That Peirce did so interpret Kant seems clear from his characterization of the critical philosophy as "Psychological Transcendentalism" which he describes as follows:

. . . there are two elements of belief; the *mental* and the *real* element; and we can *know* nothing until we can say what validity for truth the mental element has. There is no possible way of answering such a demand from *external* studies; consequently we must study the action of consciousness in order to solve the problem *quid juris*: If it cannot be solved in this way, then it is insoluable and we cannot attain cognition. This is Kant's idea. [Pr. 29f]

But here the argument becomes circular, for if the validity of all knowledge rests upon the results of a particular study of consciousness, on what does the validity of the latter rest? "Psychological transcendentalism says that the results of metaphysics are worthless, unless the study of consciousness produces a warrant for the authority of consciousness. But the authority of consciousness must be valid within the consciousness or else no science, not even psychological transcendentalism, is valid; for every science supposes that and depends upon it for validity." (Pr. 31)

If even Kant's method of proving the validity of "primal truths" was inadequate, Peirce concluded that the search for a proof was hopeless.

The different faculties have different realms by which they are distinguished. No faculty is to be trusted out of its own realm. Therefore no faculty can derive any support from another but each must stand upon its own credibility. No one faculty has more inherent credibility than another. Therefore partial skepticism is inconsistent. Total skepticism condemns itself. Therefore faith is the only consistent course.

. . . Faith is not peculiar to or more needed in one province of thought than in another. For every premiss we require faith and no where else is there any room for it.

This is overlooked by Kant and others who drew a distinction between *knowledge* and *faith*. [Pr. 38f]

The acceptance or rejection of ultimate premisses therefore cannot be justified upon purely rational grounds; it rests wholly upon an act of faith.

The problem of the truth status of primal statements constitutes one of the rocks upon which Peirce's early system went to pieces. Within the system there would appear to be no way in which it can be solved. Peirce's doctrines of cognition and inference lead to the conclusion that knowledge must form an axiomatized system, some of the axioms of which are universal. Are these axioms true or not? If not, then our knowledge is false. If true, then how is their truth to be proven? Had Peirce adopted Kant's phenomenalism he could have used the Kantian proof of synthetic a priori judgments, but since he thought that the method of the *Critique* was circular, he was forced to reject it. Peirce was therefore left with no means of establishing his premisses except by an appeal to faith, and even at the age of twenty-two he could hardly have been entirely happy with such a solution.

Peirce's denial of the critical position both widens and narrows the scope of metaphysics; on the one hand, it affirms that we do deal with things-in-themselves, but on the other hand, by making inquiry into the truth of the premisses impossible, it limits metaphysics to the logical analysis of concepts. Logic, therefore, must serve as the key to ontology. Actually, what Peirce meant by "logic" at this period included what he later called "semiotic" and it is principally from the analysis of signs that his early ontology is derived. Thus the distinction which he called "The Key-stone of this System" [6] is between the potentially thought and the potentially thought-of — between that which is capable of being a sign and that which is capable of being the object of a sign. The consequences of this distinction are traced in the following delightfully lucid passage.

*Proposition.* All unthought is thought-of.
Proof. We can sometimes think of the unthinkable as thought; we have, for instance, a conception of the conception Infinity, though we cannot attain that conception.

To think of a thing is to think in such a way that our conception has a

[6] July 1, 1860, fragment, IB2 Box 8.

2 7

relation to that thing. . . any unthought which is not thought of as thought, is by the relation of complete negation, negatively thought of as unthought.
Cor. I. Only the phenomena can be thought of as thought, the things in themselves are thought of as unthought.
Cor. II. All *neumena* (things-in-themselves) are unconditioned because they cannot even be thought of as thought.
Cor. III. All thought is thereby thought of, for it would not be in our consciousness unless we were conscious of it. Hence, all things in heaven and earth are thought of, however small our experience may be.
Cor. IV. Whatever is unthought is apprehended, for as I showed before all falsehood is partial truth.[7]

Whatever is thought-of can be normally thought of. Normal thought is true. Therefore all the unconditioned is apprehended and may be so without error. To formulate it: Whatever is unintelligible is true. [Pr. 47f]

Since this cryptic passage involves some of Peirce's most basic ideas, a rather detailed analysis of it is necessary, and first of all we must clarify the meaning of the terms "thought" and "thought-of." A "thought" means for Peirce something realized in consciousness at one time. Thus he remarks, "A quality I can think. A thing I can think of," [8] and again, "All that we are conscious is conditioned. All that we are conscious *of* is unconditioned." [9] Bearing in mind the sense given "conditioned" and "unconditioned" above, it is clear that the grammatical incorrectness of the first sentence expresses the philosophically important point that the conditioned is actually in the consciousness. Thoughts therefore are concrete mental entities — states of consciousness — having a definite temporal and spatial location.[10]

Peirce's theory of the object of a representation was derived from Kant's theory of the transcendental object.

---

[7] "Whatever claims to be a representation (a portrait for example) is a representation. Truth is that which, claiming to be a representation, is a representation. Therefore Truth has no absolute antithesis. Falsehood also claims to be a representation. It is an imperfect *copy* of truth." (Pr. 42)

[8] Untitled fragment, c. June 1859, IB2 Box 8.

[9] "Comparison of our Knowledge of God and of other Substances," July 25, 1859, IB2 Box 8.

[10] The precise origin of this concept of the thought is uncertain, but it is probably derived from a combination of two Kantian ideas: first, the notion that "any and every cognitive state" (KS 81) has a representative function, and second the belief that our concepts are a species of natural phenomena capable of objective empirical study (KS 279ff). These two ideas seem to have led to the conclusion that the concept is identical with the mental entity which has the representative function, and hence that all concepts are images or mental entities of some sort.

All representations have, as representations, their object, and can themselves in turn become objects of other representations. Appearances are the sole objects which can be given to us immediately, and that in them which relates immediately to the object is called intuition. But these appearances are not things in themselves; they are only representations, which in turn have their object — an object which cannot itself be intuited by us . . . [A108f]

There are accordingly two sorts of entities which can be objects of representation. First, all thoughts may themselves be thought of and hence may be objects. Second, that which "cannot itself be intuited by us" — the transcendental object or thing-in-itself — may be such an object. In the first case Peirce speaks of that which is "thought of as thought"; in the latter, of that which is "thought of as unthought" — i.e., as nonmental.

When a thing is thought of, it is thought of through its properties, but these properties are not discriminated from the thing. In order that we should become aware of our thoughts themselves, an act of abstraction is required. But, according to Peirce, the process of abstraction may be carried a step further.

A thought is not a thing. Several things may have some quality in common. That is a thought. All the consciousnesses which contain this thought also have the thought of which they are only expressions. Thought therefore is not personal. But pure form.
Thing
Feeling
Pure Form [11]

Such a pure form is an abstraction. "An abstraction, however, is no longer a modification of consciousness at all, for it has no longer the accident of belonging to a special time, to a special person, and to a special subject of thought . . . . Nobody can think pure abstraction on account of the necessity of doing it at a particular time, etc." [12] Since abstractions are eternal and are not localized in space, it is obvious that no abstraction can be fully realized in human consciousness. What is actually in consciousness may be an instance of an abstraction but it cannot be the abstraction itself. As Peirce remarks,

[11] "On Classification," n.d., fragment, p. 1, IB2 Box 8. This paper seems to be an alternative draft of a section of the "Principles" and was therefore probably written in the summer of 1861.

[12] "Analysis of Creation," c. 1861, fragment, pp. 1f, IB2 Box 8.

"The *necessity* for instance which I think today or tomorrow is not the same thing as that immutable, impersonal necessity which I am thinking *of*." [13] How then can we have knowledge of abstractions?

Peirce here found himself in something of a dilemma. Having identified thought with the content of consciousness at a particular moment, he could not identify the abstraction with the thought. Yet his only other recourse is to hold that abstractions are not in consciousness, and this raised the problem as to how we can know them. Peirce's answer is that it is not necessary for us to conceive something in order to be able to define it and reason about it. For example, we cannot conceive a four-sided triangle, yet we can reason about it and show that it is absurd. Why then can we not analyze an abstract conception such as infinity? He says:

If we can think of a good man, it is because in the first place we have a notion of *man* and in the second place we have the conception *good* and in the third place we can form the synthesis of these two. This synthesis I express by saying [that] an influxual dependency of good and man is conceived of. Influxual dependency is of three kinds: — 1st, Negative as when we say the *man is not good*. 2nd, Limited as when we say *he is good*, third infinite when we give the conception good in all its extent to *man*. Infinity, then, is only to be predicated of qualities, and only of qualities conceived to be possessed. We can therefore analyze the conception of infinity — we can state its relations to other conceptions although the conception itself we never have. . . .

Pseudo-conceptions or conceptions that we cannot think are of two kinds. The first is where the conceptions into which we analyze the pseudo-conception in definition refuse to be combined and are contradictory. And I will in another place give a *formal* proof that such conceptions represent no thing and are not had.

The second case is where the elementary conceptions do not refuse to be combined, but where our power of synthesizing is inadequate and the combination never can be completed.[14]

This passage is based upon that all-pervading axiom of the Kantian approach, that cognition involves the bringing of the manifold to unity. This principle is so interpreted as to mean that it would be a psychological impossibility for the mind to entertain a self-contradictory idea, since such an idea would have to be one whose "elements" could not be brought to unity and therefore there could be no cognition of such a

[13] *Ibid.*, p. 1.
[14] "Why We Can Reason on the Infinite," October 25, 1859, IB2 Box 8.

thing. The second form of pseudo-idea, however, involves no contradiction; it merely requires an act of synthesis beyond the powers of our faculties. But if the synthesis is not completed then the idea is not in consciousness; how then can we be said to know it? "When a thing influences the soul, its effect comes into the field of consciousness or it does not. In the former case we call the modification of consciousness a true thought; in the latter we may call the effect of the influence an unconscious idea." [15] It is therefore possible for the mind to entertain ideas which cannot come to consciousness. Since all thought is thought-of, we must be able to think of these unconscious ideas, but we need not be able to think them.

Now the obvious difficulty with such a theory is that if we cannot conceive the idea, how is it possible to know whether or not it is true? Peirce argues as follows:

. . . we call a judgement untrue when from its contradicting some other judgement, we conclude [that] in the framing of it, our faculties did not act in the normal way. Now to whatever is thought-of there is a normal way of thinking-of; and that normal way gives a true thought of the thing; and that is an apprehension of the thing. And so even when the normal way of thinking of a thing gives an unintelligible result, it is either because it can't be thought of or because we have an unconscious idea of it; In the first case we have no thought of it by Corollary III it does not exist and therefore hence we have a true thought of it. In the latter case, the unconscious idea accords with the definition of a true representation.[16]

To say that the "normal way of thinking" yields true statements is to say that we accept on faith the results of thinking, which, as we saw above, Peirce had already done. The presumption is therefore that every statement is true unless it contradicts another statement. In particular, therefore, meaningless assertions are true so long as they contradict no other assertions, and hence "whatever is unintelligible is true" — if it contradicts nothing else.

Peirce's analysis of conceptions yields three classes of entities — the thing, the thought, and the abstraction. And furthermore, Peirce holds that this enumeration of what there is, is complete. For since all thought can be thought-of and all unthought can be thought of, and the

[15] "That Infinity is an Unconscious Idea," October 25, 1859, fragment, IB2 Box 8.

[16] "Elucidation of the Essay headed 'All Unthought is Thought-of,'" June 30, 1860, IB2 Box 8.

thought and the unthought exhaust the universe, it follows that whatever is, is thought-of. Thus early had Peirce formulated the principle that there is no incognizable.

The doctrine of the three universes of entities is one of the most persistent of all Peircean ideas. Although he later made many changes in the details, the basic idea goes back at least to 1857, when he first began to use the personal pronouns I, Thou, and It to designate the abstract world, the mental world, and the sense world respectively.[17] By 1861, they had become full-fledged ontological categories, and in the conclusion of the "Principles" Peirce elaborated them as follows.

*Idealism.* The only possible definition of the person (self) is that which one thinks of when he closes his senses and excludes all thought but simple consciousness. That is, it is the thought-of, when the only thought-of is the thought. By Cor. III nothing external to the self exists.
*Materialism.* Matter is substance whose existence is not subject to mental conditions. By Cor. II Nothing but matter exists and the soul is matter.
*Realistic Pantheism.* From Idealism, it follows that nothing exists which is not of-thinkable as thought. From Materialism, it follows that nothing but the unthought exists. That which being unthinkable is of-thinkable as thought is Perfection. In Chapter III of the Introduction, it was shown that Perfection is God.[18] Hence, nothing exists but God.
Here then we have three worlds Matter, Mind, God, mutually excluding and including each other . . . [Pr. 48][19]

Although Peirce denied that the question of the ultimate truth of the axioms of knowledge can be answered, this did not preclude some attempt to explain how the three universes are related. The last paragraph of the "Principles" affirms: "Given three worlds completely unrelated except in identity of substance. Everything which springs up freely in one of these, the Mind, does so from the very nature and substance thereof. Verity is unity of substance.[20] It is clear that these data answer the question, How Innate Notions can be True to External Fact. The connection between mind and matter is thus a pre-established Harmony." (Pr. 48) This statement reaffirms Peirce's faith that the

---

[17] "The Synonyms of the English Language classed according to their meaning on a definite and stated philosophy," October 13, 1857, IB2 Box 8.

[18] This chapter either was not written or the manuscript has not survived.

[19] Thus Peirce wrote of himself: — "List of Horrid Things I am: Realist, Materialist, Transcendentalist, Idealist." Quoted in Weiner, *Evolution*, p. 73.

[20] "An invariable connection in the nature of things is unity of substance." (Pr. 43)

three universes are so related as to yield true knowledge, but it tells us nothing about the nature of this relation itself. If, as Peirce affirms, there are synthetic a priori propositions, then even though their truth must be accepted on faith, the problem of explaining their origin and nature still remains. Hence the famous question, how are synthetic a priori judgments possible, was as crucial for Peirce as it was for Kant.

Peirce has told us that "I was a passionate devotee of Kant, at least as regarded the Transcendental Analytic in the *Critic of the Pure Reason.* I believed more implicitly in the two tables of the Functions of Judgment and the Categories than if they had been brought down from Sinai." (4.2) The latter sentence indicates that it was the metaphysical deduction of the categories which he found most interesting and in view of his interpretation of Kant's position this is hardly surprising. The metaphysical deduction is concerned with the discovery of the categories whereas the transcendental deduction is concerned with proving the necessity of their existence and involves Kant's phenomenalism in its most pronounced form. Since Peirce did not accept Kant's phenomenalistic position it is not surprising that arguments based chiefly upon it had little influence upon him.

The basic argument of the metaphysical deduction is too well known to need description here, but there are several points concerning its interpretation which require some comment. Among these is that of the precise meanings which ought to be given to the terms "analytic" and "synthetic" in this context. Kant speaks of the unity achieved by combining concepts into a proposition as "analytical" unity, which he contrasts with the "synthetic" unity of the manifold. The text is as follows: "The same understanding, through the same operations by which in concepts, by means of analytical unity, it produced the logical form of a judgment, also introduces a transcendental content into its representations, by means of the synthetic unity of the manifold in intuition in general." (A79 B105) Kant would seem to be distinguishing here between the kind of unity which is achieved by uniting concepts into a judgment and that which is achieved in uniting the manifold. In the first case, he would seem to mean that since class concepts express common properties of things, they serve to unite the objects to which they refer and hence to impose a kind of unity. Yet class concepts are found by abstraction, which is a form of analysis, and so the unity achieved in uniting them into a judgment is an "analytical" unity only.[21] But since "as regards *content* no concepts can first arise by way of analysis" (A77 B103), every judgment must be preceded by a synthesis by which the manifold is combined into an object containing the properties that are to be abstracted. It is to make possible this synthesis in intuition that the categories are required, for a category is *"a pure concept of the necessary synthetic unity which is present in every object of experience."* (P. 258)

Peirce tells us that he honored Kant's categories as if they were the Ten Commandments: no sooner had he learned of them than he set about their revision. "Now Kant points out certain relations between the categories. I detected others; but these others, if they had any orderly relation to a system of conceptions, at all, belonged to a larger system than that of Kant's list." (4.2) The relations which seem to have struck him first are evident in the table of categories itself — namely, the fact that the twelve categories fall so neatly into four classes of three each. Actually, since the headings of the four classes are the more general conceptions, they can be regarded as constituting the categories, of which the Kantian categories are subcategories. This idea Peirce first developed in 1859.

Quantity, Quality, Relation, and Modality are not very good names for the Categories. They should express four conceptions which have each three stages, but they do rather express the stage of the Conception. Quality is a good name. But Quantity is the stage of perfection of Thing. I will therefor give them new names, and lest these should be objected to I will invent symbols to express them.

| Nullity [*crossed out*] | Simplicity I will represent by ○ |
| Positivity | . |
| Perfection | ⊙ |

Thing Quality Dependence Fact I will represent by letters which shall not stand for any particular names, nor interfere with logical letters but which yet shall be easy to remember viz; SPQR

---

[21] H. J. Paton, *Kant's Metaphysic of Experience* (New York, 1951), I, 288. (This work will hereafter be cited in the text as "P" followed by the page number.) See, however, KS 179ff. Kemp Smith's interpretation presupposes a knowledge of the chronology of composition and hence was not available to Peirce.

Then these will be compounded thus

| Unity | OS = 1 | Negation | OP | Dependence of Effect | ⊙Q | Possibility | OR |
|-------|--------|----------|-----|----------------------|-----|-------------|-----|
| Plurality | ·S = n | Affirmation | .P | Dependence of Community | OQ | Necessity | .R |
| Totality | ⊙S | Infinity ⊙P = ∞ | | Dependence of Accident | .Q | Actuality | OR |

Those persons who consider the letters SPQR as fanciful and foolish, can pretend they stand for Subjectum, Predicatum, Quo, and Realitas.[22]

It should be noted first of all that this system involves a rather drastic reordering of Kant's table.[23] Only the category of quantity is unchanged. The categories of quality have been replaced by the corresponding forms of judgment with "negation" and "affirmation" interchanged. (A70 B95) The order of the categories of relation has been precisely reversed. The categories of modality have been altered both in substance and order: "existence" has been eliminated and "actuality" introduced instead; "contingency," "non-existence," and "impossibility" have been eliminated, and "necessity" has been moved to the second place in the list. Actually, the latter change was soon reversed and the usual order of the three is possibility, actuality, necessity.[24]

These changes in the actual list of categories and the introduction of the concept of stages clearly mark a break with Kant's own theory. Where did Peirce get the idea of the stages, and what did he hope to accomplish by its introduction? Several sources appear to be involved here, one of which is the following passage in the *Critique*:

. . . in view of the fact that all *a priori* division of concepts must be by dichotomy, it is significant that in each class the number of the categories is always the same, namely, three. Further, it may be observed that the third category in each class always arises from the combination of the second category with the first. . . . It must not be supposed, however, that the third category is therefore merely a derivative, and not a primary, concept of the pure understanding. For the combination of the first and second concepts, in order that the third may be produced, requires a special act of the understanding, which is not identical with that which is exercised in the case of the first and the second. [B110f]

[22] "New Names and Symbols for Kant's Categories," May 21, 1859, IB2 Box 8.
[23] The original table (A80 B106) is as follows:

| *Quantity* | *Quality* | *Relation* | *Modality* |
|------------|-----------|------------|------------|
| Unity | Reality | Of Inherence and Subsistence | Possibility: Impossibility |
| Plurality | Negation | Of Causality and Dependence | Existence: Non-Existence |
| Totality | Limitation | Of Community | Necessity: Contingency |

[24] In all writings after May 22, 1859, necessity is regarded as the third category.

This passage clearly suggests the idea of the stages and the mode of compounding them which Peirce used, and is probably the source of this much of his theory. But the reordering of the categories, and the specific assignment of particular concepts to each stage, remain to be explained. And this problem involves the question of the origin of Peirce's three categories.

We have seen above that the analysis of conceptions — which Peirce calls "metaphysics" — yields three classes of entities: the I, the Thou, and the It. We also saw that Peirce regarded theology, psychology, and cosmology as branches of metaphysics, and that he was particularly interested in the latter two.[25] Kant describes his three transcendental sciences as follows: "The thinking subject is the object of *psychology*, the sum-total of all appearances (the world) is the object of *cosmology*, and the thing which contains the highest condition of the possibility of all that can be thought (the being of all beings) the object of *theology*." (A334 B391) The objects so described are clearly very similar to, if not identical with, mind, matter, and God: and indeed, unless we are to regard Peirce's statement concerning his early interests as completely false, there is no alternative but to regard the I, It, and Thou as the Peircean equivalents of Kant's classes of transcendental ideas. There is nothing else in the early system which can be equated with these classes.

The hypothesis that Peirce derived his categories from Kant's classes of transcendental ideas receives support from a variety of further evidence — some direct and some quite indirect. Of the latter variety is the matter of the date at which Peirce first formulated his theory. The ontological use of the three pronouns is to be found in the earliest philosophic paper of Peirce's that I have seen — dated October 13, 1857.[26] Peirce was then but eighteen years old and a junior in college. The only philosopher he is known to have studied by that time is Kant,[27] and if the three worlds derive from Kant, it is very hard to see how they could have come from any other source than the transcendental ideas.

[25] See above, pp. 20, 32.   [26] "Synonyms."

[27] Peirce began the study of Kant in 1855. See Goudge, *The Thought of C. S. Peirce*, p. 349. His first college course in philosophy was not begun until the fall of 1858. See *Harvard Catalogue*, 1855–56, pp. 28, 31; 1856–57, pp. 28f; 1857–58, pp. 29f; 1858–59, pp. 30f. The only other philosopher he is known to have read at this time is Schiller, and he had read only the *Aesthetische Briefe*.

The question of the date of origin of the theory is at most indirect evidence for the hypothesis; there is however more direct evidence. Peirce trichotomizes the table of categories by assigning one category from each class to each stage. Exactly the same method is employed by Kant in the Dialectic where the table of categories is trichotomized by the transcendental sciences. Thus the thinking subject is one, simple, substance, and related to possible objects (A344 B402); the world is plural, infinite, caused, and existent. (A415 B443) The categorical pattern is dropped when Kant reaches God, but if it were carried through we would have totality, reality, community, and necessity correlated with the divine: in fact this is virtually asserted in A571–583, B599–611. (KS 440) Thus there is a striking analogy between Kant's method of relating the categories and the transcendental sciences and Peirce's method of relating the categories and the stages.

But the analogy can be made even stronger. For Peirce's stages are correlated with the I, the It, and the Thou, and it is this correlation which explains his reordering of the categories in Kant's table. The perfect is, of course, God (Pr. 48); the positive is the Thou or mind; and the null or simple is the It or sense. It will be recalled that the I is the world of abstraction — actually, it is correlated with God only in the sense that the abstraction is regarded as an idea in the divine mind. It will also be recalled that among the predicates of abstractions which differentiate them from thoughts is their freedom from time; viewed from a temporal point of view they are infinite. Things out of us, on the other hand, are "negatively thought-of" — hence "negation" ought to apply to the It. And similarly, what we can think we have a "positive conception" of, hence "affirmation" belongs to the Thou. Roughly the same argument can be applied to quantity: totality since it can be infinite must be perfect.[28] This being granted, the plural would have to be the positive and the one the simple or null. The category of relation receives its order from the fact that Peirce regards "influx," or the inherence of a quality, as being a relation independent of time and space, and hence perfect.[29] The ordering of causality and community is, I think, quite arbitrary, but

---

[28] See the discussion of infinity below, pp. 42ff.
[29] "Derivation not in time is the relation of accident to substance." (Pr. 44)

since causality asserts a stronger dependence than community Peirce makes it the second stage. The ordering of the modalities reveals an interesting equivocation as to whether actuality or necessity is the perfect. In the earliest papers Peirce held that actuality could not be positive "since it does not admit of more or less." [30] Later, however, he made necessity the perfect and actuality the positive. It thus appears that in trichotomizing the tables of categories Peirce is relating those concepts to his ontological categories of mind, matter, and God. The analogy to Kant's method is so close that it amounts to identity.

Finally, and yet stronger, there is the evidence afforded by Peirce's treatment of the Dialectic. Although Peirce was a close student of Kant, he rejected both the Aesthetic and the Dialectic and called himself a "devotee" of the Analytic only. (4.2) In terms of what has already been said of Peirce's interpretation of Kant this is not surprising, for both the Aesthetic and the Dialectic are devoted to proving the ideality of appearances. Indeed, Kant spells out this fact in the Prolegomena in no uncertain terms.

Now he has the freedom to choose one of these eight propositions (the theses and the antitheses of the Antinomies) at his pleasure, to accept it without proof . . . and then attack my proof of the contrary. If I can still rescue this proposition and show in this way that according to principles which every dogmatic metaphysics must necessarily recognize, the contrary of the proposition he has adopted can be proved equally clearly, then it is established that there is a hereditary fault in metaphysics which cannot be explained, much less removed, except by ascending to its birthplace, pure reason itself.[31]

As Martin points out, "The full development of the antinomies in the Transcendental Dialectic makes it completely impossible to hold the old conception of mathematical and scientific truth as an insight into the divine plan of the world." [32] Since we already have excellent reason to believe that Peirce did hold just this view of truth,[32a] it is obvious that the argument of the Dialectic would not be congenial to him.

[30] "Of the Stages of the Category of Modality or Chance," May 22, 1859, p. 3, IB2 Box 8.
[31] Quoted in Gottfried Martin, *Kant's Metaphysics and Theory of Science,* trans. P. G. Lucas (Manchester, 1955), p. 56.
[32] *Ibid.,* p. 62.
[32a] See above, p. 16.

In a paper entitled "That There is No Need of Transcendental-ism," [33] written on May 21, 1859, Peirce attacked Kant's argument.

There can be no need of a Transcendental Philosophy if right reason does not lead to contradictions of *a priori* principles.

For the principle of the syllogism itself we must assume to be right in all cases since it is that which we use and the only thing we can use in refuting any use of reason.

Therefore the premisses must be false. That is to say the observation is false. Not the facts themselves for facts have no truth or falsity but only judgements. Therefore the observing power or that by which the mind modifies the fact the *a priori* conception must contain the falsity.

The falsity must be made evident by the transcendentalist to a mind still using the *a priori* conceptions that is they must be made to contradict each other.

A judgement cannot in the right use of reason be false to the phenomenon but only to the noumenon. All *a priori* conceptions are merely phenomena. The premisses cannot be false to those. The conclusion cannot be false to those if we can believe anything whatever on any grounds whatever.

Therefore there is no need of a deduction of conceptions.

What Peirce is asserting here is that a priori principles can result in contradiction only if our logic is incorrect or our premises false. Since our logic must be regarded as correct it follows that the premises are false. But what is meant by "premiss" here? Peirce cannot mean the eight propositions of the antinomies, which obviously are contradictory; he must therefore mean either some four of these eight, or the synthetic a priori judgments of the understanding. If he means the latter, then he must also hold that there is no real distinction between reason and understanding, and moreover that the propositions of reason are derived from the categories. This latter assertion could in fact be based upon a literal reading of Kant's architectonic which regards the trichotomizing of the categories by the transcendental sciences as indicating that these sciences arise from the application of those concepts to the objects of the sciences. (A345 B403) That Peirce adopted such an interpretation is implied by his completion of the trichotomic pattern and is confirmed by his handling of infinity, as we shall see below. Moreover, once the critical point of view is abandoned and the distinction between the empirical and transcen-

[33] IB2 Box 8.

dental object is rejected, there is no reason to separate reason and understanding or to regard the one as less trustworthy than the other. It therefore seems clear that we must take "premiss" here as referring to the principles of the understanding.[34]

Recalling now the interpretation which Peirce gave to Kant's critical philosophy in calling it "psychological transcendentalism," the argument would appear to be the following. By the constitution of our minds, we must think in terms of the twelve categories. Therefore anything *as thought* is thought of in terms of the categories and no judgment concerning such a phenomenal object can contradict the principles of the understanding. If our judgments are false, then, they must be false to the unthought object of thought which is not subject to the conditions of thought. But how could such a falsehood be known? "We call a judgement untrue when from its contradicting some other judgement, we conclude [that] in the framing of it, our faculties did not act in the normal way." [35] Such a falsehood then could only be known by contradiction: that is, by our thinking of it in a way other than that which the constitution of our mind permits, and this cannot occur.[36] A deduction — i.e., warrant — for the categories is therefore unnecessary since nothing can contradict them.[37]

Peirce's position in regard to the antinomies is quite consistent with his uncritical realism. Having adopted the position that the relation between mind and matter is a divinely ordained harmony, he could hardly fail to reject the Dialectic. But it also reveals a basic ambiguity in his early thought which was to continue to haunt him for years. Peirce's early thought is antiphenomenalistic in that he rejects Kant's division between the phenomenal object and the *Ding an sich* and holds that we do know things as they really are. To this extent Peirce is a realist. But he also holds that whatever is, is thought-of, so that nothing exists apart from its relation to the mind, and, as the argument above shows, that things must be as our knowledge represents

[34] The fact that Peirce interchanges "principle" and "judgement" in the quoted passage indicates that the particular meaning which Kant gave to "principle" is not involved. (A299–302 B356–359)

[35] Peirce, "Elucidation of the Essay etc."

[36] Obviously the whole argument assumes, what was to be proven, that the principles of the understanding are consistent with each other.

[37] This belief seems to underlie Peirce's almost complete neglect of the transcendental deduction.

them to be, because the constitution of our minds forbids their ever being known to be otherwise. These arguments are phenomenalistic — indeed, idealistic. The appeal to a pre-established harmony is thus unnecessary, for disharmony is impossible, and after 1862 Peirce abandoned the doctrine entirely. The fact that it was invoked at all was probably due more to the influence of his father [38] than to the necessities of his own position.

But the solution of the antinomies is not quite so simple: there still remain the actual contradictions to be dealt with, for if in fact such contradictions exist, Peirce's position cannot stand. There are two early papers dealing explicitly with this problem, but regrettably neither of them is dated. Both were almost certainly written at the same time [39] and both, I think, were composed before July of 1859 — but this latter assertion is based solely upon inference from their content. The most explicit of these papers is as follows:

4. If there are any two contradictory propositions [which] are both repugnant to reason, 1 reason is impotent as an *a priori* judge of that kind of truth and 2 Contradictions to reason need not disturb a belief in either contradictory proposition.
5. That the Absolute and Infinite exists and that ditto does not exist are contradictory and both repugnant to reason.
    Therefore human reason is impotent as an *a priori* judge of truth concerning the Absolute and Infinite.
6. No clash with reason need disturb a man's belief either in the Existence or Non-Existence of the Absolute and Infinite.
7. The Absolute and Infinite is the Fundamental attribute of God . . .
8. = 6.
    Therefore 1. Human reason is impotent as an *a priori* judge of truth concerning God or is impotent in Theology.
    2. Reasoning should not disturb either a Theists or Atheists belief.[40]

This passage is of interest for several reasons. First, the only propositions which Peirce regards as leading to difficulties are those regarding the infinite and the absolute. These include both some of the antinomies

[38] See above, pp. 14f.
[39] Both essays contain marginal page references which match in such a way that they must refer to the same book. What book this was I do not know — it was apparently not the *Critique*. The presence of these references strongly suggests that these essays were written in immediate response to reading the book and therefore they were written at the same time.
[40] Untitled fragment, n.d., IB2 Box 8.

and the ideal of reason. The antinomies which do not involve these two notions — e.g., the third — are passed over in silence. It would appear then that Peirce regarded the contradictions of reason as the results of reasoning about God and his attributes — not as inevitable consequences of an hereditary fault in reason itself. This point of view is more compatible with Peirce's basically romantic view than is Kant's. Furthermore, it denies to philosophy not all three transcendental sciences but theology only. This prohibition against the mixing of matters religious and matters philosophic Peirce explicitly adopted in the "Principles" (Pr. 12f) and affirmed ever after. In later years he found added reasons for wishing to enforce such a separation, but the original division came from Kant.

The virtues of this argument for Peirce were not unmixed. On the one hand, it is clear that Peirce was concerned to protect his religion against the encroachments of positivism. In an essay on positivism written at about this time, Peirce assailed the positivistic position as "fatal to religion" and argued that "it is possible . . . for scientific men to occupy another position equally advantageous in reference to scientific research and not so destructive of religious faith." [41] For a student at Lawrence Scientific School who believed that "we awake to reflection and find ourselves theists," [42] the Kantian divorce between theology and philosophy had advantages which the years of furious controversy over the religious implications of evolution would only serve to augment. Nevertheless, Peirce's formulation raised some pressing problems in regard to the way in which the limits of human knowledge were to be defined. Unless Peirce is to admit an incognizable reality, it becomes essential to show that in some sense we do have knowledge of God; and unless he is to qualify his rejection of transcendentalism, that knowledge must not be contradictory.

The four categories which Peirce correlated with the perfect were totality, infinity, inherence, and necessity. Peirce chose infinity as typical of these [43] and by July of 1859 was wrestling with the problem

---

[41] "Essay on Positivism," c. 1860, p.o. IB2 Box 8.

[42] *Ibid.*, p. 13.

[43] "The Infinite, The Type of the Perfect," July 3, 1860, IB2 Box 8. The choice of infinity as typical was apparently made at least a year earlier but the explicit statement that it was so being used did not come until 1860.

of how the infinite can be known. On the twenty-fifth of that month
Peirce produced the first version of "all unthought is thought-of,"
which he concluded with the remark: *"Ergo,* All the Unconditioned
is apprehended, or Whatever is normally unintelligible is true. Accordingly, no proof is needed of the existence of *infinite* space, which is an
incomprehensible truth." [44] The latter sentence, of course, refers directly to the first antinomy. On October 23 he was still baffled: "I
have shown 1859 July 25 that all things are apprehended by us; still
we are not conscious of the infinite. To solve this paradox." [45] Two
days later, he propounded the concept of the two kinds of pseudo-
ideas.

What can be discussed? We can syllogise on whatever we can define. We can
define many things of which we cannot conceive. What we define is never a
thing but an idea or a pseudo-idea. Now we can define ideas which we cannot
think; thus a four sided triangle is a defined pseudo-idea, and we can reason
upon it and show that it is an absurdity. . . .
    Pseudo-conceptions or conceptions that we cannot think are of two kinds.
The first is where the conceptions into which we analyze the pseudo-conception
in definition refuse to be combined and are contradictory. . . .
    The second case is where the elementary conceptions do not refuse to be
combined, but where our power of synthesizing is inadequate and the combination never can be completed. Such are the four grand ideas
    Unity
    Reality or Infinity
    Substance
    Necessity [46]

The theory of unconscious ideas was thus created by Peirce in part
at least as a response to the problem of the Dialectic, and constitutes
in fact a kind of compromise between his Kantian and his romantic
heritage. On the one hand, we are denied positive knowledge of God;
on the other, God does directly influence our consciousness. We are
able to apprehend God, although we cannot truly know God. So ideal
a solution is accomplished only at a tremendous cost — namely, the
introduction of faith where most philosophies would demand proof —
but this was a solution for which Peirce was prepared to pay dearly.

[44] "All Unthought is Thought-of," IB2 Box 8.
[45] "The Nature of our Knowledge of the Infinite," October 23, 1859, IB2 Box 8.
[46] "Why We Can Reason on the Infinite."

And actually the concept of truth here used is simply an extension of that already employed in discussing the antinomies — the false is the contradictory.

But does this not return us to the point at which we began? For Peirce has now argued that contradiction arises only in regard to the infinite and absolute, and that our ideas of the infinite are true if not contradictory. From this it follows that our knowledge of the infinite is false. To avoid this conclusion Peirce must show that the antinomies can be resolved and that what appear to be contradictions in fact result from the inability of our faculties to complete the synthesis. I have already noted that Peirce does not deal with the problem of freedom and hence gives no solution to the third antinomy. Nor does he deal in these early papers with the second, although in later papers he affirms the antithesis.[47] He does, however, deal directly with the first and fourth antinomies and in such a way as to reject both theses and antitheses. Thus Peirce: "The Necessary Sequence of Cause and effect is inseparable from time, therefore, this began when time began and therefore time also was *created* when the Universe was created. Therefore the whole sequence of Causation in time has the dependence of Creation, which is Influx. Therefore since the Universe has been a-going from everlasting the amount of spiritual Manifestation is *Infinite*. Q.E.D."[48] The position here taken differs fundamentally from the Kantian in its treatment of infinity, for what Peirce is asserting is that the infinite may be treated as a totality. He states:

> In mathematics then the term order, applied to infinity, implies that infinite quantities are not all equally large and that one may even be infinitely larger than another. The reasoning by which these conclusions are reached is as follows.
>
> Since infinite extensive quantities are still extensive quantities, whatever is true of extensive quantities in general is true of those that are infinite. So that . . . since if a and b are extensive quantities and if $b > 0$, $b + a > a$ it follows that since $\infty > 0$ we may make $a = \infty_1$, $b = \infty_2$ and then $\infty_1 + \infty_2 > \infty_2$; but from the nature of infinity (that it is Perfect in degree) $\infty_1 + \infty_2 = \infty_3$. Therefore $\infty_3 > \infty_1$ or all infinity is not equal.[49]

[47] See p. 382.　　　[48] "Proof of the Infinite Nature of the Creator," n.d., IB2 Box 8.
[49] "The Orders of Mathematical Infinity," July 13, 1860, IB2 Box 8. From the point of view of the modern theory of transfinite numbers Peirce's arguments are of course in error.

It is therefore possible for the series of causes to be infinite — i.e., unbounded — yet for there to exist something before this series. This fact is particularly important because it indicates Peirce's complete freedom from the intuitionistic strain in Kant [50] — an indication which is amply borne out in later writings.

Peirce's answer to the fourth antinomy is contained in the quotation just given, and consists in asserting the existence of a necessary being outside the world. The argument rests upon the notion of influx (inherence) as a relation independent of time and space. Creation is the realization of the divine logos; causality is a relation of dependence in time. Hence it is possible to affirm that God created the world but not that He is the first cause since He is not in time. Rather the causal sequence is itself the product of realizing a form in a substance in time. Time — and the causal sequence — are infinite because without limit, yet created by an independent being. While philosophically open to question, this solution is entirely consistent with an orthodox Christian view which regards God as existing free from time and space.

Peirce's rejection of the argument for the ideality of appearances in the Dialectic leads one to expect a similar reaction to the Aesthetic and, as the comments above concerning time and space indicate, one would be right. Instead of regarding these as forms of intuition, Peirce gives them the same status as the categories and relates them to the triadic pattern of the stages. The third stage he uniformly regards as independent of time and space. Since Kant himself used time as the form of inner sense and space as the form of outer sense, Peirce had another triad ready-made. Here, however, there are three very serious difficulties. First, in Kant's theory intuitions can be presented to us which are in time but not in space,[51] but there are no intuitions in space which are not also in time. (A33f B5of) Peirce ought to have correlated space with the It, time with the Thou, and that which is neither time nor space — call it "absoluteness" — with the I. But this would annihilate any sense of sequence among the stages since

---

[50] Kant explicitly denies that infinity forms a total and hence that there can be infinite numbers. (B111) Peirce seems never to have held this doctrine.

[51] Compare, however, B156. Kant evidently did not hold that time was prior to space and hence Peirce's correlation of time with the first stage is not justifiable on Kantian grounds.

space would precede time. Accordingly, Peirce took the course in these early papers of correlating time with It and space with Thou. The correlation is weak — it is almost obvious that community should correspond to space and causality to time — but the trichotomic pattern had here become a mould into which Peirce was trying to cram everything in an effort to give order to his early ideas.

The second difficulty, however, is far more fundamental. The very possibility of the Kantian philosophy depends upon the fact that intuitions come to us under the forms of time and space, and that this pure manifold can be synthesized a priori. (P. 292) Were it not for this, there would be no way "in which we can account for a *necessary* agreement of experience with the concepts of its objects . . ." (B166) By placing time and space on the same footing as the categories, Peirce leaves himself open to a basic objection, which is tellingly stated by Kant himself.

A middle course may be proposed between the two above mentioned, namely, that the categories are . . . subjective dispositions of thought, implanted in us from the first moment of our existence, and so ordered by our Creator that their employment is in complete harmony with the laws of nature in accordance with which experience proceeds — a kind of *preformation-system* of pure reason . . . there is this decisive objection against the suggested middle course, that the *necessity* of the categories, which belongs to their very conception, would then have to be sacrificed. [B167]

Peirce's system is precisely such a middle course, and, so far as I can see, there is no answer which Peirce can return to Kant's objection. Not only can Peirce not demonstrate the necessity of the categories, his handling of the Aesthetic also means that even mathematical propositions lose their necessary character. Yet strangely enough Peirce does not discuss this objection nor is there any evidence that he saw its force at this time. And this omission is the stranger the more one reflects upon the fact that Kant's argument for the necessity of the categories as conditions of the possibility of experience comes as close as any argument in the *Critique* to being a pragmatic argument.[52] It is clear that Peirce's handling of the Dialectic was based upon a complete understanding of the argument and was the result of a de-

[52] This was pointed out to me by R. S. Wells.

liberate desire to overthrow Kant's conclusion. But in the case of the Aesthetic it seems as if Peirce had somehow failed to grasp the full meaning of the argument. This would appear to be the only explanation of his failure to see the objections to his own position.[53]

Peirce's treatment of the Aesthetic also leads to a further problem. By correlating time and space with two of the three universes and leaving one universe independent of either form, he has created a situation in which no a priori synthesis involving abstraction is possible. Yet it is one of the most pressing problems of his early system to explain how the three universes are combined. "How shall an abstraction or meaning emerge in a modification of consciousness? By the law of the preservation of forms only by being before connected with a thing-or-things. Then it appears in a modification of consciousness by means of abstraction." [54]

Two different problems are here involved: first, how is abstraction combined with sense, and second, how is the thought derived from this combination? Assuming that Peirce's theory here follows the form of the metaphysical deduction it is in the first of these that the categories ought to find application. But without the pure forms of intuition through which to make such application, it is clear that Peirce faces a critical situation.

We have seen above that Peirce has a method of property abstraction which enables him to derive an abstraction from objects.[55] It is one of the most serious difficulties of his early philosophy that he has no inverse to this method, or rather, that what he took to be the inverse is actually something different. Thus Peirce seeks to solve the problem of synthesizing the abstraction and sense by what he calls "expression":

Abstraction, therefore, to become modification of consciousness needs to be combined with that which modification of consciousness as yet unrelated to any abstraction is, that is to the perfectly unthought manifold of sensation. Well, how shall abstraction be combined with manifold of sensation? By

[53] One hypothesis which would help to explain this state of affairs is that Peirce read only the first edition of the *Critique*. But this hypothesis will not stand, for in his own manuscript translation of the early portions of the *Critique*, Peirce explicitly states that he is using both editions. C. S. Peirce, "Translation of the Transcendental Deduction of the Categories as It Appears in the First Edition of the Critic," n.d., IB2 Box 8.

[54] "Of Language," c. 1861, fragment, p. 1, IB2 Box 8.

[55] See above, p. 29.

existing as a form for matter, by *expression*. The first condition of creation is then expression.

I shall formalize the mode by which this conception has been arrived at in order that there may be no doubt regarding the sequence of thought.

*Formula of Thought*. 1. Whence is B. 2. B pure simple perfect is A. 3. A is no longer B. Why? 4. A to become B must be joined to B in its *null* form C. What C is. 5. What is the process by which A is combined with C? It is B 2nd.[56]

From this it is clear that "expression" involves the joining of the perfect to the null to create the positive. But what is meant by "expression" itself? He says:

Even to be conscious of this thought it must be expressed. It must be realized in a substance. It implies a capacity of the substance to receive it. That is the subject must already have certain predicates as conditions to its receiving the given predicate.

Substance
Predicate
Predicable making Predicate
. . . We thus see that the predicate really modifies another predicate.[57]

The difficulty here is that Peirce is confusing two different forms of predication. The first is the relation which holds between an individual and a property, or a member of a class and the class itself, and which is usually called "inherence" or "membership." This relation could connect the abstraction and the thing. The second is the relation which holds between two classes when whatever is a member of one is also a member of the other, or between two properties when the one is predicable of anything of which the other is predicable. This is the relation which Peirce calls "expression," and this relation will not connect the abstraction with the thing. For this second relation can hold only between entities of the same logical type: hence to show that x is an A one must show that x is a B and that whatever is a B is also an A. Thus attribution through "expression" must result in an infinite regress, for to justify the application of any predicate one must first justify the application of some other predicate which implies the first. This is precisely the difficulty upon which Peirce has stumbled above.

[56] "Analysis of Creation," c 1861, fragment, p. 1, IB2 Box 8.
[57] "On Classification," p. 1.

The failure of the early system to resolve these problems is well illustrated by a paper entitled "The Modus of the It." In this paper Peirce is trying to explain how abstraction is combined with sense so as to become thought, and he attempts to describe this synthesis in terms of the categories. But within each category there are three stages, and each category itself must therefore be expressed. But then each category must be implied by a prior one which in turn must find expression, and so on. Thus Peirce:

> There are three Celestial Worlds. 1. that whose heaven is a speck, or the manifold of sense. 2 That whose heaven is of extensive manifestation or the world of consciousness. 3. That whose heaven is of immense manifestation or the world of abstraction.
> Consciousness is the only one of the worlds which is real tangible to us. How shall sense become consciousness? This is not meant as a skeptical question; I ask it of faith.
> The relations of the triad being apprehended, it will be clear that which is in the sensible world can only enter the mental world by having in it a *revelation* which is in the abstract world.[58]

There are however three abstract revelations — arbitrariness, dependence, and absoluteness, of which only dependence is revelation to us "because to the arbitrariness was joined absolute existence." Now there are three kinds of absolute existence — possibility, actuality, and necessity. Again, we know only actuality and this is due to the fact that to possibility was joined "necessary mode." There are three such necessary modes — community, causality, and influx (inherence), and so on through the three influxes (negation, affirmation, infinite), the three infinite qualities (unity, plurality, totality), the three total shapes (elementariness, extension, immensity), the three immense manifestations (time, space, heaven), and finally to the conclusion that "time becomes space by conjunction with a heavenly world. That of consciousness. And this turns the IT to THOU." [59] The fact that the merry-go-round stops at all seems to be due more to a power failure than to logical necessity. In one diagram of 1859, Peirce depicted eight trichotomies arranged in a circle about a center which was labeled "IT." [60]

---

[58] "The Modus of the It," c. 1861, fragment, p. 1, IB2 Box 8.
[59] *Ibid.*, p. 4.
[60] Untitled diagram, June 1, 1859, IB2 Box 8.

The same difficulties which plague the theory of synthetic unity also apply to the theory of analytic unity. The latter doctrine is to be found in several early papers, usually under the title "Analysis of Creation." A fairly typical example is the following.

The abstraction must be expressed. Suppose that condition complied with, how does it pass into consciousness? By the operation of abstracting. This is as follows. From two things which are alike in one respect and different in others we can separate mentally the unlike elements from the like and distinguish each separately. If we consider each compound as an expression, the peculiar meaning, of each will be its peculiarity; the common abstraction will be the condition of the abstraction of the meaning, that is the language. If the object expressed purely, all the abstraction it contained (the expression) would be meaning. Pure expression, therefore, is pure meaning. But this the mind would not notice for the mind notices through resemblance and difference.

Language is an abstraction not capable of realization alone, but combined (in a way of which we shall think directly) with other abstractions gives them realizability. Geometrical figures, letters, conversation, music are such languages. We seem to see their analogies in Vegetables, Animals, Chemical Compounds, Nebular systems etc.[61]

There are several peculiarly interesting features of this passage. In the first place, the process of deriving the concept is clearly modeled on a mixture of definition by genus and differentia and property abstraction. The "meaning" as here defined is the defining property of the product class of all the classes of which the given object is a member. This is the same class which would be yielded by definition by genus and differentia, but it is specified differently — namely, by its own defining property instead of the conjunction of those of the other classes. It is obvious that Peirce is using the terms "language," "expression," and "meaning" in a quite extended sense here, and it seems likely that by the "meaning" of an *object* what he really means is the essence. Certainly the property he obtains is one which would imply every other property of the thing, which is one way of specifying essence. Nature, therefore, must be a language, in which the objects which we experience are really embodiments or expressions of the ideas in the divine mind. Peirce thus agrees with the three famous propositions of Emerson:

[61] C. S. Peirce, "Analysis of Creation," c. 1861, fragment, pp. 2f, IB2 Box 8.

1. Words are signs of natural facts.
2. Particular natural facts are symbols of particular spiritual facts.
3. Nature is the symbol of spirit.[62]

But this position again involves stratification difficulties. Ordinarily the meaning of a term must be of the same logical type as that term, yet the process Peirce describes should yield a property of higher type. For example, his theory would make the meaning of man to be "rational animality" instead of "rational animal." His illustrations show that he is thinking of meaning as the abstraction embodied in the thing, yet his process of embodiment requires that subject and predicate have the same type. In short, the theory seeks to combine entities of different type through relations which hold only among entities of the same type and the result is of course a confusion of significant distinctions.

By the end of 1861 the inadequacy of the first system must have been evident to Peirce, and accordingly in June of 1862 he embarked upon a new tack in his quest for a solution to the problem of the categories. In a paper entitled "The Nature of the Perfect," [63] Peirce sets forth a series of propositions and proofs which runs as follows. The first assertion is that "there are elementary conceptions" and is proved on the argument that a concept is elementary if it is not composed of other concepts. The second proposition is in apparent contradiction to the first: "Every conception is of boundless complication in its own nature." The proof for this — so far as there is one — is that there are only three ways in which thoughts can be compounded; first, by both being thought simultaneously; second, by one being a thought of the other; third, by both being thought through a third. But the first way does not really compound thoughts — both may remain independent. The third way merely combines the first two ways. "Therefore conceptions can only be compounded by one's being a thought of the other." But, he continues, "That the of-thought should be true, it must be dependent upon the thought. It has a relation thereto of secondary to primary. When one thing has a relation to another, that wherein it has the relation must be complex, and the related members must have something in common. Hence two simple

---

[62] Ralph Waldo Emerson, *Nature, Addresses and Lectures* (Boston, 1885), p. 31.
[63] N.d., IB2 Box 8.

thoughts cannot have a relation in their own nature." The remainder of this paper requires quotation:

Proposition. The field of thought is extensive;
Proof. An extensive field is a total which has subjective elements *ad libitum* all of which are perfectly related to the others and any one of which supposes all the others. Such are time and space.
There are elementary conceptions.
Whatever is thought at once is an elementary conception.
Conceptions are infinitely complicate and every conception related in its very conception to every other.
Therefore etc.
Since conceptions are typical of abstractions the world of abstractions is constructed in the same way.
#2. The world composed of Numbers.
The final elements of abstraction since they contain in themselves the relations to one another can contain nothing else (being simple) and hence are nothing but relations.
The final elements being relations contain the idea of numbers and hence can contain nothing else.
Hence for every number there can be but one simple relation.
For 1. Ego
Two-fold. Primary and Secondary
Fourfold. Metaphysical Mathematical Dynam. Phys.

The omission of the threefold is, I believe, purely accidental. In a brief paper of June 8, 1862, Peirce supplies it:

I now make out the following as irreducible conceptions:

I

Cardinal              Secondary
Sensation      Conception      Abstraction
Metaphysical    Dynamical    Mathematical    Physical
10 in all.[64]

These ten conceptions therefore are Peirce's first attempt to formulate a new list of categories, and they therefore require rather careful analysis.

The proposition "The field of thought is extensive" is adapted from Kant's "All intuitions are extensive magnitudes." (A162) Similarly, a "field" is a "total" which is the highest stage of quantity and therefore a "magnitude." The concept of "extension" comes directly from

[64] Untitled fragment, June 8, 1862. Quoted in Wiener, *Evolution*, p. 74.

Kant: "I entitle a magnitude extensive when the representation of the parts makes possible, and therefore necessarily precedes, the representation of the whole. I cannot represent to myself a line, however small, without drawing it in thought, that is, generating from a point all its parts one after another." (A162 B203) The concepts corresponding to the fourfold are also borrowed from the same source. Thus Kant:

> All combination (*conjunctio*) is either composition (*compositio*) or connection (*nexus*). The former is the synthesis of the manifold where its constituents do not necessarily belong to one another. For example, the two triangles into which a square is divided by its diagonal do not necessarily belong to one another. Such also is the synthesis of the *homogeneous* in everything which can be *mathematically* treated. This synthesis can itself be divided into that of *aggregation* and that of *coalition*, the former applying to *extensive* and the latter to *intensive* quantities. The second mode of combination (*nexus*) is the synthesis of the manifold so far as its constituents *necessarily belong to one another*, as, for example, the accident to some substance, or the effect to the cause. It is therefore synthesis of that which, though *heterogeneous*, is yet represented as combined *a priori*. This combination, as not being arbitrary and as concerning the connection of the *existence* of the manifold, I entitle *dynamical*. Such connection can itself, in turn, be divided into the *physical* connection of the appearances with one another, and their *metaphysical* connection in the *a priori* faculty of knowledge. [B201f]

Peirce's ten conceptions thus recapitulate much of his earlier thought. The "secondary" is the thought; the "primary" or "cardinal" the thought-of; hence the first three conceptions give us the I, the It, and the Thou. The next three give us the corresponding entities as derived from the analysis of conceptions, and the last four give us the Kantian table of categories in its application to the manifold.

But there are new and striking features to Peirce's treatment. First of all, Peirce is here concerned with the problem of the simple or elementary idea. An idea is "simple" if it comprehends no other idea — if it is not a thought of another thought. This definition is confused and does not really serve to distinguish the concepts Peirce wishes to distinguish but the general intent is clear: the nearer to pure intuition a thought is, the simpler it is. The second proposition does not really contradict the first, because the terms are being taken in different senses. A thought may be simple — i.e., contain no other thought, yet "contain" infinitely complex intuitions. This becomes clear in the third proposition. Recalling Kant's statement — "all intuitions are extensive magnitudes" — the point is that the simple conception must somehow comprehend the infinitely complex manifold of intuition. Moreover, since thoughts are abstracted from things, and abstractions are abstracted from thoughts, the relation between thought and thing may be taken as typical of that between abstraction and thought: hence the last sentence of Section 1.

In Section 2, Peirce comes to grips once more with the Modus of the It, but these remarks show a genuine advance. The helpless wandering among endless triads (1.563) is gone; instead Peirce has begun to clarify the nature of his problem. If an extensive magnitude is to be brought to unity, its parts must be related; hence whatever combines them must involve relations and "being simple" can involve nothing else. Again, relations are monadic, dyadic, triadic, etc. — i.e., they involve the notion of number, and "being simple" can contain nothing else. Now number is perfect quantity and quantity is that which applies directly to the substance — the It. Hence what is, is number and to each number there must correspond a relation which, somehow, unifies the manifold to which the number refers.

So far Peirce had come by June of 1862. His problems were still unsolved — indeed unformulated — yet the superiority of the 1862 paper over the "Modus of the It" is clear. He had begun to think through the problems which confronted him and to discern the direction in which his answers must lie.

# III

# *Origins of the Second System, 1862–1867*

THE paper on the nature of the perfect marks Peirce's final rejection of his first system — a rejection due chiefly to its failure to answer the problem of the categories. In his autobiographical sketch, Peirce has told us of his attempts to solve this riddle: "Here there was a problem to which I devoted three hours a day for two years, rising from it, at length, with the demonstrative certitude that there was something wrong about Kant's formal logic." (4.2) We are not told which two years these were, but the most likely guess is 1862–63. Peirce had begun the study of logic by 1864,[1] and according to his account this should have occurred at the end of the two years' work on the categories.

Peirce also neglects to tell us precisely how "the demonstrative certitude that there was something wrong about Kant's formal logic" (4.2) was reached, but the most plausible hypothesis as to the sequence of events would appear to be the following. We have noted already that Peirce accepted Kant's argument of the metaphysical deduction as a revelation from God. (4.2) Since the crux of this argument is the relation between the logical forms of judgment and the categories, any alterations which Peirce found it necessary to make in the table of categories would have to be interpreted as indicating an inadequacy in the table of the forms of judgment. This line of reasoning finds expression in one of the early drafts of the paper on the "New List of Categories," and may actually describe the course which Peirce's thought followed.

Kant first formed a table of the various logical divisions of judgment, and then deduced his categories directly from these. . . . The correspondences between the functions of judgment and the categories are obvious and certain. So far the method is perfect. Its defect is that it affords no warrant for the

---

[1] "A Treatise on the Major Premisses of the Science of Finite Subjects, (Nature)," fragment, August 4, 1864, IB2 Box 8.

correctness of the preliminary table, and does not display that direct reference to the unity of consistency which alone gives validity to the categories. [D2p1]

It was to find such a warrant that Peirce undertook the study of logic.

The authorities to whom Peirce turned for instruction in logic were Aristotle and the Scholastics. Indeed, his interest in Scholastic thought seems to have originated at this time: the papers written before 1862 are free of Scholastic terminology, while those composed after 1865 are replete with it. We do not have a complete list of the authors Peirce read, but we do know that by 1867 he had studied at least Aristotle (Pr. 1), Boethius (2.391), Anselm (5.213n1), Abelard (1.551n1), Peter of Spain (2.800n1), John of Salisbury (5.215n1), Duns Scotus,[2] Aquinas (2.393), Ockham (2.393), and probably others.

If Peirce's investigation into logic was begun in order to correct the table of functions of judgment, then his first interest was the theory of the proposition. The study of Scotus, however, convinced him that the proper object of logic was the syllogism and that the study of the syllogism ought to precede the study of the proposition since the only differences among propositions that are logically significant are those which affect their role as components of syllogisms.[3]

For a student of Kant, the implications of this doctrine are immense. From the standpoint of the metaphysical deduction, the universality and necessity of the categories rest upon the universality and necessity of the forms of propositions, and these in turn rest upon the joint assertion that thought at all is thought in propositions, and that this classification of propositions is correct. But if in fact the significance of propositional form depends upon its use in inference, then the correctness of *this* classification depends upon the further premises that all thought is inference and that these particular forms are necessary for inference. Thus Peirce remarks: "It is necessary to reduce all our actions to logical processes so that to do anything is but to take another step in the chain of inference. Thus only can we effect that complete reciprocity between Thought and its Object which it was Kant's Copernican step to announce."[4] The development of this insight leads naturally to the question of the classification of the forms of syllogisms.

---

[2] "A System of Logic. Chapter 1. Syllogism," n.d., pp. 2f, IB2 Box 8.
[3] *Ibid.*
[4] "Logic: 1865–1867," December 13, 1865, IB2 Box 8.

Kant himself had dealt with this problem of the classification of arguments in two works which were of particular importance to Peirce. The first of these, "The Mistaken Subtlety of the Four Syllogistic Figures," [5] attacks the notion that there are four independent figures. Although Peirce interpreted Kant as asserting that all figures are reducible to the first (4.2), this is true only in a rather special sense of "reducible." Kant does not assert that the second, third, and fourth figures are "nothing but" the first; rather what he does assert is that inference in these three figures can be analyzed into a combination of two types of inference — first, one or more immediate inferences (inferences by conversion or contraposition) and second, a first figure inference.[6] Thus the inference in *Celantes*

No spirit is divisible
All matter is divisible
Consequently, No matter is a spirit

becomes

No spirit is divisible
and therefore, Nothing divisible is a spirit;

and

Nothing divisible is a spirit
All matter is divisible
Therefore No matter is a spirit.[7]

The difference between the first and the other figures is thus that the first is "pure" and the others compound. By a "pure inference" Kant means one which proceeds solely upon one of two rules of inference: *"An attribute of an attribute is an attribute of the thing itself"* (the *nota notae*) and *"whatever is inconsistent with the attribute of a thing is inconsistent with the thing itself."* [8] All figures but the first involve not only one of these rules but also an immediate inference.

---

[5] Immanuel Kant, "Die falsche Spitzfindigkeit der vier Syllogistischen Figuren," 1762, in *Immanuel Kant Werke*, ed. Buchenau (Berlin, 1912), II, 49–65. In the following discussion I have used the translation in Immanuel Kant, "The Mistaken Subtlety of the Four Syllogistic Figures" in *Kant's Introduction to Logic and His Essay on the Mistaken Subtlety of the Four Figures*, trans. Thomas Kingsmill Abbott (London, 1885).

[6] *Ibid.*, pp. 84–88.

[7] *Ibid.*, p. 85.

[8] *Ibid.*, pp. 81–83.

The second work in which Kant deals with the forms of syllogism is the Transcendental Dialectic of the *Critique of Pure Reason*. Here he distinguishes three independent syllogistic forms — the categorical, hypothetical, and disjunctive — corresponding to the three forms of relation. (A304 B361) These are not figures of the syllogism since with sufficient wrenching they can be forced into the traditional figures; rather their status as independent forms of inference depends entirely upon the form of the propositions occurring in them.

The significance of these inferential forms lies in the connection which Kant drew between them and the transcendental ideas. In what is perhaps the most outrageous example of overzealous devotion to his architectonic in the whole *Critique*, Kant derived the three transcendental sciences from the three dialectical syllogisms which are in turn derived from the three forms of relation:

. . . that it can be shown how reason, simply by the synthetic employment of that very function of which it makes use in categorical syllogisms, is necessarily brought to the concept of the absolute unity of the *thinking subject*, how the logical procedure used in hypothetical syllogisms leads to the idea of the completely unconditioned *in a series* of given conditions, and finally how the mere form of the disjunctive syllogism must necessarily involve the highest concept of reason, that of a *being of all beings* . . . [A335f B392f]

Peirce, whose passion for architectonics outran even Kant's, thus found in the Dialectic a suggestion for a theory which would correlate inferential forms, propositional forms, categories, and transcendental sciences.

But before this great design could be completed, there were certain difficulties which had to be resolved. Kant's theory holds that differences in inferential forms are derived from differences in propositional forms — hence that there are distinct hypothetical, disjunctive, and categorical syllogisms. But Scotus had brought Peirce to precisely the opposite conclusion: the logically significant propositional forms must be derived from the forms of inference. Thus from Peirce's point of view the division of inference into categorical, hypothetical, and disjunctive was unsatisfactory. What he required was a classification of forms based upon genuine distinctions among the rules of inferences or syllogistic figures themselves. But the possibility of such a classification was denied by Kant's argument of the "Mistaken Subtlety."

Peirce's objection to Kant's triad of dialectical syllogisms received complete confirmation when — probably in mid-1865 — he came to the conclusion that:

Every syllogism can be put into a hypothetical form thus

| | | |
|---|---|---|
| Y is X | | If Y then X |
| Z is Y | becomes | but Y (under Z) |
| Z is X | | Therefore X (under Z)[9] |

After translating all four figures into hypotheticals, Peirce remarks:

The third and fourth figures are therefore hypothetical in their conclusions, and the third is only probable.

Arguments in the first figure are *a priori* because they proceed from *protases*. Arguments in the second figure are *a posteriori* because they proceed from *apodoses*. The two kinds of arguments are alike as to their major premiss, they differ in their minor premiss which in the one case is the statement of a cause and in the other of an effect. The terms *a priori* and *a posteriori* applied to conceptions show whether these are conceptions of causes or of effects — of protases or apodoses . . .[10]

The significance of these remarks should be at once apparent. First, Peirce clearly had not discovered the relation between deduction, induction, and hypothesis and the three figures when this was written; rather the discovery here described probably led to the correlation of inferential and syllogistic forms. Second, this reduction depends upon the conversion of categoricals into hypotheticals. The fact that Peirce does not bother to discuss disjunctives suggests that he had already learned of material implication and so knew disjunctives were reducible — indeed, he must have known this from Prantl if from no other source. Third, and most important, although Peirce's reduction of categoricals is *formally* similar to that we use today, the interpretation which he gave to it is not the same as ours. In the Kantian tables, the relation which corresponds to hypotheticals is causality, and Peirce so interprets it here. To say "If X then Y" thus means "X is the cause of Y." In a paper probably written late in 1865, Peirce makes this quite

[9] "Distinction between *A Priori* and *A Posteriori*," n.d., fragment, IB2 Box 8. Peirce's terminology is far from clear. By "Y (under Z)" he evidently meant "under the hypothesis that Z is true," — i.e., "Y is true if Z is." But since by the *modus ponens* X is assertable if Y is, and since Y is true if Z is, then X is true if Z is — i.e., "under Z." It is evidently the *modus ponens* which Peirce is emphasizing as the hypothetical form.
[10] *Ibid.*

59

explicit: "In every proposition whether extensive or intensive the subject is represented as the cause of the predicate . . . this is an axiom and the fact that certain propositions are designed to be clearly false representations in this respect, does not alter its character. To say 'Boston is a city' is the same as 'If Boston (is) then a city (is) . . . "[11] Thus although Peirce's theory of the proposition is formally similar to the modern one, it is philosophically radically different.

Precisely when Peirce discovered that deduction, induction, and hypothesis could be correlated with the three figures of the syllogism, we do not know, but all available evidence points toward 1865. Peirce has left us an account of the discovery in which he states that it was occasioned by his reading of Boole's *Laws of Thought*.[12] Boole's treatment of probability led Peirce to ask, what is induction?

I endeavored to formulate the process syllogistically; and I found that it would be defined as the *inference* of the major premiss of a syllogism from its minor premiss and conclusion. Now this was exactly what Aristotle said it was in the 23rd chapter of the second book of the Prior Analytics . . . Aristotle's example is

Whatever has no bile is long-lived,
Thus, man, the horse, the mule has no bile;
Whence, man, the horse, the mule, is long-lived.

From the first two propositions the third follows *deductively*; but by induction we infer the first from the second and third. With this hint as to the nature of induction, I at once remarked that if this be so there ought to be a form of inference which infers the Minor premiss from the major and the conclusion. Moreover, Aristotle was the last of men to fail to see this. I looked along further and found that . . . Aristotle opens the 25th [chapter] with a description of the inference of the minor premiss from the major and the conclusion.[13]

This account is probably accurate. Even though Peirce had already come to regard the second, third, and fourth figures as a posteriori and hypothetical, and probably would have made the discovery in any case, Boole was very likely the immediate stimulus.

Once this correlation was made and combined with Peirce's causal theory of the proposition, a rather striking interpretation of the syllogistic figures resulted:

[11] "On the Distinction between *A Priori* and *A Posteriori*," n.d., p. 1, IB2 Box 8.
[12] George Boole, *An Investigation of the Laws of Thought* (New York, n.d.).
[13] Lowell Lectures, 1903, vol. I, no. 8, pp. 12–16, IB2 Box 4.

Reasoning *a priori* is inferring an effect from its cause. Reasoning *a posteriori* is inferring a cause from its effect. There is clearly a third way of reasoning, which consists in inferring a mutual connection between the several effects of one cause; this is *induction* (or *analogy*). . . . All arguments in the first figure are really *a priori*, for in the major Y is made the subject and hence the cause and in the minor it is predicated, whence the effect is predicated. So even if no conclusion can be validly drawn . . . the train of thought is from cause to effect. All arguments in the second figure are really *a posteriori*. . . . All arguments in the third figure are really *inductive* . . .[14]

But now Peirce found himself confronted by a twofold dilemma. In the first place, the reduction of the dialectical syllogisms to a single form together with the discovery of the new interpretation of the three figures appeared to show that there were genuine differences between the principles of the three figures — a position in flat contradiction with Kant's argument in the "Mistaken Subtlety." In the second place, even if Peirce could show the existence of three distinct principles of inference, still, in order to carry out the architectonic design suggested by Kant, he had to derive the table of the functions of judgment from these principles. Yet the reduction of the dialectical syllogisms to hypotheticals had been accomplished only by denying that Kant's classification of propositional forms was correct. In short, the more Peirce strove to realize Kant's dream of an all-embracing architectonic philosophy, the more the logical foundations of that dream seemed to crumble.

Faced with these difficulties, Peirce resorted to a highly dubious course: he tried to distinguish the real from the logical in such a way as to make his logic yield the Kantian tables. The three figures are autonomous forms, he asserted, because their reduction is accomplished only by limitation or negation (conversion or contraposition) and these are purely logical operations which have no real counterparts.[15] By an argument based on a similar division, he sought to show that the three figures afford the necessary warrant for the functions of judgment.

Let us now apply the distinction between the logical and representative or real to the functions of judgement.

A proposition is really universal when it is in the object represented through as much of the subject as in the representation. It is really particular when it is in the object represented through a part of the subject represented

[14] "On the Distinction Between &c.," pp. 1f.
[15] *Ibid.*, pp. 2f.

in the representation. It is really singular when in the object it is in one unit of the subject as much as in another yet not in all the subject as represented.

A conclusion logically *a posteriori* is really singular. . . .

A conclusion logically inductive is really particular. . . .

A conclusion logically *a priori* is really universal . . .[16]

Thus in the case of the inductive conclusion, Peirce holds that from the premisses

No savages can prove their immortality
Yet all savages aspire to immortality

we may prove a priori that "some who aspire to immortality cannot prove their immortality" or inductively that "all who aspire to immortality cannot prove their immortality." But he holds, "We have no ground for inferring with the least probability that this conclusion is true in all cases. Hence our conclusion is really particular." [17] This argument is of course fallacious. The conclusion is not really particular; all that is shown is that if it were particular the inference would be "really" deductive.

By similar arguments, iterated for each form of judgment, Peirce ultimately reaches the conclusion:

Logically *a priori* conclusions are really universal, affirmative, categorical, apodictic

Logically inductive conclusions are really particular, infinite, hypothetical, assertorical

Logically *a posteriori* conclusions are really singular, negative, disjunctive, problematical.

It is clear that these differences do not proceed from differences in the premisses, because either premiss of each species of syllogism may be a premiss of a syllogism of one of the other kinds. Hence, the difference must proceed from the character of the act of the inference. Hence, inference is of three kinds, and proceeds from three principles to each of which will attach those functions of judgement which are found in the conclusions of the syllogism it rules over. These principles are not conclusions of a syllogism. Hence, there are principles which have the a priori, a posteriori and inductive, characters directly and not inferentially.[18]

As a fulfillment of the Kantian architectonic, this argument must

[16] *Ibid.*, pp. 3f.

[17] *Ibid.*, p. 4.

[18] *Ibid.*, p. 5.

be counted as a failure. Not only are the specific proofs invalid and at times farfetched, but the general principle of dividing the logical from the real actually undercuts the point of the whole undertaking. If there are logical forms without real analogues, it would seem impossible to base a table of categories upon such forms. Nevertheless, as the last paragraph shows, Peirce had seen the direction in which his answer had to lie. The three figures must involve three distinct rules of inference, and Kant's "Mistaken Subtlety" must be itself mistaken.

Early in 1866, therefore, Peirce made a detailed analysis of Kant's article and of the relation among the syllogistic figures, and he did indeed succeed in proving that each figure involves an independent principle of inference. For although any syllogism of the second or third figure can be reduced to one of the first, the argument by which this reduction is made must be in the figure from which it is being reduced. "Hence, it is proved that every figure involves the principle of the first figure, but the second and third figures contain other principles, besides." (2.807) By November of 1866, when the "Memoranda Concerning the Aristotelian Syllogism" (2.792–807) was published, Peirce had found the forms of inference upon which the functions of judgment and the categories had to be based, and he was now ready to attempt his own metaphysical deduction.

But at the same time, Peirce had come to another, and even more significant, conclusion. On November 14, 1865, he wrote in his commonplace book, "There is no difference logically between hypotheticals and categoricals. The subject is a sign of the predicate, the antecedent of the consequent; and this is the only point that concerns logic." [19] That all propositions were of one form Peirce had already surmised, but heretofore he had interpreted the relation between subject and predicate as causality. The substitution of the sign relation for causality marks a fundamental advance. Years later Peirce wrote in his autobiographical sketch: "This led me to see that the relation between subject and predicate, or antecedent and consequent, is essentially the same as that between premiss and conclusion." (4.3) Just how soon this reduction of illation to the sign relation was achieved we do not know, but it was probably not until after the discovery of the error in the "Mistaken Subtlety." The significance of that error lies in the fact that the three

[19] "Logic: 1865–1867."

forms of inference are shown to be distinct; but the reduction of illation in general to signhood shows that these forms are but varieties of a single yet more basic relation, so that much of the significance of that discovery is lost. Indeed, if both inference and judgment are but instances of the same fundamental relation, then clearly it is this relation which must be the basic form of thought upon which any categorical system would have to be reared.

That this relation should turn out to be the sign relation must have appeared peculiarly striking to Peirce, for from the very earliest of his writings in 1859 he had tended to use linguistic or semiotic terms in describing the combination of the abstraction with the thing. The theory of "expression" described above shows his preference for this sort of formulation, and it is easy to see that a Platonistic philosophy such as Peirce's early system would find a symbolic formulation particularly congenial. For if there are independently existing archetypal ideas the knowledge of them must come either through direct intuition or through concretes which embody them. In the first case, some faculty of intuitive knowledge or spiritual insight must be postulated, but to this extreme of absolute idealism Peirce was never willing to go. In the latter case, empirical objects must be viewed as symbols which express the divine ideas. Thus Peirce's early papers formulate the problem as one of "expression" or "manifestation."

There is also another and even more important role which the sign relation plays in Peirce's early philosophy. As I have noted above, Peirce followed Kant in holding that thought was a species of natural phenomena capable of empirical study. Combining this with the equally Kantian doctrine that all thoughts are representations, Peirce came to the conclusion that thoughts are individual entities — states of mind — which are representations and which have a specific temporal and spatial position.[20]

Such a theory of thought made it thoroughly natural that the basic relation among thoughts should be one of representation or signhood. Moreover, it enabled Peirce to give a rather unique semiotic interpretation to Kant's phenomenalism. Peirce had interpreted the critical position as meaning that as a matter of psychological fact, certain "forms" must apply to all objects of our experience. But this new theory sugges-

[20] See above, pp. 28f.

ted that these forms could be regarded as laws of combination and reference governing our representations. That is to say, if indeed there are "forms" which necessarily apply to all objects of our experience, these forms must manifest themselves by admitting or prohibiting certain kinds and combinations of representations. Thus the science of representations — of second intentions — must yield to us all the a priori knowledge there can be, and as regards the relation of representations to their objects this science is logic, for as the schoolmen had already taught Peirce, "Logic is said to treat of second intentions as applied to first." (1.559) Thus Kant was right in holding that logic is the key to the categories.[21]

With the final clarification of the relation between logic and the categories, Peirce turned to his own metaphysical deduction. It will be recalled that Peirce had criticized Kant because he gave no warrant for the original table of forms of judgment and because his method "does not display that direct reference to the unity of consistency which alone gives validity to the categories." (D2) According to Peirce's new theory, however, the problem of the forms of judgment ceased to be important, for since all forms of propositions and all forms of inferences are instances of the same sign relation, whatever holds of this relation in general will hold of all instances of it. Since, then, the unity to which the understanding reduces the manifold is that of a proposition, the categories — so far as they constitute simply the concepts of connection among signs and their objects necessary to that unity — may be discovered by the analysis of the structure of that proposition which brings the manifold to unity. (1.550)

Nevertheless, Peirce does in fact make an important assumption concerning propositional form: namely, he assumes that all propositions are fundamentally of the subject-predicate type. Although De Morgan had sent him a copy of his paper on the logic of relations in 1866, Peirce continued to hold through 1867 that the subject-predicate form was fundamental. This assumption plays an important part in the derivation of the categories since it serves to define the general form of the proposition which the categories must yield.

Peirce published his paper "On a New List of Categories" in May of

[21] "Logic of Science," Lecture X, "Grounds of Induction," c. 1866–1867, especially the last page, IB2 Box 10.

1867.[22] This paper may justly be regarded as the summation of the first decade of his philosophic work, for the problems of the categories had been his central concern since 1857. Thus in one sense the early papers on "Analysis of Creation" and "The Modus of the It" may be viewed as forerunners of the "New List." But the final formulation of the argument cannot have been begun until the reduction of predication to the sign relation, and this probably did not occur until 1865. There exist four manuscripts which can be identified with certainty as stages in this final formulation.[23] None of these manuscripts are dated, so that the order in which they were composed has to be established by internal evidence. That this can be done is owing to the fact that the theory of the categories was not completely thought out until the third or fourth of these drafts — in the first draft, for example, reference to an interpretant is not distinguished from reference to a correlate. Yet even in the final formulation, Peirce's writing retained much of the hieroglyphic quality which characterized his early writings. Certainly of all Peirce's published papers there is none which is so cryptic in its statement of essentials, so ambiguous in its definition of terms, so obscure in its formulation of the central doctrine, or so important in its content. A rather detailed analysis of this paper will therefore be necessary.

Although the general problem of the categories has been discussed in preceding chapters, it may be convenient to review some aspects of it before turning to the "New List." In the metaphysical deduction, Kant distinguished two kinds of unity, both of which are involved in the reduction of the manifold to the unity of a proposition. "Analytic Unity" — the unity which holds among *concepts* in a proposition (P. 253–256) — is described by Kant as follows: "all judgments are functions of unity among our representations; instead of an immediate representation, a *higher* representation, which comprises the immediate representation and various others, is used in knowing the object, and thereby much possible knowledge is collected into one." (A69 B93) Thus, for example, in the sentence, "all bodies are divisible," "divisible" is a higher concept which comprises "body" as well as other concepts. (A68 B93) Unity, in this sense, then, is the thinking together of

---

[22] *Proceedings* of the American Academy of Arts and Sciences, VII, 287–298 (May 1867).
[23] See Appendix.

many objects through a common property, and it is Kant's contention that every proposition involves such a unification of individuals by universal or general concepts. (P. 253) Since such general concepts are obtained by abstraction, which is an act of analysis, the unity so produced is called an "analytic" unity. (P. 256 A78f B104f)

"Synthetic" unity is the unity which holds among intuitions and which brings them under concepts. It is therefore the kind of unity which unites the manifold directly and for which the categories are required. Thus Kant defines "synthesis" as follows: "By *synthesis*, in its most general sense, I understand the act of putting different representations together, and of grasping what is manifold in them in one (act of) knowledge." (A77 B103) It is the synthesis of intuition which gives us an object which can be analyzed; without a prior synthetic unity of the manifold, there could be no concept of an object to be brought under higher concepts. It is the concepts of connection necessary for this synthesis which are supplied by the categories. (P. 266–279 A76–80 B102–106)

Kant regarded both analytic and synthetic unity as necessary to the reduction of the manifold to the unity of a proposition. But it is one of the more striking features of the "New List" that no such division between kinds of unity appears. The entire argument of the paper assumes that there is but one form of unity and one process of combination by which that unity is produced. From this fact it might easily be concluded that Peirce either was ignorant of Kant's distinction between the two kinds of unity, or else that he rejected it as invalid. Yet Peirce's early papers dealing with the categories appear to involve this distinction or one very close to it. For example, the paper entitled "Modus of the It" seems clearly to be concerned with the question of synthetic unity,[24] while those entitled "Analysis of Creation" and "Classification" appear to relate to analytic unity.[25] Moreover, in the second draft of the "New List," Peirce writes as follows: "The distinction between imagining and conceiving is part of the very alphabet of philosophy. To imagine is [to] reproduce in the mind elementary sensible intuitions and to take them up in some order so as to make an image. To conceive is to collect under a supposition, to make a hypothesis, and therefore

---

[24] See above, pp. 49f.
[25] See above, pp. 48, 50f.

cannot dispense with the use of words." (D2p3) This passage certainly implies that there are two distinct kinds of synthesis: one in intuition through imagination and one in concepts. Yet in this same draft Peirce's deduction of the categories proceeds on the assumption that there is but one process of unification. How is this paradox to be explained? The answer, I believe, lies in the chronological relations between Peirce's theory of the categories and his theory of cognition, and in the conditions under which the "New List" was written.

Peirce's theory of cognition is formulated in three papers published in 1868. A more detailed analysis of these papers will be given below; for the present purpose it will suffice to indicate the role which intuition plays in that theory. Peirce formulates the distinction between intuition and conception in terms of their representative character, and so stated it comes to this: "The term *intuition* will be taken as signifying a cognition not determined by a previous cognition of the same object, and therefore so determined by something out of consciousness" (5.213), while a concept is always determined by a previous cognition. Peirce then argues at some length that every cognition is determined by a previous cognition of the same object, and he therefore concludes that there is no such thing as intuition.

It is obvious that upon this theory of cognition, to speak of a synthesis of impressions or intuitions is nonsense, for there is nothing of the sort to be synthesized. Since the avowed purpose of the "New List" is the discovery of the conceptions required to reduce "the manifold of sensuous impressions" (1.545) to unity, it would therefore seem that the theory of the categories must have been formulated before the theory of cognition. Yet all the available evidence indicates that the two were formulated simultaneously. The first paragraph of the paper of 1868 — from which the definition of intuition given above is taken — is rewritten from the opening paragraphs of the fourth draft of the "New List"; both contain the same definition of intuition. Moreover, in that draft, not only does Peirce carefully avoid committing himself to the existence of intuitions but he defines the question of their existence as follows: "Whether there be any such ultimate premisses is a difficult question. It amounts, however, merely to this; whether the boundary of consciousness is in consciousness or out of it." (D4p1) At least by May of 1867 — the month in which the "New List" was published —

Peirce had definitely concluded that the boundary lies without. For during the winter of 1866–67 he lectured at Harvard on the logic of science,[26] and in the tenth lecture of this series Peirce explicitly denies the existence of any cognition not determined by a previous cognition.[27] Accordingly, we may conclude that the theory of the categories and the theory of cognition were formulated at about the same time, and we may therefore expect that they will be consistent with each other. Indeed, since the theory of the categories is a part of the theory of cognition it seems unlikely that Peirce could have come to two diametrically opposed conclusions on the same question at the same time.

The fact that Peirce repeatedly refers to impressions in the "New List" at the same time that he was denying them elsewhere is not, I think, the result of contradiction but rather of the hectic period of intellectual activity during which this paper was written. Peirce denies the existence of cognitions not determined by a previous cognition — in this sense there are no intuitions; but he does not deny the existence of any nonconceptual stimuli to mental action. What he means by "the manifold of sensuous impressions" is actually something very close to the set of all nerve excitations at a given time. His retention of the term "impression" in this restricted sense is confusing but understandable; the Kantian terms were convenient and he had no others readily available.

Peirce's concept of impressions and their relation to concepts at this time finds its clearest statement in one of the early lectures in the Harvard series where he discusses the problem of the formation and introduction of concepts.

Names are commonly assigned, in our day, as synonyms for longer and more inconvenient names. . . . But it is plain that in the early youth of language, and of each man, many names must be adopted which have no equivalents at all. Now I maintain that *such* adoption of names is a hypothetic process. Before a name connoting certain characters is invented, those characters cannot be thought of, in themselves, at all. The object is thought through these characters, and is thus thought as determined in a certain mode; but to think it as one of the things which have these characters in common, or to think of the things which have these characters in common as being in any other [way]

---

[26] Wiener, *Evolution*, p. 75.

[27] "Lectures on Logic Given at the Lowell Institute, 1866–67," Lecture X, first page, IB2 Box 10.

determined or undetermined is to possess a term which connotes these characters.[28]

The word, therefore, cannot be introduced by a deductive argument
since such an argument requires a major premiss already containing the
term. He continues:

The only premiss which is held previously to the conclusion is that "this thing
is thus." We may however assume that "whatever has this name is thus," and
at the same moment infer by hypothesis that, "This thing has this name."
Such a hypothetic process is . . . the only one which can yield that conclusion. The major proposition "whatever should have this name would be thus,"
is inferred at the same moment by induction from the same fact together with
the hypothetic inference.[29]

The argument is a *petitio principii*, but Peirce defends it on the ground
that induction and hypothesis are not forms of demonstration; all that
is required of them is that the proposition to which they lead must be
such that, when taken as a premiss, a certain fact can be derived from
it.[30] Hence he holds that the adopting of the proposition "This thing is
one of those which have this name" is the result of hypothetic reasoning
and therefore of an inference.

The hypothesis so derived, however, differs from other hypotheses
in two respects: it is vacuous and it is certain. For since the hypothesis
simply introduces a word to connote certain properties, it asserts nothing, and therefore there is nothing in the conclusion which can be
denied. Hence Peirce calls it "a *nominal* in opposition to an *intellectual*
hypothesis." [31]

The significance of Peirce's argument becomes clear when he turns
to the question of perceptual judgments. The argument is worth quoting.

By a sensation, is understood, as it seems to me, a mental representation
determined by the character of a movement of the nerves, but without any
understanding of this character. We see that a certain thing is blue, but we do
not thus judge anything of it, not contained in the impressions, which we thus
explain, except that it is one of those things to which by the constitution of
our nature we give the innate name or sensation blue. A judgment of sensa-

[28] "Appendix. No. 2," n.d., pp. 3f, IB2 Box 8.
[29] *Ibid.*, p. 5.
[30] *Ibid.*, pp. 5f.
[31] *Ibid.*, pp. 7f.

tion is thus only a constitutional nominal hypothesis; and the impressions themselves have no character which would make it illogical for the sensation of blue to arise when that of yellow now does and *vice versa*. Undoubtedly, our impressions have one character when we see blue and another when we see yellow; that is to say, the elementary excitations produced by each instantaneous state of the ganglion have different relations; but those impressions cannot be colour for they are instantaneous while colour can only arise from the relative states of the nerve at different times. If there are no such instantaneous states, that does not affect the conclusion at all; still colour requires a certain lapse of time, and all the sensations in the sum of lesser times will contain all the matter of receptivity, but yet no colour.[32]

For Peirce, then, color is a concept which is applied to the manifold of impressions as an explaining hypothesis; it is not therefore an impression itself. The term "impression" is thus restricted to the instantaneous neurological stimuli which occasion the concept and are related by it. That this is the sense in which Peirce employs the term "impression" in the "New List" is made clear in the opening sections of draft four:

. . . the simplest colour is almost as complicated as a piece of music. Colour depends upon the *relations* between different parts of the impression; and, therefore, the differences between colours are the differences between harmonies; and to see this difference we must have the elementary impressions whose relation makes the harmony. So that colour is not an impression, but an inference. [D4p2]

If impression is to be understood in this sense, it is clear that Peirce's comments about the synthesis in imagination in draft two must be rejected as a momentary lapse into a purely Kantian frame of reference from which he was rapidly emerging. For to reproduce and combine the impressions into an image, those impressions would have to be compared and reflected upon. But according to the theory of draft four, this would mean that these impressions had become conceptions. Thus: "No one can know what an Impression is like, in itself; for a recognized difference between two impressions would be a difference between them *as compared*, that is as mediately known, and not between them *in themselves*." (D4p2) And, "Any reflection upon an impression, since it is a step toward bringing it to the unity of consistency, is a conception." (D4p5)

On the other hand, comparison and reflection would be impossible

[32] *Ibid.*

if in some way impressions were not held before the mind. In drafts one and two, Peirce appears to be thinking of the concept applied directly to the impressions, which must presumably be brought before us by the prior synthesis of apprehension and imagination. In drafts three and four, however, the notion of what is present in general is developed into the notion of substance, which appears in the "New List" as follows:

> That universal conception which is nearest to sense is that of *the present, in general*. This is a conception, because it is universal. But as the act of *attention* has no connotation at all, but is the pure denotative power of the mind, that is to say, the power which directs the mind to an object, in contradistinction to the power of thinking any predicate of that object — so the conception of *what is present in general*, which is nothing but the general recognition of what is contained in attention, has no connotation, and therefore no proper unity. This conception of the present in general, of IT in general, is rendered in philosophical language by the word "substance" in one of its meanings. Before any comparison or discrimination can be made between what is present, what is present must have been recognized as such, as *it*, and subsequently the metaphysical parts which are recognized by abstraction are attributed to this *it*, but the *it* cannot itself be made a predicate. [1.547]

"The present in general" is a concept but one without unity. Certainly apprehension and reproduction of the manifold are required, but this appears to be an aggregation of elements rather than a synthesis; even to combine these elements into an image is for Peirce to enter the realm of concepts. For this very reason, I think, Peirce's use of the term "it" is highly misleading since "it" is easily confused with the variable of quantification theory. "The present in general" is a concept capable of being the subject of a traditional proposition, and although it is used here as the subject of a perceptual judgment, Peirce does not distinguish its relation to its predicate from the relation of "stove" to "black," as he makes quite clear in the next paragraph. (1.548)

Nevertheless, the use of terms such as "nearest to sense" and "furthest from sense" demonstrates that Peirce is involved in stratification difficulties. This paragraph (1.547) and several others — viz. 1.548, 1.551 — derive heavily from A67–69 B92–94 of the *Critique* and so from Kant's theory of analytic unity. When Kant states that "divisible" is a concept *"higher"* than "body," it is implied that "divisible" is more abstract than "body." Again, to speak of concepts as "immediate" or "mediate," or as being "nearer" or "further" from sense, implies a scale of abstraction running upward from sense. But "divisibility" is not more abstract than "body"; Kant, and Peirce after him, is here confounding membership with inclusion, and hence abstraction with generality. We have seen above how this confusion plagued Peirce's early work; it is no less present here. Peirce is actually discussing a relation among concepts of the same type, yet he regards the predicate as more abstract than the subject.

The concept "furthest from sense" is not, as one might have thought, the predicate, but the copula. The copula is used here solely to connote "being," which is then further determined by the predicate. (1.548) This interpretation of the copula is not unique to Peirce — it was known in the Middle Ages but was regarded as too weak to be of much use.[33] Peirce adopted it for just this reason. He was seeking the most complete possible analysis of the connections within a proposition; hence he requires a conception of the copula which is as weak as possible. The less he must assume in the copula itself, the more there remains to analyze.

The unity of a proposition is achieved by applying being to substance. Since these two concepts are respectively the "nearest to sense" and "the furthest from sense" all other elements of the proposition must lie between them. "Thus substance and being are the beginning and end of all conception." (1.548) The stage is thus set for the next two paragraphs, in the first of which (1.549) Peirce develops his theory of abstraction through which, as he explains in the second (1.550), he will obtain his categories. By abstraction or "precision," Peirce means a mental separation which "arises from *attention to* one element and *neglect of* the other." (1.549) In this sense "attention" means the *"supposition* of one part of an object, without any supposition of the other." (1.549) Hence, space may be prescinded from color, because it is possible to suppose a state of things in which space would not be colored; but color cannot be prescinded from space since in every state of things colors must occur in space (1.549n1 D4pp3–4).

It is by precision that the categories are to be found, for:

[33] Ernest A. Moody, *Truth and Consequence in Medieval Logic* (Amsterdam, 1953), p. 33.

Elementary conceptions . . . are produced for the first time according to a general law, the condition of which is the existence of certain impressions. Now if a conception does not reduce the impressions upon which it follows to unity, it is a mere arbitrary addition to these latter; and elementary conceptions do not arise thus arbitrarily. But if the impressions could be definitely comprehended without the conception, this latter would not reduce them to unity. Hence, the impressions (or more immediate conceptions) cannot be definitely conceived or attended to, to the neglect of an elementary conception which reduces them to unity. On the other hand, when such a conception has once been obtained, there is, in general, no reason why the premisses which have occasioned it should not be neglected, and therefore the explaining conception may frequently be prescinded from the more immediate ones and from the impressions. [1.549]

From this it follows that however many categorical conceptions lie between being and substance, each is "more immediate" than its successor and therefore cannot be prescinded from that successor. But each conception is more mediate than its predecessor and therefore can be prescinded from that predecessor. The application of being to substance therefore is either made directly, or it is justified by an intermediate conception already joined to substance, the presence of which is a condition of the application of being. This intermediate conception cannot be supposed without the concept of being since it is more immediate than being, but the latter can be prescinded from the former. Now this intermediate conception either unites the manifold directly, or it is united to the manifold by a yet more immediate concept, and so on. By repeated precisions of the more for the less mediate, we may eventually find that concept which does unite the manifold directly, and this will be the last concept in passing from being to substance.

Peirce now proceeds to the determination of the first category. The expression "this is" is not a proposition for it does not tell us what or how this is; accordingly, some determination of being is required to constitute a predicate. "A proposition always has, besides a term to express the substance, another to express the quality of that substance; and the function of the conception of being is to unite the quality to the substance. Quality, therefore, in its very widest sense, is the first conception in order in passing from being to substance." (1.551) A quality in the sense in which Peirce here employs this term is the embodiment of an abstraction: *"Embodying blackness is the equivalent of black.*

74

. . . Moreover, the conception of a pure abstraction is indispensable, because we cannot comprehend an agreement of two things, except as an agreement in some *respect*, and this respect is such a pure abstraction as blackness. Such a pure abstraction, reference to which constitutes a *quality*, or general attribute, may be term a *ground*." (1.551) The ground is the abstraction, not the quality; the quality is that which refers to the ground. Hence a quality exists at a level of abstraction below that of the pure abstract property itself. Now the application of this quality to the subject is, Peirce states, hypothetical.

A proposition asserts the applicability of a mediate conception to a more immediate one. . . . The mediate conception, then, in order to be *asserted* to be applicable to the other, must first be considered without regard to this circumstance, and taken immediately. But, taken immediately, it transcends what is given (the more immediate conception), and its applicability to the latter is hypothetical. (1.551)

The mediate concept is therefore more than a clarification of the immediate one, for, in that case, the judgment would be analytic. Quite the contrary, it explains the immediate conception, and is therefore a hypothesis. What, then, is the occasion for making such a hypothesis? Peirce describes it as follows:

Empirical psychology has established the fact that we can know a quality only by means of its contrast with or similarity to another. By contrast and agreement a thing is referred to a correlate, if this term may be used in a wider sense than usual. The occasion of the introduction of the conception of reference to a ground is the reference to a correlate, and this is, therefore, the next conception in order.

Reference to a correlate cannot be prescinded from reference to a ground; but reference to a ground may be prescinded from reference to a correlate.

The occasion of reference to a correlate is obviously by comparison. [1.552f]

It is in respect to the second and third categories that the real problems in the interpretation of the "New List" arise. In the passage just quoted, what is being compared with what? From the first sentence it seems that the quality itself is being compared to another quality — the antecedent of "its" can only be "quality." Yet this interpretation contradicts other passages in the "New List" where the correlate is spoken of as the *object* (1.559) and as an *other*. (1.556) Nor is it

75

clear what kind of relation is established by this comparison. "Relate" and "correlate" are Peirce's names for the two terms of a relation, and this relation, we are told, is occasioned by comparison. Yet since quality can be prescinded from it, the relation must be one of similarity or agreement, for a quality is an agreement (1.551) and only in relations of agreement can the quality be prescinded. (1.558) From this it follows that "relate and correlate are not distinguished" (1.558) — the relation is commutative. But can the relation of symbol to object or of self to other be commutative? "The occasion of reference to a correlate is obviously by comparison" (1.553) but what is compared, or how, is very far from being obvious.

Peirce's theory of the relation between comparison and quality is ultimately derived, I believe, from Kant. In the *Logic*, Kant attributes the origin of concepts to three acts of the understanding — comparison, reflexion, and abstraction. These are described as follows:

Die logischen Verstandes-Actus, wodurch Begriffe ihrer Form nach erzeugt werden, sind:
1) die Comparation, d.i. die Vergleichung der Vorstellungen unter einander im Verhältnisse zur Einheit des Bewusstseyns;
2) die Reflexion, d.i. die Ueberlegung, wie verschiedene Vorstellungen in Einem Bewusstseyn begriffen seyn können; und endlich
3) die Abstraction oder die Absonderung alles Uebrigen, worinn die gegebenen Vorstellungen sich unterscheiden.[34]

Although Kant regarded the origin of concepts as a logical question (P 198–203) and Peirce as a psychological one, both are concerned with the determination of the actual process whereby concepts are produced. In Anmerk. 1, Kant describes comparison in detail.

Um aus Vorstellungen Begriffe zu machen, muss man also compariren, reflectiren und abstrahiren können; denn diese drey logische Operationen des Verstandes sind die wesentlichen und allgemeinen Bedingungen zu Erzeugung eines jeden Begriffs überhaupt. — Ich sehe z.B. eine Fichte, eine Weide und eine Linde. Indem ich diese Gegenstände zu-

To form a concept out of representations, one must therefore be able to compare, reflect and abstract; because these three logical operations of the understanding are the essential and universal conditions for the making of any and every concept.* I see, e.g., a spruce, a willow and a lime tree. By first comparing these objects among themselves, I observe

[34] Immanuel Kant, *Logik: ein Handbuch zu Vorlesungen* (Königsberg, 1800), p. 145.

vörderst unter einander vergleiche, bemerke ich, dass sie von einander verschieden sind in Ansehung des Stammes, der Aeste, der Blätter u. dgl. m; nun reflectire ich aber hiernächst nur auf das, was sie unter sich gemein haben, den Stamm, die Aeste, die Blätter selbst und abstrahire von der Grösse, der Figur derselben u.s.w.; so bekomme ich einen Bergriff vom Baume.

that they are different from each other in regard to [the size and shape of**] their trunks, their branches, their leaves etc.; now after this I again reflect what they have in common among themselves, the same trunks, the branches, the leaves, and abstract from the size and shape etc.; so I obtain a concept of a tree.[35]

The concept is thus obtained by an abstraction which results from the comparison of objects to which that concept applies. Thus the spruce, the willow, and the lime are all trees — although they differ from each other in certain other respects. It is particularly important to note than Kant does not require the three trees to be contrasted with something not a tree — presumably the relevant common properties can simply be recognized.

To this description of the process of concept formation serious objections can be raised. The number of properties common to the three trees is infinite; how is it that the conception of tree is abstracted from them rather than some other? Indeed, some philosophers have held that the abstraction of a concept requires three objects, two of which possess the property in question and one of which does not. During his early years, Peirce seems to have wavered between these two views,[36] but in a manuscript written in 1864 or 1865, he declared for the latter position. Adopting from the Scholastics the term *ens* to mean whatever may be an object of thought, he asserts two principles which he calls the first and second principles of logic. The first is, that "something or other is true of every *ens*." [37] This actually amounts to saying that every *ens* has a quality or every subject a predicate. Thus we already have substance and quality. The second principle is, "For everything which is true of an *ens*, something must be true of a pair of *entia* of which this is one." [38] That is, a quality can only become known

---

[35] *Ibid.*, p. 146. *Following Paton, *Kant's Metaphysic of Experience*, I, 199n5. ** Following Paton, I, 199n2.

[36] See above, pp. 29, 50.

[37] "Certain Fundamental Conceptions," n.d., p. 2, IB2 Box 8.

[38] *Ibid.*, p. 3.

by comparing its subject of inhesion to another subject. This is made clear in the final paragraph, where Peirce writes:

. . . the most important distinction [between relations] is between those whose relates are the same as their correlates, and these are called *agreements* and those whose relates are not the same as their correlates and these are called *oppositions*. An agreement is the relation which subsists among any number of entia in consequence of their having some absolute quality in common. All other relations are oppositions. A quality only inheres in its subject by virtue of relations of each of these two kinds. This is a supplement and completion of the second principle of logic.[39]

Thus one can only discriminate a quality from its subject by comparing the subject to something else which has that quality, and to something else which does not have it. The first comparison separates qualities from the thing; the second indicates which quality is to be taken. Both comparisons are necessary. The "correlate" or object not possessing the property Peirce calls the "suffering object." He says:

Thus, the sentence, this is blue, is complete in itself. But if we retrace our steps we observe that we said, everything is such as it is in comparison with something else. This is an old and established axiom. Now, we may have used suffering object in too wide a sense, but in such sense as we have used it, it is evident that anything *not blue* might be added as the suffering object of the above sentence. In fact, the effect of this ancient maxim is that "*blue*" *means* "blue in comparison to" and therefore requires a suffering object.[40]

The origin of the term "suffering object" I have not been able to determine; I suspect it is derived from the root meaning "to bear under" — hence to receive the action. What is essential to note is that the object so designated does not possess the property — the relation is one of opposition.

By the time Peirce wrote the third draft of the "New List," however, he had reversed his position.

Of whatever kind anything is, it is in comparison with something else; Quality is only the outside of substance and implies therefore something without. This notion which appears as Relation or Act — according as it is viewed subjectively or objectively, is the second generalization which that of Quality enables us to make. What is must not only have a *ground* but also and there-

---

[39] *Ibid.*, p. 5.
[40] "Logic. Chapter 2," fragment, n.d, IB2 Box 8.

fore, an *object*. This *object,* regarded abstractly, is matter . . . the reference to the object is the suffering object. [D3]

Since reference to a ground is prescinded from reference to the suffering object, it is clear that both relate and correlate possess the quality — that is, the relation is now one of agreement. And this view is continued in draft four, where Peirce describes reference to a correlate as follows:

All students of philosophy know that we can become aware of any quality only through the relation of its subject of inhesion to something else; and it is an equally familiar fact that no relation can have place without a quality or reference to a *ground*. The occasion of the introduction of reference to a ground, therefore, is generalization or contrast.

In generalization and contrast, the primary substance has annexed to it a correlate. Reference to a correlate, then, is the next conception in order after reference to a ground. This conception is so easy to seize that no elucidation of it is needed. It cannot be prescinded from reference to a ground, although this latter can be prescinded from it. [D4p11f]

Here there can be no doubt that the relation is one of agreement between two objects.

The reason for Peirce's vacillation over the meaning of comparison becomes clear only in relation to Kant's theory of analytic unity. The description which Kant gives of the origin of concepts harmonizes perfectly with that theory; the concept arises as the common property of a plurality of objects, and this plurality is unified by being thought through the concept. Although I believe Peirce was right in feeling that Kant's theory was inadequate and that contrast with an object to which the concept does not apply is essential to its abstraction, it is clear that such a contrast requires the addition of an element which cannot be reduced by that concept to the unity of consistency. Accordingly, it is far more convenient to regard the suffering object as an entity possessing the property in question, and therefore to define the unity of the proposition as analytic unity in the sense of Kant. Thus in 1.559 Peirce writes: "In a proposition, the term which separately indicates the object of the symbol is termed the subject, and that which indicates the ground is termed the predicate. The objects indicated by the subject (which are always potentially a plurality — at least, of phases or appearances) are therefore stated by the proposition to be related to one another on the ground of the character indicated by the predicate." But in draft three a new question is raised by the sentence, "The *object,* regarded abstractly, is matter." The term "matter" as it is used here is subject to the same ambiguity that it has in the *Critique;* it may refer to the impressions of the manifold, or to the object of the symbol, and these are not necessarily the same. (P. 193f) In the former sense, quality may be regarded as a relation among impressions, and it is thus that Peirce describes color in the above quoted passage on the nature of sensation.[41] In the latter sense, quality may be regarded as a relation between subject and object; it is in this sense that Peirce speaks when he asserts that the relation of symbol to object is made through the logos or pure abstraction: "A Logos is a form constituting the relation between an object and a representation regarded as actual." [42]

This interpretation of quality as a relation between subject and object also finds justification in the writings of Kant, for the opening section of the famous article on the "Mistaken Subtlety" reads as follows:

| | |
|---|---|
| Etwas als ein Merkmal mit einem Dinge vergleichen heisst urteilen. Das Ding selber ist das Subjekt, das Merkmal das Prädikat. Die Vergleichung wird durch das Verbindungszeichen *ist* oder *sind* ausgedrückt, welches, wenn es schlechthin gebraucht wird, das Prädikat als ein Merkmal des Subjekts bezeichnet, ist es aber mit dem Zeichen der Verneinung behaftet, des Prädikat als ein dem Subjekt entgegengesetztes Merkmal zu erkennen gibt. | Judgment is the comparison of a thing with some mark (or attribute). The thing itself is the Subject, the mark (or attribute) is the Predicate. The comparison is expressed by the word "is," which when used alone indicates that the predicate is a mark (or attribute) of the subject, but when combined with the sign of negation states that the predicate is a mark opposed to the subject.[43] |

Thus a similarity based on comparison may be taken as justifying the application of quality to substance. This usage is adopted by Peirce himself in the following statement: "Every judgment expresses a relation of ideas, and consequently involves a comparison of them, and a

[41] See above, p. 71. See also D4p2.
[42] "Grounds of Induction," p. 4.
[43] *Werke,* II, p. 51 ; Kant, *Introduction to Logic,* p. 79.

thinking of them together. Every thinking of ideas together is a process of subsumption. Consequently every proposition or expression of a judgment may be put into the form A is a case under B . . ." [44] Accordingly, the ground may be taken to relate subject and object, subject and predicate, or object and predicate as well as the objects and impressions referred to.

From a logical point of view, this position is of course a gross violation of the requirements of stratification, but it is a violation which is sanctioned by the maxim *nota notae est nota rei ipsius* which both Kant and Peirce affirmed. Indeed, in that very article on the "Mistaken Subtlety" Kant had asserted: "We see that the first and universal rule of all affirmative ratiocination is, *An attribute of an attribute is an attribute of the thing itself.*" [45] It is to these stratification difficulties that the ambiguity of the second category is largely due. For since subject, object, impressions, and sign are all spoken of as "subsumed" under the attribute, all may be said to agree in respect to that attribute, and accordingly any of them might stand as relate or as correlate. Which of these various interpretations is to be regarded as the correct one can only be determined by the examination of the third category.

Reference to an interpretant was the last of the categories to reach a clear form in Peirce's mind. Thus the first draft of the "New List" contains only reference to a ground and reference to a correlate.

Now generalization is of related things; so that the function of the conception of a ground or character is to unite relate and correlate; it is justified therefore by the fact that without it reference to a correlate is unintelligible. I hold that that which immediately justifies an abstraction is the next highest element of cognition. Accordingly, next to possession of a character or reference to a ground comes reference to a correlate. This reference to a correlate is itself not given in the sensation, but requires an act of comparison, that is a determining of the imagination of one term by that of another. One term is united to the imagination by the reference of it to its correlate. The function, therefore, of the reference to a correlate is to perform the junction, and it is justified by the fact that the reference to the determinable image is only intelligible by saying that A refers to B as its correlate. Now, the reference to a determinable image though not intelligible in the sensation (for sense does not understand) is yet just what constitutes sensation. This therefore completes the chain of elementary conceptions. [D1]

[44] "Chapter 8. Of the Copula," fragment, p. 1, IB2 Box 8.
[45] *Introduction to Logic,* p. 81.

This passage throws considerable light on the nature of Peirce's theory. "Comparison" is clearly being employed here as the basis for the subsumption of one representation under another. Hence it is by comparison that impressions are brought together and "referred" to an image as correlate. There is thus a double meaning to "comparison": there is a comparison among impressions which shows them to have a common property, and there is a comparison between the impressions and the image which justifies bringing the former under the latter.

In the second draft, Peirce achieves a clearer statement.

Now, generalization is from related things; so that the immediate function of reference to a ground is to unite relate and correlate, and hence its introduction is justified by the fact that without it reference to a correlate is unintelligible. Accordingly, reference to a correlate is the second conception with content. This conception is itself not given in sensation, but is the result of comparison. Now comparison is the determination of a representation by the medium of that which is present, in contradistinction to its determination simply by that which is present. For example, I put A into relation to B, when in contemplating A, I as it were see B through it. The representation determined by the medium of A, may be called its *correspondent*. Then the immediate function of reference to a correlate is to conjoin that which is presented with its correspondent, and the introduction of the former conception is justified by the fact that only by it is the latter made representable. Accordingly reference to a correspondent is the third conception with content. This conception is itself not in what is immediately present in its elements. But it is directly applied to the immediately present in general; for the bringing of the elementary sensations together into a notion of the immediately present in general, requires the introduction of the conception that this general represents its particulars, and in the conception of representation that of image determined as correspondent is contained. [D2p2]

Here the distinction between the two forms of comparison is made somewhat clearer; and the notion of the general representing its particulars is distinguished as an independent concept, but the basis of the representative relation is still comparison.

In the third draft, still greater clarity is achieved. Peirce abandons the locution of "seeing through" and states his case wholly in terms of the representative relation. "What is, has a *ground*, since it has also an *object*, has in the third place a *subject*. This *subject*, which must not be supposed to be a mind, though it may be a human representation and which is only that which is determined by the representation to agree with it in its reference to the object on that ground, — this subject is an abstraction which the philosophers have left too much out of account." (D3) Note here that it is the subject of the sentence which determines the "subject" — i.e., interpretant — thus illustrating again the fact that subject and predicate are each representations of the other.[46]

The clearest of all Peirce's statements is to be found, I believe, in the fourth draft.

. . . it will be found that every comparison requires, besides the related thing, the ground and the correlate, also a *mediating representation which represents the relate to be a representation of the same correlate which this mediating representation itself represents*. Such a mediating representation, I call an *interpretant*, because it fulfills the office of an interpreter who says that a foreigner says the same thing which he himself says.

Every reference to a correlate, then, unites to the substance a reference to an interpretant; which is, therefore, the next conception in the order we have adopted.

It must not be supposed that in giving a definition of interpretant, we admit at all that reference to an interpretant is a compound conception. This definition is only a verbal one; for the conception of representation which it introduces itself contains that of reference to an interpretant. Reference to an interpretant, is simply the *addressing* of an impression to a conception. To *address* or *appeal to,* is an act we, in fact, suppose everything to perform, whether we attend to the circumstance or not. It is unanalysable, I think; though it may be expressed more perspicuously by a periphrasis, as above.

It may perhaps be objected, that since an interpretant is necessarily a correlate, reference to an interpretant is merely a particular determination of the conception of reference to a correlate, and should not be coordinated with the latter. But an interpretant is not referred to as establishing a relation to a correlate, in so far as it is a correlate; it is not therefore *quatenus ipsum* a correlate. [D4p12f]

In the last paragraph Peirce finally achieves a successful articulation of the relation between the interpretant and the act of comparison — namely, it is the interpretant which creates the relation between relate and correlate by bringing them into comparison. Thus, in another paper, he writes, "That to which a thing stands for something is that which brings the thing into comparison with that for which it stands." [47] But it is the third paragraph which is of particular interest, for this

[46] See above, p. 63.
[47] "Logic of Science," chap. I, sixth page, IB2 Box 10.

is Peirce's clearest statement of what he means by the expression "reference to" which occurs in the definition of every category. The notion of "addressing" or "appealing to" Peirce regards as primitive and incapable of analysis. Although it requires that reference to an interpretant must be taken in a slightly different sense than reference to a ground and reference to a correlate, the only adequate interpretation for this notion would seem to be "to stand for." Thus a quality stands for an abstraction, a relate stands for its correlate, and impressions stand for something to their interpreting conception. Such an interpretation is consistent with Peirce's statement that the sign relation is fundamental, since a sign is that which stands for something to some one in some respect. And moreover it suggests a very plausible source for Peirce's third category — the Scholastic theory of supposition.

Recalling that Peirce went to school to the Scholastics to acquire a knowledge of logic, it is hardly surprising that his theory of the proposition should be indebted to theirs. This theory, which was called the theory of supposition, is well stated by Jean Buridan: "Supposition, as here understood, is the interpretation of a term in a proposition for some thing or things such that, if it or they be indicated by the pronoun 'this' or 'these' or an equivalent, that term is truly affirmed of the pronoun by way of the copula of that proposition." [48] As Moody points out:

In saying that a term has supposition relatively to another term, *for* some thing or things, the medieval logicians were expressing an analysis of propositions of subject-predicate form similar to that which is now effected through the use of quantified variables — e.g. '(x).Fx ⊃ Gx', or '(Ex): Fx. Gx'. The word "thing", as used in the definition of supposition, functions as a pronominal identification of the terms for a common value in their extensional domain.[49]

When Buridan's definition of supposition is compared with Peirce's definition of the interpretant in italics above, the similarity is obvious. The relation of predicate to subject is established by the predicate representing (asserting) its relate (subject) to be a representation of (to stand for) the same correlate (object) which this representation it-

[48] Moody, *Truth and Consequence*, p. 21.
[49] *Ibid.*, p. 22.

self represents (stands for).[50] In both cases, identity of the extensional domain is asserted, but Peirce regards the interpreting representation as *creating* the relation of subject and object. Thus e.g., "the interpretation of a term in a proposition for some thing" means to Peirce that an interpreting representation makes this interpretation. But then that term must be similarly interpreted by another interpreting representation, and so on *ad infinitum*.

If this interpretation is correct, it now becomes possible to clarify the meaning of the second category. In both draft four and the "New List" itself, Peirce specifies that it is the impressions which are referred to the interpretant. "But the moment there are several impressions, that is a manifoldness of impressions, we have a feeling of complication or confusedness, which leads us to differentiate this impression from that, and they require to be brought to unity. Now they are not brought to unity until we conceive them together as being *ours*, that is, until we refer them to a conception as their interpretant." (D4p14) Since the manifold can be thought of initially only as the present in general possessing no unity, it is the manifoldness of the present in general which is now unified by the interpretant, and this is achieved by the interpretant referring what is present to the correlate. This position differs from that of the second draft, where the correspondent unites impression and concept, for that position assumes that the impressions can be thought of apart from the concept. In draft four and the "New List" itself, however, the reduction of the impressions in the manifold — i.e., of the manifoldness of the present — is achieved by their being referred to the interpretant which refers them to the correlate. That is, the impressions are thought together as representing an object represented by the interpretant itself. So in draft four Peirce asserts: "An interpretant, is a representation which represents that that which is referred to it is a representation of the same object, which it does itself represent." (D4p15) It seems clear then that the relate and correlate of category three must be taken to refer to subject and object — indeed, I think that this is the only plausible interpretation of the italicized definition of the interpretant. But if this is true for the

---

[50] That "represent" is used equivocally in this passage appears to me incontestable: I can find no univocal interpretation which is plausible. This reading is also consistent with Peirce's contention that every proposition asserts its own truth (5.340) and that the interpretant is predicated of the sign it interprets. (5.284)

third category it is true for the second, for each category is obtained by precision from those below it. Accordingly, the relate and correlate mentioned in the last category must be the same as those mentioned in the second, for the second is obtained from the third by neglecting the interpretant and attending to what is left. Since then, relate and correlate in the third category must be interpreted to mean subject and object, this is the interpretation which must be given to them in the second as well.

From this position it follows that the unity of the manifold is produced by the referring of the impressions to an object by the interpretant. But when category two is examined, it is difficult to see how such a reading can be justified, for again in draft four Peirce asserts, "A correlate is a second substance with which the first is in comparison." Are we then to believe that the present in general is compared to a second substance which is also its object? This would require that there be already in consciousness a "substance" possessing the same property as the given substance, yet designated by it. This is, I believe, what Peirce is saying.

This strange doctrine of Peirce's is closely related to Kant's synthesis of recognition. I have suggested above that the theory of substance involves implicitly a synthesis of apprehension and reproduction. The theory of the interpretant appears to involve equally the synthesis of recognition, for the burden of that synthesis is precisely the unification of the manifold by referring impressions to an object. Peirce's description of the process whereby the interpretant unites the manifold is thus very close to Kant's account of his third synthesis, but there is a fundamental difference between the two in respect to the object. Kant regards the final object in this synthesis as the transcendental object, but Peirce explicitly denies the possibility of a representation which refers directly to an object out of consciousness; "A cognition not so determined [i.e., by previous cognitions], and therefore determined directly by the transcendental object, is to be termed an *intuition.*" (5.213) In denying the existence of intuition therefore, Peirce must hold that every cognition is determined by a preceding cognition — i.e., that the object is always a representation. Accordingly, we must understand Peirce to be asserting that the unity of the manifold is achieved by our interpreting these impressions to stand for an object which we already conceive, and therefore to be asserting as well both that every cognition presupposes a cognition, and hence that there is no first cognition, and that we never have a direct cognition of the external object. Thus in the second of the papers of 1868, Peirce develops this second category in the following way:

> The next question is: For what does the thought-sign stand — what does it name — what is its *suppositum?* The outward thing, undoubtedly, when a real outward thing is thought of. But still, as the thought is determined by a previous thought of the same object, it only refers to the thing through denoting this previous thought. Let us suppose, for example, that Toussaint is thought of, and first thought of as a *negro*, but not distinctly as a man. If this distinctness is afterwards added, it is through the thought that a *negro* is a *man*; that is to say, the subsequent thought, *man*, refers to the outward thing by being predicated of that previous thought, *negro*, which has been had of that thing. If we afterwards think of Toussaint as a general, then we think that this negro, this man, was a general. And so in every case the subsequent thought denotes what was thought in the previous thought. [5.285]

How then is the actual unification of the manifold achieved? The present in general must be compared to some known object which possesses the quality — say, blue; and it must be recognized that what is present in general is what one would expect to be present if one were now cognizing a blue thing. That is, the hypothesis that what is present stands for a blue thing explains what is present and so reduces it to unity. But the inference of such a hypothesis requires a recognition of similarity between the effects of blue things and what is present in general: i.e., The present in general is thus,

Blue things are thus,

∴ The present in general is a blue thing, or

This (thing) is blue.

It is not the impressions which are blue, for they can have no color, but the object to which we refer them. Hence the object is contained under the subject of the major premiss.

As we have already seen, the fundamental problem which Peirce's theory of the categories must answer is, how is the abstraction related to the thing. Is the answer of the "New List" really adequate for this purpose? Two kinds of adequacy must be here distinguished — the logical and the metaphysical. From the logical point of view, what is necessary is a concept of the union of abstraction and thing precise enough to serve as a basis for formal reasoning. The concept of representation, which Peirce employs for this purpose, does not meet the requirement, for it does not enable one to discriminate between inclusion and membership. When Peirce discovered quantification in 1885 he introduced some clarification of this situation, but as we will see below he never developed an adequate distinction between the two forms of connection.

The second kind of adequacy required of the categories is metaphysical: they must resolve the problem of the relation of the three universes. The "It" appears in the "New List" as the object. The "I," or pure abstraction, is of course the ground (1.551), while the "Thou" appears as the interpretant. Since these are the three references of the sign, it is the sign itself that is the glue which holds this multiple universe together. Peirce spells this out in some detail in a paper of 1866.

A symbol in general and as such has three relations. The first is its relation to the pure Idea or Logos and this (from the analogy of the grammatical terms for the pronouns I, It, Thou) I call its relation to the first person, since it is its relation to its own essence. The second is its relation to the consciousness as being thinkable, or to any language as being translatable which I call its relation to the second person, since it refers to its power of appealing to a mind. The third is its relation to its object, which I call its relation to the third person or It.[51]

This passage suggests that the terms "Firstness," "Secondness," and "Thirdness" were first derived from the names of the pronouns and only later matched with the number of entities connected by the relations. This hypothesis is consistent with the fact that in 1866 the distinction between interpretant and correlate was not formulated. The second and third referred to above are not the same as the second and third of the "New List": rather the second person here is the interpretant of the "New List" and the third person is the substance. But as Peirce developed his categorical theory during the winter of 1866–67, he found that the terms "First," "Second," and "Third" could be given a numerical sense and applied to the new categories. (1.556) One sees here a typically Peircean procedure: having set forth a doctrine with appropriate terminology, Peirce revises and refines the

---

[51] "Logic of Science," Lecture I, 1866, p. 9, IB2 Box 10.

content of the doctrine while retaining the form and terminology unchanged. Thus, extensive revisions of position pass unnoticed under a shell of changeless terminology, to the utter confusion of the reader.

From a metaphysical point of view, the "New List" of categories is simply a continuation of Peirce's early papers on the "Analysis of Creation." Peirce speaks of bringing the manifold to the "unity of consistency" (D4p2), but "consistency is the intellectual character of a thing; that is, is its expressing something." (5.315) Accordingly, the unity is achieved by the embodying of the abstraction in the thing through the interpretant. But this unity is of a more than personal nature, for as Peirce wrote in 1866:

. . . it becomes important to distinguish two kinds of self-knowledge — two selves, if you please, one known immediately and the other mediately. The mediate knowledge of self is not the inner world . . . is not something presented to us but is a mere product of active thought. We find that every judgment is subject to a condition of consistency; its elements must be capable of being brought to a unity. This consistent unity since it belongs to all our judgments may be said to belong to us. Or rather since it belongs to the judgments of all mankind, we may be said to belong to it. But the world of self the world of feelings does not contain such a unity. Much rather does this unity contain the feelings.[52]

The world of feelings, or inward world, "is then the world of memory for it is clear that we can remember nothing except what is within. But the world of memory is the world of time hence the inward world and the world of time are the same." [53] Similarly, space is used to characterize the world of sense or the outward world. Both distinctions are clearly derived from Kant's theory of the inner and outer sense. Peirce then goes on to remark that:

We have now considered that experience as determination of the modifying object and of the modified soul; now, I say, it may be and is naturally regarded as also a determination of an idea of the Universal Mind; a pre-existent, archetypal Idea. Arithmetic, the laws of number *was* before anything to number or any mind to number had been created. It *was* though it did not *exist*. It was not a *fact* nor a thought, but it was an unuttered word. . . . We feel an experience to be a determination of such an archetypal Logos, by

---

[52] *Ibid.*, p. 5½.
[53] *Ibid.*

virtue of its *depth of tone,* logical *intention,* and thereby it is in the *logical world.*[54]

The transcendental unity of apperception has here become the transcendent unity of apperception in the divine mind. If the idea of the three pronouns originated — as seems very likely — with Kant's use of the "I think," Peirce is interpreting the "I" as referring to God. The bringing of the manifold to the unity of consistency therefore is the union of the pure idea in God's mind with sensory data so that it may be a concept for us. The pure idea then forms the meaning of the sign whose matter is given through the senses, and whose interpretant is a similar concept. Viewed "in their transcendental (or rhetorical) transformation" (D3) — i.e., as objectively real — this position requires every entity to be a realization of a divine idea, and hence an expression of that idea which constitutes its essence. What there are, therefore, are signs, and from a metaphysical point of view Peirce is committed to an extreme semiotic idealism not unlike Berkeley's. It was for precisely this reason that Peirce chose a review of Berkeley's works as the appropriate place to make the case for realism.

Peirce's theory at this point represents a unique fusion of previously disparate elements of his thought. By converting his preformitarian Kantianism into a semiotic phenomenalism, he can argue that whatever holds of signs in general must hold for all experience. Then, by explicating the idea of a sign in such a way that the statement of what a sign is involves reference to each of his three universes, he can derive his categories by precision from the sign relation, and the three universes by precision from the categories. He states:

A representation is anything which may be regarded as standing for something else. Matter or thing is that for which a representation might stand prescinded from all that could constitute a relation with any representation. A form is the relation between a representation and thing prescinded from both representation and thing. An image is a representation's prescinded from thing and form.

Derived directly from this abstractest triad was another less abstract. This is Object — Equivalent Representation — Logos. The *object* is the thing corresponding to a representation regarded as actual. The equivalent representation is a representation in any language equivalent to a representation

[54] *Ibid.,* p. 6.

regarded as actual. A Logos is a form constituting the relation between an object and a representation regarded as actual.

Every symbol may be said in three different senses to be determined by its *object*, its *equivalent representation*, and its *logos*. It stands for its *object*, it translates its *equivalent representation*, it realizes its logos.

As every symbol is determined in these three ways, Symbols, as such, are subject to three laws one of which is the condition sine qua non of its standing for anything, the second of its translating anything, and the third of its realizing anything. The first law is Logic, the second Universal Rhetoric, the third Universal Grammar.[55]

Thus by an extraordinary feat of ingenuity Peirce appears to derive his architectonic, and the multiple ontology which it is to support, from a rigorous analysis of the concept of representation. And this derivation is carried out purely in phenomenalistic terms without as yet claiming reality for anything. Peirce's strategy is now clear: he will elaborate his system first as a theory of signs, and then define reality in such a way as to prove that the three references of the sign are real.

The presupposition underlying the categories is that whatever a priori conditions may be true of thought must manifest themselves as laws governing symbols. In view of the triple reference of symbols, there are therefore laws governing their relations to their ground, their object, and their interpretants. To the investigation of each of these relations Peirce assigns a particular science — to the first, speculative grammar; to the second, logic; and to the third, speculative rhetoric. These sciences are clearly the Peircean equivalents of Kant's transcendental sciences, but the concept of them as "speculative" is derived from Scotus. As Gilson has put it: "Avec la grammaire et le rhétorique, la logique a en commun ce caractère de spéculer, non sur le réel, comme font la mathématique, la physique et la métaphysique, mais sur de simples contenus de la raison." [56] These contents of the mind are representations.

Peirce describes speculative grammar as treating "of the formal conditions of symbols having meaning, that is of the reference of symbols in general to their grounds or imputed characters . . ." (1.559),

[55] "Grounds of Induction," pp. 4ff.

[56] Etienne Gilson, *Jean Duns Scot. Introduction à ses Positions Fondamentales* (Paris, 1952), p. 107.

91

thereby indicating how far he was from the idea of pragmatism in 1867. "Meaning," as here used, is the abstraction — just as it was in the papers of 1859 — and has nothing to do with future consequences. Logic, Peirce regards as treating "of the formal conditions of the truth of symbols" (1.559) and therefore "of second intentions as applied to first" (1.559), or of the relation of symbols to their objects. Rhetoric deals with the reference to the interpretant — the "power of appealing to a mind." (1.559) These three "transcendental sciences" were projected in the "New List," but neither grammar nor rhetoric received much development in the late 1860's; Peirce was mainly concerned with logic.

Logic deals with the reference of symbols to their objects, and Peirce turned at once to the question of how their reference is made. Since the categories are the fundamental modes of connection among signs and their referents, they must also afford the basic combinatory principles within each of the three sciences. In the "New List," Peirce distinguished three ways in which a sign can refer to its object. The first is by a real resemblance — the possession of a common property. In this sense, any real similarity constitutes a basis for reference, and a representation which refers to its object in this way may be called a "likeness." (1.558) An example of a likeness might be a man and his photograph. Obviously, this relation is derived from the category of quality. The second way is by a correspondence in fact between representation and object. Such signs Peirce calls "indices." (1.558) This classification is clearly a generalization from the idea of reference to a correlate — of denotation. The third form of connection is by convention, or imputed character. Since such a representation is a representation solely because an interpretant so regards it, this category arises from reference to an interpretant. Signs of this ilk Peirce calls "symbols." (1.558) All words — with the possible exception of ejaculations — are symbols. The inclusion of pure likenesses and indices in the enumeration is for the sake of completeness — Peirce's real interest is in symbols.

Within the subcategory of symbols, the categories again furnish the basic varieties. Thus we have a threefold division of symbols into terms, propositions, and arguments: the term refers directly to its ground; the proposition directly to its ground and correlate; and the argument to ground, correlate, and interpretant. (1.559) Similarly, each of these three classes must yield to trichotomy on the same plan. Of particular interest here are the trichotomies of breadth, depth, and information, and of induction, deduction, and abduction.

By the "depth" of a term, Peirce means the connotation — all the qualities which can be predicated of it. The depth is the meaning. By the "breadth," Peirce means the objects of which the term is true — the denotation or extension. Clearly, breadth and depth are related to object and quality; one therefore expects a further characteristic corresponding to the interpretant and this is forthcoming in the concept of "information." Peirce speaks of the information as the "sum of synthetical propositions in which the symbol is subject or predicate, or the *information* concerning the symbol." (2.418) This concept of information is more than a fiction fulfilling a relentless architectonic, for it serves to clarify the relation between breadth and depth. Kant had asserted that breadth and depth were inversely proportional to one another. As Peirce points out, this is not strictly true: the term "men less than 200 years old" has the same extension as "men" but not the same connotation. The proper relation Peirce asserts to be given by the formula: Breadth $\times$ Depth = Information. (2.419) The inverse proportionality is only true therefore in a fixed state of information.

The theory of breadth, depth, and information was rapidly extended to propositions. Peirce divided propositions into analytic, extensive, and synthetic on the basis of the relations among the breadth, depth, and information of their two terms. An analytic — or connotative — proposition he defined as one "immediately determinative only of connotation" [57] — i.e., only connotations are involved and the depth of the subject is determined by that of the predicate. In extensive propositions, the extensions or breadth only are involved, and a relation is asserted to hold among the extensions of the two terms. He continues:

Synthetic intensive propositions (are those) which are immediately determinative both of denotation and connotation and therefore also of information and may be called informative propositions.

Thus if I say No Britons are slaves, I hereby make non-slave to be an addi-

[57] "Grounds of Induction," p. 7.

tional mark of Britons and also exclude slaves from those objects which are Britons.[58]

There is no fourth form, for if there were, the connotation of the subject would have to be determined by the denotation of the predicate. But "a symbol *denotes* by virtue of *connoting* and not *vice versa*, hence the object of connotation determines the object of denotation and not *vice versa*. . . . Whence if one of the terms is an object of connotation and the other an object of denotation, the latter is the subject and not the former." [59]

Having already proven that there were irreducible forms of inference, Peirce had his trichotomy of arguments ready made; the problem was to derive it from the categories. Since all inference is now to be regarded as an instance of the sign relation, the differences among signs must afford the key to the differences among inferential forms, and each reference of a sign — taken as a middle term — should afford a way of combining the other two. Thus e.g., induction can be regarded as the production of a proposition "all M is P" — by taking as middle term the subjects of M and P; thus:

$S^i$, $S^{ii}$, $S^{iii}$, $S^{iv}$ are taken as samples of the collection M
$S^i$, $S^{ii}$, $S^{iii}$, $S^{iv}$ are P
Therefore all M is P.

The S's thus justify the application of P to M by serving to establish a partial identity of their extensional domains. Hence the connection is made through the object as middle term. In hypothesis, the juncture is effected through the predicate; thus:

All M is $P^i$, $P^{ii}$, $P^{iii}$, $P^{iv}$
S is $P^i$, $P^{ii}$, $P^{iii}$, $P^{iv}$
S is M.

Here the identity of the qualities serves to combine S and M. In deduction the middle term is the subject of one premiss and the predicate of the other; therefore it cannot be the quality or the thing but must be viewed as the symbol or thought itself which operates as combinor. Thus the categories can be shown to yield even the forms of inference.[60]

[58] *Ibid.*
[59] *Ibid.*, p. 3.
[60] *Ibid.*, pp. 11–15.

# PART TWO

# IV

# *The Middle Years*

DURING the years from 1867 to 1880, Peirce's mature achievements began to fulfill his early promise. By 1869 he had attained sufficient stature in philosophy to be chosen "as one of a select group which included Ralph Waldo Emerson, George Park Fisher, James Elliott Cabot, and John Fiske" [1] to give the Harvard University lectures in philosophy. Moreover, his scientific ability received new recognition when in that same year he was made assistant at the Harvard Observatory and in late 1870 he and his wife were sent to Sicily on a Coast Survey expedition to observe the eclipse of the sun.[2] Returning early in 1871, Peirce continued his work for the observatory and undertook a program of photometric research which was to result in the only book he published during his lifetime. Little had been done on the subject when Peirce began his observations, and he had to face not only the task of making the observations but also that of devising an adequate means of measurement. In his attempts to reform the existing scales of magnitudes, Peirce introduced the idea of using the wave length of light as a standard unit of measure, a procedure which has since played an important part in metrology. Between 1871 and 1875 he measured the light of 494 stars, using an apparatus which he built himself, and the results obtained are still of value. As the historian of the observatory notes, "It is obvious that the work of Peirce during the years 1871 to 1875 was of a pioneer nature." [3]

During the late sixties Peirce had become a friend of William James and of the James family. Henry James the elder was America's leading Swedenborgian and Peirce found his religious ideas more palatable than those of the theologians, while in his son William, Peirce found

---

[1] Weiss, "Peirce," p. 399.
[2] Solon I. Bailey, *The History and Work of the Harvard Observatory 1839–1927* (New York, 1931), p. 53.
[3] Bailey, *Harvard Observatory*, p. 125.

the man who was to be his closest friend for over forty years. After Peirce returned from Europe in 1871, he, James, and several of their friends began to hold periodic discussions on philosophy. "After my return, a knot of us, Chauncy Wright, Nicholas St. John Green, William James, and others, including occasionally Francis Ellingwood Abbot and John Fiske,[4] used frequently to meet to discuss fundamental questions." [5] Thus was born the first and most famous of Peirce's metaphysical clubs. Historically, the importance of the club arises from the fact that there, in 1872 or 1873,[6] the idea of pragmatism was born. According to Peirce's account, Green was the one who first suggested it.

. . . the man who made the deepest impression upon me, and that in the direction of Pragmatism, was Nicholas St. John Green . . . the oldest member of the club, a profound lawyer, and an admirer particularly of Alexander Bain.[7]

The particular point that had been made by Bain and that had most struck Green, and through him, the rest of us, was the insistence that what a man really believes is what he would be ready to act upon, and to risk much upon.[8]

Peirce tells us that he wrote out a statement of pragmatism for the club, which later formed the basis for his famous paper, "How To Make Our Ideas Clear."

But for Peirce the most important feature of the club was the general issue under debate. Wright and Peirce were both physical scientists, and James was a psychologist, Abbot and Fiske, although the former was an editor and theologian and the latter a historian, were both greatly interested in science, and Green, Warner, and Holmes were lawyers who were much concerned over the social implications of science. All of them were interested in science and the scientific method. Wright, a follower of Mill, was a nominalist and a believer in the philosophic neutrality of science. He consistently attacked those who tried

[4] Oliver Wendell Holmes and Joseph Warner also attended.
[5] Wiener, *Evolution*, p. 21. This book is devoted to a study of the club and its relation to pragmatism.
[6] Peirce gives the date as 1872 ("Essays toward the Interpretation of our Thoughts," April 5, 1909, IB2 Box 11), but the earliest statement of the principle that I have found is 1873. (7. 358–361)
[7] "Essays toward the Interpretation etc.," p. 2.
[8] "Pragmatism Made Easy," p. 5, IB1 Box 1.

to erect cosmic systems on the basis of evolution (among whom of course were Peirce, Fiske, and Abbot) and maintained that "behind the bare phenomenal facts . . . there is *nothing*."[9] James regarded him as an arch apostle of positivism — an opinion also shared by Peirce. In the discussions Wright played the part of a boxing master for both Peirce and James, consistently attacking the realism to which both of them, as well as Abbot, already adhered. This was a "metaphysical club" in a strange sense, then, for instead of spinning systems these men were arguing over the legitimacy of metaphysics itself. Wright denied it; Peirce, James, and Abbot affirmed it, and each sought to support his position by the authority of science and the scientific method. It is not surprising therefore that the upshot of these discussions should have been the formulation of a theory of inquiry which was designed to be both adequate for science and consistent with a realistic metaphysic.

During the seventies Peirce was reformulating his own version of realism and was becoming increasingly occupied with the nominalist-realist controversy. The significance of the controversy for him went far beyond academic philosophy, and involved both religious and social questions. Peirce was one of that generation of scientific men who, like Andrew Dickson White, saw the conflict between the churches and science as a warfare between science and theology rather than between science and religion.[10] Although he opposed dogmatic theology vigorously, he was equally opposed to any philosophy which closed the door on religion. In the early sixties Peirce wrote an essay on positivism in which he attacked Comte and his followers for doing just this.

A Positivist to be consequent [consistent] should hold that all religious belief is superstition, and that all superstitions which do not come into conflict with any scientifically known fact are on one level of credibility. . . .

If therefore I am asked as a theist what I have to reply to the arguments of the positivist against religion, I reply in the first place, that positivism is only a particular species of metaphysics. . . . We awake to reflection and find ourselves theists.[11]

Because Peirce considered religion an affair of the heart he denied the

[9] Perry, *James*, I, 522.
[10] Andrew Dickson White, *A History of the Warfare of Science with Theology* (New York, 1955), pp. ixff.
[11] "Essay on Positivism," pp. 9, 14, IB2 Box 8.

possibility of metaphysical proofs of religious questions. But he was equally insistent that metaphysics should not adopt principles which precluded religion. Such Peirce believed were the nominalist reduction of the abstract to the sensory and the general to the individual.

So long as there is a dispute between nominalism and realism . . . a man as he gradually comes to feel the profound hostility of the two tendencies will, if he is not less than man, become engaged with one or other and can no more obey both than he can serve God and Mammon. . . . The question whether the *genus homo* has any existence except as individuals, is the question whether there is anything of any more dignity, worth, and importance than individual happiness, individual aspirations, and individual life. Whether men really have anything in common, so that the *community* is to be considered as an end in itself, and if so, what the relative value of the two factors is, is the most fundamental practical question in regard to every public institution the constitution of which we have it in our power to influence. [8.38]

Remembering that this passage was written in the year 1871, when Grant was President of the United States and the day of rugged individualism was already under way, one can see why Peirce considered the issue of such transcendent importance. The controversy between nominalism and realism was not a tilt in an ivory tower; it was in Peirce's eyes the fundamental question of the age. The utilitarian economics of Bentham and Marshall was as much the logical result of Ockham's denial of universals as was the positivist's denial of religion and Wright's denial of metaphysics. To attack one was to attack all, and the issue was one to which no man of the late nineteenth century could be blind.

But the issue had a special significance for Peirce. By training and profession he was a physical scientist, and he was always to see himself as first of all a man of science. Yet the impact of science was clearly the most important single reason for the triumph of the doctrines to which Peirce was most deeply opposed.

The doctrine of the correlation of forces, the discoveries of Helmholz, and the hypotheses of Liebig and of Darwin, have all that character of explaining familiar phenomena apparently of a peculiar kind by extending the operation of simple mechanical principles, which belongs to nominalism. Or if the nominalistic character of these doctrines themselves cannot be detected, it will at least be admitted that they are observed to carry along with them those daughters of nominalism, — sensationalism, phenomenalism, individualism, and materialism. That physical science is necessarily connected with doctrines of a debasing moral tendency will be believed by few. But if we hold that such an effect will not be produced by these doctrines on a mind which really understands them, we are accepting this belief, not on experience, which is rather against it, but on the strength of our general faith that what is really true it is good to believe and evil to reject . . . it is allowable to suppose that science has no essential affinity with the philosophical views with which it seems to be every year more associated. . . Yet a man who enters into the scientific thought of the day and has not materialistic tendencies, is getting to be an impossibility. [8.38]

To have devoted one's life to a labor, the accomplishment of which threatens to destroy the ideals in which one believes most deeply, is to find oneself in an intolerable position. This was the position in which Peirce, and the scientists who, like Peirce, were deeply concerned with the implications of their work, found themselves in the second half of the nineteenth century. While the issue was usually formulated in the context of the dispute over evolution, it went far deeper. Peirce was one of the first to see that it was not Darwin's theory, or any other particular theory, that was important — it was the method pursued. (1.33) So long as the scientific method could be founded upon nominalistic grounds, so long nominalism would rule the field.

Years later Peirce wrote: "I must count it as one of the most fortunate circumstances of a life which the study of scientific philosophy in a religious spirit has steeped in its joy, that I was able to know something of the inwardness of the early growth of several of the great ideas of the Nineteenth century." [12] As a scientist among scientists, he was impressed by the lack of individualism, the selfless devotion to the discovery of truth, which he observed among his colleagues. The sense of cooperation, the respect for the opinions of colleagues, and the ceaseless striving to reach agreement seemed to him the exact antithesis of the individualism which the results of science were being used to support. The true spirit of science it seemed to him was the spirit of religious devotion to the discovery of universal truth. (1.32–34) And this same spirit he found exemplified in the work of the medieval Scholastic philosophers. "Think of the spirit in which Duns Scotus must have worked, who wrote his thirteen volumes in folio, in a style

[12] Peirce, "Pragmatism Made Easy," pp. 3f.

as condensed as the most condensed parts of Aristotle, before the age of thirty-four." (8.11)

Indeed, if anyone wishes to know what a scholastic commentary is like, and what the tone of thought in it is, he has only to contemplate a Gothic cathedral. The first quality of either is a religious devotion, truly heroic. . . . Nothing is more striking in either of the great intellectual products of that age, than the complete absence of self-conceit on the part of the artist or philosopher. That anything of value can be added to his sacred and catholic work by its having the smack of individuality about it, is what he has never conceived. His work is not designed to embody *his* ideas, but the universal truth; . . . Finally, there is nothing in which the scholastic philosophy and the Gothic architecture resemble one another more than in the gradually increasing sense of immensity which impresses the mind of the student as he learns to appreciate the real dimensions and cost of each. [8.11]

Peirce was convinced that modern science was just as realistic and just as fundamentally opposed to nominalism as had been the philosophy of the Scholastics, and it became the labor of his life to prove that the one afforded the only true basis for the other.

During the period from 1871 to 1875 Peirce had continued his work for the Coast Survey, and in 1875 he went to Europe with his wife as the first American delegate to the International Geodetic Conference. From the standpoint of his scientific work, the trip was a complete success. He presented a paper concerning his own work with pendulums at the meeting and showed that pendulum experiments were subject to a hitherto undetected error. The paper aroused considerable opposition and a heated discussion, but two years later, after others had had a chance to check his results, he received a vote of approval from the congress.[13]

But on the personal side, the trip was something less than ideal. By December, Peirce was in Paris, and Melusina had returned to the United States. They were never to live together again. The causes of the separation are hidden under that queer blanket of obscurity which Peirce's friends and family have thrown over his life. The only reference which Peirce left concerning it is contained in the following passage:

---

[13] Peirce's pendulum work has won recognition from Plantamour, Cellerier, and Helmert.

Many a man has cherished for years as his hobby some vague shadow of an idea, too meaningless to be positively false; he has, nevertheless, passionately loved it, has made it his companion by day and by night, and has given to it his strength and his life, leaving all other occupations for its sake, and in short has lived with it and for it, until it has become, as it were, flesh of his flesh and bone of his bone; and then he has waked up some bright morning to find it gone, clean vanished away like the beautiful Melusina of the fable, and the essence of his life gone with it. I have myself known such a man; and who can tell how many histories of circle-squarers, metaphysicians, astrologers, and what not, may not be told in the old German story? [5.393] [14]

Peirce spent the winter in Paris doing pendulum work and dining occasionally with Henry James. The latter wrote home that "he is a very good fellow, and one must appreciate his mental ability; but he has too little social talent, too little art of making himself agreeable. He had, however, a very lonely and dreary winter here. . . . " [15] Peirce remained in Europe until at least July of 1876 working on official business for the Coast Survey. But during this time he was apparently in constant difficulty over money and was living well beyond the salary he was receiving. The exact reasons for these difficulties are unclear, but Peirce apparently had to go into debt to make up the survey deficit.[16] Thus began a long history of money troubles which were to plague him throughout his life. Peirce had evidently a temperamental incapacity to handle money, and once away from Cambridge he ran at once to extravagance.

Peirce returned to the United States briefly in 1876 but sailed for Europe in 1877 to attend another geodetic conference. It was on this voyage that he wrote his famous paper, "How to Make Our Ideas Clear." He says:

In the autumn of 1877 I took passage for Plymouth, England. There were

[14] The fable is that of Raymond of Poitou, who wins and weds Melusina, subject to the condition that on a particular day of the week he will not see her. For a time they live happily, but one day Raymond forgets the condition and breaks in upon her on the specified day. He then discovers that she is a water nymph, and, the condition being broken, she disappears never to return again. (S. Baring-Gould, *Curious Myths of the Middle Ages*, Second Series, Philadelphia, 1868, pp. 207–258.) The reader is left to draw his own conclusions.

[15] Perry, *James*, I, 367.

[16] C. S. Peirce to C. P. Patterson, July 6, 1876, Coast Survey Assistants N to Z, 1876, Records of the United States Coast and Geodetic Survey, National Archives, Washington, D.C.

only four first-cabin passengers beside myself, two ladies travelling separately alone and two gentlemen travelling separately, equally unprotected. They found themselves very congenial and paired off. This left me the smoking room entirely to myself; and I occupied myself by writing an article in which I enunciated a logical maxim for making ideas clear, which I called *Pragmatism*.[17]

During the 1870's, Peirce had tried to obtain teaching positions without success, and his friend William James now took a hand. In November of 1875 James wrote to Daniel Gilman recommending Peirce for a position at Johns Hopkins.[18] Gilman was then gathering a staff for the new university, and was impressed by Peirce's record and recommendations. In 1879, he received the appointment as lecturer on logic at a salary of $1500.[19]

The Johns Hopkins University was the realization of Peirce's dream of a community of scholars. The men whom Gilman brought together were a truly remarkable group. Gildersleeve headed the classics department; Remsen, the chemistry department; Rowland, the physics department; Adams, the history department; and G. Stanley Hall, the psychology department. George Morris and Peirce shared the philosophy department, and a young poet named Sidney Lanier had charge of English literature. Among the visiting lecturers were Lord Kelvin, Arthur Cayley, William James, and Josiah Willard Gibbs. But the strongest department of all was mathematics. Here Gilman managed to secure James Joseph Sylvester, one of the world's foremost mathematicians. Under Sylvester's direction, the Hopkins mathematics department became almost at once the mathematical center of America, and to it came a host of bright young students, some of whom were also interested in logic. The list of fellows and students with whom Peirce had contact, either through his classes or through the metaphysical club which he founded in 1879, includes Christine Ladd, Oscar Mitchell, Thomas Craig, Josiah Royce, John Dewey, Thorstein Veblen, Alan Marquand, George Halsted, Joseph Jastrow, and Lester Ward — to name only the more famous. Among his younger colleagues on the fac-

[17] "Sketch of some proposed chapters on the Sect of Philosophy Called Pragmatism," p. 1, IBI Box 2.
[18] Philip Wiener and Frederic Young, *Studies in the Philosophy of Charles Sanders Peirce* (Cambridge, Mass., 1952), pp. 363f.
[19] F. M. Thorn to Gilman, July 25, 1885, Gilman Papers.

ulty were Fabian Franklin and William E. Story — both to become noted mathematicians.[20]

Peirce's courses were as popular as could be expected from their abstract character. He was a good teacher and was well liked by his students.[21] In 1883 he edited a collection of essays by his students — including two of his own — which testifies to the high quality of his instruction.[22] Two of these papers were particularly outstanding — Christine Ladd's and O. H. Mitchell's, the latter of which broke ground on quantification theory.

Peirce continued his work for the Coast Survey and was periodically in Europe during these years. On April 24, 1883, he divorced Melusina Peirce and on April 30, 1883, he married Juliette Froissy (Mme Pourtalai),[23] a French woman whom he had known at least since 1878 and quite probably earlier. In October of that year the Peirces rented a house on Calvert Street and planned to make their home in Baltimore. To all appearances, Peirce was now well on the way to success. He had received a raise (to $2500) and although on yearly tenure his position seemed secure.[24] He was publishing steadily and his scientific work with the survey continued to go well. His domestic problems seemed to have been solved, and he was now a happily married and highly respected man. For the time at least Peirce's star seemed to be steadily rising.

[20] *The President's Report*, The Johns Hopkins University, 1876–1885. *The Johns Hopkins University Circular*, no. 1 (December 1879), p. 2; no. 2 (1880), p. 13; Max Fisch and Jackson I. Cope, "Peirce at the Johns Hopkins University," in Wiener and Young, *Studies*, pp. 277–311. The account of Peirce's career at Hopkins given by Fisch and Cope is thorough and detailed and the reader is referred to it for information beyond the brief sketch I have given here.

[21] Joseph Jastrow, "Charles S. Peirce as a Teacher," *Journal of Philosophy, Psychology and Scientific Method*, Vol. XIII, 723–726 (December 21, 1916).

[22] *Studies in Logic by Members of the Johns Hopkins University* (Boston, 1883).

[23] C. S. Peirce to Gilman, April 30, 1883, Gilman Papers.

[24] C. S. Peirce to G. W. Brown, October 1884, The Johns Hopkins University Library.

# V

## *The New Theory of Cognition, 1867–1870*

OF the four manuscript versions of the "New List," one bears no heading, two are entitled "Chapter I," and one is entitled "Introduction." [1] Presumably, then, the "New List" was originally conceived as the introduction to a more extended work. This work was apparently to have been on logic, but, understanding that term as broadly as he did, Peirce would have included more than his purely formal papers, and it is likely that the three papers of 1868 — "Questions Concerning Certain Faculties Claimed for Man" (5.213–263), "Some Consequences of Four Incapacities" (5.264–317), and "Grounds of Validity of the Laws of Logic" (5.318–357) — were also destined for this volume. This is the more likely since these papers are in fact developments of the doctrine contained in the "New List."

The categorical theory of the "New List" involves a semiotic phenomenalism of a radical variety. The phenomena of experience are conceived as representations which are connected with each other through the representative relation. Since the categories constitute the fundamental concepts of connection involved in representation itself, it is clear that these categories must apply throughout the phenomenal world. A basis is thereby laid for a system of a priori knowledge, since whatever holds of signs generally must also hold for all phenomenal experience. But before proceeding to the delineation of such a system there were several prior questions which had to be dealt with. First, granted that the categories apply to all phenomena, do they apply to all knowledge? That is to say, are there things-in-themselves of which we have knowledge, or are there innate principles not derived from sense experience? Closely related is the problem of intuition, for by

[1] See Appendix.

106

intuition Peirce means an effect determined directly by the thing-in-itself. Thirdly, the nature of cognition and of the cognitive process remain to be determined. And finally, the ontological status of the object of cognition must be decided. Clearly, the answers to these questions involve both a theory of cognition and a theory of reality, and it was to the elaboration of these that Peirce turned in 1868.

The theories which are presented in the papers of 1868 are stated to be attacks upon the philosophic point of view which Peirce called the "spirit of Cartesianism." [2] (5.264) What Peirce meant by this "spirit" was really nominalism (5.310), and the specific doctrines which he assails are those which he regarded as leading inevitably to a nominalistic view. Indeed, Peirce's bias is evident from the very form of the first paper, for it is modeled on that of a Scholastic commentary. The seven questions advanced might have been phrased by Aquinas or Scotus:

1. Whether by the simple contemplation of a cognition, independently of any previous knowledge and without reasoning from signs, we are enabled rightly to judge whether that cognition has been determined by a previous cognition or whether it refers immediately to its object. [5.213]
2. Whether we have an intuitive self-consciousness. [5.224]
3. Whether we have an intuitive power of distinguishing between the subjective elements of different kinds of cognitions. [5.237]
4. Whether we have any power of introspection, or whether our whole knowledge of the internal world is derived from the observation of external facts. [5.243]
5. Whether we can think without signs. [5.249]
6. Whether a sign can have any meaning, if by its definition it is a sign of something absolutely incognizable. [5.253]
7. Whether there is any cognition not determined by a previous cognition. [5.258]

These are followed by an argument for the affirmative and a proof of the negative in the best Scholastic style.

But it would be a mistake to believe that Peirce is concerned only with the medieval controversy or with Descartes' own work. For among the spiritual progeny of Descartes, Peirce included all the British empiricists who, if they were not overtly nominalists, yet subscribed

---

[2] For an excellent evaluation of Peirce's attack on Cartesianism, see W. B. Gallie, *Peirce and Pragmatism* (Harmondsworth, Middlesex, 1952), chap. 3.

to doctrines tending in that direction.[3] It is for this reason that Peirce chose a review of Fraser's edition of Berkeley as the appropriate place to make his strongest argument for realism. (8.7–38) And it is also for this reason that so many of Peirce's writings of this period can be read as direct replies to Hume. Thus Peirce is writing for a contemporary audience and his arguments are directed as much against modern empiricists as against Descartes.

By answering the seven questions in the negative, Peirce establishes the following four propositions:

1. We have no power of Introspection, but all knowledge of the internal world is derived by hypothetical reasoning from our knowledge of external facts.
2. We have no power of Intuition, but every cognition is determined logically by previous cognitions.
3. We have no power of thinking without signs.
4. We have no conception of the absolutely incognizable. [5.265]

The second principle is aimed directly at the theory of the transcendental object, for as Peirce remarks, "A cognition not so determined [by a previous cognition], and therefore determined directly by the transcendental object, is to be termed an *intuition*." (5.213) It is essential to realize that Peirce quite literally regards the existence of intuition as involving the existence of the transcendental object and therefore as a fallacy leading to nominalism. It is for this reason that he regards the British empiricists as fundamentally nominalists. For the Lockean theory of cognition holds that all knowledge originates in experience in the form of simple ideas or immediate perceptions. These simple ideas are either sensations referring to external things or reflections referring to the operations of our own minds. Sensations, according to Locke, are caused by the direct action of external realities upon our senses. Some of the ideas so produced may be regarded as copies of the qualities of the reality — these are the primary qualities — but others — the secondary qualities — do not resemble anything in the reality but correspond to it as its constant effects. Hence in both cases we do perceive the real in our first impressions. It may be regarded as the contribution of Berkeley to have proven that the real is never perceived but must be inferred through the principle of

[3] See above, p. 100.

causality; and it may be regarded as the contribution of Hume to have demonstrated that this inference is invalid. Accordingly, the existence of the real cannot be proved. Peirce believed that even Kant fell into this trap when he postulated the transcendental object as the object of intuition. (5.213) Any system, Peirce maintains, that begins with percepts relating directly to the real object faces the same fate, for the accuracy of those perceptions cannot be proven and one is driven inevitably into solipsism. (8.12)

The denial of intuition is Peirce's boldest stroke against the British school, for Locke, Berkeley, and Hume all require the existence of intuition as an axiom. Thus Hume based his whole argument upon "our fundamental principle, *that all ideas are copy'd from impressions*," [4] where by "impressions" is meant "all our sensations, passions, and emotions, as they make their first appearance in the soul." [5] To deny this principle undercuts the whole *Treatise*.

There are two arguments for the existence of intuition which Peirce must meet, one direct and the other indirect. The direct argument is that we have the power of distinguishing an intuition from a derived conclusion by inspection. Peirce shows this to be false by pointing out that in fact people cannot differentiate what they have seen from what they have inferred, and therefore the difference is at least not self-evident. If there are intuitions, therefore, they are not immediately recognizable as such but their existence must be inferred, and this leads to the indirect argument. (5.213ff)

Since there is a time before which we have no cognition of an object, and since we do cognize the object subsequently, it can be argued that the process of cognizing that object must begin at some point between these two times. But if there were no first cognition or intuition, this process could never have begun and we should never come to know the object. Peirce's answer to this argument is as follows:

. . . let any horizontal line represent a cognition, and let the length of the line serve to measure (so to speak) the liveliness of consciousness in that cognition. A point, having no length, will, on this principle, represent an object quite out of consciousness. Let one horizontal line below another represent a cognition which determines the cognition represented by that other and which has

---

[4] David Hume, *A Treatise of Human Nature* (Oxford, 1949), p. 163.
[5] *Ibid.*, p. 1.

the same object as the latter. Let the finite distance between two such lines represent that they are two different cognitions. . . . To say, then, that if there be a state of cognition by which all subsequent cognitions of a certain object are not determined, there must subsequently be some cognition of that object not determined by previous cognitions of the same object, is to say that when that triangle is dipped into the water there must be a sectional line made by the surface of the water lower than which no surface line had been made in that way. But draw the horizontal line where you will, as many horizontal lines as you please can be assigned at finite distances below it and below one another. For any such section is at some distance above the apex, otherwise it is not a line. Let this distance be *a*. Then there have been similar sections at the distances $\frac{1}{2}a$, $\frac{1}{4}a$, $\frac{1}{8}a$, $\frac{1}{16}a$, above the apex, and so on as fas as you please. [5.263]

This argument holds, it should be noted, just in case the analogy between the thought process and the triangle holds, i.e., just in case the variations in liveliness are continuous, and individual cognitions are without temporal dimension. It is by no means clear that the first assertion is warranted, and its intrusion merely serves to obscure the issue: the real question is, whether the series of cognitions must have a first member. If, as Peirce asserts, this series is continuous, it may be represented by a line, and the question then is, must the line contain its own limit? In 1868, Peirce held that it need not: granted that there is no least finite interval required for a cognition, the series may converge to a limit outside itself. The difficulties of explaining how cognition arises are thus analogous to those of Achilles and the tortoise, to which Peirce proposed the following solution.

. . . the reasoning in this sophism may be exhibited as follows: We start with the series of numbers,

$$\frac{1}{2}a$$
$$\frac{1}{2}a + \frac{1}{4}a$$
$$\frac{1}{2}a + \frac{1}{4}a + \frac{1}{8}a$$
$$\frac{1}{2}a + \frac{1}{4}a + \frac{1}{8}a + \frac{1}{16}a$$
$$\text{etc. etc. etc.}$$

Then, the implied argument is
    Any number of the series is less than *a;*
    But any number you please is less than the number of terms of this series:
    Hence, any number you please is less than *a*.
    This involves an obvious confusion between the number of terms and the
    value of the greatest term. [5.333]

Although there is an interpretation of the Achilles for which this solution is correct,[6] it does not resolve Peirce's problem, for it assumes the very point at issue — namely, that there is no minimum finite interval.

From the denial of intuition in general the denial of particular intuitions of one's self and of the subjective elements of cognition follows at once. Accordingly, the second, third, and fourth of the seven questions must be answered in the negative, and these answers are summarized in the first of the four propositions. Yet since we do in fact have knowledge of the internal world, Peirce must either show that such knowledge can be inferred from external facts or postulate a power of introspection to account for them. In taking the former alternative, the chief difficulty is to explain how self-consciousness can arise as a product of hypothetic reasoning. Peirce's argument is genetic. He first maintains that self-consciousness cannot be proven to exist in very young children. If this be granted, then the problem is to show that by the time children do manifest this consciousness, the conception of self would have arisen by hypothesis to explain facts which they would necessarily have encountered. But in the course of maturation, every child discovers ignorance and error, and must suppose a self in which these qualities inhere. Thus the conception of self may be regarded as a hypothesis to explain ignorance and error, and no faculty of introspection need be postulated. (5.225–237)

The third proposition affirms that all thoughts are signs. The justification for this doctrine Peirce develops in the following passage:

. . . since an idea consists only in what is thought at a particular moment it is only what it is thought to be at the moment it is thought. . . . Thus, the idea of one moment is in no way the same as or similar to the idea of another moment (apart from what the idea suggests to the mind). The same idea cannot therefore be said to exist in different moments but each idea must be strictly momentary; but a state of mind which does not exist for any space of time however short does not exist at all. For nothing is true of a point of time which is not true of a lapse of time except what is contained in saying it is the ideal limit of an interval. Accordingly an idea which should exist only for one moment, which should never before that have had any existence in the mind in any preceding time however close before and which should never have any existence in any succeeding time no matter how close after would have no existence whatever; and therefore an idea apart from what it represents and suggests to the mind, apart from its calling up to the mind another

[6] Bertrand Russell, *Our Knowledge of the External World* (London, 1952), pp. 177f.

idea, does not exist in the mind at all. It is therefore an essential property of an idea that it should address itself to the mind at another time. Thus an idea is in the strictest sense a representation and the statement that it is necessary that a representation should excite an idea in the mind different from its own idea is reduced to the statement that a representation is something which produces another representation of the same object and in this second or interpreting representation the first representation is represented as representing a certain object. This second representation must itself have an interpreting representation and so on *ad infinitum* so that the whole process of representation never reaches a completion.[7]

This passage makes clear several important principles of Peirce's theory. First, cognition is "momentary" — i.e., there is no least finite interval required for a cognition. Second, every thought is a sign. Third, the thought process is identical with the process of sign translation. Fourth, this process is without end. Thought is therefore a process infinite in both directions wherein each sign is suggested to the mind by its predecessors and in turn calls up its own successors.

The last of the four propositions — that we have no conception of the absolutely incognizable — Peirce had held for some years. The argument which he advances here rests upon the assertion that "all our conceptions are obtained by abstractions and combinations of cognitions first occurring in judgments of experience. Accordingly, there can be no conception of the absolutely incognizable, since nothing of that sort occurs in experience. But the meaning of a term is the conception which it conveys. Hence, a term can have no such meaning." (5.255) Since Peirce defines "cognizable" as synonymous with "experienceable," it is obvious that the two have the same extension. If, however, it be argued that we must have a concept of the incognizable because we have a concept of "cognizable" and a concept of "not" and therefore we must have a concept of their compound, Peirce's answer is that the term "not" is to be interpreted either syncategorematically, in which case it is not a concept (5.256), or as a concept of the cognizable: "*Not*, then, or *what is other than*, if a concept, is a concept of the cognizable. Hence, not-cognizable, if a concept . . . is, at least, self-contradictory." (5.257) Thus cognizability and being are synonymous and the denial of cognizability is either meaningless or impossible.

[7] "On Representations," 1873, pp. 4–6, IB2 Box 8.

Peirce's argument concerning negation is of particular interest since it marks a reversal of one of his early doctrines. In 1861 he had held that negative and universal statements cannot be derived from experience and therefore must be obtained from principles innate in the mind.[8] In the foregoing argument, however, he holds that all concepts occur first in judgments of perception. What is involved here is nothing less than the universality of the categories, which have been proven true only of perceptual experience. When Peirce asserted the existence of innate principles in 1861, he did so on the basis of two premises; viz. that all mental processes are inferential, and that all inference is reducible to Barbara. The first of these premises he continued to hold: illation, as he affirms at the end of the "New List" (1.559), is simply a form of sign translation. But the second premiss he rejected when he discovered the three forms of inference. The question is thereby posed whether or not the inclusion of ampliative inference among the forms of sign translation enables him to account for all the forms of statements which we have without postulating innate principles.

It is something of a historical tragedy that Peirce should have used the terms "hypothesis" and "induction" as names for his two forms of ampliative inference, for his choice of terminology has helped to obscure his meaning. Since we today use the term "hypothesis," or rather "hypothetical reasoning," to mean postulation — the "free creation of a postulate" — and "induction" to mean the confirmation of a hypothesis, it is easy to assume that this is also what Peirce meant. So far as his writings before 1880 are concerned, nothing could be further from the truth.[9] In his usage, both "hypothetical" and "inductive" reasoning are concerned with the process by which we create postulates. The difference between them has to do with the way in which this postulate is obtained. In hypothetical reasoning, a relation is postulated between two terms which occur in the premises as subjects:

M is, for instance, $P^i$, $P^{ii}$, $P^{iii}$, and $P^{iv}$;
S is $P^i$, $P^{ii}$, $P^{iii}$, and $P^{iv}$:
$\therefore$ S is M [1.559]

[8] See above, p. 22.
[9] In later writings, however, Peirce did use "induction" and "hypothesis" in the modern sense. Cf. 2.755.

and any such inference is hypothetical. In inductive inference, on the other hand, a relation is postulated to hold between two terms which occur in the premisses as predicates:

$S^i$, $S^{ii}$, $S^{iii}$, and $S^{iv}$ are taken as samples of the collection M;
$S^i$, $S^{ii}$, $S^{iii}$, and $S^{iv}$ are P:
∴ All M is P [1.559]

and any such inference is inductive. In neither case is any question of confirmation involved: these are methods of forming postulates not of testing them. Obviously, these are not demonstrative forms of argument; their conclusions are at best probable. But the consideration of their validity must be postponed until we have examined Peirce's theory of reality.

The problem which now confronts Peirce is that of reducing all forms of mental action to one of the three kinds of inference. It would seem at first sight that at least two separate types of processes are required: those of sign introduction and those of sign translation. But the denial of intuition means that every cognition is in some sense determined by a previous one, and the introduction of a new term may therefore be regarded as the upshot of hypothetic reasoning, even if it is only of the constitutional nominal variety.[10] Thus hypothesis serves to account for perceptual judgments and for the introduction of minor premisses in general. The introduction of a new universal statement to serve as a major premiss may be regarded as the result of induction, and deductive reasoning may then account for the conclusions derived. Accordingly, it would appear that there is no form of declarative statement which cannot be obtained by one of these three processes, and therefore, so far as the content of consciousness is concerned, there is no reason to suppose other processes.

The obvious objection to this argument is that although any declarative statement may be so derived it need not be, and that the existence of fallacies shows other processes at work. But in reply, Peirce asks under what conditions an inference can be false. According to Peirce, an inference consists of the premisses, the conclusion, and the leading principle or rule of inference according to which the conclusion follows from the premisses. (2.465f) Accordingly, Peirce argues in-

[10] See above, pp. 69–71.

genuously that every fallacious argument must be of one of four kinds: "1. Those whose premisses are false; 2. Those which have some little force, though only a little; 3. Those which result from confusion of one proposition with another; 4. Those which result from the indistinct apprehension, wrong application, or falsity, of a rule of inference." (5.282) For in any other case, a false conclusion would have to be drawn from a true premiss clearly understood by a valid rule of inference and this is impossible. But if the premisses are false, either the conclusion was validly drawn, or the error results in one of the other three ways. If the argument has some force the reasoning is valid probable inference. If the error results from confusion, "this confusion must be owing to a resemblance between two propositions; that is to say, the person reasoning, seeing that one proposition has some of the characters which belong to the other, concludes that it has all the essential characters of the other, and is equivalent to it. Now this is a hypothetic inference . . ." (5.282), and though the particular conclusion may be false yet the form is a valid one. Finally, in the last kind, the fallacy results either from confusion as to the rule, in which case it is a fallacy of the third kind, or from adopting a false rule which serves as a premiss, and hence comes under the first case. "In every fallacy, therefore, possible to the mind of man, the procedure of the mind conforms to the formula of valid inference." (5.282)

By these arguments Peirce seeks to show that all thoughts are signs and all thought processes are inferences. Yet seemingly opposed to this point of view is the time-honored dogma of British empiricism that all thoughts suggest other thoughts only through the three principles of association — resemblance, contiguity, and causality. To this dogma Peirce graciously accedes, but he goes on to argue that all association by the three principles is in fact inference. For the association of *ideas* Peirce substitutes the association of *judgments*, since concepts occur only as constituents of propositions. He then argues as follows:

The association of ideas is said to proceed according to three principles — those of resemblance, of contiguity, and of causality. But it would be equally true to say that signs denote what they do on the three principles of resemblance, contiguity, and causality. There can be no question that anything *is* a sign of whatever is associated with it by resemblance, by contiguity, or by causality: nor can there be any doubt that any sign recalls the thing signified. So, then, the association of ideas consists in this, that a judgment occasions another judgment of which it is the sign. Now this is nothing less nor more than inference. [5.307]

The design of this argument is a thing of beauty, for what Peirce is maintaining is that these three principles are really the leading principles of the three forms of inference. But this would mean that they are real general rules or laws governing the translation of signs, and so would undercut the materialism of the associationist psychology. Unfortunately, however, the details are far from being well developed. That the association of two terms by resemblance is hypothesis Peirce can plausibly maintain; but the other two arguments are weak. The relation of induction to contiguity is based on a very forced rendering of denotation, and requires considerable clarification; similarly, the relation of deduction to causality is very unclear. The development of these two parts of the argument had to await the completion of the theory of habit in the 1870's. Nevertheless the intent of Peirce's argument is clear, whatever its failings — namely, to show that all the psychological processes postulated by the associationists are really inferential.

But Hume had demonstrated that our concepts of causal connection are in reality reducible to invariable sequences of discrete and separate existences which have occurred repeatedly in our experience and so become habitual. If this is so, Peirce's theory of inference has covertly reintroduced the banished first impressions by the back door. Yet Peirce was fully aware of this difficulty — indeed, I believe it was partly to meet just these arguments of Hume that he developed the theory of habit and the new theory of inquiry in the 1870's. That the principles of inference are merely "habits" Peirce also affirms, but "habits" in the sense of Duns Scotus.

The term "habit" is hoary with philosophic usage. Far from being introduced by the nineteenth-century physiologists, it was a technical term of medieval philosophy and was employed by all the great Scholastics. Scotus' use of it was described by Peirce in his review of Berkeley in 1870.

There are two ways in which a thing may be in the mind, — *habitualiter* and *actualiter*. A notion is in the mind *actualiter* when it is actually conceived; it is in the mind *habitualiter* when it can directly produce a conception. It is by virtue of mental association (we moderns should say), that things are in the mind *habitualiter*. In the Aristotelian philosophy, the intellect is regarded as being to the soul what the eye is to the body. The mind *perceives* likenesses and other relations in the objects of sense, and thus just as sense affords sensible images of things, so the intellect affords intelligible images of them. It is as such a *species intelligibilis* that Scotus supposes that a conception exists which is in the mind *habitualiter*, not *actualiter*. This *species* is in the mind, in the sense of being the immediate object of knowledge, but its existence in the mind is independent of *consciousness*. Now that the *actual* cognition of the universal is necessary to its existence, Scotus denies. The subject of science is universal; and if the existence of [the] universal were dependent upon what we happened to be thinking, science would not relate to anything real. On the other hand, he admits that the universal must be in the mind *habitualiter* . . . [8.18]

This concept is in fact very similar to that of the "Unconscious Idea" which Peirce had employed in 1859 and 1860 to explain how abstractions can inhere in the soul. Since such abstractions are never fully realized in consciousness, they cannot be present *actualiter*; on the other hand, since instances of them are realized in consciousness, they must be present in some sense. Thus for example when a man is said to "know" French what is meant is not that the whole language is present to his mind at once, but that he can understand any word in it.

As early as 1867 Peirce had begun to identify the mode in which generals inhere in the mind with habits. (5.297f) Yet until the early seventies the notion remains confused. For there are two sorts of entities to which Peirce wishes to assign this status and these two are not wholly compatible. In the first place, a *species intelligibilis* in Scotus' sense would be a class property such as "man." Here again one senses a confusion over levels of abstraction. I suspect that what Peirce really means is "manness" conceived as the essence of man and that it is this property which serves as the rule governing association by resemblance. This would be consistent with his statement that it is impossible to conceive of agreement except as comparison in some respect, and that this respect constitutes a pure abstraction. (1.551) It would also be in line with his prior use of "concept" to designate a mental entity — a conception *actualiter* — and "Unconscious Idea" for the abstraction which is independent of consciousness. But in the second place the rules of inference, or "leading principles," must have this status, since such rules must be continuously operating throughout the process of inference or sign translation. What Peirce has not yet fully clarified is the difference between the habitual presence of a class property and the habit or rule itself, and this clarification was not forthcoming until the early seventies.

Peirce's theory is thus an attempt to show that all mental action, including that traditionally called association, may be reduced to one of the three forms of inference, and so may be regarded as a form of sign translation operating under general laws of thought. Accordingly, since the forms of inference are based upon the categories, it is shown that not only do the categories supply the concepts involved in individual propositions but they supply as well all concepts of connection among propositions, and hence the universality of the categories is assured.

Yet several problems remain to be settled. One of these was succinctly stated by Hume as follows:

If perceptions are distinct existences, they form a whole only by being connected together. But no connexions among distinct existences are ever discoverable by human understanding. . . . In short there are two principles, which I cannot render consistent; nor is it in my power to renounce either of them, viz. *that all our distinct perceptions are distinct existences,* and *that the mind never perceives any real connexion among distinct existences.* . . . For my part, I must plead the privilege of a skeptic, and confess, that this difficulty is too hard for my understanding.[11]

It would appear that this difficulty applies to Peirce's theory in full force, for the denial of intuition commits him to the position that ideas have no temporal duration and that "an idea consists only in what is thought at a particular moment."[12] Yet Peirce is also committed to a precisely contradictory view, for in discussing the theory of perceptual judgments he states explicitly that concepts are distinguished from impressions by the fact that they do require time.[13] Moreover, if ideas are not present during some period of time, it is impossible to explain association by resemblance. Similarity is impossible without comparison: the idea called up must be compared with that in the mind

[11] Hume, *Treatise,* pp. 635f.
[12] "On Representations," pp. 4–6.
[13] See above, p. 71.

and this requires presence during a lapse of time. Thus Peirce remarks that unless there is continuity in thought:

It follows that no idea could determine another, because this implies that one follows after the other according to a general rule, by which every similar idea would be followed by a similar consequent. But where there is no similarity there can be no general rule. Such a mind could certainly not be a logical one. Indeed, if as it seems natural to admit resemblances and differences can only be known through a process of comparison, it could have no consciousness at all.[14]

Nor could there be any mental connections or memory, for ideas wholly instantaneous must be utterly discrete and separate and could not be connected with others except through relations. But relations would be impossible, for they would have to embrace two different ideas and hence could not be instantaneous.

Thus Peirce is seemingly caught in a contradiction from which there is no escape. On the one hand, he is committed to the belief that ideas occupy no finite time, and on the other, that they do occupy time. Yet Peirce did not regard this situation as contradictory, for he believed that it could be resolved through the concept of continuity:

. . . we may content ourselves with the simpler conception of an indefinite continuity in consciousness. It will easily be seen that when this conception is once grasped the process of the determination of one idea by another becomes explicable. What is present to the mind during the whole of an interval of time is something generally consisting of what there was in common in what was present to the mind during the parts of that interval. And this may be the same with what is present to the mind during any interval of time, — or if not the same, at least similar — that is, the two may be such that they have much in common.[15]

This argument has the appearance of escaping the difficulty simply by asserting that it does not exist, yet it must be recognized that Peirce's theory was solidly grounded in the mathematics of his time. The theory here involved is that of the real infinitesimal, or infinitely small quantity, of the infinitesimal calculus. The theory of infinitesimals is rejected today, having been replaced by the theory of limits, but in the 1870's it was still widely held by mathematicians. Although Cauchy's

---

[14] "Chapter 4. The Conception of Time Essential to Logic," 1873, p. 4, IB2 Box 8.
[15] Untitled manuscript, 1873, 6th page, IB2 Box 8.

works of the 1820's had done much to show the superiority of the theory of limits, it was not until the work of Weierstrass became widely known that this superiority was generally acknowledged.[16] Meanwhile, many mathematicians of the older generation remained staunch in their defense of infinitesimals, and among the staunchest of these was Benjamin Peirce.[17] To the end of his life, Charles never abandoned the theory.

The classical theory of infinitesimals regards the infinitesimal as the reciprocal of the infinite, so that if $a$ is finite, $x$ infinite, and $i$ infinitesimal, $a/x = i$ and conversely $a/i = x$. Moreover, infinitesimals are themselves capable of division: thus $(a/x)/x = i^2$. According to Price:

Hence then it appears, that there will be a scale of infinities and of infinitesimals in regular sequence: such that an infinite of the $n$th order must be infinitely subdivided to produce an infinity of the $(n - 1)$th order, and infinitely quantupled to produce one of the $(n + 1)$th order: infinitesimals also bear such relations to those, on either side of them in the scale, that they are infinitesimal parts of the one, and the aggregate of an infinity of the other. Thus . . . if $i$ be the symbol of an infinitesimal, $i^0$ will represent the finite quantity, and the scale will be

$$i^{-n}, \ldots i^{-2}, i^{-1}, i^0, i^1, i^2, \ldots i^n$$

the order . . . being a descending one.[18]

Under such a scheme it is clear that continuity must be defined as Peirce defines it: "A continuum such as we suppose time and space to be, is defined as something any part of which itself has parts of the same kind." [19] Thus every interval is capable of division into infinitesimal intervals and each such infinitesimal interval may be divided into infinitesimals of the next order.

The theory of infinitesimals thus appears to resolve all Peirce's problems at one stroke. His argument against the existence of a first cognition continues to hold since there is no minimum finite interval required for cognition, but the difficulties of incomparability are

[16] Carl Boyer, *The Concepts of the Calculus* (New York, 1949), pp. 271–288. Bell, *Men of Mathematics*, pp. 492f.

[17] Cf. Benjamin Peirce, *An Elementary Treatise on Plane and Solid Geometry* (Boston, 1841), Preface.

[18] Bartholomew Price, *A Treatise on Infinitesimal Calculus*, vol. I: *Differential Calculus*, 2nd ed. (Oxford, 1857), p. 20.

[19] Untitled manuscript, March 8, 1873, p. 1, IB2 Box 8.

avoided by positing presence through an infinitesimal interval. Accordingly Peirce can deny the existence of intuition yet retain the ordinary processes of mental operation unimpaired.

Yet can Peirce really hold that thought is continuous? In 1868 he hedged on this all important point.

There is reason to believe that the action of the mind is, as it were, a continuous movement. Now the doctrine embodied in syllogistic formulae (so far as it applies to the mind at all) is, that if two successive positions, occupied by the mind in this movement, be taken, they will be found to have certain relations. It is true that no number of successions of position can make up a continuous movement; and this, I suppose, is what is meant by saying that a syllogism is a dead formula, while thinking is a living process. But the reply is that the syllogism is not intended to represent the mind, as to its life or deadness, but only as to the relation of its different judgments concerning the same thing. And it should be added that the relation between syllogism and thought does not spring from considerations of formal logic, but from those of psychology. [5.329]

But this is not adequate. For Peirce has explicitly asserted that thoughts are signs, that thinking is the translation of signs, and that this translation is inference. From this it follows that the process of inference cannot be analogous to thinking — it is thinking; and it either is or is not continuous.

Peirce goes on to remark:

All the arguments of Zeno depend on supposing that a *continuum* has ultimate parts. But a *continuum* is precisely that, every part of which has parts, in the same sense. Hence, he makes out his contradictions only by making a self-contradictory supposition. In ordinary and mathematical language, we allow ourselves to speak of such parts — *points* — and whenever we are led into contradiction thereby, we have simply to express ourselves more accurately to resolve the difficulty. [5.335]

But here again the relation of the continuous and discontinuous is left undefined. Is it a metaphor to speak of distinct thoughts or signs, and in what would the more accurate expression consist? To these questions, Peirce had as yet no answer.

Thus by 1868 Peirce had already become involved in the problems of infinity and continuity — problems to which he had as yet no very adequate answers. Not until the 1880's, when he came upon the work of Georg Cantor, was he able to make substantial progress in these areas. Meanwhile the relation of inference to the thought process required further clarification. So, too, did the nature of habit: is a habit a property or a rule, and what is its ontological status? And finally, what grounds can be alleged for believing that either generals or objects are real? These are the primary problems to which Peirce turned in the years between 1868 and 1878.

# VI

# *The Theory of Reality*

PEIRCE'S theory of the categories provides the basis for his theory of cognition, and the theory of cognition in turn provides the basis for the theory of reality. Accordingly, the latter theory is first presented as a corollary in the second of the 1868 papers on cognition. (5.311ff) The fullest exposition of the new doctrine, however, occurs in the review of Berkeley in 1871 where Peirce describes his own theory as follows:

> This theory involves a phenomenalism. But it is the phenomenalism of Kant, and not that of Hume. Indeed, what Kant called his Copernican step was precisely the passage from the nominalistic to the realistic view of reality. It was the essence of his philosophy to regard the real object as determined by the mind. That was nothing else than to consider every conception and intuition which enters necessarily into the experience of an object, and which is not transitory and accidental, as having objective validity. In short, it was to regard the reality as the normal product of mental action, and not as the incognizable cause of it. [8.15]

There are two parts to the problem of reality — are there real objects? and are there real universals? Peirce's writings of the decade 1868–1878 may be regarded as an attempt to answer both questions in the affirmative — an attempt which failed. The rock upon which Peirce's first system went to pieces was the problem of the categories; that upon which his second system foundered was the problem of reality.

Peirce's argument for the existence of real objects is based upon his phenomenalistic belief that our knowledge is not a sensory copy of the cause of sensation but the product of a synthesis of sense experience carried out by the mind. (8.12–16) Concepts serve to reduce sense experience to unity and are justified only by the unity they produce. (1.545) This is equivalent to saying that concepts arise by hypothesis to give coherence to what would otherwise be an unintelligible chaos of sense data. I hypothesize the existence of an object $x$ in order to explain why I now have certain sensations, and I refer these sensations to $x$ as cause. What justifies my hypothesis is the fact that it gives coherence to my experience — that is, that these sensations continue to occur together as if they were the effects of one cause. The test of truth, then, is coherence: a true proposition is one which gives coherence to experience.

To say that the proposition, "There is an $x$ which is so and so," is true is to say that there really is such an $x$. (3.93n1) This real is that which is asserted to exist in a true proposition, and therefore that which must be postulated to explain our experience. Thus Peirce writes:

. . . if we mount the stream of thought instead of descending it, we see each thought caused by previous thought, until at last we reach the original sensations, which it is supposed themselves are caused by something external. In using the word "supposed," I do not wish to imply that there is any room for doubt in the matter; but only that the external realities are not themselves the immediate object of thought but are only what it is necessary to suppose exists to account for the phenomena of sensation. We find in this stream of thought, in this succession of images, a certain coherency, harmony, or consistency, which cannot be due entirely to the laws of association themselves; but which extends to the additions which are made to the body of our thought from without. And it is this coherency of experience which demonstrates the existence of a reality; or something permanent and fixed, to which our thought and experience, more or less perfectly, corresponds.[1]

The existence of the real object is thus hypothetically affirmed in order to explain the regularities of phenomena and thereby to make our experience intelligible.

Although Peirce's phenomenalism differs from Kant's in some respects, both agree concerning the possibility of a priori knowledge. For Peirce it is the facts that all thoughts are signs and that the relations among thoughts are sign relations that make this possible, for it follows that whatever must be true of the object of a sign must be true of any object we can know. One of the most important a priori truths so

---

[1] "Chapter 4. (2nd draft)," 1873, pp. 6f, IB2 Box 8. Although this statement was written five years after the 1868 papers, its position in respect to the object is I believe that which is implicit in both the "New List" and the review of Berkeley and therefore that which Peirce held in 1868.

derived is the reality of generals. Peirce states his position in the review of Berkeley:

> It is plain that this view of reality is inevitably realistic; because general conceptions enter into all judgments, and therefore into true opinions. Consequently a thing in the general is as real as in the concrete. It is perfectly true that all white things have whiteness in them, for that is only saying, in another form of words, that all white things are white; but since it is true that real things possess whiteness, whiteness is real. It is a real which only exists by virtue of an act of thought knowing it, but that thought is not an arbitrary or accidental one dependent on any idiosyncrasies, but one which will hold in the final opinion. [8.14]

A more detailed form of this argument is to be found in the second paper on cognition where Peirce undertakes to refute Berkeley's doctrine that every cognition must be utterly determinate. If we have an "image, or absolutely singular representation," (5.298) Peirce points out, it would have to be "absolutely determinate in all respects. Every possible character, or the negative thereof, must be true of such an image." (5.299) But "this being so, it is apparent that no man has a *true* image of the road to his office, or of any other real thing. Indeed he has no image of it at all unless he can not only recognize it, but imagines it (truly or falsely) in all its infinite details. This being the case, it becomes very doubtful whether we ever have any such thing as an image in our imagination." (5.300) The argument is supported by the fact that we never become aware of any such infinity of detail in a given cognition, and therefore no ground can be alleged for believing it to exist. But if there are no wholly determinate cognitions, then a most important conclusion follows:

> But it follows that since no cognition of ours is absolutely determinate, generals must have a real existence. Now this scholastic realism is usually set down as a belief in metaphysical fictions. But, in fact, a realist is simply one who knows no more recondite reality than that which is represented in a true representation. Since, therefore, the word "man" is true of something, that which "man" means is real. The nominalist must admit that man is truly applicable to something; but he believes that there is beneath this a thing in itself, an incognizable reality. His is the metaphysical figment. Modern nominalists are mostly superficial men, who do not know, as the more thorough Roscellinus and Occam did, that a reality which has no representation is one which has no relation and no quality. The great argument for nominalism is that there is no man unless there is some particular man. That, however, does

not affect the realism of Scotus; for although there is no man of whom all further determination can be denied, yet there is a man, abstraction being made of all further determination. There is a real difference between man irrespective of what the other determinations may be, and man with this or that particular series of determinations, although undoubtedly this difference is only relative to the mind and not *in re*. Such is the position of Scotus. Occam's great objection is, there can be no real distinction which is not *in re*, in the thing-in-itself; but this begs the question for it is itself based only on the notion that reality is something independent of representative relation. [5.312]

This passage, which appeared in 1868, is Peirce's first avowal of Scotian realism — an avowal which was reaffirmed in the review of Berkeley in 1871 and many times after that. Yet in these same papers, Peirce is equally explicit in avowing his Kantian phenomenalism. That one can be both a Kantian and a Scotian is an assertion which will be greeted with some interest by the proponents of either view, and accordingly the nature of Peirce's Scholasticism must be examined with some care.

Duns Scotus was not a phenomenalist; neither was he a Platonist. He belonged to that school of medieval philosophers who believed that universals were real because they corresponded to something out of the mind, but who did not believe that that correspondent was a Platonic form.[2] Boehner has described Scotus' theory as follows:

The nature of a thing, its real essence, is naturally prior to its singularity and its universality. That is explained by referring to Avicenna who says in the fifth book of his Metaphysics: "Horseness, for instance, is only horseness. It is from itself, neither one nor many, neither universal nor particular." That means, if you understand it correctly, adds Scotus: "Horseness is by itself not one horseness by numerical unity, nor is it actually universal in the manner of a universal made by the intellect (but he excludes: "non ut objectum intellectus"), nor is horseness by itself particular or singular." Though it never really exists without being singular or universal, nevertheless, by itself, it is neither singular nor universal; it is rather naturally prior to both its singularity and universality. Because of this priority by nature over singularity and universality, the common nature is the "quod quid est," the quiddity or whatness. As such it is, by itself, the object of the intellect, and, if taken as such, it falls under the consideration of the metaphysician. . . . This "natura communis" exists really in singular things; it is not numerically one in all

[2] Edward Carter Moore, "The Scholastic Realism of C. S. Peirce," *Philosophy and Phenomenological Research*, XII, 408 (March 1952).

singular things, but each singular thing has its own common nature, which is singularized by the individual difference. This common nature existing in singular things is the basis of our abstraction, and it is the basis of our intuitive knowledge as well, though only in so far as it exists, not, however, in its singularity. . . . Hence the process of abstraction has to explain the mode of universality which is added to this common nature, as the principle of individuation has to explain the mode of singularity which is added to the common nature. But the mode of commonness of this nature has not to be explained, since the nature, the "natura communis," is common by itself.[3]

Scotus thus solves the problem of universals by redefining it. The correspondence of concept and thing is now easily explained since each is a form of the same nature. But what has now to be explained is how this common nature comes to have different forms — that is, how this nature is generalized into the universal and singularized into a particular.

When a cognition takes place, Scotus holds that what is perceived — the content of the cognition — is the common nature. But as perceived, the common nature is not universal; rather it must be converted into a universal through abstraction. This act of abstraction, however, does not consist in simply eliminating the particularizing determinations, for if it did the common nature would be universal in itself, and this Scotus denies. On the contrary, the production of universality involves the addition of something positive to the common nature by the spontaneous activity of the intellect. Boehner continues:

Universality is an addition made by the intellect to the cognition of the common nature; it is an ens rationis, a second intention, and it means that the common nature is predicable about many things. Hence abstraction is the act by which the intellectus agens produces the universality of the known common nature by bringing it into the relation of predicability with every singular possessing the same common nature.[4]

If the common nature is not in itself universal, neither is it singular, and Scotus must also explain the process by which it is individuated. Scotus was dissatisfied with the Thomistic theory that matter is the individuating principle, and he therefore took a radically different

---

[3] Philotheus Boehner, O.F.M., "The History of the Franciscan School, Part III: Duns Scotus," mimeographed (New York, 1945). Remimeographed, Duns Scotus College, Detroit, Michigan, 1946, pp. 42f.
[4] *Ibid.*, pp. 44f.

course. He conceives the *quiddity* as prior to determination and allows it to be individuated not only by the addition of further determinations but ultimately by a nonqualitative positive addition called *haecceity*. This notion seems to have originated in a theological dispute concerning the freedom of God's will. Scotus maintained, as against Thomas, that although God cannot act contrary to his own nature, yet his own nature does not completely determine his actions. In any particular case, God has alternative possibilities of action, and which of these He will follow depends entirely upon an arbitrary decision of his free will. Among these particular cases are acts of creation: although God creates the essences of things by reason, He creates their existence by arbitrary fiat. Hence existence contains an arbitrary, nonintellectual element which is inexplicable. Species exist by virtue of an intelligible essence — individual things by virtue of an arbitrary *thisness* or *haecceity*. *This* stone is this stone and not another — its *thisness*, its brute matter-of-fact existence, cannot be deduced from any antecedent reasons but can only be known by experience. Individuality, therefore, is not merely limitation; it is also something positive in itself, and the addition of this positive element completes the singularization of the common nature.[5]

The singular so produced is truly singular by numerical unity, yet this fact does not prevent it from being the real counterpart of the universal in the mind, for its common nature and its *haecceity* remain distinct. To explain how that which is singular may contain distinct elements, Scotus introduced a new form of distinction which he called a "formal" distinction and which serves as an intermediary between the two traditional Scholastic distinctions — the real distinction and the logical distinction. A real distinction holds between two objects when they can exist independently of one another — it is thus both a conceptual distinction and a distinction *in re*. A logical distinction, on the other hand, is a distinction made only by the mind with no basis in fact, as e.g., between the *definiendum* and the *definiens*. A formal distinction as defined by Scotus is a distinction made by the mind which has a basis in fact, but which does not suppose the things distinguished to be capable of existing separately. Scotus' best example

---

[5] *Ibid.*, p. 104. Robert L. Calhoun, "Lectures on the History of Christian Doctrine," Yale Lectures, 1948, privately printed, pp. 334–337.

of such a distinction is of course that between the persons of the Trinity: if this distinction were real there would be three gods; if it were logical there would be no basis in fact for it. Hence it must be formal. Such too is the nature of the distinction between common nature and *haecceity* in the singular. Neither component ever exists alone so they are separated only by the mind, yet the distinction has a basis *in re* and it is just this fact which enables Scotus to regard the common nature of the singular as the correspondent of the universal and so to maintain the reality of universals.[6]

That Peirce was influenced by these doctrines of Scotus we know from his own statements as well as from the studies of his commentators — particularly those of E. C. Moore. Thus Peirce's categories of Firstness, Secondness, and Thirdness seem to correspond to the common nature, *haecceity*, and the universal respectively, his concept of precision resembles Scotus' formal distinction, and his theory of abstraction seems similar to Scotus' method of deriving universality.[7] That these similarities exist, and that Peirce did in fact derive some of his ideas from the great Scholastic, is, I believe, true. Yet once again the question of time must be raised, for these correspondences hold good chiefly for the period after 1885. Until then the concept of *haecceity* plays no part in Peirce's philosophy. Firstness and Thirdness remain defined as they were in the "New List," and precision is not identical with formal distinction. It is only with the reformulation of the categories around 1885 that these analogies become operative; our problem now is to determine what if any relation there is between Peirce and Scotus during the 1870's.

Let us look first at the relation between Scotus' theory of the formal distinction and Peirce's theory of precision. That Peirce's theory is actually derived from Scotus' cannot be shown, although some of his later writings suggest this possibility. (1.549n1) Nevertheless, there is certainly a very striking parallel between the three forms of distinction used by Scotus — real, formal, and logical, and the three forms of distinction discussed by Peirce in the "New List."

Discrimination has to do merely with the senses of terms, and only draws a

---

[6] Edward Carter Moore, "Metaphysics and Pragmatism in the Philosophy of C. S. Peirce," unpublished doctoral dissertation, University of Michigan, 1950, pp. 14–16, 90–96.
[7] Moore, "The Scholastic Realism," pp. 409–412.

distinction in meaning. Dissociation is that separation which, in the absence of a constant association, is permitted by the law of the association of images. It is the consciousness of one thing, without the necessary simultaneous consciousness of the other. Abstraction or precision, therefore, supposes a greater separation than discrimination, but a less separation than dissociation. Thus I can discriminate red from blue, space from color, and color from space, but not red from color. I can prescind red from blue, and space from color (as is manifest from the fact that I actually believe there is an uncolored space between my face and the wall); but I cannot prescind color from space, nor red from color. I can dissociate red from blue, but not space from color, color from space, nor red from color. [1.549]

The parallel is sufficiently close to suggest that Peirce's theory may be the result of redefining Scotus' distinctions so as to make them consistent with phenomenalism. In order to define the nature of the Scholastic distinctions, it is necessary to contrast the degree of separation made by the mind with the degree of separation which actually exists *in re*. But in Peirce's theory, such a contrast cannot be stated, for to talk of a separation *in re* apart from the mind is to talk of a separation *an sich*. Thus in reply to Occam, Peirce writes: "Occam's great objection is, there can be no real distinction which is not *in re*, in the thing-in-itself; but this begs the question for it is itself based only on the notion that reality is something independent of the representative relation." (5.312) If the concept of a real distinction is translated into Peirce's theory, therefore, it must be formulated as a distinction holding among things as represented, and the simplest such formulation would be as the distinction between two things each of which can be conceived to exist separately. This problem does not arise with the logical distinction which supposes no division *in re* and which may therefore be translated as a discrimination of meaning, but it does recur with the formal distinction. If the formal distinction is to preserve its position as a mediator between the other two, it would seem natural to define it as the distinction between two things when at least one of them can be conceived to exist without the other. Accordingly, Peirce defines precision as the *"supposition* of one part of an object, without any supposition of the other." (1.549) Clearly, there are two forms of precision — one where each element can be conceived to exist independently, and one where only one element can be so conceived. (1.549) In the former case, the elements are also dissociable (e.g., red and blue); in the latter they are not (e.g., space from color) but they can be discriminated. Thus it seems very likely that what Peirce has done is to take from Scotus a theory of the degrees of differentiation which he needed for his own purposes, and to reinterpret it so as to make it consistent with his own phenomenalism.

That Peirce's categories bear any such relation to Scotus' elements of cognition, however, seems very dubious, at least for the period of the 1870's. As we have seen above, Peirce's categories antedate his knowledge of Scotus, so no question of origin is involved — the most that can be claimed is an influence. But there is very little real evidence of such an influence, as may be seen by examining the content of each category in some detail.

As previously noted, the term *haecceity* does not occur in Peirce's writing prior to 1890. If, therefore, the concept of *haecceity* influenced Peirce, the existence of that influence must be proven on other grounds. Clearly, such an influence — if it exists — should be most evident in Peirce's theory of individuation. Yet the theory of individuation which Peirce actually propounded at this time is chiefly distinguished by the complete absence of any positive individuating principle. Thus in 1870 Peirce wrote:

The absolute individual can not only not be realized in sense or thought, but cannot exist, properly speaking. For whatever lasts for any time, however short, is capable of logical division, because in that time it will undergo some change in its relations. But what does not exist for any time, however short, does not exist at all. All, therefore, that we perceive or think, or that exists, is general. So far there is truth in the doctrine of scholastic realism. But all that exists is infinitely determinate, and the infinitely determinate is the absolutely individual. This seems paradoxical, but the contradiction is easily resolved. That which exists is the object of a true conception. This conception may be made more determinate than any assignable conception; and therefore it is never so determinate that it is capable of no further determination. [3.93n1]

There is, then, no true singular — no true individual, except in a wholly ideal sense. (5.299f) Metaphysically speaking, this argument depends upon Peirce's theory of continuity which was outlined in a foregoing section;[8] namely, that a true continuum is one every interval of which

[8] See above, pp. 120f.

is infinitely divisible into parts of the same kind. Taken together with the assertions that time is continuous and that every cognition occupies an interval of time — assertions which we have seen that Peirce also advanced [9] — this implies that absolute individuality cannot be realized. For if any quality is predicable of the object, the object endured during some continuous interval of time. But divide that interval as you like, there will still remain a continuous interval during which it existed and which is capable of further division. Hence absolute determination and so absolute individuality are inherently unattainable. But this position flatly contradicts the position of Scotus.

On the other hand, Peirce's concept of universality, or generality, is very similar to that held by Scotus and most Scholastics. The universal is an *ens rationis*, an abstract property, such as *whiteness, blackness, manness,* etc.[10] Thus in affirming his realism, Peirce writes: "It is perfectly true that all white things have whiteness in them, for that is only saying, in another form of words, that all white things are white; but since it is true that real things possess whiteness, whiteness is real." (8.14) There is a clear analogy between universality so defined and the ground referred to by a Firstness, for as defined in the "New List" the ground is precisely such an abstract property. (1.551) But there is no apparent analogy between this concept of the universal and the Thirdness of the "New List." Whether such a connection emerges with the birth of pragmatism is a question into which we shall enquire in due course, but it suffices to point out that Thirdness, in the sense of the "New List," has no analogue in Scotus; there is nothing precisely corresponding to Peirce's concept of representation in Scotus unless it be the theory of supposition, and this is a doctrine common to many medieval logicians.[11]

We are left then with the problem of the common nature. Again, since Peirce never employed this term, the influence of the concept — if any — must be inferred. For Duns Scotus the common nature is the

---

[9] See above, pp. 118–120.

[10] "Universality is an addition made by the intellect to the cognition of the common nature; it is an ens rationis, a second intention, and it means that the common nature is predicable about many things. Hence abstraction is the act by which the intellectus agens produces the universality of the known common nature by bringing it into the relation of predicability with every singular possessing the same common nature." Boehner, "Scotus," pp. 44f. See also Moore, "The Scholastic Realism," pp. 410f.

[11] Moody, *Truth and Consequence,* pp. 18ff.

*quod quid est* of cognition, and if there is an analogous concept in Peirce's theory, that concept should play the same role in the cognitive process. In the preceding section we have examined Peirce's 1868 papers on cognition, but these papers define his position chiefly by negation; they tell us what a cognition is not, but not what it is. A more positive statement is now desirable, and accordingly three questions must be asked: what is a cognition? what is its *quiddity?* and what is it a cognition of?

A cognition is always a proposition. But what is a proposition? In 1867 and 1868 Peirce believed that every proposition was fundamentally of the subject-predicate form (2.472; 1.559), and this assumption, as noted above, underlies the "New List." [12] Yet De Morgan's paper on the logic of relations had been in Peirce's hands since 1866 (1.562), and although the full significance of that paper had still not dawned upon him in 1867, it must have done so very shortly thereafter. Certainly by 1870, when he published his first major paper on the logic of relations (3.45–149), Peirce had abandoned his allegiance to the subject-predicate form. But in so far as the subject-predicate theory of the proposition is a premiss of the "New List" — and so of the 1868 theory of cognition — any change in that doctrine requires a reconsideration of the categories and the cognitive theory. There are then two cognitive theories — one belonging to the period 1867–1870, and the other to the period 1871–1880. To the analysis of this later theory we shall turn in another section, but for the present we must restrict our attention to the period 1867–1870, during which Peirce first declared himself a Scotian. And during this period, a cognition is to be regarded as a proposition of the subject-predicate form.

The *quod quid est* of a cognition must be a quality, since what the cognition does is to affirm a quality of an object. (1.559; 2.415) [13] But what a quality is, is not so clear. We have seen above that Peirce regards the abstract property as the true universal. Quality is usually regarded as the embodiment of this abstraction. Thus he asserts, *"Embodying blackness* is the equivalent of *black"* (1.551), and again he states that the two sentences, "This is white" and "This possesses

[12] See above, pp. 65f.

[13] Thomas A. Goudge, "Peirce's Theory of Abstraction," in Wiener and Young, *Studies*, p. 123.

whiteness" are equivalent. (8.14) There are also passages where Peirce speaks of the abstraction as the "meaning" of the quality (1.559), but this is probably only a loose way of saying that it is the essence. All concepts — at least all class concepts — are regarded as qualities, and all qualities are conceptual. This includes even qualities forming the predicates of judgments of sensation or perceptual judgments, for these sensations are not "sense qualities" in the sense of being the matter of sensation, as e.g., would be true of the fictitious first impressions of sense, but they are concepts introduced as hypotheses. Thus quality may range from the relatively abstract to the relatively concrete, but it is always conceptual.

Peirce adds considerable confusion to the status of quality when he states that qualities are only known as abstractions from things compared. (1.551f) The kind of abstraction involved here is precision (1.558),[14] not what Peirce later called "hypostatic" abstraction,[15] and precision is ambiguous as to type. When I prescind space from color, I am not abstracting a property — I am ignoring a differentia; but if I were to prescind red from two apples, I would seem to be abstracting a property. In the latter case we have a true difference in level of abstractness while in the former we have only a difference in degree of specification. This is the same confusion of generality and abstractness which we have seen before.[16] In general, Peirce does regard increasing generality as involving increasing abstractness, but the nature of the relation between the two terms is never really made clear.

If quality is the *quod quid est* of cognition, then, if there is an analogue to the common nature in Peirce's system, it must be quality. Yet there would appear to be severe difficulties in such a position. For Scotus the whole point of the common nature is that it exists in the thing out of the mind and serves as the correspondent for the universal in the mind. If it did not exist in the thing out of the mind it would be useless, for it would not guarantee the reality of the universal. That it exists in the thing is shown by its being perceived — i.e., the cognition is an immediate perception of the thing as it is.[17] But it appears as though Peirce both does and does not accept this position. On the one

[14] Goudge, "Peirce's Theory of Abstraction," p. 123.
[15] *Ibid.*, p. 124.
[16] See above, pp. 72f.
[17] Moore, "The Scholastic Realism," p. 410.

hand, he explicitly states that he holds the theory of immediate perception (8.16), yet on the other hand his whole theory of cognition contradicts this theory, for the quality is not a copy of its cause directly transmitted through the senses, but a hypothesis introduced by the mind.

We are thus brought to the third question, what is a cognition a cognition of? And this question may be answered by referring again to Peirce's bizarre doctrine that there is no first cognition. Let us suppose that there is a first cognition. Then the subject of that cognition would clearly have to be directly known in the first impressions of sense, and the cognition would consist of a proposition asserting some quality, received as a first impression, to be true of that thing. But as Peirce points out, what would be in the first impression would be only an effect of the thing — the thing itself we should not really know at all. Thus, as Kant says, the transcendental object is an object never intuited by us (A109), and it is therefore incognizable. Accordingly, we should never know if the first cognition were true, and we should be immediately reduced to the classic epistemological dilemma.

Peirce's theory holds that the object of any true cognition must be a real object. But what is a real object? That there is any such object is a hypothesis introduced by us to give coherence to experience. The object therefore is posited, or hypothesized — it is a construct having explanatory value. But this means that the object is as we conceive it to be, since it is only as we conceive it that its existence is postulated. If therefore we attribute whiteness to an object, and the statement asserting the attribution is true in the sense of giving coherence to our experience, then the object is white. To identify the present in general as standing for an object is therefore to refer it to an object as conceived and hence as conceived in a previous thought. But in this sense it is perfectly true that Peirce believed in immediate perception, for the thing is as we perceive it to be.

Yet Peirce's denial of a first cognition involves something more than this. He has shown that the existence of a first impression would be very unfortunate, but has he really shown that there cannot be such an impression? Recalling that he defines impressions to mean neural stimuli which are instantaneous, as distinct from qualities which require time, Peirce must show that it is impossible to think of a first impression. Any thought — including sense qualities — is a concept, and such concepts arise only when we need to reduce the manifold to unity. (1.545) If there were but one impression, there would be no concept. (1.554) There are, then, many impressions for every cognition. Let us assume that there is a first impression which is cognized. Then that cognition must state " '$i_1$' is the first impression." '$i_1$' is therefore a concept designating $i_1$. But this is impossible since even the concept of the present in general, which Peirce regards as the concept "nearest to sense," is a concept of many elements present together. (1.547) Thus as Peirce remarks: "That which exists is the object of a true conception. This conception may be made more determinate than any assignable conception; and therefore it is never so determinate that it is capable of no further determination." (3.93n1) The first impression then cannot be known because there is in Peirce's system no way to designate a wholly singular object. And this means that there is no sign capable of making such a reference, and therefore no index — at least in the later sense of the term.

This point is actually quite obvious, for the later theory of the index is so closely tied to the theory of *haecceity* that the absence of the one almost implies the absence of the other. Yet because Peirce introduced the terms "likeness," "index," and "symbol" in the "New List," and because he gave a definition of the index which sounds very much like the definition he used later (viz., "Those [representations] whose relation to their objects consists in a correspondence in fact" [1.558]) the differences are not at once apparent. But what Peirce means by the index in 1867 is the term which functions as the subject of the proposition and which indicates the object. Such a term is always a concept, even in the case of "it," or the present in general, and always denotes a plurality of things. (1.547; 1.559) Thus, although Peirce's logic of 1870 contains individual variables, the values of these variables are not interpreted as being completely singular but rather as entities capable of further determination which for purposes of convenience we treat as singular. (3.93–96) Even traditionally singular terms such as proper names are not regarded as naming absolute individuals, for, as the famous case of Philip drunk and Philip sober indicates (1.494), such individuals are divisible. (2.415)

It seems clear that this theory of individuality is the result of the same confusion between abstraction and generality, or conversely between individuality and specification, which we have seen at work before. Peirce has failed to differentiate between the individual and its unit class; instead of segregating a domain of individuals, then one of classes of individuals, then one of classes of classes of individuals, etc., he has only a domain of classes. To reach the individual he must specify the class so as to reach the unit class, but, lacking any positive concept of the individual, he is forced to define the unit class as the product class of an infinite number of classes, which obviously leads to an infinite regress and ultimately to the definition of the individual as the limit of an endless process. It is this fact which gives to Peirce's whole discussion of denotation its highly ambiguous character — it is never clear whether the object denoted is an individual thing, another concept, or whatever is denoted by another concept. Since the thing and the unit class are not clearly discriminated, Peirce seems to be talking about a concept even when he is talking about the thing, for since the thing is as it is thought to be, it must be like the concept, and so comparable to it. Nor does his logic of individual terms serve to clarify the situation since his postulates relating to these terms do little more than translate the *nota notae* into symbols. (3.96) But this leaves Peirce in the position of trying to explain supposition without an individual variable. Thus instead of interpreting "Some S is P" as "(Ex). 'S' stands for x. 'P' stands for x," [18] Peirce must say, " 'S' stands for the same correlate that 'P' stands for." But for what correlate is that? Peirce must answer either "for M," which is a concept and therefore must already be known, or "for the correlate that 'M' stands for," which leads to a regress. Thus Peirce's doctrine that the subject refers to the object only through a prior sign is seen to be the result of the fact that there is no way of referring to the object except through a concept.

That Peirce's theory of cognition should turn out to be built upon logical notions, whether correct or not, is a further confirmation of the hypothesis that his system is constructed on the architectonic plan. But in view of the foregoing, another consequence of this hypothesis now becomes evident. The addition of the logic of relations in 1870 must lead to some changes in the theory of cognition, but even more basic changes would have to follow should quantification theory be

[18] Following Moody, *Truth and Consequence*, p. 35.

added. For in that case the problem of individuation would have to be reconsidered, and some positive concept of individuality added. Peirce had discovered quantification by 1885. It is not surprising therefore that he should have begun to use *haecceity* as a means of characterizing individuals shortly thereafter.

Peirce's theory of the object, whatever its logical difficulties, thus appears to support the analogy between quality and the common nature. Yet since Peirce asserts that quality is the result of comparison, the question arises whether quality is not the universal while some more immediate form serves as the common nature. Moore [19] has particularly stressed the importance of a passage written by Peirce in 1867 in this connection:

> General terms denote several things. Each of these things has in itself no qualities, but only a certain concrete form which belongs to itself alone. This was one of the points brought out in the controversy in reference to the nature of universals. As Sir William Hamilton says, not even the humanity of Leibniz belongs to Newton, but a different humanity. It is only by abstraction, by an oversight, that two things can be said to have common characters. [2.415] [20]

This passage certainly has some similarities to Scotus, for as Boehner remarks, "This 'natura communis' . . . is not numerically one in all singular things, but each singular thing has its own common nature, which is singularized by the individual difference." [21] Yet I think Moore's reading is doubtful. It is first to be remarked that the only example of such a concrete form which Peirce cites is a proper name

---

[19] Moore, "The Scholastic Realism," p. 411.

[20] William Hamilton, *Discussions on Philosophy and Literature* (New York, 1853), p. 630. The passage referred to occurs in Hamilton's defense of his doctrine of the quantification of the predicate against the attacks of De Morgan, and the particular point at issue is the application of the *nota notae* to the proposition, "Newton is not Leibniz." Hamilton states the *nota notae* as: *"The predicate of the predicate is, with the predicate, affirmed or denied, of the subject."* (p. 629) Then the argument is as follows. In the proposition, "Newton is not Leibniz," "Newton" is the subject and "Leibniz" is the predicate. The predicate being denied of the subject, the predicate of the predicate is also denied. But Leibniz was a mathematician. Therefore, Newton was not a mathematician, which is false. What this proves to the satisfaction of Sir William is that in the proposition, "Leibniz is a mathematician," the predicate is existentially quantified i.e., "Leibniz is some mathematician" — and that particular mathematician we do indeed deny of Newton. (p. 630) This illustrates the necessity of what Hamilton calls the "parti-partial negative proposition" — "Some X's are not some Y's." (p. 626)

[21] Boehner, "Scotus," pp. 42f.

— Napoleon (2.415); and whatever else "Napoleon" may be it is not a common nature. Moreover, this passage occurs in a discussion of substantial breadth and depth — that is, breadth and depth in a state of information so complete as to be "the state in which the information would amount to an absolute intuition of all there is, so that the things we should know would be the very substances themselves, and the qualities we should know would be the very concrete forms themselves." (2.409) Certainly the concrete forms, if they are known only in an ideal state of information, are not the *quiddity* of ordinary cognition. Rather, this sounds far more like the theory of substantial form than the common nature.

But there is a third objection to the analogy between quality and the common nature which I believe is fatal. Universals are real according to Scotus because there is in the singular out of the mind a common nature which is neither singular nor universal and which is the correspondent of the universal in the mind. But this is not Peirce's position. For Peirce the reality of universals holds because all judgments contain general terms, and no matter how far determination is carried the true singular is never realized. (3.93; 5.299–306; 5.312) The real object is therefore not truly singular; it contains not a neutral essence but a universal. Thus Peirce asserts, "All, therefore, that we perceive or think, or that exists, is general." (3.93n1) And even Peirce's own avowal of Scotian realism illustrates this difference:

The great argument for nominalism is that there is no man unless there is some particular man. That, however, does not affect the realism of Scotus; for although there is no man of whom all further determination can be denied, yet there is a man, abstraction being made of all further determination. There is a real difference between man irrespective of what the other determinations may be, and man with this or that particular series of determinations, although undoubtedly this difference is only relative to the mind and not *in re*. Such is the position of Scotus. [5.312]

But this is not really Scotian realism, for as Boehner points out, Scotus does not obtain the universal from the particular by ignoring the particularizing determinations, since if it were so obtained the common nature would be universal in itself.[22] Yet this is precisely what Peirce

[22] *Ibid.*, p. 44.

asserts. Moreover, a difference relative to the mind is, for a phenomenalist, a true difference, and what is universal relative to the mind is truly universal. Thus even in 1867 Peirce's realism was of a far more extreme variety than the moderate realism of Scotus.

We are thus brought back to the fact that the ultimate ground of Peirce's realism of the 1868–1870 period is the indeterminateness of the phenomena — or, stated in terms of the theory of thought-signs, the fact that every judgment involves general terms. Since the real is what is thought in a true cognition, and since every cognition refers a quality to an object, it follows that if any cognition is true then there are both real generals and real objects. Now the truth of a cognition consists in its giving coherence to experience, so the hypothesis that there is a real object of a given description is confirmed by the fact that it accords with and explains our phenomenal experience. The object, whose existence we hypothesize to explain why we perceive as we do, is as we conceive it to be, yet our conception of it is the result of a process of inference. That is to say, although we hypothesize that the object antedates and causes our sensations, yet in formulating our theory the sensations occur first and the concept of the object is added subsequently by hypothetical reasoning. The order of cognition is thus the reverse of the postulated causal order: in the latter the object exists before it affects us and initiates the cognitive process; in the former the concept of the object is the final product of a process of reasoning which begins with sensation. Thus Peirce remarks that the realities which our sensations signify are not "the unknowable cause of sensation, but *noumena*, or intelligible conceptions which are the last products of the mental action which is set in motion by sensation." (8.13)

Peirce presents his definition of the real as a consequence of this theory of cognition. Having rejected all incognizables, Peirce requires a way of distinguishing the real from the unreal in purely phenomenalistic terms, and it is the theory of the object as an explaining construct which provides it. For if the hypothesis of the object is inadequate, or incomplete, or false, this can only become known by the failure of the hypothesis to reduce experience to order — i.e., by the fact that the hypothesis will have to be modified. On the other hand, a hypothesis which will never be modified must be true. Accordingly, the real object is the object of a proposition which will stand in the long run. And so among the consequences of four incapacities which Peirce enumerated in 1868 was the following definition of the real:

The real, then, is that which, sooner or later, information and reasoning would finally result in, and which is therefore independent of the vagaries of me and you. Thus, the very origin of the conception of reality shows that this conception essentially involves the notion of a COMMUNITY, without definite limits, and capable of a definite increase of knowledge. And so those two series of cognition — the real and the unreal — consist of those which, at a time sufficiently future, the community will always continue to re-affirm; and of those which, under the same conditions, will ever after be denied. Now, a proposition whose falsity can never be discovered, and the error of which therefore is absolutely incognizable, contains, upon our principle, absolutely no error. Consequently, that which is thought in these cognitions is the real, as it really is. There is nothing, then, to prevent our knowing outward things as they really are, and it is most likely that we do thus know them in numberless cases, although we can never be absolutely certain of doing so in any special case. [5.311]

This passage contains two distinct criteria of reality: first, what will ultimately be agreed upon; second, what is independent of what you, I, or any group less than the community may think. These criteria are not synonymous: the second involves the first, but not the converse. Freedom from the vagaries of you and me does not differ essentially from freedom from errors made at any one time. In both cases, the point is that while any finite number of inquiries may go wrong, the infinite extension of the process must bring us to agreement at last. But the second criterion does involve an important extra element — namely, the community. After all, when we have traversed the ground required to prove that other minds are real — i.e., that there is a community — we have gone just about the whole way. If the definition of reality essentially involves the reality of the community — and the reality of the community obviously cannot be proven by an appeal to the community — then it appears to involve the notion of reality to begin with.

Whether or not this objection is valid depends upon whether or not the investigation must actually go on forever. The assumption that the community exists is required by Peirce because the individual investigator will not live forever and the process of investigation must be infinite. But this assumption is unnecessary if the ultimate agreement is ideal, for the infinite will never come, and all that is required is the concept of an infinite series of investigations. Such a concept does not require a community, or any other inquirer. We can certainly talk meaningfully of an infinite series of experiments or inductions without introducing someone to perform them, just as we can talk meaningfully of an infinite series of additions without an adder to add. Thus it is not really necessary to assume that the community is real; all that is required to define the concept of reality is the concept of such an infinite series, and if we can conceive any infinite series we can certainly conceive this one.

The status of the community in Peirce's theory is a matter of considerable complexity. Although Peirce usually employs this concept in discussing the real, the usage is not invariable; thus in 1870 he wrote: "Then by the truth concerning a thing we do not mean how any man is affected by a thing. Nor how a majority is affected. But how a man would be affected after sufficient experience discussion and reasoning." [23] It is clear that the concept under discussion here is that for which the community is usually introduced, but in this case Peirce is content to deal with an immortal man. The critical point, then, becomes whether Peirce is actually committed to holding that inquiry will in fact go on forever, in which case he will have to show that some inquirer will exist, or whether the infinite extension simply defines an ideal limit. This question cannot be settled simply by asking whether or not Peirce believes the community to be real, for, as I will try to demonstrate below, there are other reasons for holding the community to be real which have nothing to do with inquiry. Thus Peirce will maintain the reality of the community in any case, whether its existence is a presupposition or a consequence of the theory of agreement. What must be determined therefore is what the theory of agreement itself presupposes.

One of Peirce's clearest statements of the theory of agreement is given in the following extended quotation:

It may seem conceivable that any two investigators must traverse the same path, and that all their successive steps must be the same if their conclusions are to agree. This however is very far from being the fact. We may

[23] "Notes for Lectures on Logic to begin First Term 1870–1871," IB2 Box 10. Cf. also 5.384.

with equal certainty infer the rotation of the earth from the diurnal motions of the heavenly bodies or from the manner of swinging a pendulum. Nor do observers in different situations or at different times ever observe the same facts. . . . The final conclusion of an investigation then depends entirely upon observations, and these observations are entirely private and peculiar for each investigator. Yet the conclusions themselves necessarily agree, if the process has been carried far enough. As *fate* in the fairy stories is the inevitableness of a certain result, which will surely be brought about however the antecedent conditions may be, so we may say that there is something like this in the fact that two series of sensations without any similarity perceived by two minds will ultimately lead them with perfect certainty to one conclusion.

It is true that we may avoid this strange and paradoxical way of conceiving the fact, since we are clearly warranted by it in saying that there are certain external realities, whose characters do not depend on what we think about them and that these things cause our mental affections from which by the logical process we arrive at a knowledge of how the external things are. Thus, our sensations are as various as our relations to the external things but the cause of the agreement in our final conclusions is the identity of the real external object which through the affections of sense has been the origin of them.[24]

This passage contains several points of considerable importance. Peirce is asserting that the effect an object has upon the perceiver is not determined by the object alone but depends also upon the perceiver and the relations between perceiver and object. And since these relations can never be precisely the same for different men or at different times, no two observers, and no one observer at different times, ever see the same thing. This doctrine, which Peirce called the principle of the relativity of sensation, would seem to imply that ultimate agreement is impossible, yet Peirce drew just the opposite conclusion. For the fact that sensations are relative to the observer does not mean that objects do not have invariable effects: it only means that what those effects will be depends upon the conditions prevailing at the time of observation. Thus although the presence of an S does not imply that I have sensations A and B and . . . and K, yet the presence of an S under conditions $C^1$ . . . $C^n$ (including my relation to the object) does imply

---

[24] "Of Reality," 1873, pp. 4–6, IB2 Box 8. That Peirce's position on these aspects of the theory of reality was the same in 1873 as in 1868 may be substantiated by comparing 8.12–13 (1871) and by the fact that the doctrine of the relativity of sensation goes back to about 1865.

that I have these sensations. Therefore the following hypothetic inference becomes possible:

The presence of an S under condition $C^1$ . . . $C^n$ is always
followed by the perceptions A and . . . and K
I perceive A and . . . and K
Conditions $C^1$ . . . $C^n$ prevail
Therefore, there is an S here.

Thus the postulate of the existence of the object, together with the laws of perception and the statement of the relevant conditions, does yield a coherent explanation of our sense experience.

So far Peirce's position is very similar to that held by his father, Benjamin Peirce. But Benjamin Peirce had explained the convergence of inquiry by asserting that our knowledge is a true copy of things as they are — an assertion which he justified by an appeal to a pre-established harmony.[25] Such was not the course taken by his son. Not only does Charles explicitly deny the existence of the pre-established harmony (5.353); he states that it is the fact that the agreement will come which justifies us in asserting the existence of external realities. But if the real is what will be thought in that theory to which investigation will ultimately converge, and if it is asserted that there is a reality, then it is asserted that the ultimate agreement will be reached. Yet how can Peirce possibly prove this?

It is essential to distinguish two different questions which are involved in this statement of the problem. There is, first, the question of whether or not inquiry will go on forever. I think it is quite obvious that Peirce can neither know nor prove that it will, and he himself admitted this on several occasions. (2.654n; 5.357) But there is a second and more important question: if it were to go on forever, would agreement be reached? After all, there is no reason why one could not inquire forever and never come to agreement; convergence is in no sense a necessary property of every infinite series, as every mathematician knows. Accordingly, unless there is something peculiar about this series which implies that agreement will be reached, an infinite inquiry might very well be futile.

There are two ways in which Peirce might have attempted to prove that infinite inquiry would yield agreement. First, such a proof might

[25] See above, p. 14.

be attempted directly in terms of some character of the cognitive process. In this case, it would be necessary to show that the nature of cognition, or the method of inquiry, is such that, if persisted in long enough, it must yield agreement. But as we have seen above, the process of cognition is inference, so that the problem is that of showing that the three forms of inference, repeatedly applied, necessarily lead to one conclusion. Such a conclusion would be by definition the truth, so the problem is synonymous with that of the grounds of validity of the laws of logic, and particularly of synthetic logic. This problem Peirce regarded as one of the most fundamental in philosophy, for as he remarked in 1868:

According to Kant, the central question of philosophy is "How are synthetical judgments *a priori* possible?" But antecedently to this comes the question how synthetical judgments in general, and still more generally, how synthetical reasoning is possible at all. When the answer to the general problem has been obtained, the particular one will be comparatively simple. This is the lock upon the door of philosophy. [5.348]

Thus the question is whether or not the validity of synthetic inference can be demonstrated without assuming the existence of the real.

Peirce's answer to this question is that it cannot, and the argument is as follows. "All probable inference, whether induction or hypothesis," Peirce states, "is inference from the parts to the whole" (5.349), where by "whole" is meant "class," and "part" is used ambiguously to mean both "member" and "subclass." Since induction and hypothesis are species of the same genus, Peirce presents his argument in terms of induction and leaves it to the reader to derive an analogous proof for hypothesis. Then the argument that the validity of induction depends upon the existence of the real is this:

. . . since all the members of any class are the same as all that are to be known; and since from any part of those which are to be known an induction is competent to the rest, in the long run any one member of a class will occur as the subject of a premiss of a possible induction as often as any other, and, therefore, the validity of induction depends simply upon the fact that the parts make up and constitute the whole. This in its turn depends simply upon there being such a state of things that any general terms are possible. But it has been shown . . . that being at all is being in general. And thus this part of the validity of induction depends merely on there being any reality. [5.349]

What Peirce is trying to show is that if there is any real class of things, then the defining character of that class is discoverable by induction. The first premiss limits the contents of any possible class to things which will be known — a limitation which follows as a corollary from the denial of incognizables. The second premiss asserts that from any member or subclass an induction is "competent" to the containing class. But the meaning of "competent" is confusing. Obviously, if it means "valid," then the validity of induction is assumed as a premiss and the whole argument is circular. There is, however, another possible interpretation. By the "validity" of induction, Peirce means the probability of inductive arguments yielding true conclusions — i.e., the ratio of the number of cases in which inductive arguments yield true conclusions to the number of cases in which inductive arguments are employed. Clearly, "validity" in this sense is inapplicable to a particular inductive argument. But there is a distinction between a "correct" and an "incorrect" inductive argument, as e.g.:

$$
\left.\begin{array}{l} S^i, S^{ii}, S^{iii} \text{ are M} \\ S^i, S^{ii}, S^{iii} \text{ are P} \\ \therefore \text{ P is M} \end{array}\right\} \text{ is correct but} \qquad \left.\begin{array}{l} S^i, S^{ii}, S^{iii} \text{ are M} \\ Q^i, Q^{ii}, Q^{iii} \text{ are P} \\ \therefore \text{ P is M} \end{array}\right\} \text{ is not.}
$$

In this sense, one might speak of "correctness" or "competence" without assuming validity. I believe therefore that what Peirce means is that any "part" of a class may serve as the subject of the premises of a "correct" induction.

From the premisses that

> Any part of a class may occur as subject of the premisses of an induction regarding the rest.

and

> Every part of a class will be known

it follows that

> Any part of those which will be known may occur as subject of the premisses of an induction regarding the rest.

But how does Peirce reach the conclusion that each part will occur as often as any other? The only plausible answer that I can think of depends upon the following theorem established by Boole: in any finite class from which samples of a fixed size are drawn but to which each sample is returned before the next draw, so that members once drawn in one sample may be drawn again in another, the probability that any given member will be twice drawn goes to zero as the number of members of the class goes to infinity.[26] This would appear to be what Peirce meant when he said, *"In the long run* any one member of a class will occur as the subject of the premiss of a possible induction as often as any other" (italics mine). And the final conclusion — "the validity of induction depends simply upon the fact that the parts make up and constitute the whole" — then follows without difficulty by the principle that what is true of each is true of all.

In the last sentence of the quoted passage, Peirce points out that his argument for the validity of induction depends upon there being real classes. But the question of whether or not there are real classes is the question of whether or not general terms are true of anything real, and accordingly the question of whether or not there is anything real. Thus the validity of induction assumes the existence of real things and cannot be used to prove its own premiss.

There is, however, a second way in which Peirce can attempt to prove the existence of the real — namely, by showing that the contrary hypothesis leads to contradiction. In fact, Peirce gives three arguments of this sort, two of which may be considered together. First, assume that the objects of thought are not real. In what would their lack of reality consist? Clearly, in the characters of those objects of thought depending upon what we know of them. From this it follows that after an induction has discovered some character of objects, that character must change. But this relation between our knowledge and the changes in the order of things would be a law for such a universe, and would therefore be discoverable by induction. Therefore it would cease to operate when discovered; but this would be another law also discoverable by induction. And so on. Accordingly, we should be able to discover the nature of such a world by induction and so to reach agreement. But this is contrary to hypothesis. (5.352)

The second argument is similar. Suppose that there is no reality. Then if our experience is not of real things, it is illusory. But either this illusion holds for all men, or it does not. If it does, it is real by definition. If it does not, it is independent of the thought of all except those

<hr/>

[26] Boole, *Laws*, p. 371. In this same paper, Peirce cites Boole's argument on p. 370 of the *Laws*. (5.345n1)

who hold it. Therefore, the existence of the illusion is a real fact, and something is real. But this is contrary to hypothesis. (5.352)

Both arguments involve an equivocation. In stating the problem Peirce defines "reality" as that which will ultimately be agreed upon (5.351) but in answering it he defines it as that which is independent of what any limited group may think. If the former definition is substituted for the latter in the two arguments given above, both are seen to fail. This is obvious in the first case where if agreement will never be reached, no induction will hold good in the long run. And it is equally true in the second, for to agree that there is an illusion is to agree.

Peirce's third argument has more to commend it. Again using induction as typical of synthetic inference, Peirce argues that it is impossible to conceive of a world in which induction would fail as often as hold good. For what could such a world be? Clearly, it must be one in which no universal proposition holds good. But this could occur only if every possible combination of characters occurs with equal frequency.

But this would not be disorder, but the simplest order; it would not be unintelligible, but, on the contrary, everything conceivable would be found in it with equal frequency. The notion, therefore, of a universe in which probable arguments should fail as often as hold true, is absurd. We can suppose it in general terms, but we cannot specify how it should be other than self-contradictory. [5.345]

From this it follows that the supposition that there is a possible universe in which induction would be invalid is self-contradictory, and, therefore, that in every possible world induction is valid. Therefore, we have a criterion for the admission of possible worlds — namely, that induction must be valid in them. To prove his theory of reality therefore Peirce has to show that his theory of the real affords an adequate basis for induction, and that no other theory does so. But the first proposition he had already established to his satisfaction, while the second is supported by the following argument.

But now let up suppose the idealistic theory of reality, which I have in this paper taken for granted to be false. In that case, inductions would not be true unless the world were so constituted that every object should be presented in experience as often as any other; and further, unless we were so constituted that we had no more tendency to make bad inductions than good ones. These facts might be explained by the benevolence of the Creator; but, as has already been argued, they could not explain, but are absolutely refuted by the fact that no state of things can be conceived in which probable arguments should not lead to the truth. This affords a most important argument in favor of that theory of reality, and thus of those denials of certain faculties from which it was deduced, as well as of the general style of philosophizing by which those denials were reached. [5.353]

Thus e.g., if there are incognizables, so that the members of a class are not limited to these that will be known, then we can never know, even in the long run, that we have examined enough cases, nor can we generalize from our sample without gratuitously assuming its randomness. Accordingly, Peirce holds that his theory affords a basis for induction, that no other theory does, and therefore, since induction must be valid, his theory is true.

It seems clear that in 1868 Peirce regarded his theory of reality as a consequence of the denial of incognizables and therefore as susceptible of proof. Yet it is equally clear that the arguments he advances fall far short of the mark. The denial of incognizables is perfectly consistent with the nonexistence of external realities — indeed, it is perfectly consistent with an extreme solipsism — and the specific proofs of reality which Peirce advances involve either an equivocation in the definition of reality or some very doubtful assumptions concerning the impossibility of a universe in which induction fails. Moreover, even if Peirce could show that given a real class, we can always discover some property or other of its members by induction, there is nothing to show that the property so found would be unique. For induction is here defined, not as a method of testing the incidence of a predesignated character, but as a method of discovering a character of a class by the examination of its members. But since there is a possible infinity of characters having the same extension, induction need never lead to agreement. That Peirce did not see this was probably due to the fact that he was still under the spell of the Scholastic theory of essence and therefore assumed that the property investigated would be the defining property of a natural class; but the result is that his argument at best fails to prove that agreement will be reached.

Thus at the close of the 1860's the problem of the existence of real things stands as the most serious unresolved difficulty confronting

Peirce's philosophy. According to the architectonic plan, the theory of the real should be a corollary from the theory of cognition, yet Peirce's attempts so to derive it had not yet proven successful. And it is clear that unless some proof of the reality of objects is forthcoming, Peirce's metaphysical realism also fails and his position degenerates into that very phenomenalism of Hume which he so abhorred.

# VII

# *The Theory of Inquiry, 1871–1879*

It must have been in 1866 that Professor De Morgan honored the unknown beginner in philosophy that I then was . . . by sending me a copy of
his memoir "On the Logic of Relations, etc." I at once fell to upon it; and before many weeks had come to see in it, as De Morgan had already seen, a
brilliant and astonishing illumination of every corner and every vista of logic.
[1.562]

PEIRCE began the study of logic in the early 1860's when, as a
result of the failure of his first system, he came to the "demonstrative certitude that there was something wrong about Kant's formal
logic." (4.2) The logical questions in which he was chiefly interested,
therefore, were those of propositional and syllogistic form, and it was
natural that for instruction in these subjects he should have turned to
the classical logic of Aristotle and the Scholastics. During the years
from 1862 to 1867, Peirce read widely in medieval logic and became
thoroughly imbued with the subject-predicate theory of the proposition. His discovery of Boole's work in 1865 did not alter this situation,
for although Boole made brilliant innovations which greatly extended
the scope of the traditional logic, he did not break with the classical
theory of the proposition. Indeed, so well entrenched was the belief
that every proposition must be of the subject-predicate form that De
Morgan himself in his epoch-making paper on the logic of relations retained the established terms even while he greatly extended their meaning.[1] Thus it is not surprising that when Peirce read De Morgan's paper
in 1866, he did not immediately see all the implications involved in the
admission of relative propositions. Before these implications would
become manifest a more detailed investigation of the theory of relations

---

[1] Augustus De Morgan, "On the Syllogism IV, and the Logic of Relations," read
April 1860, *Cambridge Philosophical Transactions*, X, 341.

was required, but such an investigation Peirce did not make at once. His logical papers of 1867 and 1868 are concerned either with questions of classical logic ("Memoranda Concerning the Aristotelian Syllogism" [2.792–807], "On The Natural Classification of Arguments" [2.461–516], "Upon Logical Comprehension and Extension" [2.391–426] or with extensions of Boole's calculus ("On an Improvement in Boole's Calculus of Logic" [3.1–19], "Upon the Logic of Mathematics" [3.20–44]) and include only casual mention of relations. It was not until 1869 and 1870 that Peirce began his serious investigation of the new field of logic and became fully aware of its great significance. And accordingly it is only after the publication of his paper "Description of a Notation for the Logic of Relatives, etc." (3.45–149) that the effects of the new logic become evident in his other philosophic writings.

The discovery of the calculus of relations was one of the most important events in Peirce's philosophic career. For although Peirce's contributions to logic were many and varied, it is primarily upon his work in relations that his fame as a logician is based. To De Morgan belongs the credit for originating modern relation theory, but it was Peirce who developed it, and virtually all of the calculus of relations of the Boole-Schröder algebra was his creation. Not until the *Principia* appeared was Peirce's work superseded and then only by a theory based in large part upon his own.[2]

But there is another reason for the importance of this event. To anyone who believes in the architectonic theory of philosophy, the discovery of new logical forms implies the existence of corresponding philosophical concepts. In the preceding part, I have tried to show that Peirce's theory of the categories is based very largely upon the notions of classical logic, and particularly upon the subject-predicate theory of the proposition. And since the 1868 theory of cognition is based upon the "New List," and the theory of reality upon the theory of cognition, it is not an exaggeration to say that the subject-predicate theory of the proposition is one of the fundamental premises of Peirce's philosophy in the late 1860's. But the discovery of the logic of relations

---

[2] C. I. Lewis, *A Survey of Symbolic Logic* (Berkeley, 1918), pp. 79ff; *Chance, Love and Logic*, Morris R. Cohen, ed. (New York, 1949), p. xxiv; I. M. Bochenski, *Formale Logik* (Munich, 1956), pp. 436ff.

152

introduces propositions which are not reducible to the subject-predicate form, and accordingly it becomes an open question whether a set of categories derived from that form will also apply to relative propositions.

Once Peirce was thoroughly in command of the new logic, it cannot have taken him long to see what the answer to the question had to be. The argument of the "New List" depends upon the definition of the categories as the concepts of connection which unite Being to Substance: it is upon this definition that the method of finding the categories and the completeness of the list depend. But the concepts of Substance and Being are clearly derived from those of Subject and Predicate. With the admission of propositions not of the subject-predicate form, Substance and Being lose their universality, and therefore the proof of the universality of the categories also fails. Nor is there any way of generalizing the notion of propositional form so as to include relative propositions which will leave the "New List" intact. For if dyadic and triadic relations are admitted as propositional constituents fully as abstract as quality, the concepts which had before served to join the abstract element to the manifold must now themselves be joined by something else. Indeed, the categories now become simply three kinds of predicates, and the question of how these predicates are applied to the manifold is left untouched. Thus the "New List" collapses entirely once the new logic is admitted.

Peirce now found himself facing an extremely unwelcome choice: he had either to reject the architectonic theory of philosophy, or to revise the whole of his second system. Although this was the second time in his career that he had laboriously constructed an architectonic system only to see its foundations crumble before his eyes, there is no evidence that Peirce even considered abandoning the architectonic theory. Instead he set to work at once upon a complete revision of his second system. The theories of the categories, cognition, and reality had all to be reworked so as to make them consistent with the new logic.

One of the most critical problems raised by the new logic concerns the definition of meaning. We have seen above that Peirce's early writings are not completely consistent in regard to meaning. Usually Peirce defines the meaning of a concept as a second concept which is conveyed to the mind by the first (5.255), but he also speaks of it as the abstraction of which the concept is the embodiment.[3] The inconsistency of these two definitions is hidden by the fact that the processes of definition and abstraction are not clearly distinguished; hence to define by genus and differentia is to define by "higher" and more abstract concepts.[4] It is this fact which makes it possible for Peirce to regard the essence of a thing as the meaning of the concept of the thing. The essence then is qualitative, it is a substantial form in the Scholastic sense constituting the nature or principle of operation of the thing.

But the introduction of relative propositions makes necessary a revision of this theory. For if relations are as abstract and as fundamental as qualities, the meaning of a concept, or the essence of the object of a concept, may very well consist in its relations to other objects or in the relations among its states at different times. In particular, there is no reason why the operations of a thing may not be the foundation of its embodied quality rather than the embodied quality being the foundation of the operation of a thing. That is to say, there is no reason why a law governing the operation of a thing, and therefore asserting an invariant relation among several of its states, should not be as essential as any abstract property which it may embody.

The analogy between a general law and a habit was first pointed out by Peirce in 1868 when, as a part of his thesis that every modification of consciousness is the result of inference (5.298), he showed that habits could be regarded as general rules derived by induction. (5.297) Three years later, in the review of Berkeley, Peirce returned to the subject of habit from a fresh perspective. In discussing the Scholastic notion of intelligible species as developed by Scotus, Peirce notes that such universals exist in the mind *habitualiter* — i.e., although not actualized in consciousness, they are in the mind in the sense of being able to produce a conception. (8.18) As pointed out above, this theory is quite similar to Peirce's own early theory of the unconscious idea, whereby he had sought to explain how eternal abstractions can be in the mind even though they cannot be fully realized in consciousness.[5] All that remains, then, is for Peirce to extend the concept of essence to include laws, and the essence of a thing then may be identified with the habits it involves.

[3] See above, p. 51.
[4] See above, pp. 51, 66.
[5] See above, p. 31.

A tentative step in this direction is to be found in Peirce's 1871 review of Berkeley where, in stating his theory of reality, he writes as follows:

What is the POWER of external things, to affect the senses? To say that people sleep after taking opium because it has a soporific *power*, is that to say anything in the world but that people sleep after taking opium because they sleep after taking opium? To assert the existence of a power or potency, is it to assert the existence of anything actual? Or to say that a thing has a potential existence, is it to say that it has an actual existence? In other words, is the present existence of a power anything in the world but a regularity in future events relating to a certain thing regarded as an element which is to be taken account of beforehand, in the conception of that thing? If not, to assert that there are external things which can be known only as exerting a power on our sense, is nothing different from asserting that there is a general *drift* in the history of human thought which will lead it to one general agreement, one catholic consent. And any truth more perfect than this destined conclusion, any reality more absolute than what is thought in it, is a fiction of metaphysics. [8.12]

What Peirce is asserting here is that a real object can only be known as a regularity in phenomenal experience. But since the real object is as we conceive it to be, this means that the concept of the object must be translatable into some conjunction of sense predicates. This assertion, however, must be modified in terms of Peirce's doctrine of the relativity of sensation. That doctrine is equivalent to the proposition that every property of an object is a disposition property, for how the object affects us depends upon our relations to it and the conditions at the time of perception, and therefore the occurrence of a given phenomenal property depends upon the existence of specifiable antecedent conditions. The concept of the object, then, is translatable, not simply into a conjunction of sense predicates, but rather into a conjunction of conditional propositions $C_1^1 \ldots C_1^n \supset A,\ C_2^1 \ldots C_2^m \supset B, \ldots$ relating the conditions of perception to the occurrence of sense properties. And these conditionals are of course general laws, and therefore of the nature of habits.

Between 1871 and 1872 this new concept of meaning was developed into the theory of pragmatism. This theory is Peirce's most famous doctrine. But pragmatism was made famous by William James, not by

Peirce; and it was made famous in 1898, not in 1878.[6] Surprisingly little of Peirce's own writing prior to 1898 deals with this subject, and that which does shows that pragmatism was simply a part of a theory of inquiry which Peirce developed in the 1870's. Indeed, although it is likely that Peirce did first use the term "pragmatism" to describe this theory of meaning, he did not use it in any known manuscript of the 1870's, nor, so far as I can determine, in any surviving paper written before 1898.[7] When the doctrine became famous, however, Peirce as its originator was drawn into the controversy over it and wrote a number of papers concerning its history and meaning. But these papers, it must be noted, were written twenty years after the first published statement in 1878, and during those twenty years Peirce had made substantial changes in his theory of inquiry. Accordingly, in the following discussion I shall be concerned with what Peirce said in the 1870's — not with what Peirce said twenty years later that he had meant in the 1870's.[8]

[6] William James first brought it into prominence in a lecture entitled "Philosophical Conceptions and Practical Results" delivered at the University of California in 1898. William James, *Pragmatism* (New York, 1947), p. 47. Perry, *James*, II, 325.

[7] James states incorrectly that Peirce introduced the term in the 1878 paper (James, *Pragmatism*, p. 46). But Peirce wrote to James on November 10, 1900: "Who originated the term 'pragmatism,' I or you? Where did it first appear in print? What do you understand by it?" (Perry, *James*, II, 407n5) Actually the term comes from Kant and it would be more characteristic of Peirce to so employ Kantian terms than it would be of James. The most likely hypothesis concerning the origin of the term would therefore appear to be this. From his later accounts of the origin of the theory of pragmatism (Peirce, "Essays Toward the Interpretation of Our Thoughts," April 5, 1909, pp. 1f IB2 Box 11; Peirce, "Pragmatism Made Easy," IB1 Box 1; 11–13), it is clear that the doctrine was discussed in the Metaphysical Club in 1871 or 1872, and it is also clear that Peirce wrote a paper on it which was read before the club but which has not survived. (5.13) Either in discussion or in that paper Peirce probably used the term "pragmatism." Years later, James, remembering the theory of the early 1870's and assuming that Peirce had used the same terminology in 1878, attributed the introduction of the term to the 1878 paper. The fact that Peirce did not feel it necessary to have a special designation for the theory in 1878 is one indication that he did not then regard the doctrine as separate from the general theory of inquiry. Indeed, as late as 1893, when he could have secured the insertion of the term in the *Century Dictionary*, Peirce did not consider it worth while to do so (5.13) — a fact concerning which he later (1902) remarked somewhat ruefully, "It is a singular instance of that over-modesty and unyielding self-underestimate on my part of which I am so justly proud as my principal claim to distinction that I should have omitted *pragmatism*, my own offspring, with which the world resounds." (5.13n1)

[8] For example, there has been some discussion as to whether the term "practical consequences" refers to conditional statements (*consequentiae* in the Scholastic sense) or to the consequents of conditional statements. (Cf. Goudge, *The Thought of C. S. Peirce*,

Peirce's original statement of the pragmatic maxim is as follows: "Consider what effects, which might conceivably have practical bearings, we conceive the object of our conception to have. Then, our conception of these effects is the whole of our conception of the object." (5.402) Peirce here asserts that the meaning is the concept of the effects. Does this mean, then, that the meaning is nothing but a conjunction of phenomenal qualities? It must be admitted that Peirce's statement of the maxim can be so interpreted; but the remainder of the paper makes it very clear that what he meant was a conjunction of conditionals relating conditions of perception to phenomenal qualities. Thus two paragraphs before the maxim, Peirce wrote as follows:

To develop its meaning, we have, therefore, simply to determine what habits it produces, for what a thing means is simply what habits it involves. Now, the identity of a habit depends on how it might lead us to act, not merely under such circumstances as are likely to arise, but under such as might possibly occur, no matter how improbable they may be. What the habit is depends on *when* and *how* it causes us to act. As for the *when*, every stimulus to action is derived from perception; as for the *how*, every purpose of action is to produce some sensible result. Thus, we come down to what is tangible and practical, as the root of every real distinction of thought, no matter how subtle it may be; and there is no distinction of meaning so fine as to consist in anything but a possible difference of practice. [5.400]

By a "habit," Peirce means a law or conditional relating antecedent conditions to consequent experience, and by "practical bearings" he means "sensible results." Then our conception of all such conditionals is our conception of the object.

The pragmatic theory is thus decidedly phenomenalistic. Its fundamental assertion is that the concept of the real object can be fully translated into a set of conditionals having for antecedents a statement of the conditions of perception and for consequents the phenomenal quality observed. In developing his realism Peirce had previously held that the concept of the object implied such conditionals but not conversely. Thus, the verification of the conditionals afforded a basis for the hypothetical inference:

---

p. 153.) But the term "consequences" does not occur in the 1878 version and was not introduced until twenty years later.

$$(\text{Ex})(\phi\text{x} \supset \blacksquare \ C_1^1 \ . \ . \ . \ C_1^n \supset A \blacksquare C_2^1 \ . \ . \ . \ C_2^m \supset \ B \blacksquare \ . \ . \ .)$$
$$C_1^1 \ . \ . \ . \ C_1^n \supset A$$
$$C_2^1 \ . \ . \ . \ C_2^m \supset B$$
$$\vdots$$

$$\therefore (\text{Ex}) \ \phi\text{x}.$$

By the pragmatic principle, Peirce converts this implication into a definitional identity, thereby completing the reduction of the real to the phenomenal which is implicit in the denial of the incognizable.

But although pragmatism is a direct development from Peirce's earlier work, it marks an important change in point of view — a change which is directly anti-Scholastic. Peirce's earlier writings do not involve a true Scholasticism, but they do involve the Scholastic theory of essence. Pragmatism signifies Peirce's complete break from this theory. Instead of seeking a qualitative essence from which the behavior of the thing follows, Peirce now identifies the essence with behavior. The essence of a thing is the sum of the habits it involves. Accordingly, our objective in the investigation of a thing is to discover the laws governing its behavior — i.e., its habits — not the form which serves as the basis for natural classification, for there is no such form.[9]

Pragmatism also lays to rest another problem which we have already encountered in the theory of agreement. In his earlier writings, Peirce seems to take it for granted that the conclusion of an inductive inquiry must be unique. I think the most plausible reason for this assumption is that Peirce thought of induction as the discovery of the defining property of a natural class. This was the sort of question with which he then thought that science should be concerned, and it is in these terms that he discusses induction in the 1868 paper. The problem of how to distinguish essential properties from accidental ones does not seem to have particularly troubled him, in part because the whole tradition of Scholastic thought assured him that it could be done. But with the transition to the new point of view where the thing is as it behaves, the problem of the uniqueness of the law of its behavior is raised and there were no authorities to guarantee its easy solution.

[9] This difference between Peirce and the Scholastics has been pointed out very clearly in Ralph J. Bastian, S.J., "The 'Scholastic' Realism of C. S. Peirce," *Philosophy and Phenomenological Research*, XIV, 246–249 (December 1953).

Peirce deals with this knot in a fashion worthy of Alexander — if the thing is as it behaves, then what behaves the same is the same. Two concepts, or hypotheses, which imply the same conditionals, are identical. Accordingly, if our experience admits of at least one complete explanation, then it admits of at most one, for two hypotheses explaining precisely the same observations are synonymous.

The theory of inquiry of which pragmatism is a part was also being developed in the years 1870–1872. This theory was not a rejection of the 1868 theory, although there are some significant differences, but rather the creation of a new and more general theory of inquiry within which the older theory is imbedded. Thus the denial of intuition, introspection and incognizables, and the theory of thought-signs are all preserved intact, but they are now set in a new context — the doubt-belief theory of inquiry.

The basic argument of the doubt-belief theory of inquiry is that a knowledge of the laws governing the behavior of objects has at least this practical utility — it enables us to predict what sensible experiences we will receive from an object as a consequence of actions of our own. That is, if we wish to obtain certain experiences, then a knowledge of those laws enables us to shape our actions so as to gain the desired end. The laws, then, act as rules for action, and, when adopted, as habits. Now Peirce contends that the possession of such habits is a necessity for all men, since we must constantly engage in action to satisfy desire. Such a habit when thoroughly adopted is a belief. "The feeling of believing is a more or less sure indication of there being established in our nature some habit which will determine our actions." (5.371) "Belief does not make us act at once, but puts us into such a condition that we shall behave in a certain way, when the occasion arises." (5.373) When, however, a belief fails and the expected result does not follow upon our actions, or when we are confronted with circumstances concerning which we have no belief, we are cast into a state of doubt. "Doubt is an uneasy and dissatisfied state from which we struggle to free ourselves and pass into the state of belief; while the latter is a calm and satisfactory state which we do not wish to avoid, or to change to a belief in anything else." (5.372) This struggle to attain belief, which is initiated by the irritation of doubt, Peirce calls "inquiry."

159

The irritation of doubt is the only immediate motive for the struggle to attain belief. . . . With the doubt, therefore, the struggle begins, and with the cessation of doubt it ends. Hence, the sole object of inquiry is the settlement of opinion. We may fancy that this is not enough for us, and that we seek, not merely an opinion, but a true opinion. But put this fancy to the test, and it proves groundless; for as soon as a firm belief is reached we are entirely satisfied, whether the belief be true or false. . . . The most that can be maintained is, that we seek for a belief that we shall *think* to be true. But we think each one of our beliefs to be true, and, indeed, it is mere tautology to say so. [5.375]

In a brilliant article on the genealogy of pragmatism, Max Fisch has shown that this theory of inquiry was largely derived from the writings of the English psychologist, Alexander Bain. Beginning in 1859, Bain had evolved a new theory of belief which aroused considerable interest among both philosophers and psychologists. Bain laid particular stress upon the relation of belief to action "Belief is . . . 'essentially related to Action, that is, volition. . . . Preparedness to act upon what we affirm is admitted upon all hands to be the sole, the genuine, the unmistakable criterion of belief. . . . The readiness to act is thus what makes belief something more than fancy'." [10] Like Peirce's habit, Bain's belief is " 'an attitude or disposition of preparedness to act' when occasion offers." [11] Thus our belief in a certain report regarding Africa is expressed "by saying that *if* we went to Africa we *would* do certain things in consequence of the information." [12] Both belief and habit, then, are real laws governing action which become effective whenever the conditions of the antecedent are realized. Similarly, both are purposive, relating means to ends desired. Furthermore, like habit, belief results from induction, for as Bain remarks, "belief is a primitive disposition to follow out any sequence that has been once experienced, and to expect the result." [13] Thus Bain's theory of belief forms a consistent extension and reformulation of Peirce's theory of habit.

"Disbelief is not the opposite of belief but belief of the opposite.

[10] Alexander Bain, *The Emotions and the Will* 3rd ed. (New York, 1875), pp. 505–507, quoted in Max Fisch, "Alexander Bain and the Genealogy of Pragmatism," *Journal of the History of Ideas*, XV, 423 (June 1954).

[11] Bain, *Emotions*, p. 595, in Fisch, *Bain and Pragmatism*, p. 419.

[12] Alexander Bain, *Mental and Moral Science* (New York, 1868), p. 373, in Fisch, *Bain and Pragmatism*, p. 420.

[13] Bain, *Mental and Moral Science* (London, 1872), part first, appendix, p. 100, in Fisch, *Bain and Pragmatism*, p. 422.

The real opposite of belief is doubt and uncertainty." [14] Between belief and doubt, Bain holds, there is a felt difference: belief "is the name for a serene, satisfying, and happy tone of mind" [15] whereas the state of doubt "is one of discomfort in most cases, and sometimes of the most aggravated human wretchedness." [16] The desire to escape doubt and reach belief is therefore inherent in man; indeed, belief is our natural state, for we have an initial trust or belief in the continuation of the present state and the continued efficacy of our mode of behavior. But experience disappoints us and so generates doubt, which must continue until a new pattern is established which does yield the desired result.[17]

With his usual meticulous scholarship, Fisch has demonstrated that seven members of the Metaphysical Club knew of Bain's theory and that at least Wright, Green, James, and Peirce had studied it in detail.[18] In view of Peirce's explicit acknowledgment of the influence of Bain's theory upon the development of the doctrine of pragmatism,[19] it appears incontestable that Bain was the immediate source of the doubt-belief theory of inquiry as well. But to show the source from which the theory was derived is not to show why the theory was formulated.

There are several reasons why Bain's theory should have had a special appeal for Peirce. In the first place, the theory is in many respects easily combined with Peirce's earlier theory of cognition as outlined in the papers of 1868. Thus Bain supplies a psychological foundation for Peirce's denial of Cartesian doubt, for Bain holds that men are naturally believers and that doubt is produced only by events which disrupt our beliefs — not by pretense. Even more important, however, is the similarity between Peirce's theory of reality and Bain's doctrine. In both cases the aim of inquiry is the production of agreement. For Peirce a true cognition is one which will always be reaffirmed; for Bain a true belief is one which will never be disappointed by experience. For Peirce a false cognition is one which will sometimes be rejected; for Bain a false belief is one which will be disappointed. Thus again Bain's theory completes and extends Peirce's own.

---

[14] Fisch, *Bain and Pragmatism*, p. 420.
[15] Bain, *Emotions*, p. 573, in Fisch, *Bain and Pragmatism*, p. 420.
[16] *Ibid.*
[17] Fisch, *Bain and Pragmatism*, pp. 420f.
[18] *Ibid.*, pp. 424–434.
[19] *Ibid.*, pp. 443f.

Secondly, I have tried to show above that Peirce's theory of cognition of 1868 was aimed not alone at Descartes but also at the whole of the British empirical school. Peirce's usual technique in these papers is to seem to adopt the position of his opponent and then to redefine the crucial terms so as to reach the opposite conclusion. Precisely the same technique is involved in the theory of doubt and belief. It has always been the strength of British empiricism that it admitted as real only those things which could be pointed to in the real world. From Ockham on, the British thinkers have opposed the admission of superfluous metaphysical entities. Again and again, postulated entities have been reduced to psychological or physiological associations devoid of objective validity, and claims of special faculties validating beliefs have been shown to be absurd by deriving the beliefs from pure association. Indeed, Hume — and his followers after him — had declared that any special faculties claimed for man were mythical, and that no psychological explanation of belief could be admitted which would not explain also analogous behavior in animals. Thus in the *Treatise*, Hume had used the analogy between human and animal reasoning as a test of the adequacy of any theory of mental operations.

When any hypothesis, therefore, is advanc'd to explain a mental operation, which is common to man and beasts, we must apply the same hypothesis to both; and as every true hypothesis will abide this trial, so I may venture to affirm, that no false one will ever be able to endure it. . . . Now let any philosopher make a trial, and endeavor to explain that act of the mind, which we call *belief*, and give an account of the principles, from which it is deriv'd, independent of the influence of custom on the imagination, and let his hypothesis be equally applicable to beasts as to the human species; and after he has done this, I promise to embrace his opinion.[20]

Now in fact Bain's theory — as one would expect from a physiologically inclined associationist — meets Hume's demand, for it is very similar to the rote learning theories of the behaviorists. In adopting it, therefore, Peirce seems to take the empirical, or as he would say, nominalistic, point of view. The critical difference lies in the definition of habit, for as we have already seen Peirce regards a habit as a general law or principle governing its instances — not simply as a regularity. A habit is a disposition or readiness to act which will, or would, be carried

[20] Hume, *Treatise*, pp. 177f.

out if the proper conditions are, or were to be, realized. It is therefore an active principle in nature — a real general law derived by induction from experience. Thus what Peirce is seeking to show is that a theory of belief can be formulated which meets Hume's demands but which is still realistic.

Finally, Bain's theory, precisely because it can be applied to man and beast, was particularly timely in the post-Darwinian period when an unblushing evolutionism afflicted all fields of learning. By adopting it, Peirce is able to fit his whole theory of inquiry into an evolutionary frame of reference. Beliefs may be regarded as adjustive habits while failure of adjustment leads to doubt. And the superior adjustive power of an organism endowed with the capacity to correct its patterns of action by experience makes it possible to utilize an argument from natural selection to explain how we come to be so admirably constituted. The necessity of a process of inquiry which will lead from doubt to belief may thus be based upon evolutionary arguments. Moreover, the addition of this biological perspective permits Peirce to strengthen some of his earlier doctrines. For in the first place, it provides him with a new definition of the nature of a problem — a definition subsequently developed by Dewey. A problem situation exists whenever we find our established habits of conduct inadequate to attain a desired end, regardless of how the inadequacy comes about, and the effect of a problem situation upon us is the production of doubt. This being the case, Cartesian doubt is nonsense, for there is no problem situation. But secondly, the theory provides a clarification of the nature of an answer. An answer is any rule of action which enables us to attain our desired ends. Accordingly, our objective is to find a rule which will always lead us to that which we desire. So in the investigation of a real object, our objective is a knowledge of how to act respecting that object so as to attain our desired ends. Thus, as pragmatism asserts, the concept of the object can mean nothing to us but all the habits it involves. The attainment of a stable belief — belief that will stand in the long run — is thus the goal of inquiry. Such belief we define as true, and its object as reality.

The new theory of inquiry thus has as its aim the production of agreement, or the fixation of belief. But in the discussion of the methods to be used in attaining agreement, Peirce breaks with the theory of 1868.

In the earlier theory of cognition, Peirce held that all thought is inference, and accordingly that there is but one method by which we can think. But in the new theory, Peirce presents alternative methods of fixing belief, and only one of these is the inductive method. (5.377–383) The choice among these methods is now dictated by the aims of inquiry itself — i.e., by their efficacy in settling belief. Since the aim of inquiry is everywhere the same it follows that the most adequate method for achieving this aim will ultimately be adopted by all inquirers, but this will occur as a result of normative considerations — not because we involuntarily infer, as was the case with the 1868 theory.

In several respects the paper on "The Fixation of Belief" is one of the most curious and least satisfactory that Peirce ever wrote. After an introductory statement of the doubt-belief theory of inquiry, Peirce turns to a discussion of four methods of fixing belief. These are: (1) the method of tenacity, by which any answer we may fancy is adopted and adhered to without question (5.377f); (2) the method of authority, by which an institution is empowered to create, teach, and enforce set doctrines, and all dissenters are liquidated (5.379–381); (3) the a priori method, by which we adopt an answer which seems generally "agreeable to reason" (5.382f), and (4) the scientific method. (5.382ff) It is very difficult to see how Peirce arrived at this list. It is doubtful that these "methods" are independent, for Peirce himself remarks, "This method [the a priori], therefore, does not differ in a very essential way from that of authority." (5.383) Certainly there is no historical justification for the list, and it can hardly be maintained that these are all the possible methods. Rather Peirce seems to have drawn up this list more or less arbitrarily so as to have some alternatives against which the superiority of the method of science could be shown.

That the scientific method is the only adequate means of reaching agreement and therefore the method which will prevail, Peirce seeks to show by proving that each of the alternatives will fail in the long run whereas science will not. But the arguments which are presented for this purpose are barely worthy of the name. To say that the method of tenacity fails because "the social impulse is against it" (5.378) is hardly adequate, and Peirce's confidence in the impossibility of a completely authoritarian state cannot survive twentieth-century history. In fact, Peirce takes it for granted that his reader will agree upon the inadequacy of these methods without any real proof, and he therefore makes no serious effort to provide one.

Having disposed of his straw methods, Peirce then turns to the description of the scientific method.

> To satisfy our doubts, therefore, it is necessary that a method should be found by which our beliefs may be caused by nothing human, but by some external permanency — by something upon which our thinking has no effect. . . . Such is the method of science. Its fundamental hypothesis, restated in more familiar language, is this: There are Real things, whose characters are entirely independent of our opinions about them; those realities affect our senses according to regular laws, and, though our sensations are as different as our relations to the objects, yet, by taking advantage of the laws of perception, we can ascertain by reasoning how things really are; and any man, if he have sufficient experience and reason enough about it, will be led to the one True conclusion. [5.384]

This passage summarizes succinctly the elements of Peirce's theory of inquiry and reality. The real is that which will ultimately be agreed upon; the real object causes our sensations, but despite the relativity of sensation we can by reasoning discover how things really are; and any man if he inquire long enough will reach this conclusion. But Peirce goes on to assert that the existence of the real is a presupposition of the scientific method: "It may be asked how I know that there are any realities. If this hypothesis is the sole support of my method of inquiry, my method of inquiry must not be used to support my hypothesis." (5.384) In answer to this question, Peirce enumerates four reasons for believing in the existence of real things. First, "If investigation cannot be regarded as proving that there are Real things, it at least does not lead to a contrary conclusion; but the method and the conception on which it is based remain ever in harmony. No doubts of the method, therefore, necessarily arise from its practice, as is the case with all the others." (5.384) This however comes merely to saying that the method does not lead to contradiction; it does not prove the existence of realities. Second,

The feeling which gives rise to any method of fixing belief is a dissatisfaction at two repugnant propositions. But here already is a vague concession that there is some *one* thing to which a proposition should conform. Nobody, therefore, can really doubt that there are realities, or, if he did, doubt would not be a source of dissatisfaction. The hypothesis, therefore, is one which every mind admits. So that the social impulse does not cause me to doubt it. [5.384]

But this says merely that if there were no real things, we should be frustrated. Third, "everybody uses the scientific method about a great many things, and only ceases to use it when he does not know how to apply it." (5.384) This statement is simply an appeal to common usage. And fourth, "Experience of the method has not led me to doubt it, but, on the contrary, scientific investigation has had the most wonderful triumphs in the way of settling opinion." (5.384) But this argument, if true, is an inductive argument, and therefore does employ the method to prove the hypothesis upon which the method is based.

Thus by 1873,[21] Peirce had come to see that the existence of reality cannot be derived from the theory of cognition but must be taken as an ultimate premiss.[22] This discovery can hardly have been welcome, for to assume the existence of reality as a premiss, with Peirce's definition of reality, raises again the question of the status of the infinite future. Does the assertion that there are real things imply that the ultimate agreement must actually be reached, and if so how is the present existence of a reality related to the future agreement? Peirce saw these questions quite clearly, and the manuscripts of 1873 contain various attempts to clarify the notion of reality. Thus in one paper he writes:

All that we can know or conceive of the existence of real things is involved in two premisses; first that investigation will ultimately lead to a settled opinion, and, second, that that [sic] this opinion is entirely determined by the observations. The only thing that we can infer is that the observations have such a character that they are fated to lead ultimately to one conclusion. And therefore the only distinctly conceivable sense in which we can say that the objects of the final opinion exist before that opinion is formed is that that existence consists in the fact that the observations will be such as will bring about and maintain that opinion.[23]

[21] "The Fixation of Belief" was published in 1877 as the first of the six *Popular Science Monthly* articles on scientific method. Earlier drafts of this paper, however, are to be found among the manuscripts of 1873, and there can be no doubt that the theory it involves was fully formulated at least by that date (7.313ff, 1873 folder, IB2 Box 8).

[22] In the fifth of the *Popular Science Monthly* articles, Peirce again raises the question as to whether or not there can be a world in which induction would fail. But his treatment of this question in 1878 is quite different than it had been a decade earlier. Instead of contending that a chance world would be perfectly orderly, Peirce seeks to show that such a universe is self-contradictory. (6.400–405) But he does not go on to argue that the impossibility of such a world proves his theory of reality, for the existence of reality has already been taken as a premiss beyond proof in the first paper.

[23] "Logic, Chapter 4. Of Reality," 1873, p. 7, IB2 Box 8.

But this calls for an explanation, based on the character of cognition, of how that agreement will be reached, and such an explanation Peirce is not able to provide.

Yet it is also clear that Peirce regarded his definition of reality as being that which scientists do in fact employ. This is made clear in an extremely interesting passage written in 1873.

> It is true that the belief is future and may even not ever be attained, while the reality actually exists. But the act of believing is one thing, the object of belief another. Nor need anyone who is familiar with the conceptions of physical science shrink from admitting that the existence [of] a present reality is in one sense made by a contingent event. Nobody hesitates to say that a leaden weight resting upon a table is really heavy. Yet to say that it is heavy only means that if it be so placed that it is free to move it will approach the earth. . . .
>
> Thus we find the physicists, the exactest of thinkers, holding in regard to those things which they have studied most exactly, that their existence depends upon their manifestation or rather on their manifestability. We have only to extend this conception to all real existence and to hold those two facts to be identical namely that they exist and that sufficient investigation would lead to a settled belief in them, to have our Idealistic theory of metaphysics.[24]

By "Idealistic" Peirce means "phenomenalistic," and what he is asserting here is that translation of the real into the phenomenal which we have discussed above. What is must be manifestable — i.e., cognizable. Thus, anticipating the pragmatic definition of weight in "How to Make Our Ideas Clear" (5.403), Peirce argues that weight can mean nothing but what we shall observe under certain conditions. The present weight of an object consists in what will come to be, or would come to be under test conditions. In locating ultimate reality in an ideal agreement, then, Peirce did not mean that the reality is created at the time that agreement is reached, for the agreement "may even not ever be attained." All that is required is that agreement would be attained if investigation went on forever. The electron did not begin to exist when Lorenz postulated it, although the belief in it did; and it would have been none the less real if the world had ended in 1800, for if inquiry had gone on it would have been agreed upon.

It is obvious that such a position involves an extremely heavy commitment to contrary-to-fact conditionals and disposition terms. Indeed, such a commitment is already implicit in Peirce's theory of the relativ-

[24] *Ibid.*, pp. 13f.

ity of sensation, since that doctrine implies that every property of an object is a disposition property. It is therefore essential to know under what conditions Peirce regards counterfactuals as true and disposition properties as real. Are such properties real when the object is not under test? Or, for that matter, is an object real at times when it is not cognized? To these questions Peirce's answer must clearly be yes, for, as he remarks in the passage quoted above, "the act of believing is one thing, the object of belief another." To say that John Jones is real is to say that there are possible cognitions of John Jones at times when he is not in fact cognized.[25] Thus in order to avoid saying that the real does not exist until the final opinion is reached, Peirce must endorse counterfactual postdictions.

But suppose the object were never to be tested — would it then be real? To this Peirce returned the following answer.

There is absolutely no difference between a hard thing and a soft thing so long as they are not brought to the test. Suppose, then, that a diamond could be crystallized in the midst of a cushion of soft cotton, and should remain there until it was finally burned up. Would it be false to say that that diamond was soft? . . . We may . . . ask what prevents us from saying that all hard bodies remain perfectly soft until they are touched, when their hardness increases with the pressure until they are scratched. Reflection will show that the reply is this: there would be no *falsity* in such modes of speech. They would involve a modification of our present usage of speech with regard to the words hard and soft, but not of their meanings. For they represent no fact to be different from what it is; only they involve arrangements of facts which would be exceedingly maladroit. This leads us to remark that the question of what would occur under circumstances which do not actually arise is not a question of fact, but only of the most perspicuous arrangement of them. [5.403]

From this passage it follows that not only is the diamond not hard when never tested, but it is not hard when not under test. But this contradicts the position stated above.

It is here that the seriousness of the difficulties in which Peirce is involved becomes apparent. At first glance one might think that his position in regard to the counterfactual is simply the result of a thoroughgoing empiricism which denies incognizables. But this is in-

---

[25] "An Unpsychological View of Logic. Chapter I. Definition of Logic," 1867, 7th page, IB2 Box 10.

correct; rather, his position regarding incognizables results from an implicit assumption that whatever is possible must become actual. This assumption rarely finds overt expression, although it is quite clearly stated in a passage quoted above from the review of Berkeley. (8. 12) [26] Yet it is the presupposition which underlies the assertion that what will never be cognized is incognizable.

The basis for this view of the possible is Peirce's attempt to combine realism and phenomenalism. If he is to maintain the latter doctrine, he cannot admit as an existent anything which is not manifested phenomenally. The real then is known by its sensible effects alone. But does the real consist of these sensible effects? This question is not answered by pragmatism, for pragmatism merely translates the concept into a set of conditional propositions — it does not answer the question of counterfactuals. If the real is identical with its phenomenal manifestations, it can add nothing to them and we might as well deal with the phenomena alone. But if it does not consist of its manifestations, then in what besides these manifestions does it consist? Peirce says that to say John Jones is real means that there are possible cognitions of John Jones at times when John Jones is not in fact cognized. But how is the existence of a possible cognition manifested? If it is manifested by the cognition becoming actual, then the evidence for the existence of a possible cognition is identical with that for the existence of an actual cognition, and the concept of possibility adds nothing. Indeed, as Moore has pointed out,[27] under these circumstances the concept of a possible cognition is pragmatically equivalent to that of an actual cognition. But if the cognition does not become actual, it is incognizable. Thus Peirce appears to be on the horns of a true dilemma: if a possibility is not actualized, it cannot be cognized; if it is actualized it is no longer a mere possibility.

I believe that the problem of the possible is the real reason for Peirce's addiction to the infinite future. In Peirce's system, the infinite future plays the part of the philosopher's stone: it transforms possibility into actuality without compromising either the inexhaustibility of the possible or the limitations of the actual. On the one hand, the real must be a permanent and inexhaustible possibility of sensation

---

[26] See above, p. 155.
[27] Moore, "Metaphysics and Pragmatism etc.," pp. 183 ff.

(1.487); on the other, it must be wholly cognized. These two statements can only be reconciled by postulating an infinite future in which those possibilities of sensation can be realized.

It is this theory of possibility which underlies what Manley Thompson has called "the paradox of Peirce's realism." "The paradox stated bluntly, then, is that nothing can remain ultimately unknowable only if an ultimately unknowable fact is assumed, viz., the indefinite continuation of intellectual inquiry." [28] This paradox actually involves three distinct statements: (1) everything is cognizable if and only if everything will be cognized sometime; (2) everything will be cognized sometime if and only if inquiry goes on forever; (3) it is not possible to know that inquiry will go on forever. The third proposition is the one which Thompson has stressed — namely, that the infinite continuation of inquiry is itself incognizable. Peirce seeks to avoid this difficulty by arguing that although continuation cannot be known, yet at any given time the chances of some continuation can be estimated. But this hardly meets the issue, for our estimates are at best finite and give no warrant for infinite continuation. [29] If, as Thompson holds, Peirce does require a real infinite future, there is no escape from admitting the infinite future as a rather appalling incognizable.

But in fact the infinite continuation of inquiry is not required in order that everything be cognized. For suppose that inquiry does not go on forever; does it follow that there exists an incognizable, or even an uncognized? It is clear that Peirce would have to deny such a conclusion. For in the first place, the very concept of the incognizable is self-contradictory and meaningless. (5.254–258) It is therefore impossible for cognizability to be dependent upon any contingent event, for cognizability cannot be denied. Second, it is entirely consistent with Peirce's theory to hold that no matter how long inquiry should continue no new opinion would ever be formed nor any now in existence rejected. That is, it is at least possible that we have reached complete truth now and that subsequent investigation would merely confirm our present theories. Hence, although we cannot know that we have reached such a state, it cannot be asserted that we have not; hence it cannot

[28] Manley Thompson, "The Paradox of Peirce's Realism," in Wiener and Young, *Studies*, p. 138.
[29] *Ibid.*, pp. 138f.

be asserted that there is more to be cognized. Put in another way, if inquiry were to end today, the contrary-to-fact conditional that "if inquiry had continued, we would have come to different conclusions" would be meaningless, for the only cause of our changing our conclusions would be the existence of a reality which we had not hitherto cognized. But now we can never cognize this reality and therefore it is incognizable and does not exist; hence it would not lead us to change our conclusions. The infinite continuation of inquiry is required, therefore, not to avoid the existence of incognizables, for all that is is cognized whenever inquiry ends, but to guarantee the reality of anything at all.

The problem of the infinite future is thus the problem of the existence of real things in another form, and the difficulties which it involves arise directly from the attempt to give a phenomenalistic definition of reality. Convinced that the nominalism of the British school resulted from a cognition theory which assumes incognizables, Peirce insisted that nothing can exist which is not phenomenally manifested. Accordingly, he must define the real in purely phenomenalistic terms while at the same time maintaining that the real object is something more than simply a regularity in sensation. To do this he defines the real as the permanent possibility of sensation. (1.422) But since the possible per se is not phenomenally manifest, its existence must be shown by its becoming actual, and the actualization of an inexhaustible quantity requires infinity. Accordingly, the statement that, if inquiry were to go on forever then agreement would be reached, is meaningless unless inquiry does in fact go on forever. But that this will be the case Peirce cannot prove. Thus Peirce's theory does not really escape from nominalism, except by taking the existence of the real wholly on faith. As the diamond example shows all too clearly, there is no fact to which Peirce can point to support his theory which Hume cannot admit while denying the conclusion.

The new theory of inquiry and the pragmatic theory of meaning constitute revisions of Peirce's earlier theories in the light of the new logic of relations. The fact that this revision was carried out so quickly is probably due to the stimulus of Bain's theory which served to suggest how such a revision could be effected. But important as these revisions were, the fundamental problem of the categories remained to be solved. If Peirce was to maintain his architectonic, he had to find a new set of categories based upon logic which would support his new theories of meaning and cognition. But here there was no convenient theory of Bain's to show the way and Peirce had to work out a solution for himself.

A fragment of 1875 shows the direction in which Peirce's mind was moving.

> By the third, I mean the medium or connecting bond between the absolute first and last. The beginning is first, the end second, the middle third. The end is second, the means third. The thread of life is a third; the fate that snips it, its second. A fork in the road is a third, it supposes three ways; a straight road, considered merely as a connection between two places is second, but so far as it implies passing through intermediate places it is third. Position is first, velocity or the relation of two successive positions second, acceleration or the relation of three successive positions third. But velocity in so far as it is continuous also involves a third. Continuity represents Thirdness almost to perfection. Every process comes under that head. Moderation is a kind of Thirdness. . . . Action is second, but conduct is third. Law as an active force is second, but order and legislation are third. [1.337]

This passage is an extremely interesting example of Peirce's method of readapting his earlier doctrines to meet new exigencies. The first, second, and third of this pasage are no longer those of the "New List." Substance and Being, or subject and predicate, have now been discarded and with them the hierarchy of concepts. Peirce now extends the notion of "third" as a "mediating representation," or interpretant which brings things into relation, into the notion of any medium — therefore as the relation which connects two terms. And first and second now become simply names for the terms of the relation. So in the relation schema 'xRy', x is the first member of the ordered pair x;y, y is second, and R is the connecting relation. Thus, Thirdness begins to emerge, not as the most abstract, but as the most important of the categories since it corresponds to relation. No mention is made here of Firstness as a quality nor of Secondness as *haecceity*; Peirce is solely concerned with finding an interpretation of his categorical terms which can be applied to relations.

Of particular interest in view of Peirce's subsequent history is the statement, "Continuity represents Thirdness almost to perfection." (1.337) This statement finds extension in the third of the *Popular*

*Science Monthly* papers. In the opening section of that paper, Peirce develops the importance of continuity as "the direct instrument of the finest generalizations." (2.646) To illustrate his point he employs the example of a naturalist who generalizes a class concept by extending the membership of the class to include all forms which differ from the original members only by minute variations. By this process, the naturalist "obtains, for example, an idea of a leaf which includes every part of the flower, and an idea of a vertebra which includes the skull." (2.646) Peirce then remarks:

> Now, the naturalists are the great builders of conceptions; there is no other branch of science where so much of this work is done as in theirs; and we must, in great measure, take them for our teachers in this important part of logic. And it will be found everywhere that the idea of continuity is a powerful aid to the formation of true and fruitful conceptions. . . . I propose to make a great use of this idea in the present series of papers; and the particular series of important fallacies, which, arising from a neglect of it, have desolated philosophy, must further on be closely studied. [2.646]

This passage is significant for several reasons. First, the method described is obviously that of Darwin, and the praise given it is further evidence of Peirce's full acceptance of evolution. But even more significant is the fact that Peirce's promise is not fulfilled — the idea of continuity does not play a great part in these six papers and the fallacies are not discussed. It is true that the papers are largely concerned with probability, and that, as Peirce noted, "Probability is a continuous quantity" (2.648), but in his treatment of probability its continuity plays no great part. Peirce's claims for continuity are thus programmatic: they express an intention which was not fulfilled. It seems very likely that the reason both for the claims and for the failure to fulfill them lies in the fact that in the late seventies Peirce was trying, and trying unsuccessfully, to reformulate his categorical structure. Clearly, the papers on inquiry should have been based explicitly upon a system of categories. But although Peirce was beginning to develop an interpretation of Thirdness as the analogue of relation and as somehow related to continuity, no clear-cut formulation had yet materialized to replace that of the "New List." Accordingly, Peirce's philosophy of the 1870's is truly architectonic only in intent; the theories of meaning and cognition do not rest upon a well-defined categorical structure and further revision of the system was therefore necessary which would bring it into line with the overall architectonic plan. These revisions, however, belong to the final phase of his philosophy.

The subjects to which Peirce devoted himself in the 1870's were chiefly logic, cognition, meaning, and reality. But beyond and behind these lies an ontological and religious position which also rests upon the categorical theory. We have seen above that Peirce's categories yield the three universes of thing, thought, and abstraction, and that abstraction is regarded as an archetypal idea in the divine mind. This esoteric side of Peirce's thought does not often receive overt statement in his papers, but it remains a highly important ingredient. One of the clearest indications of it occurs in the second of the 1868 papers on cognition where Peirce turns to the question, "in what does the reality of the mind consist?" (5.313) To this he replies: "We have seen that the content of consciousness, the entire phenomenal manifestation of mind, is a sign resulting from inference. Upon our principle, therefore, that the absolutely incognizable does not exist, so that the phenomenal manifestation of a substance is the substance, we must conclude that the mind is a sign developing according to the laws of inference." (5.313) This rather surprising thesis follows from Peirce's denial of introspection and intuition and his theory of thought-signs. It will be recalled that by the denial of introspection and intuition, Peirce makes it necessary for all knowledge of self to be inferred from objective data. What proves our existence is the existence of ignorance and error, for we must suppose some subject in which ignorance and error inhere.

But it follows from our own existence . . . that everything which is present to us is a phenomenal manifestation of ourselves. This does not prevent its being a phenomenon of something without us, just as a rainbow is at once a manifestation both of the sun and of the rain. When we think, then, we ourselves, as we are at that moment, appear as a sign. [5.283]

From the theory of thought-signs it follows that every conception is a sign. But a conception is simply a particular state of mind. (5.288) This state of mind then has, like every sign, three references: "first, the representative function which makes it a *representation*; second, the pure denotative application, or real connection, which brings one thought into *relation* with another; and third, the material quality, or how it feels, which gives thought its *quality*." (5.290) Thus, the feeling or emotion involved in the thought constitutes its quality. The denotative application of the sign, which directs it to its object, is attention: "Attention is the power by which thought at one time is connected with and made to relate to thought at another time; or, to apply the conception of thought as a sign, that it is the *pure demonstrative application* of a thought-sign." (5.295) And the representative function is that property by virtue of which the sign is interpreted by a subsequent sign — i.e., conveys its meaning to a subsequent sign. Thus feeling, attention, and understanding are all explicable on the theory that the mind is a developing sign. (5.313) Indeed, since the knower which knows the self is only an interpreting sign, the self known can never be other than a sign; "the man is the thought." (5.314)

The mind therefore is a sign. But it is a sign of me only in so far as I am necessary to explain ignorance and error.

The individual man, since his separate existence is manifested only by ignorance and error, so far as he is anything apart from his fellows, and from what he and they are to be, is only a negation. This is man,
". . . proud man,
Most ignorant of what he's most assured,
His glassy essence." [5.317]

The question naturally arises, therefore, what would occur if ignorance and error were eliminated? Clearly, individuality would cease to exist, but identity would not, for "the identity of a man consists in the *consistency* of what he does and thinks, and consistency is the intellectual character of a thing; that is, is its expressing something." (5.315) But to "express" in this sense is to embody an abstraction. The identity of man lies then in the abstraction he expresses in his life — that is, in his conforming his thought and action to the idea in the divine mind. Thus in so far as ignorance and error are eliminated, men are identified with each other and the divine, and since it is the sole aim of inquiry to eliminate ignorance and error, so it is the sole aim of inquiry to merge the individual with the community.

Now as this argument makes clear, the community is for Peirce more than the community of men. This is made explicit in the review of Berkeley where he wrote: "And the catholic consent which constitutes the truth is by no means to be limited to men in this earthly life or to the human race, but extends to the whole communion of minds to which we belong, including some probably whose senses are very different from ours . . ." (8.13) Like his father, Peirce was evidently willing to countenance life in other worlds and other forms.[30] But the community is pre-eminently a sort of holy community of dedicated men who by their dedication enter a kind of communion with God. It is this quasi-religious unity which Peirce so admired among the Scholastics and among modern men of science. (8.11ff)

But if inquiry thus carries religious overtones, it follows that those who inquire should be animated by such a spirit of devotion. And this is indeed the case, for as Peirce points out, according to his theory of induction the attainment of truth is guaranteed only by adhering to the inductive method in the long run. To attain that truth, therefore, the individual must merge his own interests with those of the community of investigators, and sacrifice his own partial beliefs for the attainment of ultimate truth.

But just the revelation of the possibility of this complete self-sacrifice in man, and the belief in its saving power, will serve to redeem the logicality of all men. For he who recognizes the logical necessity of complete self-identification of one's own interests with those of the community, and its potential existence in man, even if he has it not himself, will perceive that only the inferences of that man who has it are logical, and so views his own inferences as being valid only so far as they would be accepted by that man. But so far as he has this belief, he becomes identified with that man. And that ideal perfection of knowledge by which we have seen that reality is constituted must thus belong to a community in which this identification is complete. [5.356]

The discovery of the logic of relations compelled a number of changes in the theory of inquiry, but it did not lead to a change in the theory of the spirit of inquiry. Thus in the third paper of the *Popular Science Monthly* series, Peirce repeats the closing paragraphs of the 1868 paper with only slight change. (2.654) The three sentiments of "interest in an indefinite community, recognition of the possibility of this interest being made supreme, and hope in the unlimited continuance of intellectual activity, [are] indispensable requirements of

[30] See above, p. 14.

logic." (2.655) Peirce compares these sentiments to faith, hope, and charity, and he remarks that although the New Testament is not a textbook in the logic of sentiments, it "is certainly the highest existing authority in regard to the dispositions of heart which a man ought to have." (2.655)

The continuation of this ontology through the 1870's is also indicated by Peirce's famous doctrine of pragmatism. In the discussion above, I have emphasized the influence of Bain's theory and of Peirce's own doctrines of cognition and reality in the formation of this theory. But two of the key terms in the theory of pragmatism come from Kant — "practical" and "pragmatic." "By 'the practical' I mean everything that is possible through freedom," (A800 B828) and again, "A will which can be determined independently of sensuous impulses, and therefore through motives which are represented only by reason, is entitled *freewill* (*arbitrium liberum*), and everything which is bound up with this will, whether as ground or as consequence, is entitled *practical*." (A802 B830) By "practical bearings," then, I think Peirce meant bearings which have significance for actions subject to our control. This is confirmed by the meaning of pragmatic in Kant: "contingent belief, which yet forms the ground for the actual employment of means to certain actions, I entitle *pragmatic belief*." (A824 B852) And in a passage which shows very clearly why Peirce found Bain so congenial, Kant remarks, "The usual touchstone, whether that which someone asserts is merely his persuasion — or at least his subjective conviction, that is, his firm belief — is *betting*." (A824 B852) The connection between the pragmatic and the practical Kant states as follows: "When, however, the conditions of the exercise of our free will are empirical, reason can have no other than a regulative employment in regard to it, and can serve only to effect unity in its empirical laws. . . . In this field, therefore, reason can supply none but *pragmatic* laws of free action, for the attainment of those ends which are commended to us by the senses . . ." (A800 B828) Now under Peirce's theory of cognition, the conditions of the exercise of free will can only be empirical, so that all practical laws are pragmatic. Peirce's pragmatism is supposed to be a method of determining the intellectual meaning of concepts. But in what does such meaning consist? According to him:

It appears then that the intellectual significance of all thought ultimately lies in its effect upon our actions. Now in what does the intellectual character of conduct consist? Clearly in its harmony to the eye of reason; that is in the fact that the mind in contemplating it shall find a harmony of purposes in it. In other words it must be capable of rational interpretation to a future thought.[31]

That is, the objective is to introduce consistency and harmony into our conduct. The laws or habits which effect this will determine our voluntary conduct so as to satisfy our needs, and what we need to know about an object — i.e., the meaning of the object for us — will consist in how it relates to our voluntary action. Now that consistency which we shall strive to create in our conduct is no other than the consistency described in 1868 — the conforming of our conduct to "the highest existing authority in regard to the dispositions of heart which a man ought to have." (2.655)

The normative character of inquiry is thus implicit in much of Peirce's writing of the late 1860's and 1870's. But Peirce did not attempt to develop any systematic theological rationale as a consequence of this character. Rather he held true to his earlier decision to create a theory which would be consistent with religion, but which would not deal directly with religious problems.[32] This decision, based first on his interpretation of the Antinomies, was greatly strengthened during the next twenty years by the unremitting battle over evolution. I have pointed out above that Peirce first interpreted this battle as a war between science and religion, and that subsequently he came to see it as a war between science and theology, leaving religion, interpreted as a sentiment of the heart, free from attack.[33] Exactly this strategy is to be seen in the fifth of the *Popular Science Monthly* papers where Peirce writes:

[31] "That the Significance of Thought Lies in Its Reference to the Future," 1873, pp. 3f, IB2 Box 8.

[32] Thus in the fifth of the *Popular Science Monthly* articles, Peirce explicitly refuses to countenance theological arguments based on design (6.419f) and thus rejects the so-called "natural theology." The question of whether or not such theological arguments were valid was one of the most hotly debated issues of the science-religion controversy in the years after Darwin. Cf. Simon Newcomb, Noah Porter, James Freeman Clarke, James McCosh, "A Symposium: Law and Design in Nature" in Walter Muelder and Laurence Sears, eds., *The Development of American Philosophy* (Boston, 1940), pp. 195–210.

[33] See above, pp. 99f.

It seems to me that those scientific men who have sought to make out that science was not hostile to theology have not been so clear-sighted as their opponents. . . . It is true that, if the priests of any particular form of religion succeed in making it generally believed that religion cannot exist without the acceptance of certain formulas, or if they succeed in so interweaving certain dogmas with the popular religion that the people can see no essential analogy between a religion which accepts these points of faith and one which rejects them, the result may very well be to render those who cannot believe these things irreligious. Nor can we ever hope that any body of priests should consider themselves more teachers of religion in general than of the particular system of theology advocated by their own party. But no man need be excluded from participation in the common feelings, nor from so much of the public expression of them as is open to all the laity, by the unphilosophical narrowness of those who guard the mysteries of worship. Am I to be prevented from joining in that common joy at the revelation of enlightened principles of religion which we celebrate at Easter and Christmas because I think that certain scientific, logical, and metaphysical ideas which have been mixed up with these principles are untenable? No; to do so would be to estimate those errors as of more consequence than the truth — an opinion which few would admit. People who do not believe what are really the fundamental principles of Christianity are rare to find, and all but these few ought to feel at home in the churches. [6.425–427]

# PART THREE

# VIII

# *Mathematical Interlude*

I N the early nineteenth century, mathematics was usually defined as "the science of quantity," where by quantity was meant measureable or countable magnitude. Numbers were regarded as concepts abstracted from collections of things, and it was common practice to support mathematical demonstration by reference to operations upon tangible objects. Where no empirical model could be found, many mathematicians were inclined to deny the reality and validity of the mathematical processes involved.[1]

So long as mathematics confined itself to the positive integers, no serious difficulties arose to trouble this concept of the science. But negative and imaginary numbers created new problems concerning the notion of existence in mathematics. The mathematicians could not deny the immense utility of the new numbers; yet they had difficulty in finding an empirical interpretation for them. The situation in respect to negative numbers was not so serious, for a ready model was available in the form of double-entry bookkeeping; but the imaginary numbers posed insuperable problems. The square root of minus one was an entity not to be met with in everyday life, and many termed them "imaginary" or "impossible" numbers.

In England, where an unwise reverence for the fluxion notation had stifled mathematical thought since Newton's time, the issue came to the fore only in the 1820's and 1830's. A group of young men at Cambridge, under the leadership of George Peacock, sought to legitimize the impossible numbers by the introduction of what they called symbolical algebra. Peacock divided algebra into two parts — the algebra of numbers and the algebra of symbols. In the former, the permissible operations were restricted to those which could be performed

[1] Alexander Macfarlane, *Lectures on Ten British Mathematicians of the Nineteenth Century* (New York; 1916), p. 12.

upon the nonnegative integers. Thus, where $a$ and $b$ are nonnegative integers, $a + b$ and $ab$ are always permissible operations yielding non-negative integers, but $a - b$ is permissible only where $a$ is greater than or equal to $b$, and $a/b$ is permissible only if $b$ is an exact divisor of $a$.[2] In the algebra of symbols, however, full use of the inverse operations is permitted so that the negative and imaginary expressions appear. Peacock justified his new symbolic algebra by what he called the "principle of the permanence of equivalent forms," namely, "Whatever algebraical forms are equivalent when the symbols are general in form, but specific in value, will be equivalent likewise when the symbols are general in value as well as in form."[3] The importance of the principle lies in the fact that the equivalence is postulated to hold true even when expressions occur in the general form which have no direct interpretation in the algebra of nonnegative integers. That is to say, Peacock took the fundamental step of freeing algebraic symbols from intuitive meaning; it is no longer necessary that every algebraic expression have an intuitively acceptable model. The validity of the reasoning turns upon the form, not upon an intuitive interpretation.[4]

The path thus opened by Peacock was followed at once by others, of whom two, Augustus De Morgan and George Boole, deserve particular mention. De Morgan carried out Peacock's principle to its logical end, and declared the independence of algebra from the then familiar interpretations. "In abandoning the meaning of symbols, we also abandon those of the words which describe them. Thus addition is to be, for the present, a sound void of sense. It is a mode of combination represented by $+$; when $+$ receives its meaning, so also will the word addition."[5] De Morgan then went on to enunciate the fundamental principles of the new algebra. He reduced the laws of algebra to five — the law of signs, the commutative and distributive laws, the index (exponentiation) law, and the laws of reduction (viz. $a - a = 0$, $a \div a = 1$) — and after specifying symbols for variables and operations, stated, "Any system of symbols which obeys these laws and no others, except they be formed by combination of these laws, and which uses the preceding

---

[2] *Ibid.*, p. 15.
[3] *Ibid.*, p. 17.
[4] Eric Temple Bell, *The Development of Mathematics* (New York, 1945), pp. 180f.
[5] Macfarlane, *Ten British Mathematicians*, p. 25. De Morgan made an exception in the case of the symbol of identity which retained its meaning.

symbols and no others, except they be new symbols invented in abbreviation of combinations of these symbols, is symbolic algebra." [6] This statement was published in 1849, just fifteen years after Peacock had first broken the way. The shift in point of view is clear cut and obvious. Algebra is now defined as a system of symbols, having no fixed interpretation, whose relations are defined by purely formal laws. There is no reference to the meaning of the symbols, to an absolute empirical model, or to intuitive justifications. In the formulation of De Morgan, algebra becomes an abstract, formal, system.

Once algebra had been freed from the concept of quantity, it became possible to apply algebra to nonquantitative subjects. Among the first such applications to be made was the development of the algebra of logic — the forerunner of modern symbolic logic. In the year 1847 De Morgan began the work with his *Formal Logic* [7] but the man who actually carried it through was George Boole, whose *Mathematical Analysis of Logic* [8] was also published in 1847, to be followed in 1854 by *The Laws of Thought*. As Boole pointed out in the introduction to the former work: "They who are acquainted with the present state of the theory of Symbolical Algebra, are aware, that the validity of the processes of analysis does not depend upon the interpretation of the symbols which are employed, but solely upon the laws of their combination. Every system of interpretation which does not affect the truth of the relations supposed, is equally admissible . . ." [9] And Boole then showed in detail that it is possible to assign an interpretation to the symbols of a special algebra so as to yield the logic of propositions, and the algebra of classes.

The same trend toward the formalist point of view also developed in geometry, and led to equally startling results. The success of analytic geometry tended for a time to focus attention upon the metrical aspect of the subject to the exclusion of the synthetic. But by the early years of the nineteenth century, the work of Poncelet, Gergonne, and others in the development of projective geometry had made it clear that there was a distinctively geometrical subject matter which was not metrical

[6] *Ibid.*, pp. 26f.
[7] Augustus De Morgan, *Formal Logic* (London, 1847).
[8] George Boole, *The Mathematical Analysis of Logic* (Cambridge, 1847).
[9] Boole, *The Mathematical Analysis of Logic*, p. 3.

and hence not quantitative.[10] The work of Poncelet and Gergonne, and after them of Grassmann, also rid geometry of dependence upon diagrammatic constructions and upon the notion of extension. Through his "principle of continuity" — the geometrical analogue of Peacock's "Principle of the Permanence of Form" [11] — Poncelet opened the way for the introduction of imaginary or ideal elements into geometry, and thus affected the same combined liberation and formalization in the latter field which Peacock had achieved in algebra.[12] But the killing blow to the concept that geometry was dependent upon any definite subject matter was brought by Gergonne when he introduced the principle of duality in 1825.[13] The principle affirms, what is easily proved, that "to each theorem in plane [projective] geometry there necessarily corresponds another, deduced from it by simply interchanging the two words 'points' and 'lines' . . ." [14] while in three dimensional projective geometry the same duality holds in respect to the terms "points" and "planes." As Nagel has pointed out, "Everything in this history points to the view that the only identifiable subject-matter which can be assigned to demonstrative geometry is the interconnections of the symbolic operations whose properties have been formally specified." [15]

A further difficulty which the formal view of geometry had to overcome was the belief that geometry was the science of pure space — a doctrine derived from Kant and affirmed by his followers. This view was finally overthrown by the work of the geometers Lobatchewski, Bolyai, and Gauss.[16] Since early times, mathematicians had suspected that the parallel postulate of Euclidean geometry might be a theorem rather than an axiom. Accordingly, attempts had been made to show

---

[10] Ernest Nagel, "The Formation of Modern Conceptions of Formal Logic in the Development of Geometry," *Osiris*, VII, 149ff (1939). The reader is referred to this article for a detailed account of the developments I briefly summarize.

[11] *Ibid.*, pp. 159f.

[12] *Ibid.*, pp. 152–178.

[13] *Ibid.*, p. 179.

[14] *Ibid.*, p. 180.

[15] *Ibid.*, p. 178.

[16] Modern Kantians deny that their philosophy does require the a priority of Euclidean geometry. It is however a historical fact that when the non-Euclidean geometries were discovered they were regarded as disproving the Kantian theory. Philip Chapin Jones, "Kant, Euclid, and the Non-Euclideans," *Philosophy of Science*, XIII, 137–143 (April 1946).

that it was not independent of the other axioms. One method of doing this was to substitute for the axiom its negation and then to try to derive a contradiction, thus showing that the parallel axiom was implied by some of the other axioms. Research along these lines led Gauss, Lobatchewski, and Bolyai to the startling conclusion that no contradiction resulted, or, in other words, that there were perfectly consistent metrical geometries which assumed as axioms propositions denying the parallel axiom.[17] The existence of these "non-Euclidean" geometries made it clear that a priori truth could not be claimed for Euclidean geometry, nor indeed could it be said which of the alternative systems was true, for the testable consequences which resulted from them were below the limit of observation. Thus the emphasis was shifted from the truth to the formal consistency of the theories.

The method which led to the discovery of the non-Euclidean geometries depended upon the axiomatic formulation of geometry, and with the axiomization of algebra similar methods became available there. One of the most striking of the results obtained was the discovery of the system of quaternions by the great Irish mathematician Sir William Rowan Hamilton. In 1833 Hamilton had devised a method for representing complex numbers by couples of real numbers, thus giving a new interpretation to the imaginary unit $i$.[18] In the plane these couples were interpreted as lines having length and direction, and De Morgan conferred the title of "double algebra" upon the calculus of such couples.[19] The problem immediately suggested itself, was there a triple algebra resembling in outline the "double algebra"? Such an algebra, so De Morgan and his contemporaries believed, would be an algebra of vectors in three-dimensional space, and had obvious importance in the theory of vector analysis. De Morgan and many others tried in vain to solve the problem. The reason for their failure was a confusion. As Macfarlane has pointed out, "the symbol of double algebra denotes not a length and a direction; but a multiplier and *an angle*. In it the angles are confined to one plane; hence the next stage will be a *quadruple algebra*, when the axis of the plane is

---

[17] Bell, *Men of Mathematics*, pp. 294–306.

[18] C. C. MacDuffee, "Algebra's Debt to Hamilton," *Scripta Mathematica*, X, 28–30 (1944).

[19] Macfarlane, *Ten British Mathematicians*, p. 28.

made variable." [20] Hamilton alone seems to have recognized this, but for years he was unable to discover the algebra. One day while out walking, the solution suddenly came to him, and he carved upon a stone of the bridge where the discovery was made the defining equation:

$$i^2 = j^2 = k^2 = ijk = -1.^{[21]}$$

From this equation it follows that $ij = -ji$ — in other words, the resulting algebra is noncommutative with respect to multiplication.

The discovery that there was a consistent algebra which did not assume the commutative law of multiplication came as a revelation to Hamilton's contemporaries, and it opened the way for the creation of new systems of such algebras. One of the men who undertook this investigation was Benjamin Peirce, whose *Linear Associative Algebra* was an investigation of algebras which assume the associative law but not the commutative law. The discovery also led to the theory of matrices, formulated by Arthur Cayley in 1858 [22] — one of the most important advances in all of modern algebra.

In 1841 George Boole noted that if a quadratic form be subjected to a particular kind of transformation, either the discriminant of the form is unchanged, or it is altered by a factor which depends only on the coefficients contained in the transformation.[23] This discovery ushered in the theory of algebraic invariants — a theory which was to dominate English, and American, algebra for the remainder of the century and which has played a fundamental role in the development of modern algebra.[24] Boole began the development of the theory, but the lead soon passed to two men who were to make it their life's work and whose names are so closely identified with it that one historian has called them "the invariant twins" — Arthur Cayley and James Joseph Sylvester.[25]

The theory of invariants might be described as the study of those properties of an algebraic form which are preserved when the form is

---

[20] *Ibid.*, p. 28.

[21] $ij = k$, $jk = i$, $ki = j$, $ji = -k$, $kj = -i$, $ik = -j$. MacDuffee, "Algebra's Debt to Hamilton," pp. 31–33 and Robert Perceval Graves, *Life of Sir William Rowan Hamilton* (Dublin, 1885), II, 435.

[22] Arthur Cayley, "Memoir on the Theory of Matrices," *The Collected Mathematical Papers of Arthur Cayley* (Cambridge, 1889), II, 475–497.

[23] Bell, *Men of Mathematics*, pp. 389f.

[24] Bell, *The Development of Mathematics*, chap. 20.

[25] Bell, *Men of Mathematics*, p. 378.

subjected to a linear transformation. By an "algebraic form," or "quantic," is meant a homogeneous, algebraic function of any number of variables. Examples of binary forms are

$$ax^2 + 2bxy + cy^2,$$
$$ax^3 + 3bx^2y + 3cxy^2 + dy^3,$$

etc.

An invariant of such binary forms might then be defined as follows: If a binary form, $f$, be changed by a linear transformation into a new form, $F$, and a function, $I$, of the coefficients of $F$ be equal to the same function of the coefficients of $f$ multiplied by a factor depending solely on the transformation, then $I$ is called an invariant of the binary quantic $f$.[26] The basic problem of the theory is to determine all the invariants and covariants (which differ from the invariants in depending upon the variables as well as the coefficients) of a given quantic.

Much of the fundamental work of the theory was done by Cayley in his famous series of ten memoirs on quantics, published between 1854 and 1878. But for our purposes, one of these — the famous "Sixth Memoir on Quantics" [27] — is of particular importance. In this paper Cayley developed the geometrical application of the theory of invariants in a way which was to have immense importance. It was already well known that projective geometry was nonmetrical and contained no reference to distance, in which respect it differed sharply from the usual Euclidean geometry. Cayley set himself the task of "establishing the notion of distance upon purely descriptive [projective] principles." Cayley argues as follows:

I have, in all that has preceded, given the analytical theory of distance along with the geometrical theory, as well for the purpose of illustration, as because it is important to have the analytical expression of a distance in terms of the coordinates; but I consider the geometrical theory as perfectly complete in itself: the general result is as follows, viz. assuming in the plane (or space of geometry of two dimensions) a conic termed the Absolute, we may by means of this conic, by descriptive constructions, divide any line or range of points whatever, and any point or pencil of lines whatever, into an infinite series of infinitesimal elements, which are (as a definition of distance) assumed to be equal; the number of elements between two points of the range or two

[26] Adapted from J. H. Grace and A. Young, *The Algebra of Invariants* (Cambridge, 1903), pp. 3, 7.
[27] Cayley, *Mathematical Papers*, pp. 561–592.

lines of the pencil, measures the distance between the two points or lines; and by means of the quadrant, as a distance which exists as well with respect to lines as points, we are enabled to compare the distance of two lines with that of two points; and the distance of a point and a line may be represented indifferently as the distance of two points, or as the distance of two lines.[28]

Cayley argues that if the equation of the Absolute (in terms of the Cartesian coordinates of its points) is

$$(a,b,c \ ) \ x,y)^2 = o,$$

then the distance of the points $(x,y)$, $(x',y')$ is equal to a multiple of the arc having for its cosine the expression

$$\frac{(a,b,c \ ) \ x,y \ ) \ x',y')}{\sqrt{(a,b,c \ ) \ x,y)^2} \quad \sqrt{(a,b,c \ ) \ x',y')^2}}. \ [29]$$

These considerations led Cayley to remark in conclusion: "In ordinary plane geometry, the Absolute degenerates into a pair of points, viz. the points of intersection of the line infinity with any evanescent circle, or what is the same thing, the Absolute is the two circular points at infinity." And

. . . that, *in my own point of view*, the more systematic course in the present introductory memoir on the geometrical part of the subject of quantics, would have been to ignore altogether the notions of distance and metrical geometry; for the theory in effect is, that the metrical properties of the figure are not properties of the figure considered *per se* apart from everything else, but its properties when considered in connection with another figure, viz. the conic termed the Absolute. The original figure might comprise a conic; for instance, we might consider the properties of the figure formed by two or more conics, and we are then in the region of pure descriptive geometry: we pass out of it into metrical geometry by fixing upon a conic of the figure as a standard of reference and calling it the Absolute. Metrical geometry is thus a part of descriptive geometry, and descriptive geometry is *all* geometry . . .[30]

Cayley's argument thus appeared to show that metrical geometry is simply a special case of projective geometry; by a suitable choice of the Absolute conic, all of Euclidean geometry can be generated out of projective geometry. But the implications of the paper went even beyond this. As was shown by Felix Klein in 1872, various metrical geometries, Euclidean and non-Euclidean, can be obtained by Cayley's

[28] *Ibid.*, p. 591.
[29] *Ibid.*, p. 584.
[30] *Ibid.*, p. 592.

method. If the Absolute is the circular point-pair, we get Euclidean geometry; if the Absolute is real, we obtain Lobatchewski's geometry; and if it is imaginary, we obtain either spherical or elliptic geometry. Thus the seeming disorder which the advent of the non-Euclidean geometries had created is resolved, and they are shown to be merely the results of different ways of projectively defining distance.[31]

But Cayley's conclusion that "descriptive geometry is *all* geometry" involves an error. Cayley assumes that the reduction of metric to projective geometry is a logical reduction — that metrical geometry logically follows from projective geometry. This conclusion is based upon his interpretation of the definition of distance as requiring no additional postulates. The error has been pointed out by Russell. The distance function obtained depends entirely upon the Absolute, and different distance functions result for different choices of the Absolute. In order to obtain the usual metrical geometry by Cayley's method, it is necessary to choose the circular point-pair for the Absolute. The question accordingly arises as to whether this choice can be made within projective geometry — i.e., whether it is possible to specify these points by projective properties alone. Russell has shown that in fact this cannot be done, for in projective geometry the only method of distinguishing points from one another is through collineation — the points lying on the same line. But there is no projective property of a pair of points on a line which is not also shared by every other pair of collinear points. Only when we reach sets of four points does such a property emerge — the cross ratio, which is a purely projective property. The projective definition of a distance must accordingly be a definition in terms of four points, not of two. In order then to obtain a definition which is similar to the metrical definition of distance, two fixed points must be regarded as independently specified. The distance relation described by the variable points is then fixed by the choice of these two points. Hence in order to obtain any given distance relation, two points must be already independently specified, and this as we have just remarked cannot be done by projective properties alone. The definition is therefore not arbitrary — it is necessary either to introduce the notion of distance in order to make the required specification, in which case the

---

[31] Bertrand Russell, *An Essay on the Foundations of Geometry* (Cambridge, 1897), pp. 29f.

proposed reduction fails, or to introduce a postulate to the effect that the required choice can be made; and in either case a postulate is required which is not a postulate of projective geometry and which cannot be deduced from projective geometry.[32]

The relation which subsists between metrical and projective geometry is accordingly not one of logical deducibility. But there is an important relation, and it was again Cayley who first brought this relation into prominence, through his "Sixth Memoir." Namely, every postulate of projective geometry is a postulate of metrical geometry, but there are some postulates of metrical geometry which are not postulates of projective geometry. Thus any projective space, upon the addition of a distance postulate, becomes a metric space, and any metric space, upon the elimination of the distance postulate, becomes a projective space. It was on the basis of this principle that Klein was able to prove that the differences among the various metric geometries are differences among the definitions of distance.[33]

The existence of this relation led Klein to formulate a very important further generalization. In his work on the distance definition Klein had shown that there is a method of introducing numerical coordinates into projective geometry which does not presuppose the existence of a metric.[34] With these coordinates it is possible to give an analytic representation of projective geometry, and when this is done the projective geometry in its analytic form may be regarded as the theory of linear transformations. These transformations have of course a system of invariants, and the transformations themselves constitute a group.[35] These facts led Klein to a generalization of the principle of duality, based upon the close relation between a group of transformations and the properties left invariant by them. This generalization is as follows: "The geometrical properties characteristic of a geometry remain unchanged by the principal group, and the geometrical properties of a system are characterized by the fact that they remain unchanged by

[32] *Ibid.*, pp. 30–38.
[33] Nagel, "Geometry," p. 207.
[34] *Ibid.*, p. 204.
[35] Thus, *"an aggregate of transformations is called a group if the combination of two of its transformations gives again a transformation of the aggregate, and if the inverse of every transformation also belongs to the aggregate."* Felix Klein, *Elementary Mathematics from an Advanced Standpoint: Geometry* (New York, 1939), p. 132.

the transformations of the principal group." [36] Every geometry may be characterized by the relations which it explores; thus for example metrical geometry is the study of the metrical relations among the various kinds of geometrical figures. It is also possible to characterize the geometry by the transformations permitted in the system which leave these relations invariant. These two methods of characterizing the geometry are equivalent.

On the basis of this formulation Klein formulated his famous Erlanger program: *"Given any group of transformations in space which includes the principal group as a sub-group, then the invariant theory of this group gives a definite kind of geometry, and every possible geometry can be obtained in this way."* [37] This principle affords a method for the complete classification of geometries, and its application became the chief project in geometry between the day of its statement in 1872 and the end of the century.[38]

The classification in the Erlanger program is a classification by subsumption. As we have seen, metric systems may be considered as projective systems to which distance is added. The addition of such a postulate reduces the number of independent parameters on which the transformations of the system depend, and yields a narrower system. Thus, for example, metric geometry may be called the group $G_7$ because its transformations depend upon seven parameters. Projective geometry is the group $G_{15}$ and requires fifteen parameters. Topology is the widest of all such systems and is called the group $G_\infty$ because there is no finite number of such parameters.[39] From the logical point of view, the theory of the classification amounts to saying that the fewer the axioms which have to be satisfied, the less restricted will be the resulting system.[40] Thus a hierarchy is established which, beginning with the least restricted of geometries, obtains narrower and narrower systems by the addition of more and more postulates. And one of the most general geometries — the foundation assumed by many others — is topology.

[36] Felix Klein, quoted in Nagel, *Geometry*, p. 204.
[37] Klein, *Geometry*, p. 133.
[38] Bell, *Development of Mathematics*, p. 443.
[39] Klein, *Geometry*, p. 133.
[40] Bell, *Development of Mathematics*, p. 444.

# IX

# *Topology*

## *The Listing Theorem*

HISTORICALLY speaking, topology is one of the newest branches of mathematics. Although isolated results were known as early as 1640, topology was not recognized as a distinct field until the middle of the last century. Among the early workers in the subject, Euler is the most outstanding; his theorem for polyhedra, his characteristic of closed surfaces, and his work on networks analysis are still important. Beginning in 1794, and intermittently thereafter, Gauss published memoirs on the classification of knots. But not until about 1850 did interest in the subject become general. In 1847 Kirchhoff published a paper on networks, and J. B. Listing published his *Vorstudien zur Topologie*.[1] Moebius in 1858 introduced the Moebius strip. With the work of Bernhard Riemann the potentialities of the subject were realized. Riemann showed that topology could be used in the study of functions of a complex variable, thereby indicating a link with analysis which has proven of great importance. After Riemann, Klein, Poincaré, and others turned to the study of the new field.[2]

The topology created by these men was revised and rebuilt in the present century by Brouwer, Alexander, Veblen, Lefschetz, and others. The modern theory is based almost entirely on the theory of sets and has abandoned the synthetic methods used by its founders. Lefschetz thus describes it: "Topology begins where sets are implemented with some cohesive properties enabling one to define continuity. The sets are then called topological spaces. Thus topology is a branch of general

---

[1] Johann Benedict Listing, *Vorstudien zur Topologie* (Göttingen, 1848). Reprinted from the *Göttingen Studien*, 1847.

[2] For notes on the history of topology, see Bell, *Development of Mathematics*, pp. 453–468; Bell, *Men of Mathematics*, pp. 484–510; Richard Courant and Herbert Robbins, *What Is Mathematics?* (New York, 1941), pp. 235f; Albert Tucker and Herbert S. Bailey, Jr., "Topology," *Scientific American*, 182: 18–24 (January 1950).

set theory, the creation of Georg Cantor (around 1880). That his ideas have had a profound influence in all mathematics is well known. In topology this influence has been decisive." [3]

For the present, however, we must confine our attention to the early period, and particularly to the work of Johann Benedict Listing. Although Listing was one of the earliest workers in the field, he is now almost entirely forgotten. Born in 1808, he was professor of astronomy at Göttingen at the time when that university was the mathematical capital of the world. As was usual at the time, a professorship of astronomy involved the teaching of mathematics, and Listing seems to have given most of his time to the latter subject. His principal scientific work was in physiological optics [4] and topology.

The development of topology is closely connected with the history of Göttingen. Gauss appears to have initiated the interest by his work on knots, and his encouragement led Listing to publish the *Vorstudien* in 1847.[5] When Riemann came to Göttingen in the 1840's, topology was already established as an important mathematical study. Gauss encouraged Riemann to work in the field [6] and Listing also played a part in his development. Riemann was a member of Listing's seminar in 1850, and Listing undoubtedly encouraged his interest in the subject.[7]

In 1861, Listing published a second memoir, "Der Census räumlicher Complexe" in the *Göttingen Abhandlungen*.[8] Although this paper aroused little interest among mathematicians,[9] it did immediately attract the attention of Arthur Cayley. In 1861, the year Listing published, Cayley published a paper "On the Partitions of a Close" [10] which was also a generalization of Euler's theorem, and in a note, added

---

[3] Solomon Lefschetz, *Introduction to Topology* (Princeton, 1949) p. 3.

[4] Peirce, "Topical Geometry," c.1904, p.35, IA2.F.1.

[5] Courant and Robbins, *Mathematics*, p. 235.

[6] Bell, *Men of Mathematics*, pp. 491–499.

[7] *Ibid.*, p. 491.

[8] Johann Benedict Listing, "Der Census räumlicher Complexe," *Abhandlungen der K. Gesellschaft der Wissenschaft zu Göttingen*, vol. 9–10, part II, pp. 97–180. Neither of Listing's memoirs has been translated into English. In what follows I shall use a translation made by Eric Lenneburg and myself during the summer of 1952. References are to section rather than to page.

[9] The literature seems to contain almost no reference to the census theorem and practically none to Listing. Cayley's brief exposition, cited below, is the only published commentary I have found on the theorem.

[10] Arthur Cayley, "On the Partitions of a Close," *Collected Mathematical Papers*, V, 62–65.

after publication, he remarks: "The generalization which is here given of Euler's Theorem $S + F = E + 2$, is a first step toward the theory developed in Listing's memoir . . . "[11] In 1868, Cayley reported on the census theorem to the London Mathematical Society,[12] and in 1873 he published a seven-page brief of it in the *Messenger of Mathematics*.[13] Cayley's interest in the theorem was probably due to his work on the theory of trees, which had begun in 1857. As developed in his early papers,[14] this theory was purely mathematical, but in 1874 [15] and 1875 [16] he applied it with success to a problem of importance in chemistry, which Bell describes as follows:

There is, however, one problem of some chemical interest which demands topological considerations . . . for its systematic solution: given any number of atoms with assigned valences, how many distinct compounds can be made from them, on the assumption that any graphical formula satisfying the valence conditions is admitted? The combinatorial machinery for obtaining the required chemical graphs was devised by Cayley (1875) in what he called the theory of trees; it was rescued from oblivion and amplified in the 1930's by chemists when the question again became of scientific interest.[17]

The connection between the theory of trees and the Listing theorem was pointed out by Cayley in the paper of 1874, where he wrote: "the mathematical question of the determination of such forms [trees] belongs to the class of questions considered in my paper 'On the Theory of the Analytical Forms Called Trees' . . . and in some papers on Partitions in the same Journal." [18] Among these was the paper on partitions of a close already referred to.

It was only a few years after this that Peirce, Cayley, and Sylvester were to meet at Hopkins. And it was just three years after Cayley's

---

[11] *Ibid.*, V, 617.
[12] *Ibid.*, VI, 22.
[13] *Ibid.*, VIII, 540–547.
[14] *Ibid.*, IV, 112–115.
[15] *Ibid.*, IX, 202–204.
[16] *Ibid.*, IX, 427–460.
[17] Bell, *Development of Mathematics*, p. 456.
[18] Cayley, *Mathematical Papers*, IX, 203. A tree may be described as a linear figure generated by the repeated furcation of a line, and the mathematical problem is to find a general formula for the combination of these forms. The application to chemistry is made by letting the points of furcation, or "knots," represent chemical atoms, and the radiating lines the valency of the atom. The formula then gives the possible combinations which can be formed from atoms of a given valency.

application of the theory of trees to chemistry that Sylvester and Clifford conceived the idea of using chemical diagrams to represent algebraic invariants. In his paper on the chemico-algebraic theory, Sylvester refers to Cayley's trees, and speaks of his own interest in and work on the subject.[19] The chemico-algebraic theory failed to prove fruitful, but it aroused considerable interest at the time.

By training and profession Peirce was a chemist, and, although he is chiefly remembered for his philosophy, the greater part of his adult life was spent in scientific work. To the end of his life he was avidly interested in chemical theories and in relations among chemistry and other sciences. He was greatly impressed by Sylvester's idea, and his use of chemical diagrams to represent logical schemata seems to have begun at this time.[20] Among these diagrams were Cayley's "trees," which Peirce used particularly in connection with the theory of ordinal numbers,[21] and a system of valential graphs, which he used to represent logical relations and with which he tried to prove topologically the irreducibility of triadic relations.[22]

It seems very likely that it was through Cayley and Sylvester that Peirce first became interested in Listing. The date of his first reading of the memoir is unknown, but a set of notes survives which is almost certainly the product of that reading. They indicate strongly that he was not impressed. Concerning one section he commented, "Talkee, Talkee," and on another, "I don't understand this so far, at all." [23] Yet in 1904 he wrote: "There is no possible question that the most important topical investigation that has ever yet been conducted, — it is probably the most important that ever will be undertaken, — is that of Johann Benedict Listing . . . " [24] The explanation of this change of mind and of the importance of topology in Peirce's thought will become evident as we proceed, but we must first examine Listing's theorem in some detail.

---

[19] James Joseph Sylvester, "On An Application of the New Atomic Theory to the Graphical Representation of the Invariants and Covariants of Binary Quantics, — With Three Appendices," in *The Collected Mathematical Papers of James Joseph Sylvester* (Cambridge, 1909), III, 172f. See also Cayley, *op. cit.*, IX, 429.

[20] C. S. Peirce to O. H. Mitchell, December 21, 1882, Scientific Correspondence.

[21] Peirce, "Topical Geometry," pp. 24f.

[22] "On Logical Graphs," 1898, pp. 1–4, IB2 Box 5.

[23] "Notes on Listing," n.d., pp. 4, 7, IA2.

[24] "Topical Geometry," p. 35.

In 1752 the great Swiss mathematician Leonard Euler discovered a theorem which has become known as Euler's theorem for polyhedra. (Strictly speaking, the first discoverer was Descartes who knew the theorem at least as early as 1640. Euler's rediscovery, however, was completely independent.) [25] The theorem states that, if V be the number of vertices, E the number of edges, and F the number of faces of any simple polyhedron, then it is true that

$$V - E + F = 2$$

The theorem is a topological one, since it holds for any homeomorphic transformation of a polyhedron.

Listing noted that if the number "2" of Euler's formula be taken as referring to parts of the space — the one included within it, the other excluded from it — then we have the formula

$$V - E + F - S = 0,$$

where S is the number of disjoint spaces.[26] He also noted the obvious fact that the Euler theorem does not hold for all solid figures. Listing thereupon conceived the idea of so generalizing the formula that it would hold for every kind of figure composed of points, lines, surfaces, and spaces in a three-dimensional space. In order to do this, he defined points, lines, surfaces, and spaces as categories having several properties, among which would be the number of units of each class in a given figure. He thus obtained an equation of the form

$$(V \pm W) - (E \pm X) + (F \pm Y) - (S \pm Z) = 0.$$

If W, X, Y, and Z are all equal to O, the Euler formula results. The problem then is to find values for these new variables which would make them equal to O in the case of simple polyhedra, but which make the formula true of all types of spatial figures. This would give a "census-like" equation which would hold for all spatial configurations. Accordingly, he called his formula the "Census Theorem."

The final form of the census theorem is

$$a - (b - x) + (c - x' + \pi) - (d - x'' + \pi' - w) = 0.[27]$$

The left side of the equation consists of four quantities, a, $(b - x)$, $(c - x' + \pi)$, and $(d - x'' + \pi' - w)$. These quantities, which Listing calls "Curien," or Kategories, refer to points, lines, surfaces, and

---

[25] Courant and Robbins, *Mathematics*, p. 236.
[26] Listing, "Der Census räumlicher Complexe," Introduction.
[27] *Ibid.*, no. 44.

spaces respectively. The variables 'a', 'b', 'c', and 'd' designate the number of each such constituent of a figure. In a cube, for example, $a = 8$, $b = 12$, $c = 6$, $d = 2$. These obviously correspond to the variables of the Euler theorem.

Concerning the first Kategorie, that of points, Listing writes:

Points are not only the limits of lines or the intersections between two or more lines, but they are also components of bodies or surfaces where they appear as corners. Further, even on a curve or straight line (or surface) they may occur anywhere, as e.g., . . . the contact between two spheres. In the latter case the point may disappear when the two spheres separate, or it may be retained, depending on the constitution of the elements (that is to say, the elements may be so defined as to retain the point). These examples show that any point on any line or surface, or in any space, may be designated as a point which must be counted, and as such it should be differentiated from any other (uncounted) point. It therefore seems practical to call all such points, given as data for the constituents, and all other elements in so far as they count in their Kategories, *effective*; and to call all others *virtual,* which though used for certain operations, do not count in their Kategories.[28]

Regarding the second Kategorie, lines, he writes:

While the constituents of the first Kategorie (points) have a dimensionality of zero, those of the second Kategorie (lines) have a dimensionality of one. . . . As the constituents of Kategorie I form limits for the constituents of higher Kategories, so lines form the limits of surfaces and spaces. Thus the lines, or edges, of a tetrahedron limit both the sides and space. . . . Lines are limited only by points, or else they lack limits. . . . We count every line in so far as none of its inside points is effective as a constituent of the second Kategorie . . .[29]

Of the third Kategorie, surfaces, Listing writes:

Constituents having two dimensions are members of the third Kategorie. Surfaces function as limits of bodily spaces, while they themselves may be limited by points or lines. . . . Surfaces may be limited by points alone, as e.g., a spheroid with any given number of effective points on its surface, or by a line, as e.g., an ellipse, or by both lines and points. We count as a constituent of the third Kategorie every surface in which one may draw a line from any given point to any other point in this surface without having to surpass a limit of that surface. . . . The limits of a surface may be simple, multiple, or zero (the limit of a sphere is zero).[30]

[28] *Ibid.,* no. 2.
[29] *Ibid.,* no. 3.
[30] *Ibid.,* no. 4.

And of the fourth Kategorie, spaces:

Bodily spaces which are divided from one another by complexes have three dimensions, and accordingly they belong in the fourth Kategorie. All space is divided generally by complexes into separate parts — bodily spaces, or compartments (that is, the space included by the complex), and one excluded space which extends unlimited on all sides of the complex. This excluded space we call the *Amplexum*. In special (but numerous) cases, however, such a division may not be necessary: this will occur when the number of complexes is zero, or when either a complex contains no surface or the surfaces contained in it do not separate off any finite bodily space. . . . We consider the entirety of all spatial elements as belonging to one space when these spatial elements are interrelated in such a way that one can go from any one of them to any other along any path possible in the inside of that space without ever transgressing any limit.[31]

From these quotations it is clear that Listing conceives of the constituents of a Kategorie as limited by those of a lower Kategorie, and as limiting those of higher Kategories. Thus the theorem excludes to begin with such figures as cusps and nodes. The possible combinations of limits are given in the following table, where the first figures designate the constituent being limited ('2' for a line, '3' for a surface, '4' for a space) and the following figures the constituents which act as limits.[32]

| | | |
|---|---|---|
| 2,0 | 3,0,0 | 4,0,0,0 |
| 2,1 | 3,0,1 | 4,0,0,1 |
| | 3,2,0 | 4,0,2,0 |
| | 3,2,1 | 4,0,2,1 |
| | | 4,3,0,0 |
| | | 4,3,0,1 |
| | | 4,3,2,0 |
| | | 4,3,2,1. |

The three cases of null limitation will particularly concern us. (2,0) is a line which returns to itself without any effective point; (3,0,0) is a smooth, closed surface without effective points or lines, such as an unmarked sphere; (4,0,0,0) is a complete space.

Having now examined the Kategories and their relations, we must look to their components. "Among the constituents of any one Kategorie, there are subsidiary Kategories based on a distinction among

[31] *Ibid.*, no. 5.
[32] *Ibid.*, no. 6.

topological properties — i.e., such properties as do not refer to the quantity or mass or extension but solely to the mode of arrangement and the situation. The mode of connection between parts of any one constituent is what conditions the differentiation which here concerns us." [33] To explain what these topological properties are we will introduce the term "shape-class" — a term invented by Peirce rather than by Listing, and one which gives strong evidence that Peirce had conceived at least some of the ideas involved in modern topology. Unfortunately, however, Peirce failed to require that the "shape-class" induce an equivalence relation and he therefore allowed irreversible operations. Two figures belong to the same shape-class only if they may, by continuous deformation, be made to shrink to the same figure, or shape. Thus, for example, a line with one or two free ends can be shrunk by a continuous transformation to a point. It is therefore of the same shape-class as a point. A simple, bounded continuous surface may likewise be shrunk to a point and so is of the same shape-class as the line with a free end point. But a smooth, closed line or a torus cannot always shrink to a point. Thus in Figures 1 and 2 "b" is interchained by "a"

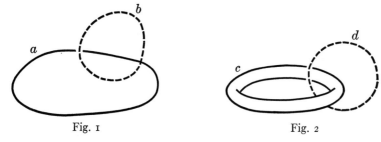

Fig. 1                              Fig. 2

and "d" by the torus "c" and this prevents their shrinking to a point. But in the two surfaces in Figures 3 and 4, the oval line "d" on "a" may

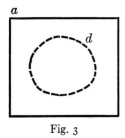

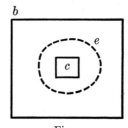

Fig. 3                              Fig. 4

[33] *Ibid.*, no. 7.

shrink to a point, but the oval "e" on "b" cannot, for the hole "c" bars the path. Figures 1, 2, and 4 then belong to a shape-class which is cyclic — they may all shrink to a cycle but not to a point. This property of a figure is called its "cyclosis," and is represented in the census equation by the variable x. As Figures 1 and 2 show, cyclosis is an attribute of lines, surfaces, and spaces, but never of points.[34]

A third shape-class is encountered in the case of a perfectly smooth sphere without effective lines or points. The sphere according to Listing wholly contains a space which prevents it from shrinking to a point. Nor can it shrink to a cyclic line. It therefore belongs to a distinct shape-class — it can shrink to at most a sphere. The property of such a figure is called its "periphraxis," and is designated by the variable $\pi$. Clearly, neither points nor lines can be periphractic, but surfaces and spaces may. In the case of spaces, this is so obvious as almost to be overlooked, for space wholly encloses all complexes. It is therefore periphractic.[35]

In the formula
$$a - (b - x) + (c - x' + \pi) - (d - x'' + \pi' - w) = 0,$$
the variable x denotes cyclosis: x is line-cyclosis, $x'$ surface cyclosis, $x''$ spatial cyclosis. The variable $\pi$ denotes periphraxis: $\pi$ is surface periphraxis, $\pi'$ spatial periphraxis. The meaning of the variable w will be made clear below.

With this understanding of the meaning of terms, Listing proceeds to the theorem itself. Listing first proves the theorem
$$a - b + c - d = 0 \qquad\qquad (1)$$
for all complexes of acyclotic, aperiphractic constituents.[36] In order to prove the general equation, he gives a procedure whereby the cyclotic and periphractic values may be equated to zero without disturbing the relative magnitudes of 'a', 'b', 'c', and 'd'. In other words, if x, $\pi$, and w all vanish, then the complex is both acyclotic and aperiphractic, and for such a complex (1) is true. Furthermore, (1) will remain true even if the vanishing of $x^n$, $\pi^n$, and w occasions changes in 'a', 'b', 'c', and 'd' so long as every increase of a positive quantity, 'a' or 'c', is balanced by an equal increase in a negative quantity, 'b' or 'd'. That this will always occur is the assertion of the theorem.

[34] *Ibid.*, nos. 7–10ff.
[35] *Ibid.*, nos. 24, 42.
[36] *Ibid.*, no. 34.

The possibility of proving this is afforded by the two facts that a constituent can only be limited by constituents of a lower Kategorie; and the first Kategorie, points, contains no attributive. Points cannot be cyclotic or periphractic. The number of points in a complex may therefore always be determined without reference to cyclosis or periphraxis, or to any other constituents of the complex. Given this definite value of 'a', we may then proceed to calculate the value of (b − x). The number 'b' is determined by inspection — likewise the number x. In order to eliminate x we invoke a process which Listing terms "dialyse." Given the cyclic line, x, as in Figure 5, let it be cut through as in Figure 6. x is then converted into a simple line with two end points

Fig. 5                               Fig. 6

which, being of the shape-class of a point, may be reduced to a point. The effect of a dialyse is thus to decrease x by one and to add one point to 'a'. We then have $(a + 1) − (b − (x − 1)) = (a + 1 − ((b + 1) − x)$. Since 'a' is positive and 'b' is negative the effect is the same as before. In a similar way, the dialyse of x′ and x″ may be shown to leave the aggregate value unchanged.[37] And since the limiting constituents are always of a lower Kategorie so that their number is determinate, no circularity arises.

Listing then considers the case of periphraxis, and we have to show that this can be eliminated without altering the value of the equation. The operation here involved is called "trema," from the Greek word "to puncture." The trema of a periphractic surface consists in puncturing the surface. The surface so produced is deformable by a continuous deformation into a plane. It is accordingly of the same shape-class as the plane, which is equivalent to a point. Hence the quantity $\pi$ is decreased by one and 'a' is increased by one. Therefore from

$$a − (b − x) + (c − x′ + \pi)$$

[37] *Ibid.*, nos. 7–12.

we have

$$(a + 1) - (b - x) + (c - x' + (\pi - 1))$$
$$(a + 1) - (b - x) + (c - 1 + \pi - x').$$

Clearly, the value of the aggregate remains unchanged.[38]

But in the trema of space we meet a new problem. Let us suppose we have three complexes, 'x', 'y', and 'z' which are not connected. The space which surrounds each complex is periphractic. If we connect the three complexes by lines to effect a trema, we will have two such lines. But the "amplexum," or infinite space, remains periphractic. In order to eliminate this final periphraxis we require a connecting line from the complex (the three now being united by connecting lines) to infinity. Listing writes:

> The consequence of the introduction of the new line is, on the one hand, an increase in the value of 'b'; on the other hand, however, if the point of departure is located in one of the *a* effective points of the complex the effect is zero, if it is located on an effective line the effect is an increase by one in the value of 'a' and 'b' simultaneously, if it is located in an effective surface the effect is an increase in the value of 'a' by one and a decrease in the value of 'c' by one: in any case, therefore, a decrease in the value (of the aggregate) by one. The other terminal point which is to be located in infinity must therefore be counted as an increase of one in the aggregate . . . from which it is apparent that the spatial infinity plays the role of a point which is located in infinite distance and with which this trematic line must connect the totality of the *p* complexions.[39]

He designates this point at infinity by w and names it "stigma." Its value must clearly be either one or zero — one if there is any complex (including empty space), zero if nothing whatever be given, not even space. Furthermore:

> This is primarily the point where the trematic line which reduces the amplexum to its aperiphractic condition finds its terminus; at the same time however the stigma must also be considered as the common limit of all constituents of the second and third Kategories which may occur in a bodily complex and which expand into infinity, so that after the introduction of w the census in its present form is also applicable to such cases as where the expansion of any constituent reaches into infinity. Instead of saying that a line or surface (curved or plane) expands into infinity at one or two or any number

---

[38] *Ibid.*, no. 24.
[39] *Ibid.*, no. 43.

of sides, we may now say that they find their limit on these sides in the stigma, which in all cases has the value one.[40]

It is thus clear that the cyclotic and periphractic values may be eliminated without changing the value of the aggregate $a - b + c - d$. Since this aggregate is always equal to zero, then it is proven that
$$a - (b - x) + (c - x' + \pi) - (d - x'' + \pi' - w) = 0,$$
or in words:

Theorem. In any given bodily complex the sum of the four contributing numbers, which have alternative signs $(+, -)$, consisting of existing points, lines, surfaces, and spaces, and which consists within each of these four Kategories of the number of constituents and the attributives determined from the modalities of cyclosis, of periphraxis, and of the expansion into infinity, is equal to zero.[41]

### The Peirce-Listing Theorem

Peirce was dissatisfied with the Listing theorem in several respects and undertook the task of revising it. First of all, he clarified the concepts involved, defined the idea of shape-class, distinguished infinite expansion from periphraxis, and made the number of constituents an attributive. We thus have the following definitions.

The Chorisy is the number of simple parts of a place of the dimensionality of the place itself which must be filled up in order to leave no room for a single *particle*. (In simpler language, it is the number of separate pieces.)

The Cyclosy is the number of simple parts of a place of dimensionality *one* less than that of the place itself which must be filled up in order to leave no room for a single *filament* that shall not be geometrically capable of shrinking indefinitely towards a point by an ordinary motion in the unoccupied place.

The Periphraxy is the number of simple parts of a place of dimensionality *two* less than that of the place itself which must be filled up in order to leave no room for a single *pellicle* that shall not be geometrically capable of shrinking indefinitely towards a line or point by an ordinary motion in the unoccupied place.

The Apeiry is the number of simple parts of a place of dimensionality *three* less than that of the place itself which must be filled up in order to leave no room for a single *solid* that shall not be geometrically capable of shrink-

[40] *Ibid.*, no. 44.
[41] *Ibid.*, no. 44.

ing indefinitely towards a surface, line, or point by an ordinary motion in the unoccupied place.[42]

In line with this revision he introduced a new notation for the theorem.[43] If $x_0$ stands for points, $x_1$ for lines, $x_2$ for surfaces, $x_3$ for spaces, X for chorisis, K for cyclosis, Π for periphraxis, and A for apeiry, then the quantities of the theorem are

$$A\, x_3 - \Pi\, x_3 + K\, x_3 - X\, x_3 = -\,(d - x'' + \pi' - w)$$
$$+\, \Pi\, x_2 - K\, x_2 + X\, x_2 = +\,(c - x' + \pi)$$
$$+\, K\, x_1 - X\, x_1 = -\,(b - x)$$
$$+\, X\, x_0 = a.$$

These quantities Peirce called the "Listing numbers" or "Listings." His statement of the census theorem is accordingly: *"The census number of a whole is equal to the sum of the census-numbers of the listings of its parts."* [44]

But Peirce was not entirely satisfied with the theorem.[45] Thus he wrote: "Listing's investigation is insufficient in that he takes no notice of topical singularities, or places where the ways of moving are greater

---

[42] "Topical Geometry," pp. 18–20. The unfortunate plethora of technical terminology is typical of Peirce's writings and is unavoidable. The requisite definitions are as follows: The terms "point," "line," "surface," and "space" designate absolute loci. No point, line, etc., can move — only things occupying points, lines, etc., are capable of motion. Dimensionality is used in the conventional sense whereby a point has zero dimensionality, a line one, a surface two, and a space three.

A "particle" is anything which occupies a single point at one time.

A "filament" is anything which occupies a single line at one time.

A "pellicle" is anything which occupies a single surface at one time.

A "solid" is anything which occupies a single space at one time.

A "place" is a line, surface, or space.

A "simple" place is one which can be generated by a single generator in a continuous motion. A simple line, for example, is generated by the continuous motion of a single particle. (These definitions are from "Topic. Chapter I. Of Point Figures," n.d., pp. 1–2, IA2.)

[43] "Topical Geometry," p. 26. Peirce often changed his terminology. "Apeiry" is often given as "immensity." The variables too are often changed, sometimes being distinguished by subscripts, sometimes not.

[44] *Ibid.*, p. 36.

[45] As a countercase to the theorem, Peirce cites the following: "For instance, the census-theorem would permit a net upon a spheroidal surface having twelve pentagonal faces, or regions, one hexagonal face, twenty-two coigns, and thirty-three boundaries. But this is easily seen to be impossible." "Of Topical Geometry, In General," n.d., p. 1. IA2. But this objection is not legitimate: Listing never said that everything for which the theorem is true is a real spatial complex but only that for all real spatial complexes the theorem is true.

or less than at ordinary points." [46] As we noted in discussing the census theorem, only limiting constituents are included. Peirce therefore attempted to generalize the theorem still further to include all shape-classes. Unfortunately, I have not found in Peirce's papers any complete treatment of this subject. That he made some attempt to carry out the plan is abundantly evident from the fragments that remain, but it is not clear how far he went with it. The theory of line singularities is well developed, that of surface singularities less so, and I have found very little on spatial singularities. I will therefore confine my remarks to a brief sketch of the theory of line singularities.

Peirce defined a topical singularity as follows:

A *topical singularity* of a figure or place, P, is a place, L, within P and of lower dimensionality than P, such that a movable object occupying L can move away from it in a separative motion so as to begin to generate a part of P, and can do this in fewer or in more ways (that is, can generate, a smaller or greater number of entirely separate parts of P) than an object of the same dimensionality as L moving in a like manner away from any neighboring place in P. The *grade* of singularity (which may also be called the singularity) is the product of the excess of the number of such beginnings of generation over those of an ordinary place in P, by the excess of the dimensionality of P over L.[47]

If we designate by 'g' the number of beginning generations, by 'd' the dimensionality, by 'p' the place, by 's' the singularity, and by 'S' the grade of singularity, then the formula for singularities is

$$(g^s - g^P) \cdot (d^P - d^s) = S.$$

The method of compounding singularities is as follows: If x is a singularity of y, and y is a singularity of z, then the grade of singularity of x considered as a singularity of z is the sum of its grade as a singularity of y and the grade of y as a singularity of z.[48]

Peirce's notation for singularities is somewhat inconsistent. The most usual is as follows:

$U^n_m$     the census value of an isolated singular point of a place of dimensionality $m$, $n$ being the order of the singularity;

$V^n_m$     the census-value of an isolated singular line, $m$ and $n$ having the same significations:

[46] "On the Problem of Map-Colouring and on Geometrical Topics, in General," n.d., p. 2, IA2. "Of Topical Geometry, In General," p. 1.
[47] "Topical Geometry," p. 13.
[48] *Ibid.*, p. 14.

$W^n$     the census-value of a singular surface, $n$ being the order of the singularity.

$^n I^l_m$     the census-value of a singular point of a singular line of a place of dimensionality $m$, $n$ being the order of singularity of the line, and $l$ that of the point.[49]

Peirce then develops the theory as follows.[50] The chorisis of a point figure must always be equal to the number of points. Therefore the chorisis of one point is one, and its census value is one. Furthermore figures of the same shape-class have the same value. Accordingly a terminated open line must be equal to one. The line has two singularities — its end points, both of which have the grade of singularity — 1. Accordingly, for such a line

$$X_1 + 2U_1{}^{-1} = 1. \tag{1}$$

Given a point which is the intersection of $\frac{1}{2}(x+2)$ lines, then there are $x+2$ free extremities, and the given point has the order (grade) x. Computed by parts, the census value is

$$(x+2) X_1 + 2 (x+2) U_1{}^{-1} - (x+1) X_0.$$

As a whole, $X_1 + (x+2) U_1{}^{-1} + U_1{}^x$.

By the census theorem these expressions are equivalent. Equating them

$$X_1 + (x+2) U_1{}^{-1} + U_1{}^x = (x+2) X_1 + 2 (x+2) U_1{}^{-1}$$
$$- (x+1) X_0,$$
$$U_1{}^x = (x+1) X_1 + (x+2) U_1{}^{-1}$$
$$- (x+1) X_0,$$
$$U_1{}^x = (x+1) X_1 + (x+2) U_1{}^{-1}$$
$$- [ (x+1) X_1 + (x+1) 2U_1{}^{-1}],$$
$$U_1{}^x = - xU_1{}^{-1}. \tag{2}$$

Given a terminated open line with an internal point, we have

by parts,    $2X_1 + 4U_1{}^{-1} - X_0,$

by whole,    $X_1 + 2U_1{}^{-1} + U_1{}^0.$

Equating    $2X_1 + 4U_1{}^{-1} - X_0 = X_1 + 2U_1{}^{-1} + U_1{}^0,$
$$X_1 + 2U_1{}^{-1} - X_0 = U_1{}^0,$$
$$X_1 + 2U_1{}^{-1} - (X_1 + 2U_1{}^{-1}) = U_1{}^0,$$
$$O = U_1{}^0. \tag{3}$$

---

[49] "Rough Sketch of Suggested Prolegomena to Your First Course in Quaternions," n.d., p. 18, IA5. The notation for higher singularities is constructed on the same plan.

[50] With several exceptions, the following theorems and proofs are from "Rough Sketch of Suggested Prolegomena etc.," pp. 19–26. Theorem (3) is from "Topical Geometry," p. 28. Theorem (6), part of the proof of (4), and the proof of (7) are mine.

Given a simple line through an outlying point of a line figure consisting of a simple line and one outlying point.

By parts: $\quad 3X_1 + 6U_1^{-1} - X_o,$

$\qquad\qquad 2X_1 + 4U_1^{-1}.$

By whole: $\quad yX_1 + 4U_1^{-1} + U_1^0,$

$\qquad\qquad yX_1 + 4U_1^{-1}.$ $\hfill$ by (3)

Equating: $\quad 2X_1 + 4U_1^{-1} = yX_1 + 4U_1^{-1},$

$\qquad\qquad\qquad 2 = y.$ $\hfill$ (4)

"Therefore," Peirce remarks, "the chorisy of a line figure is the number of separate pieces." [51]

A nonsingular cyclic line taken as L lines and points.

By parts: $\quad L(X_1 + 2U_1^{-1}) - LX_o = O.$

By whole: $\quad X_1 + K_1,$

$\qquad\qquad K_1 = -X_1.$ $\hfill$ (5)

A node on a terminated open line.

By parts: $\quad 3X_1 + 4U_1^{-1} + K_1 + U_1^0 - X_o.$

By whole: $\quad X_1 + 2U_1^{-1} + U_1^2.$

Equating: $\quad X_1 + 2U_1^{-1} + U_1^2 = 3X_1 + 4U_1^{-1} + K_1 + U_1^0 - X_o,$

$\qquad\qquad\qquad\qquad U_1^2 = 2X_1 + 2U_1^{-1} + K_1 + U_1^0 - X_o,$

$\qquad U_1^2 = X_1 + K_1 + U_1^0,$

$\qquad U_1^2 = O.$ $\hfill$ (6)

The junction of two ordinary points of a line figure by a simple line may diminish the number of parts by one. If it does not do so, it will increase the number of enclosures by one. Let us suppose that in the former case, it increases the chorisy by $-x$, and in the latter case increases the cyclosy by $y$. Thus its effect upon the census-value, calculated by parts is to add to it

$$X_1 + 2U_1^{-1} - 2X_0$$

While calculated from the whole the same addition is, in one case,

$$-xX_1 + 2U_1^1$$

Equating, we have

$$xX_1 = X_1 \text{ or } x = 1$$

In the other case, the effect on the whole is

$$yK_1 + 2U_1^1$$

and since $K_1 = -X_1$, this also gives $y = 1$. Hence the cyclosy is the number of the smallest circuits.

[51] "Rough Sketch Etc.," p. 20.

There is nothing whatever to determine the value of $X_1$, from which those of $K_1$ and $U_1{}^n$ will follow; nor is it necessary for calculating the census-value of the line figure. We may make it zero, when $K_1 = 0$, and $U_1{}^{-1} = \frac{1}{2}$, and $U_1{}^n = -n/2$, so that the census-value of the figure will be minus half the sum of the orders of the singularities. Or we may make $X_1 = 1$, when $U_1{}^n = 0$ and $K_1 = -1$ and the census-value will be the excess of the chorisy over the cyclosis. It follows that this is equal to minus half the sum of the orders of the singularities.[52]

From this Peirce proves the following theorem concerning the relation between the census value of a line and its total singularity. "The negative of what Listing calls the *Census number* of a line is, if we give a further extension to his definition, that which I would call the total *singularity* of the line; namely, it is half the sum of the excesses over two of the number of ways in which a particle could leave the different singular points of the line." (4.223) By "the sum of the excesses over two of the number of ways in which a particle could leave the different singular points of the line," Peirce means the sum of the orders of singularity, for the line-singularity formula gives

$$(g^s - g^p) \cdot (d^p - d^s) = S,$$
$$(g^s - 2) \cdot (1 - 0) = S,$$
$$(g^s - 2) = S.$$

The sum of the n singularities then will be $\lambda$, where

$$\lambda = \sum_{i=1}^{n} S_i.$$

Since $X_1 + 2U_1{}^{-1} = 1$, if $X_1 = 0$ then $U_1{}^{-1}$ must equal $\frac{1}{2}$. $U_1{}^n$ then will equal $-\frac{1}{2}n$. The general form of the line census equation is

$$X_1 + U_1{}^{-2} + \ldots = C.$$

Summing the singularities we have

$$X_1 + U_1{}^\lambda = C,$$
$$-\frac{1}{2}\lambda = C. \tag{7}$$

Peirce extended the theory of singularities to surfaces and spaces as well, and derived theorems similar to those given above. By these results he gave the census theorem a generality which it lacked as Listing conceived it. Peirce's statement of it is: "*The census-number of an aggregate is the aggregate of the census-numbers of the topical characteristics of its aggregants.*"[53] The brief outline I have given of the

[52] *Ibid.*, p. 21.
[53] "Topical Geometry," p. 27.

Peirce-Listing theorem by no means exhausts Peirce's work in topology.[54] But for our purposes, what Peirce thought about topology is more important than what Peirce did in topology, and it would not be strictly relevant to go more deeply into his technical work. We must accordingly turn to the question of the relation between topology and the rest of mathematics.

[54] Peirce was particularly interested in the four-color theorem and in problems concerning networks. The latter question led him into investigations of Riemann's theory of connectivity and the theory of valency ("The New Elements of Geometry," n.d., IA2), while he made many attempts to prove the former (cf. IA2). The fact that neither the Listing numbers nor the theory of connectivity were sufficient to prove the four-color theorem (it has never been proven) was an indication to him of the undeveloped state of topology. ("Map-Colouring," pp. 1f.) Indeed, this reflects one of the chief reasons for his interest in the subject: "What has, however, particularly attracted me to the subject is that there is no recognized method of proof in topical geometry, and that it is beset with logical difficulties." ("On Topical Geometry, In General," p. 2.)

# X

# *The Classification of Geometry*

IN preceding sections, we have seen how Klein, generalizing from Cayley's "Sixth Memoir" and Lie's theory of transformation groups, was led to define a geometry as the invariant theory of a particular group. The widest such group of transformations is the group which Klein called $G_\infty$. He characterized it as follows: "The *group of all continuous distortions* has no finite number of parameters whatever; the operations of this group depend, rather, upon arbitrary functions, or, if one wishes, upon infinitely many parameters."[1] The invariant theory of this group is "analysis situs," or topology.[2]

Since topology is the most general of all the current geometries, it ought to follow that projective geometry bears the same relation to topology that metric geometry bears to projective. This is clearly the position taken by Peirce:

> We know that Metrical Geometry is but the projective, or as I prefer to call it, the Optical Geometry, of an individual quadric locus, from or to which no part of a rigid body ever moves. . . . In like manner Optical Geometry is but a special problem of Topical Geometry; for the entire family of rays does not differ geometrically from that of any other family of unlimited lines of which there is just one through any two points of space and any four of which, no two of which cut one another, are cut by just two others.[3]

But we have yet to see how Peirce analyzed this relation.

---

[1] Klein, *Geometry*, p. 133.

[2] *Ibid.*, pp. 132f.

[3] "On Topical Geometry, In General," p. 1. The absolute, it will be recalled, is a conic. Conics are analytically described as the loci of points satisfying a quadratic, or quadric, equation. In three dimensions, this gives a quadric surface. (Cf. Courant and Robbins, *Mathematics*, p. 212.) Unlike more modern writers, Peirce uses the term "ray" to designate a straight line unlimited in both directions.

# CLASSIFICATION OF GEOMETRY

In the "New Elements of Geometry," [4] Peirce describes the relation between topology and projective geometry as follows:

. . . graphics is distinguished from Topology, or Topics, in considering especially straight lines, or rays, and *flat* surfaces, or planes. . . .

In studying the uniformity of space, we learned that there are innumerable multitudes of systems of surfaces called homoloidal systems having the following properties:

1st. Any two surfaces of one system have a line in common, and nothing else;

2nd. There is a singly-continuous multitude, or *book*, of surfaces in the system each of which contains that line;

3rd. That line contains a point in common with each of the surfaces of the system;

4th. It contains but one such point for each surface that does not belong to the *book* of such surfaces [of] which it is the *hinge*; [5]

5th. Every two points in space are contained in such a hinge of each system;

6th. No two different points are both contained in two different hinges of one system;

7th. Every such hinge and each point in space are contained in some surface of the system;

8th. No such hinge and point not contained in it are contained in two different such surfaces of the system.

These innumerable multitudes of systems of surfaces have their surfaces differently shaped, but all their properties are exactly analogous. It is, therefore, impossible to find any intrinsic property which distinguishes one from another. Some shapes appear to us simpler than others; but that is only a peculiarity of our minds, not of the object; for there is no geometrical property which distinguishes one from another. Indeed, they have no properties except such as are deducible from the eight just enumerated together with the general properties of space. Nevertheless, they are geometrically distinguishable by their relations to one another. It is, therefore, desirable to

---

[4] About 1895, Peirce and his brother James decided to revise and republish their father's *Elementary Treatise on Geometry*, 1837. The new edition, which was to have been entitled "The New Elements of Geometry," never appeared, but Charles Peirce's manuscript still survives. The work was to have been divided into subbooks and evidently Charles was to write the first three — "Topics," "Graphics," and "Metrics." The manuscript is several hundred pages in length and contains marginalia by James Peirce. The book was intended for elementary instruction and as a result many points are less thoroughly treated than one would like. The work remains, however, the nearest thing to a systematic exposition of the structure of geometry that we have from Peirce's hand.

[5] A "book" is a group of surfaces all of which intersect in one common line. This line is called the "hinge" of the book.

select one system to which the others may be referred and in terms of which they can be described.

Now when any spatial figure is imagined, it is imagined as seen . . . and thus the properties of light, so far as they are perfectly familiar, are used and, as it were, taken for granted by our imagination. . . .

A line which is the free path of light, according to our common notion of light, is some one, it may be any one, of the intersections of a certain system of surfaces of the kind described.

*Definition* 134. A *plane* is a homoloidal surface of such a system that all intersections of two planes are paths of light.

*Definition* 135. A *ray*, or unlimited straight line, is a homoloidal line the intersection of two planes, and a path of light. . . .[6]

*Definition* 136. Points, planes, and rays, are called the *chief elements*, or *dominant homoloids*, of space.[7]

It is at once apparent that none of these statements contains reference to a metric of any sort. The relation of the metric to these statements is explained as follows: "Cayley (in 1854) and Klein (more fully, in 1873) showed that metrical geometry is simply the geometry of the *firmament*, or *absolute*, or infinitely distant parts of space, which constitutes a surface which is one or another quadric surface, according to the system of measurement adopted, that is, according to the way in which rigid bodies move." [8] The eight fundamental propositions afford no method by which any particular surface may be distinguished — they rather describe surfaces of a given class. In order to get any particular surface, additional assumptions are required. Specifically, an existence postulate is necessary — the Absolute must be assumed to exist and to have just those properties which distinguish the Absolute of one metric from that of another. Thus Peirce here avoids the difficulty which Russell pointed out concerning Cayley's Absolute.

But at first glance it does appear that Peirce has fallen into a circularity concerning the definition of the straight line. For Propositions 5 and 6 together amount to the statement that through any two points there is one and only one line, a proposition which appears to be a definition of the straight line. And since, according to Peirce, "homoloidal" may mean "flat," [9] he seems also to have assumed the plane to

---

[6] "The New Elements of Geometry," pp. 169–171.

[7] *Ibid.*, p. 177.

[8] Peirce, "The New Elements of Mathematics," p. 3, IA3. This brief paper was intended as a preface to "The New Elements of Geometry."

[9] "The New Elements of Geometry," p. 41.

begin with. I believe the confusion is apparent rather than real, but to support this some explanation is required.

Every formalized system assumes in addition to its axioms some terms which are taken as primitive and undefined in the system itself. In modern topology, these primitive terms are usually "point," "open set," and a relation of a point being "in" an open set.[10] These terms together with the axioms suffice to define the notions of "line" and "surface." Further, these lines and surfaces can be classified into various equivalence classes such that by a transformation continuous in both directions any member of a given class can be transformed into any other. Thus, for example, all open lines are equivalent in this sense.

In projective geometry, on the other hand, the notions of "straight line" and "plane surface" are essential and the axioms must be so chosen as to yield them.[11] But since these terms are not topologically definable, a reduction of projective geometry to topology is necessarily incomplete. In other words, what distinguishes the group $G_{15}$ from the group $G_{\infty}$ is the fact that certain additions have been made to the axioms which allow for the definition of these concepts and of their properties.

If we simply leave these additional postulates out of account, then the projective plane becomes indistinguishable from a topological surface and the infinite straight line is simply an oval.[12] From the topologist's standpoint, then, the infinite straight line becomes "homeomorphic" to any other cyclic line, meaning that the two lines can be transformed into each other by a topological transformation.[13] Furthermore, the number of intersections is a property which is invariant under topological transformation, so that any number of homeomorphs can be found which will possess all the properties of the straight line or the plane. Peirce is quite right then in saying that there may be an innumerable number of lines and surfaces all of which have the same

---

[10] Various alternative choices are of course possible.

[11] Cf. Alfred North Whitehead, *The Axioms of Projective Geometry* (Cambridge, 1906), pp. 7f.

[12] Topologically, the straight line of projective geometry is cyclic owing to its infinite extent. Peirce's statement of this in the "New Elements" (p. 171) is: "In one respect, the *ray* of the geometer's idea differs from our notion of a path of light; and that is that after an immence prolongation, the ray is conceived to complete a circuit and return into itself."

[13] A "homeomorphism" is a one-one correspondence continuous in both directions.

intersectional properties as the plane and straight line and which are intrinsically indistinguishable within topology.[14]

I have not been able to discover who first introduced the term "homoloid," but it was brought into prominence by Cremona in 1863 who used it to denote certain curves which are transforms of straight lines and which preserve intersectional properties.[15] Since Cremona was one of the outstanding Italian geometers of the period,[16] this is probably the source of the term for Peirce, although he uses it to denote any line, surface, or solid which is a transform of a straight line, plane, or rigid solid.

The confusion of the above passage is then apparent only. The point Peirce is making is simply that since topology recognizes no dominant system of homoloids, there is no topological distinction between a straight line and any topological transform of a straight line, or between a plane and a topological transform of the plane. Topological properties alone then do not suffice to give us projective geometry. The added axioms of graphics must be introduced by postulate. Thus, as Peirce notes, topology "deals with only a portion of the hypotheses accepted in other parts of geometry. . . ." [17]

Peirce's classification of geometry therefore is based on presupposition rather than logical deduction. Topics should precede all other existing geometries because it is more general and because its axioms are presupposed in all other branches. Graphics is second, because while it assumes topology it is itself presupposed by all others. Finally, we have metrics, which presupposes both topology and graphics.

Yet Peirce also describes the differences between the branches of geometry as differences in "purity." Thus he writes:

. . . geometry or rather mathematical geometry, which deals with pure hypotheses, and unlike physical geometry, does not investigate the properties of objectively valid space — mathematical geometry, I say, consists of three branches; Topics (commonly called Topology), Graphics (or pure projective geometry), and Metrics. But metrics ought not to be regarded as pure

[14] M. H. A. Newman, *Elements of the Topology of Plane Sets of Points* (Cambridge, 1951), chaps. 4–5.

[15] Julian Lowell Coolidge, *A History of Geometrical Methods* (Oxford, 1940), pp. 285–293.

[16] Bell, *Development of Mathematics*, pp. 347f. Struik, *Concise History*, pp. 281f. Florian Cajori, *A History of Mathematics* (New York, 1919), pp. 295f.

[17] "The New Elements of Mathematics," p. 1.

geometry . . . but is the study of the graphical properties of a certain hypothetical thing. But neither ought graphics to be considered as pure geometry. It is the doctrine of a certain family of surfaces called the *planes*. But when we ask what surfaces these planes are, we find that no other purely geometrical description can be given of them than that there is a threefold continuum of them and that every three of them have one point and one only in common. But innumerable families of surfaces can be conceived of which that is true. . . . [Topics] is the study of the continuous connections and defects of continuity of loci which are free to be distorted in any way so long as the integrity of the connections and separations of all their parts is maintained. All strictly pure geometry, therefore, is topics. [4.219]

This passage certainly seems to involve a confusion between "pure" and "applied" geometry. But the opening sentence makes it quite clear that Peirce is talking about pure geometry only rather than "physical" or applied geometry, and that the differences described lie within the domain of pure geometry itself. That Peirce grasped the distinction between "pure" and "applied" geometry may be further shown by the following passage from the introduction to the "New Elements."

We all see, now, that geometry has two parts; the one deals with the *facts* about real space, the investigation of which is a physical, or perhaps a metaphysical, problem, at any rate, outside of the purview of the mathematician, who accepts the generally admitted propositions about space, without question, as his *hypotheses*, that is, as the ideal truth whose consequences are deduced in the second, or mathematical, part of geometry.[18]

Certainly there is no room for doubt as to what is meant here.

How then is this doctrine regarding the relative "purity" of the branches of pure geometry to be explained? Since it is clear that Peirce is not talking about the usual distinction between "pure" and "applied," it might be thought that he is using "pure" in this context simply as a synonym for generality and that he is therefore only reaffirming the thesis that topology is presupposed by all the other branches of geometry. In this sense the axioms of pure geometry would be only those which are required to define the subject matter of all geometries, and any additional postulates would be arbitrary additions or "impurities." This interpretation is partially borne out by the following statement:

. . . projective geometry is but a problem in topology, the science of spatial connections, better called *synectics*. The plural form is recommended by the

[18] *Ibid.*, p. 1.

circumstance that besides the pure doctrine unlimited by any special hypotheses as to the shape, or morphoidal character, or better the *synexis* of space, two alternative hypotheses come before us for studying real space.

*Pure synectics* is the science of the connections of the parts of true continua, in general. What a true continuum is will be defined below.

A *synectic singularity* of any continuum, A, is a continuum, say B, forming a part of A, of fewer dimensions than A, whose synectic relations to A are different from those of any other part of A in the immediate neighbourhood of B.[19]

The passage is fragmentary and does not give the promised definition, but it does show that there is such a thing as a "pure" branch of geometry and that it is the addition of special and limiting hypotheses which violates the purity. But in order to see why these limiting hypotheses should be regarded as introducing impurities, it is necessary to look more closely at Peirce's interpretation of their content.

Before doing so, however, there is a particularly important feature of the passage quoted above which must be remarked — the use of the term "synectics" as a synonym for topology. This term is derived from the Greek roots "syn" meaning "with" and "echein," "to hold" — hence to hold together or be continuous. Another derivative of the same roots in the term "synechism," which Peirce used as a name for his later philosophy. And this fact strongly suggests that Peirce's topology, as the foundation of all geometry, is closely related to his basic philosophic doctrines. Concerning synechism, Peirce wrote: "It [synechism] carries along with it the following doctrines: first, a logical realism of the most pronounced type; second, objective idealism; third, tychism, with its consequent thorough-going evolutionism." (6. 163) If one wanted a three-line summary of Peirce's major philosophic beliefs, one could ask for little more. The hypotheses which underlie geometry are the hypotheses which underlie Peirce's philosophy.

[19] Peirce, "On Synectics, otherwise Called Topology or Topic," n.d., pp. 1f, IA2.

# XI

# On the Hypotheses Which Lie at the Basis of Geometry

ON June 10, 1854, Bernhard Riemann delivered his probationary lecture as a candidate for an unpaid lectureship at Göttingen. The title of the paper was "Ueber die Hypothesen welche der Geometrie zu Grunde Liegen." It is reported that the lecture won enthusiastic praise from Gauss [1] and after its publication in 1867 it won similar praise throughout the mathematical world. One of the first to appreciate its importance was the English mathematician and friend of the Peirce family, William Kingdon Clifford. A first-rate mathematician himself, Clifford recognized the great importance of Riemann's lecture and in 1873 he translated it into English.[2] It is quite probable that Clifford's praise of Riemann's work influenced Peirce's judgment of it. Concerning him, Peirce wrote, "Bernhard Riemann is recognized by all mathematicians as *the* highest authority upon the philosophy of geometry." [3] Since Peirce's views on the foundations of geometry are based on Riemann's, we must examine the latter's theory in some detail.

Riemann opened his lecture with the following much-quoted passage.

It is known that geometry assumes, as things given, both the notion of space and the first principles of constructions in space. She gives definitions of them which are merely nominal, while the true determinations appear in the form of axioms. The relation of these assumptions remains consequently in darkness; we neither perceive whether and how far their connection is necessary, nor, *a priori*, whether it is possible.[4]

[1] Bell, *Men of Mathematics*, pp. 496–499.
[2] Bernhard Riemann, "On the Hypotheses Which Lie at the Basis of Geometry," trans. W. K. Clifford, *Nature*, VIII, 14–17, 36f (May 1873).
[3] "Critic of Arguments. Synthetic Propositions *a priori*," p. 10, IB2 Box 12.
[4] Riemann, "Hypotheses," p. 14.

"From Euclid to Legendre," Riemann declares, nothing has been done to remove this obscurity. He continues:

The reason of this is doubtless that the general notion of multiply extended magnitudes (in which space-magnitudes are included) remained entirely unworked. I have in the first place, therefore, set myself the task of constructing the notion of a multiply extended magnitude out of general notions of magnitude. It will follow from this that a multiply extended magnitude is capable of different measure-relations, and consequently that space is only a particular case of a triply extended magnitude. But hence flows as a necessary consequence that the propositions of geometry cannot be derived from general notions of magnitude, but that the properties which distinguish space from other conceivable triply extended magnitudes are only to be deduced from experience. Thus arises the problem, to discover the simplest matters of fact from which the measure-relations of space may be determined; a problem which from the nature of the case is not completely determinate, since there may be several systems of matters of fact which suffice to determine the measure-relations of space — the most important system for our present purpose being that which Euclid has laid down as a foundation. These matters of fact are — like all matters of fact — not necessary, but only of empirical certainty; they are hypotheses. We may therefore investigate their probability, which within the limits of observation is of course very great . . . [5]

He then proceeded to consider separately the notion of an n-ply extended magnitude, and of the measure relations possible in such a manifold. In explicating the former Riemann states:

Magnitude-notions are only possible where there is an antecedent general notion which admits of different specialisations. According as there exists among these specialisations a continuous path from one to another or not, they form a *continuous* or *discrete* manifoldness: the individual specialisations are called in the first case points, in the second case elements, of the manifoldness.[6]

As examples of notions whose specializations form a continuous manifoldness Riemann offers positions and colors. He then continues:

Definite portions of a manifoldness, distinguished by a mark or by a boundary, are called Quanta. Their comparison with regard to quantity is accomplished in the case of discrete magnitudes by counting, in the case of continuous magnitudes by measuring. Measure consists in the superposition of the magnitudes to be compared; it therefore requires a means of using one magnitude as the standard for another.[7]

[5] *Ibid.*, pp. 14f.
[6] *Ibid.*, p. 15.
[7] *Ibid.*, p. 15.

Riemann then shows how an n-ply extended manifold may be constructed and determination of place in it reduced to determinations of quantity. He then faces the question of the measure relations possible in such a manifold. Mathematically, this portion of the essay is of great significance, but the technical development need not concern us here. The basic idea may be summarized as follows. Riemann notes that measurement requires quantity to be independent of place and he accordingly adopts the hypothesis that the length of lines is independent of their position so that every line is measurable by every other. If we define distance as the square root of a quadratic function of the coordinates then Riemann shows that for the length of a line to be independent of its position, the space in which the line lies must have constant curvature. "The common character of these continua whose curvature is constant may also be expressed thus, that figures may be moved in them without stretching . . . whence it follows that in aggregates with constant curvature figures may have any arbitrary position given them." [8]

In the final section of the essay Riemann turns to the question of the application of his technical apparatus to empirical space for the determination of its metric properties. In a space of constant curvature in which line length is independent of position, the empirical truth of the Euclidean axiom that the sum of the angles of a triangle is equal to two right angles is sufficient to determine the metric properties of that space.[9] But such empirical determinations run into difficulty in the cases of the infinitely great and the infinitely small. "The questions about the infinitely great are for the interpretation of nature useless questions," [10] according to Riemann, but the same is not true on the side of the infinitely small. He continues:

If we suppose that bodies exist independently of position, the curvature is everywhere constant, and it then results from astronomical measurements that it cannot be different from zero; or at any rate its reciprocal must be an area in comparison with which the range of our telescopes may be neglected. But if this independence of bodies from position does not exist, we cannot draw conclusions from metric relations of the great, to those of the infinitely

---

[8] *Ibid.*, p. 17. For discussions of this portion of Riemann's paper see Russell, *Foundations of Geometry*, pp. 15–22; Bell, *Men of Mathematics*, pp. 503–509.

[9] Riemann, "Hypotheses," p. 36.

[10] *Ibid.*, p. 36.

small; in that case the curvature at each point may have an arbitrary value in three directions, provided that the total curvature of every measurable portion of space does not differ sensibly from zero. . . . Now it seems that the empirical notions on which the metrical determinations of space are founded, the notion of a solid body and a ray of light, cease to be valid for the infinitely small. We are therefore quite at liberty to suppose that the metric relations of space in the infinitely small do not conform to the hypotheses of geometry; and we ought in fact to suppose it, if we can thereby obtain a simpler explanation of phenomena.

The question of the validity of the hypotheses of geometry in the infinitely small is bound up with the question of the ground of the metric relations of space. In this last question . . . is found the application of the remark made above; that in a discrete manifoldness, the ground of its metric relations is given in the notion of it, while in a continuous manifoldness, this ground must come from outside. Either therefore the reality which underlies space must form a discrete manifoldness, or we must seek the ground of its metric relations outside it, in binding forces which act upon it.[11]

But the final answer to this question, Riemann asserts, must come from physics rather than from pure mathematics.

This paper of Riemann's is among the most famous in modern mathematics. Nevertheless, as the rather extensive quotations given above should make clear, Riemann's statement of his position is cryptic in the extreme, and it is far from easy to be sure of his exact meaning. Riemann asserts that the notion of "space" is included under that of magnitude — i.e., that "space" is a species of magnitude. In order to distinguish space from other magnitudes, some differentia is required which will single out just the entity we want. These differentiae are, Riemann asserts, "matters of fact." But the meaning of "matters of fact" in this context is not clear. It is evident that Riemann recognizes different "empirical" hypotheses — those of Euclidean and non-Euclidean geometries — as determining different metrics. Yet he speaks of the measure relations of space as if there were but one possible alternative. The obvious conclusion would be that he is talking about physical space — that the problem of the paper is to provide a method for determining which of the different metric geometries is true of physical space. The problem so stated is a problem of physical geometry rather than of pure geometry, and it seems perfectly clear from the last section of the paper — the application to physical space of

[11] *Ibid.*, p. 37.

the technical apparatus developed in the earlier sections — that this is what Riemann was trying to do. Indeed, his closing sentence, "This leads us into the domain of another science, of physic," [12] seems to prove this, and historically the great significance of this paper is that it provided the theoretical basis for just such a test in the form of the general theory of relativity.[13] But if this interpretation is correct, then how is one to explain the statement that space in general is distinguished from other triply extended magnitudes such as color solely by empirical propositions? For clearly the difference between space and color is not of the same sort as the difference between Euclidean and non-Euclidean geometry. It seems as though two different questions are being discussed at once — (1) the question of the logical relation between the concept of magnitude and the axioms of geometry, and (2) the question of the empirical truth of the axioms of geometry. Both of these fall under Riemann's concept of "matters of fact" and are not clearly distinguished in the paper.

Whether or not this interpretation is a justifiable explication of Riemann's intent, it is clearly the interpretation adopted by Peirce. Thus he writes:

That geometry contains propositions which may be understood to be synthetical judgments *a priori*, I will not dispute. Such are the propositions that the sum of the three angles of a triangle is invariably and unconditionally equal to 180°. . . . But the difficulty is that, considered as applicable to the real world, they are *false*. *Possibly* the three angles of every triangle make exactly 180°; but nothing more unlikely can be conceived. It is false to say it is necessarily so. Considered, on the other hand, as purely formal, these propositions are merely ideal. Some of them define an ideal hypothesis (in the mathematical sense), and the rest are deductions from those definitions . . .[14]

And continues:

Thus, it seems clear to me that the proposition in question [7 + 5 = 12] is analytical or explicatory; . . . Some have been of the opinion that while arithmetical propositions are analytical, geometrical ones are synthetic. But I am certain they are all of the same character. Unquestionably it was Riemann's opinion that all the synthetic propositions of geometry are "matters of fact," and "like all matters of fact not necessary, but only empirically

[12] *Ibid.*, p. 37.
[13] Bell, *Men of Mathematics*, pp. 508f.
[14] Peirce, "Critic of Arguments," p. 1.

223

certain; they are hypotheses." This I substantially agree with. Considered as *pure* mathematics, they define an ideal space, with which the real space approximately agrees. As Riemann also says: "Geometry assumes, as things given, both the notion of space, and the first principles of spatial constructions. She gives definitions of them that are merely nominal, while the true determinations appear in the form of axioms." [15]

Peirce here draws a sharp distinction between physical or applied geometry, and pure geometry. The empirical statements of the former lose their empirical character by being considered as ideal hypotheses. Pure mathematics consists in the explication of these initial hypotheses without regard to their empirical validity.

Adopting this view, we may restate Riemann's thesis as follows: Let all the axioms of all geometries be conceived as adjectives predicated of space. By hypothesis, space is a species of magnitude. Then some predicates of space are predicates of all magnitudes and some are not. Required: to determine which predicates of space are true of all magnitudes and which are not; and to determine which of the latter class are true of empirical space.

Now the point at which the sharpest criticisms of Riemann's paper have been leveled is precisely this assumption that space is a species of magnitude. As Russell wrote of this paper:

The resulting formulation of the axioms — while, from the mathematical standpoint of metrical Geometry, it was almost wholly laudable — must, from the standpoint of philosophy, be regarded, in my opinion, as a *petitio principii*. For when we have arrived at regarding spatial figures as magnitudes, we have already traversed the most difficult part of the ground. The axioms of metrical Geometry — and it is metrical Geometry, exclusively, which is considered in Riemann's Essay — will appear . . . to be divisible into two classes. Of these, the first class — which contains the axioms common to Euclid and Metageometry, the only axioms seriously discussed by Riemann — are not the results of measurement, nor of any conception of magnitude, but are conditions to be fulfilled before measurement becomes possible. The second class only — those which express the difference between Euclidean and non-Euclidean spaces — can be deduced as results of measurement or of conceptions of magnitude. [16]

The first class are of course the axioms of projective geometry which, as we have seen, contain no metrical conceptions at all. If Riemann

[15] *Ibid.*, pp. 9–11.
[16] Russell, *Foundations of Geometry*, pp. 63f.

does assume that he is already dealing with magnitudes before he introduces measurement, then clearly the argument is circular. But Riemann's position is not quite this clear. Speaking of magnitude he writes:

Grössenbegriffe sind nur da möglich, wo sich ein allgemeiner Begriff vorfindet, der verschiedene Bestimmungsweisen zulässt. Je nachdem unter diesen Bestimmungsweisen von einer zu einer andern ein stetiger Uebergang stattfindet oder nicht, bilden sie eine stetige oder discrete Mannigfaltigkeit; die einzelnen Bestimmungsweisen heissen im erstern Falle Punkte, im letztern Elemente dieser Mannigfaltigkeit.[17]

Magnitude-notions are only possible where there is an antecedent general notion which admits of different specialisations. According as there exists among these specialisations a continuous path from one to another or not, they form a *continuous* or *discrete* manifoldness: the individual specialisations are called in the first case points, in the second case elements, of the manifoldness.[18]

There is however a basic ambiguity in the use of these terms "magnitude" and "manifold." As Stallo points out, Riemann's term *Mannigfaltigkeiten* means "varieties, multiplicities, used in the sense of multiples — Helmholtz translates 'aggregates.' "[19] Cantor used this term to mean class or set in his early papers, only later replacing it by "Menge,"[20] and Peirce in discussing Cantor's theory refers to it as Cantor's theory of "manifolds." (4.121) Taking manifold in the sense of aggregate, there is clearly a difference between "magnitude" and "aggregate" which is obscured in Riemann's statement:

Definite portions of a manifoldness, distinguished by a mark or by a boundary, are called Quanta. Their comparison with regard to quantity is accomplished in the case of discrete magnitudes by counting, in the case of continuous magnitudes by measuring. Measure consists in the superposition of the magnitudes to be compared; it therefore requires a means of using one magnitude as the standard for another.[21]

A "magnitude" is not an "aggregate." An "aggregate" is a class; a

[17] Bernhard Riemann, *Collected Works of Bernhard Riemann*, ed. Heinrich Weber (New York, 1953), p. 273.

[18] Riemann, "Hypotheses," p. 15.

[19] J. B. Stallo, *The Concepts and Theories of Modern Physics* (New York, 1882), p. 253n.

[20] A. A. Fraenkel, *Abstract Set Theory* (Amsterdam, 1953), p. 4n2.

[21] Riemann, "Hypotheses," p. 15.

"magnitude" is a property of that class. The attribution of magnitude to an aggregate is the result of a process either of counting or of measuring, and measurement consists in the superposition not of magnitudes but of aggregates. For space to be a magnitude there must already exist measure relations which give the aggregate a magnitude. Certainly it would appear that Russell is right in holding that Riemann's argument is circular.

But there is another way of regarding Riemann's argument which eliminates these difficulties — namely, to regard it as concerned only with the relation of space to the class of triply extended manifolds or aggregates. So regarded, space and color are both triply extended continuous manifolds and whatever holds good of all such manifolds will hold equally good of them. Riemann's argument would imply that the axioms of projective geometry are true of all triply extended manifolds, but Peirce, carrying the reduction through more fully, held that only topical geometry is pure geometry — i.e., deals with pure continua. It was for this reason that he called the pure branch of geometry "synectics." Now it follows from this that the theorems of pure geometry such as the Listing theorem must hold good for all continua, at least in three dimensions. This is in fact Peirce's position, for he holds that wherever continua are met with it is necessary to determine their Listings, and he applies this to the case of color as well as space.[22] Thus topics (i.e., Peirce's shape-class geometry) acquires a status quite unique in geometry: not only is it the basis of all current geometries — the group $G_\infty$ — but it is also the mathematics of pure continua, spatial or not, and hence, from the synechistic point of view, of the whole universe.

To distinguish space from other triply extended continua, some differentiating factors must be found which will suffice to select out space from the other members of the set. We have seen that Riemann employed the term "matter of fact" in so broad a sense as to include these differentia. So, I believe, did Peirce. What differentiates space from other continua is the existence within space of *haecceities*, for which space provides a form permitting their realization.[23] Similarly, it is the contents introduced by hypothesis which differentiate the

[22] "Considerations for Eight Lectures," n.d., p. 2, IB3.
[23] See below, p. 381.

various geometries from one another. Thus topologically considered, space contains no dominant system of homoloids. All lines not self-returning, all surfaces not periphractic, are equivalent, and nothing distinguishes the plane or straight line from any other figures of the same shape-class. To distinguish the straight line from other lines, according to Peirce, it is necessary to hypothesize the existence of something in that space which would effect the distinction — i.e., light rays which travel in straight lines. This is why Peirce called projective geometry optical geometry.[24] So long as we remain in the domain of mathematics only, this hypothesis is ideal; we do not inquire, or care, whether it is true. But when we do come to the question of whether or not projective geometry is true of real space, we identify the path of our hypothetical light ray with that of the real physical entity called a light ray. Actually, Peirce also identifies the straight line with the path of a particle unacted upon by any force. (6.82) I suspect that he regarded the straightness of the path of a light ray as ultimately reducible to the first law of motion, although he nowhere says this; if not, it must be taken as a matter of sheer coincidence that the two paths coincide. That space should possess such existents is, even in the ideal form of pure mathematics, an arbitrary fact. These existents are *haecceities*, in no sense required by the concept of space itself. I think that this is what Peirce meant when he said that projective geometry was not *pure* geometry in the same sense that topics is: it requires the introduction of an arbitrary factor which distinguishes one system of homoloids from the others.

If this is true of projective geometry, it is equally true of metric geometry, but in a more complex sense. There are two distinct sorts of matters of fact to be considered here: those which distinguish a metric space in general from a projective space, and those which determine which of several possible metrics that space shall possess. Cayley had shown in his famous "Memoir" that the metric properties of a space depend upon the existence of the Absolute; which metric applies depends upon the characteristics of the Absolute. Now if these are matters of fact, then "pure" metric geometry, like "pure" projective geometry, is simply the system into which these hypotheses are introduced but treated only as ideal. But if metric geometry is true of

[24] "Logic of Continuity," n.d., pp. 3ff, IB3.

real space, then Cayley's Absolute really exists. It is worth quoting Peirce's statement of this in detail:

Since space has only the being of a law, its places cannot have distinct identities in themselves, for distinct identity belongs only to existent things. Hence place is only relative. But since, at the same time, different motions must be comparable in quantity, and this comparison cannot be effected by the moving and reacting particles themselves, it follows that another object must be placed in space to which all motion is referred. And since this object compares generally and thus partakes of the nature of a law, it must unlike the moving and reacting bodies be continuous. It is a corrected equivalent of that which has been called the body *alpha*. It is the firmament, or Cayley's Absolute. Since this is to determine every motion, it follows that it is a locus which every straight line cuts, and because space is a law of twoness only, and for other reasons, every straight line must cut it in two points. It is therefore a real quadratic locus, severing space into two parts, and the space of existence must be infinite and limited in every direction. [6.82; cf. 1.504]

Real space does possess metric properties,[25] and these properties, like the projective properties, are due to the entities which exist in space. As Riemann had asserted, "Either therefore the reality which underlies space must form a discrete manifoldness, or we must seek the ground of its metric relations outside it, in binding forces which act upon it." [26] This Peirce took to mean in the contents of space.

Peirce's theory of geometry is a combination of the work of Cayley, Klein, Listing, and Riemann. Following Cayley and Klein, he classifies the geometries in terms of presupposition and thus achieves an ordering in which the metric geometries are derived from projective geometry and projective geometry from topics. But Peirce regards both metric and projective geometry as the results of introducing arbitrarily chosen existents into pure space — it is topology alone which deals with pure continua. Topology therefore lies at the basis of the whole structure of geometries. Yet topology, too, has its presuppositions — notably, the notion of continuity. If synectics is to serve as the basis for synechism, it is obviously necessary to develop an adequate definition of the continuum which will be applicable both to analysis and to geometry. Accordingly, having reviewed Peirce's writings on geometry, we must turn to his views on mathematics in general and the theory of sets in particular.

[25] See below, p. 383.
[26] Riemann, "Hypotheses," p. 37.

# XII

# *Pure Mathematics*

Mathematics is the science which draws necessary conclusions.

This definition of mathematics is wider than that which is ordinarily given, and by which its range is limited to quantitative research. The ordinary definition, like those of other sciences, is objective; whereas this is subjective.[1]

THIS justly famous definition of mathematics was propounded in 1870 by Benjamin Peirce. Instead of defining mathematics by its subject matter, it rather makes the essential character of the science lie in the method it uses. Mathematics is the practice of necessary reasoning, not the study of it; and whatever science uses necessary reasoning thereby uses mathematics.[2]

The elder Peirce's definition met the wholehearted approval of his son. Recalling the time of its formulation, Charles Peirce later wrote:

At the time my father was writing this book, I was writing my paper on the logic of relations that was published in the 9th volume of the *Memoirs of the American Academy*. There was no collaboration, but there were frequent conversations on the allied subjects, especially about the algebra. The only way in which I think that anything I said influenced anything in my father's book (except that it was partly on my urgent prayer that he undertook the research) was that when at one time he seemed inclined to the opinion which Dedekind long afterward embraced,[3] I argued strenuously against it, and thus he came to take the middle ground of his definition. In truth, no two things could be more directly opposite than the cast of mind of the logician and that of the mathematician. . . . The mathematician's interest in a reasoning is as a means of solving problems. . . . The logician, on the other

---

[1] Benjamin Peirce, "Linear Associative Algebra," *American Journal of Mathematics*, IV, 97 (1881), with notes and addenda by C. S. Peirce.

[2] *Ibid.*, pp. 97f.

[3] I.e., the logistic view. Cf. Richard Dedekind, *Was Sind und was Sollen die Zahlen?* (Brunswick, 1888).

hand, is interested in picking a method to pieces and in finding out what its essential ingredients are.[4]

The study of necessary reasoning thus falls to the logician; its practice to the mathematician. Indeed, Peirce notes, "Mathematics might be called an art instead of a science were it not that the last achievement that it has in view is an achievement of knowing." [5]

It follows from this view that mathematics must be a purely deductive discipline. (4.233) Yet Peirce has so often emphasized the importance of observation, induction, and experimentation in mathematical reasoning that many of his commentators have been led to impute to him an intuitionistic and empirical doctrine.[6] The reason for this emphasis on observation seems quite clear; Peirce is seeking to explain how it can be that mathematics is both analytic and yet constantly yields new discoveries. Thus he writes:

> It has long been a puzzle how it could be that, on the one hand, mathematics is purely deductive in its nature, and draws its conclusions apodictically, while on the other hand, its presents as rich and apparently unending a series of surprising discoveries as any observational science. . . . The truth, however, appears to be that all deductive reasoning, even simple syllogism, involves an element of observation; namely, deduction consists in constructing an icon or diagram the relation of whose parts shall present a complete analogy with those of the parts of the object of reasoning, of experimenting upon this image in the imagination, and of observing the result so as to discover unnoticed and hidden relations among the parts. [3.363]

It should be noted here that Peirce extends this conception of deductive reasoning as observational to logic as well as to mathematics, and it does not therefore serve to distinguish them, nor does it affect the relations between them. The observational character of the reasoning is not opposed to its deductive character. Regardless of observation, no transformation may be performed which is not legitimate under the transformation rules of the system.[7] In emphasizing the importance of observation, then, Peirce was attacking the naive concept of analyticity, not the concept of formal rigor. Thus he writes:

[4] "Notes on Peirce's *Linear Associative Algebra*," n.d., pp. 3f, IA5.
[5] *Ibid.*, p. 4.
[6] Goudge, *The Thought of C. S. Peirce*, pp. 55f. Arthur Burks, "The Logical Foundations of the Philosophy of Charles Sanders Peirce," unpublished dissertation, University of Michigan, June 1941, chap. III.
[7] Justus Buchler, *Charles Peirce's Empiricism* (New York, 1939), pp. 214–219.

. . . neither Kant nor the scholastics provide for the fact that an indefinitely complicated proposition, very far from obvious, may often be deduced by mathematical reasoning, or necessary deduction, by the logic of relatives, from a definition of the utmost simplicity, without assuming any hypothesis whatever . . . ; and this may contain many notions not explicit in the definition. [2.361]

The logic of relatives . . . shows accordingly that deductive reasoning is really quite different from what it was supposed by Kant to be; and this explains how it is that he and others have taken various mathematical propositions to be synthetical which in their ideal sense, as propositions of pure mathematics, are in truth only analytical. [6.595]

It is Kant's notion of the analytic statement as one in which the predicate is "confusedly thought" in the subject that is under attack here. The kind of analyticity which Peirce assails is psychological, not logical. The emphasis on observation is necessary to explain why our deductions surprise us, not why they are deductions.

Yet there are passages in Peirce's writings where he appears to deny the deductive character of mathematics altogether. Thus he speaks of mathematical reasoning as a kind of "ideal induction" (3.531), as not absolutely certain (4.478), and as resting upon experimentation with diagrams. (3.556) Certainly such statements seem to argue an empirical or intuitionistic approach and to deny the purely deductive character of the reasoning.

The question of error is the most easily answered. Peirce does not deny the apodictic character of the reasoning; all he maintains is the rather obvious point that mathematicians do make errors in calculation and that accordingly it is at least possible that every mathematician has made an error every time he has added two and two. Thus Peirce remarks, "It is *possible* — barely possible" (4.478) that all have blundered, but neither Peirce nor anyone else considered it very likely.

The other points are of more importance, particularly because in arguing for them Peirce cites the authority of Kant (3.556f) and so lays himself open to the charge of intuitionism. That Peirce rejected any dependence of mathematics upon space, time, or any "form of intuition" is quite clear from his attack on Hamilton and De Morgan for holding just such views. (3.556f) And that he rejected the thesis that mathematics involves induction and hypothesis in any sense that is opposed to deduction becomes clear from his remarks on Sylvester, who was, in Peirce's experience, probably the strongest advocate of that position.[8] Thus Peirce writes:

> 5th. Is not the definition [his father's] too narrow in that induction, hypothesis, and every variety of reasoning is used in mathematics? . . .
> The fifth question is raised by a remark of Sylvester. But the reply is that all those other kinds of reasoning are in mathematics merely ancillary and provisional. Neither Sylvester nor any mathematician is satisfied until they have been swept away and replaced by demonstrations.[9]

No matter how useful induction may be in mathematics, the final justification must always be in terms of deduction. Yet this does not explain the role of the diagram, nor the "induction-like" character which Peirce attributes to formal reasoning.

The crux of Peirce's argument is given in the following passage:

> Demonstration of the sort called mathematical is founded on supposition of particular cases. The geometrician draws a figure; the algebraist assumes a letter to signify a certain quantity fulfilling the required conditions. But while the mathematician supposes a particular case, his hypothesis is yet perfectly general, because he considers no characters of the individual case but those which must belong to every such case. The advantage of his procedure lies in the fact that the logical laws of individual terms are simpler than those which relate to general terms, because individuals are either identical or mutually exclusive, and cannot intersect or be subordinated to one another as classes can. . . .
> The old logics distinguish between *individuum signatum* and *individuum vagum.* "Julius Caesar" is an example of the former; "a certain man," of the latter. The *individuum vagum*, in the days when such conceptions were exactly investigated, occasioned great difficulty from its having a certain generality, being capable, apparently, of logical division. If we include under *individuum vagum* such a term as "any individual man," these difficulties appear in a strong light, for what is true of any individual man is true of all men. Such a term is in one sense not an individual term; for it represents every man. But it represents each man as capable of being denoted by a term which is individual; and so, though it is not itself an individual term, it stands for any one of a class of such terms. . . . The letters which the mathematician uses (whether in algebra or in geometry) are such individuals by second intention. . . . All the formal logical laws relating to individuals will hold good of such individuals by second intention, and at the same time a universal

[8] Sylvester, *Mathematical Papers*, II, 719–731.
[9] "Notes on Peirce's Algebra," pp. 1f, 4.

proposition may at any moment be substituted for a proposition about such an individual, for nothing can be predicated of such an individual which cannot be predicated of the whole class. [3.92–94] [10]

As Lewis notes, what Peirce is discussing here is the concept of the variable. The geometer's figure is always a particular figure, a particular triangle for example, but it is used to stand for any one of a class of triangles having a similar form. When we construct such a diagram, Peirce points out, we construct it according to the conditions which define the class, and although the figure will have certain peculiarities (i.e., the color of the ink in which it is drawn) these are neglected. Thus Peirce asserts:

. . . every deductive inference is performed, and can only be performed, by imagining an instance in which the premisses are true and *observing* by contemplation of the image that the conclusion is true. The image, as *singular*, must of course have determinations that the premisses as *general*, have nothing to do with. But we satisfy ourselves that the particular determinations of the image chosen, so far as they go beyond the premisses, could make no difference.[11]

What is relevant is the form of the figure, for it is this which makes it possible for us to consider the figure as "any one" of the members of the class. (3.363; 3.560) Peirce expresses this by saying that the form of the icon is also its object (4.531) — an expression which is not wholly satisfactory but which makes the point.

What is true of the figure is true also of the formula and of the whole of a formal argument. Thus Peirce writes: "Every inference involves the judgment that, if *such* propositions as the premisses are true, then a proposition related to them, as the conclusion is, must be, or is likely to be, true. The principle implied in this judgment, respecting a genus of argument, is termed the *leading principle* of the argument." (2.462) Every valid inference is a member of a class of valid inferences, and given any one member, all others can be obtained from this one by the substitution of terms. The logical leading principle is a formal schema which defines the logical form of the various individual members of the class. (2.465ff) What Peirce calls an icon then

[10] Quoted in Lewis, *Survey*, pp. 93f.
[11] C. S. Peirce to Judge Francis Russell, September 18, 1908, p. 3, Scientific Correspondence.

is a sign which expresses the form of its object, and hence it may stand for any object which has a given form. Thus Peirce states: "Reasoning, nay, Logic generally, hinges entirely on Forms. You, Reader, will not need to be told that a regularly stated Syllogism is a Diagram; . . . No pure Icons represent anything but Forms; no pure Forms are represented by anything but Icons." (4.544) A diagram is not a pure icon, but it is chiefly an icon and it is this fact which accounts for its importance in mathematics. "Now since a diagram, though it will ordinarily have Symbolide Features, as well as features approaching the nature of Indices, is nevertheless in the main an Icon of the forms of relations in the constitution of its Object, the appropriateness of it for the representation of necessary inference is easily seen." (4.531)

Mr. Arthur Burks has termed the icon a "specific universal" since it is a specific thing which can stand for any member of a class. But Mr. Burks takes it as a particular member of a class, and interprets its function as that of a sample from which the general rule is derived by induction. Mr. Burks accordingly takes Peirce's comments about the inductive character of mathematics at face value, and interprets him as saying that mathematical theorems are derived by the empirical study of icons.[12] But I think that this is clearly not what Peirce means. For in constructing the icon, we do not construct one particular case under the hypothesis, we rather construct any particular case under the hypothesis. And it is only because of this fact that the mathematician can afford to neglect such individual characters of his constructs as the color of the ink. (5.8) Doubtless considerable ingenuity and experiment are required for the solution of any problem, and doubtless too one must always make sure that particular features of the symbolism do not influence the results — as e.g., in the famous case of the Peano ? operator[12a] — but this certainly does not make the reasoning inductive.

When Peirce speaks of mathematical reasoning as being inductive he is speaking loosely, for, he comments, "As for such general perceptions [those of iconic reasoning] being inductive, I might treat

[12] Burks, *Logical Foundations*, pp. 82–128.
[12a] Carl G. Hempel, *Fundamentals of Concept Formation in Empirical Science*, International Encyclopedia of Unified Science, vol. II, no. 7 (Chicago, 1955), p. 19.

the question from a technical standpoint and show that the essential characters of induction are wanting." (5.149) The analogy to induction consists in the fact that we do deal with the particular case; the difference is that we deal with any particular case.

The conception of pure mathematics which thus emerges from Peirce's writings appears to be that of a purely formal deductive system.[13] The premisses of such a system are to be regarded as postulates: "Mathematics studies nothing but pure hypotheses, and is the only science which never inquires what the actual facts are . . ." (3.560) The truth or falsehood of the premisses is not a relevant consideration for pure mathematics; it becomes relevant only when the system is applied. The application, however, is the business of the physicist or whatever scientist it may be who makes the application, not of the pure mathematician. (3.560)

Since the system is purely formal, the meanings of the terms which occur in its postulates and theorems are strictly irrelevant, or rather these terms are best conceived as uninterpreted variables.

A proposition is not a statement of perfectly pure mathematics until it is devoid of all definite meaning, and comes to this — that a property of a certain icon is pointed out and declared to belong to anything like it, of which instances are given. [5.567]
. . . In pure algebra, the symbols have no other meaning than that which the formulae impose upon them. In other words, they signify any relations which follow the same laws. Anything more definite detracts needlessly and injuriously from the generality and utility of the algebra. [4.314]

The only definitions which mar this "dignified meaninglessness of pure algebra" (4.314) are thus the implicit definitions which the postulates impose upon their terms. Alternatively, the postulates may be taken as implicitly defining the object or objects to which they apply, in the sense in which Riemann pointed out that the axioms of geometry afford a definition of space. This was usually the way in which Peirce interpreted them, as is illustrated by his comments in an early paper of 1867. "The object of the present paper is to show that there are certain general propositions from which the truths of mathematics follow syllogistically, and that these propositions may be taken as definitions of the objects under the consideration of the mathematician

---

[13] This statement will be qualified in certain respects below.

without involving any assumption in reference to experience or intuition." (3.20)

Since Peirce makes necessary reasoning synonymous with mathematics, it is clear that formal logic must be regarded as a case of applied mathematics. Thus he comments that logic "has a mathematical branch. But so much may be said of every science. There is a mathematical logic, just as there is a mathematical optics and a mathematical economics. Mathematical logic is formal logic. Formal logic, however developed, is mathematics." (4.240) And from this fact it is clear that the certainty of mathematics cannot be guaranteed by logic; rather the certainty of both must rest upon some other and common ground. What is required here is a definition of the notion of mathematical truth, and this in turn involves the question of a theory of proof. To these questions Peirce has given no wholly satisfactory answer. It is, I think, clear from his writings that he takes mathematical truth as meaning provability; thus he notes that the only disputes which can arise in mathematics are those concerning the question as to whether or not a given consequence follows from given hypotheses. And in this case, "because this dispute relates merely to the consequence of a hypothesis, the mere careful study of the hypothesis, which is pure mathematics, resolves it . . ." (1.247) But Peirce does not go on to develop a theory of proof. Rather he seems driven back upon the ground of self-evidence.

We simply perceive that two certain propositions in flat contradiction to one another cannot both be true. . . . We simply recognize a mathematical necessity. Mathematics is not subject to logic. Logic depends on mathematics. The recognition of mathematical necessity is performed in a perfectly satisfactory manner antecedent to any study of logic. Mathematical reasoning derives no warrant from logic. It needs no warrant. It is evident in itself. It does not relate to any matter of fact, but merely to whether one supposition excludes another. Since we ourselves create these suppositions, we are competent to answer them. [2.191]

That the truth of a mathematical theory lies in its consistency is a doctrine that few would question, but that the consistency of a theory is self-evident is a doctrine that Peirce, after his attack on the naivete of the Kantian concept of analyticity, should never have advanced. And indeed, Peirce is not this naive, for what he appears to mean here is not that we know by inspection that a theory is consistent, but that we should assume its consistency until we find a contradiction. (2.192) Then and only then does the consistency question become a genuine one, and in that case the ordinary processes of mathematical reasoning are sufficient to resolve it. To support this argument he appeals to history, and cites the fact that whenever a question of the validity of a mathematical proof has arisen, it has been speedily resolved by the mathematicians themselves without appeal to any but mathematical principles. (1.248; 4.243)

It must be granted that Peirce is partly right. We now know that constructive consistency proofs for arithmetic systems are impossible and that in most cases we must simply wait and see whether or not a contradiction turns up. But the fact that Peirce is right must be regarded as being of the general nature of an unearned run. There is no evidence that Peirce knew of the existence of undecidable statements, or that he considered the question of proof theory very thoroughly or carefully. Thus, although he must have known from Klein's work that models could be used to prove consistency,[14] he never attempted to employ them in his own work, and he comments in a rather derogatory fashion that "what people call an 'interpretation' is a thing totally irrelevant, except that it may show by an example that no slip of logic has been committed." (4.130) But to show this is, after all, a rather important matter.

Looking back across the fifty years of unresolved mathematical dispute which Weyl has well termed the "crisis" in mathematics,[15] Peirce's treatment of the consistency question seems incredibly cavalier. In fairness it should be remarked that that crisis was just beginning in Peirce's time and that he never appreciated the genuine seriousness of it. But his theory still leaves us with a trial and error method which affords little security.

[14] Courant and Robbins, *Mathematics*, pp. 220ff.
[15] Herman Weyl, "Mathematics and Logic," *American Mathematical Monthly*, LIII, 13 (1946).

# XIII

## *Number*

I N the preceding section, I developed Peirce's theory of the nature of mathematics in terms of an uninterpreted postulational system. For the purposes of algebra, such "dignified meaninglessness" suffices; for purposes of the arithmetic of daily life it does not. For in that arithmetic, certain primitive concepts such as "number" and "O" and "successor," which are not simply uninterpreted variables, are required. As Russell has remarked:

It might be suggested that, instead of setting up "O", "number" and "successor" as terms of which we know the meaning although we cannot define them, we might let them stand for *any* three terms that verify Peano's five axioms. They will then no longer be terms which have a meaning that is definite though undefined: they will be "variables" . . . But from two points of view [such a procedure] fails to give an adequate basis for arithmetic. In the first place, it does not enable us to know whether there are any sets of terms verifying Peano's axioms; it does not even give the faintest suggestion of any way of discovering whether there are such sets. In the second place . . . we want our numbers to be such as can be used for counting common objects, and this requires that our numbers should have a *definite* meaning, not merely that they should have certain formal properties.[1]

Peirce's theory is a highly formalistic one, but the formalism stops short of that of the modern formalists. He did not regard numbers simply as variables — rather he considered them to be a peculiar sort of abstract object. Thus he writes:

This system [of number] is a cluster of ideas of individual things; but it is not a cluster of real things. It thus belongs to the world of ideas, or Inner World. Nor does the mathematician, though he "creates the idea *for himself*," create it absolutely. Whatever it may contain of (that which is) im-

[1] Bertrand Russell, *Introduction to Mathematical Philosophy* (London, 1950), pp. 9f.

pertinent (to mathematics) is soilure from (elsewhere). The idea in its purity is an eternal being of the Inner World. [4.161]

This passage at once raises three questions. Are numbers real? What is the meaning of the phrase "eternal being of the Inner World"? And what is meant by "create"?

The consideration of the last question must be postponed until we have examined Peirce's theory in detail, but the first two may be considered here. Numbers are not external, but they are real.

Of the three Universes of Experience familiar to us all, the first comprises all mere Ideas, those airy nothings to which the mind of poet, pure mathematician, or another *might* give local habitation and a name within that mind. Their very airy-nothingness, the fact that their Being consists in mere capability of getting thought, not in anybody's Actually thinking them, saves their Reality. [6.455]

Numbers are "ideas" and as such they belong to a different "universe of experience" then do facts or laws. This "Universe of Ideas," Peirce calls the "Platonic world of pure forms" (4.118), and its inhabitants are abstract and eternal entities. Peirce also calls it the "Inner World" — a name which is apt to be misleading because he also uses the term "inner world" to designate the world of memory which is not eternal but is rather characterized by its relation to time.[1a] In the passage quoted above, the term "Inner World" is used in a pre-"New List" sense as referring not to the world of self but to the world of "logos" or realm of pure, eternal abstractions. Such abstract entities are never known in their entirety — they are realized only in instances and their reality consists precisely in the possibility of these instances, in their "capability of getting thought," rather than in their actually being thought.

This doctrine is remarkable in several respects. In the first place, it is only with respect to mathematics that this early Platonism is retained in Peirce's thought after 1885. Mathematical entities therefore form a unique class in Peirce's ontology and are quite distinct from any other sort of entity which his later system contains. Peirce himself remarked this fact when, in the prospectus for his twelve-volume *Principles of Philosophy*, he entitled the fourth volume, *Plato's World: An Elucidation of the Ideas of Modern Mathematics.* (8.G. c.1893)

[1a] See above, p. 89.

Secondly, this theory introduces confusion into the theory of the categories. Since Peirce's unwavering allegiance to the architectonic plan required that numbers too should fall within the categorical schema, they are classed as Firsts. But since Firsts are represented by icons, and, as we have seen above,[2] icons also serve as variables, Peirce's dictum that mathematical propositions are iconic now becomes ambiguous in an almost vicious sense since it is easy to conclude either that Peirce is a pure formalist or that all icons are Platonic entities. But in the first case, numbers would not be eternal, abstract properties or Platonic ideas, in contradiction to Peirce's statements above, while in the second, iconic reasoning would be reasoning about one individual in a class, not about any individual in a class, and this is contrary to Peirce's views as we saw in the last chapter. Here as in so many other cases, the categorical schema fails to preserve significant distinctions and so helps to obscure what it is that Peirce is talking about.

Peirce's theory of number is one of the chief supports upon which his later philosophy is based. But before turning to the exposition of the theory itself, it is important to determine both the extent and the limits of his knowledge of contemporary work on classes and numbers. We know that he was thoroughly familiar with Dedekind's *Was sind und was sollen die Zahlen?* (4.239; 4.331) We also know that he had become acquainted with the work of Cantor in 1884 [3] when he read at least some of the papers in volume II of *Acta Mathematica*.[4] It is impossible to be sure just which or how many of these papers Peirce read, but since his chief interest was in Cantor's theory of continuity it is likely that he read only "Sur les ensembles infinis et linéaires des points; parts i–iv" and "Sur divers théorèmes de la théorie des ensembles de points situés dans un espace continu à *n* dimensions." The former paper is of course the first four sections of

[2] See above, pp. 233f.

[3] Peirce, "Multitude and Continuity," notes for a lecture at Harvard, May 15, 1903. p. 7, Peirce Papers, Houghton Library.

[4] Peirce, "Map Colouring," p. 2. These are, "Sur une propriété du système de tous les nombres algébriques réels," pp. 305–310; "Une contribution à la théorie des ensembles," pp. 311–328; "Sur les séries trigonométriques," pp. 329–335; "Extension d'un théorème de la théorie des séries trigonométriques," pp. 336–348; "Sur les ensembles infinis et linéaires de points, i–iv," pp. 349–380; "Fondements d'une théorie générale des ensembles," pp. 381–408; "Sur divers théorèmes de la théorie des ensembles de points situés dans un espace continu à *n* dimensions," pp. 409–414.

the *Über unendliche, lineare Punktmannichfaltigkeiten.* Subsequently, Peirce also read Cantor's *Zur Lehre vom Transfiniten* and the papers in volume 49 of *Mathematische Annalen* — namely *Beiträge zur Begrundung der Transfiniten Mengenlehre,* and also Schoenflies' *Die Entwickelung der Lehre von den Punktmannigfaltigkeiten.*[5] There is good reason to believe, however, that Peirce read selectively and skipped over a good deal of the content of these papers, for as we shall see below he either did not know about some of Cantor's discoveries which are described in these papers or else he very badly misunderstood what he read. On the whole, though, it can be said that Peirce apparently saw enough of Cantor's writings to be familiar with his major doctrines. On the other hand, I have found no references to Frege in any of Peirce's writings and it seems virtually certain that Peirce knew nothing of his work. More important, however, is the question of Peirce's knowledge of Russell. Although Peirce wrote a review of Russell's *Principles of Mathematics* in 1903, the notice is so brief and cursory that I am convinced he never read the book.[6] For not only does Peirce never mention Frege, of whom he could not have failed to learn from the *Principles* — he also somehow managed not to learn of the paradox. In all Peirce's writings I have found but one reference to Russell's paradox, and this reference occurs in a manuscript written sometime after 1910 and is based on information derived from reviews of the *Principia,* not from the *Principles* nor from the *Principia* itself. This passage I quote in entirety:

In two recent notices of Russell and Whitehead's last volume I have seen the following set down as self-contradictory. I change only the wording.
    If any $x$ does not include itself, it includes $w$, it does [sic].

[5] Peirce to Judge Russell, September 18, 1908, p. 6.

[6] Peirce, "Review of V. Welby's *What is Meaning* and Bertrand Russell's *The Principles of Mathematics,*" *Nation,* 77: 308–309 (October 15, 1903). Peirce's copy of Russell's *Principles* is now in the hands of Mr. Victor Lenzen, through whose kindness, and the good offices of Professor Max Fisch, I have been able to examine it. The volume contains several annotations in Peirce's hand. These annotations are all in the chapter on logic: they begin on page 13 with the discussion of the proposition and end on page 24 with dyadic relations. There is no evidence that Peirce read anything but these few pages, in which as it happens there is no discussion of the paradox and but one casual reference to Frege, and his comments are highly contemptuous of Russell's work. Moreover, the hand in which the annotations are written is tremulous, indicating that they were written very late in Peirce's life — certainly after the appearance of the *Nation* review. The evidence afforded by the annotations is therefore consistent with the assertions that the review was written without having read the book, and that Peirce never understood the paradox. [Mr. Lenzen has subsequently given the book to the Harvard University Library.]

If any $x$ includes $w$ it does not include itself.

But suppose that, in place of the logical relation of inclusion, we substitute an ordinary relation between individuals. We shall so get such a pair of propositions as the following: Whatever is not a lover of itself is a lover of $w$. If anything is a lover of $w$, it is not a lover of itself. These two propositions simply imply that anything of this nature of $w$ is not self-identical. It is perhaps of a general nature, such as an abstraction. There are many things that have to be reasoned about that are not exactly *existent*.

In mathematics such apparently self-contradictory assertions are often made, but are easily interpreted so as to remove their self-contradictory sound.[7]

This statement of the paradox is incorrect as is easily seen by comparing it with Russell's statement: "Let $w$ be the class of all those classes which are not members of themselves. Then, whatever class $x$ may be, '$x$ is a $w$' is equivalent to '$x$ is not an $x$.' Hence, giving to $x$ the value $w$, '$w$ is a $w$' is equivalent to '$w$ is not a $w$'." [8] Peirce's rendering of the paradox makes it equivalent to the paradox of the barber; consider the barber who lives in a certain town and who shaves all and only those male residents of the town who do not shave themselves. Does the barber shave himself or not? This, however, is not a genuine paradox. All that is shown is that the supposition that there is such a barber leads to a contradiction, and from this it merely follows that there is no such barber. What is required to make the paradox genuine is a reason for holding that there must be such a barber. Russell's paradox, on the other hand, is genuine, for not only is it shown that the supposition that there is a class of all classes not members of themselves must lead to contradiction, but the theory of classes affords reasons for saying that there must be such a class. Yet in changing "only the wording" Peirce manages to omit this portion of the paradox despite the fact that his own theory of classes involves the same principle. Thus although Peirce saw correctly that the problem raised by the paradox is the problem of the mathematical existence of such paradoxical entities, he failed to see that their existence was required by principles fundamental to his own system as well as Russell's. Since this passage was written within four years of Peirce's

[7] Peirce, "Mr. Bertrand Russell's Paradox," fragment, IB2 Box 7.

[8] Alfred North Whitehead and Bertrand Russell, *Principia Mathematica* (Cambridge, 1950), I, 60.

death, it seems very doubtful that he ever knew what Russell's paradox was. It is therefore not surprising that he fell repeatedly into difficulties from which this knowledge could have saved him.[9]

Peirce has given several constructions for what he called a system of pure number.[10] One of the simplest of these may be rendered as follows. He first defines a "sequence," which consists of any number of objects connected by a relation, which is called a "relation of sequence," and which is such that:

Precept I. If A is any object of the sequence whatever and B is any object of the sequence whatever, either A is not R to B or else B is not R to A.[11]

Precept II. If A is any object of the sequence whatever, B is any such object, and C is any such object, then, so far as Precept I permits, either A is R to B, or B is R to C, or C is R to A. [3.562B] [12]

As Peirce points out, we may interpret the relation, R, either as "follows" or as "precedes": he chooses to interpret it as "follows." The "sequence may or may not have an absolute end; that is, a member which is followed by no member; and it may or may not have an absolute beginning; that is, a member which follows no member." He then defines the relation "follows hard after," viz. if A and B are two members of the sequence, and B follows A, then B follows hard after A if and only if there is no member C of the sequence which follows A and does not follow B. (3.562C) Peirce then defines a "simple sparse sequence" as follows: "Let us call a sequence of which every member follows hard after a second, and is itself followed hard after by a third, a *sparse* sequence; and let us call a sparse sequence which cannot be broken into parts which want either beginning or end (except so far as they may retain the infinity of the total sequence), a *simple* sparse

---

[9] Cf., e.g., pp. 246f. below.

[10] Cf. 4.16off.

[11] A is R to B means A stands to B is the relation R, and A is R'd by B means that A stands to B is the converse of the relation R.

[12] From these precepts transitivity follows:

I. (A)(B) $\sim$ ARBv $\sim$ BRA

II. (A)(B)(C) ARBvBRCvCRA

| 3 | CRB & BRA | Hyp. |
|---|---|---|
| 4 | $\sim$ BRC | I, 3, A:C, modus tollendo ponens |
| 5 | $\sim$ ARB | I, 3, modus tollendo ponens |
| 6 | CRA | II, 4, 5, modus tollendo ponens |
| 7 | (A) (B) (C) CRB & BRA $\supset$ CRA | 3–6, condit. proof. |

sequence." (3.562F) This affords Peirce the means of defining a system of pure number — "Then the system of pure number may be defined as a simple sparse sequence, having an absolute beginning, called *zero*, but no absolute end." (3.562F) He then proves the principle of mathematical induction as a theorem (3.562G), and gives recursive definitions of sum and product. (3.562H–562I) As Peirce has elsewhere shown, this system is adequate for the construction of rational and real numbers. (4.677–681)

It is instructive to compare this system with the Peano axioms. Assuming as primitive the terms "number," "zero," and "successor," these are

(1) O is a number.
(2) The successor of any number is a number.
(3) No two numbers have the same successor.
(4) O is not the successor of any number.
(5) Any property which belongs to O, and also to the successor of every number which has the property, belongs to all numbers.[13]

(5) is the induction principle which Peirce proves as a theorem. (4) and (1) are guaranteed by definition. (3) is obtained by the following reasoning. The "successor" of a number, $a$, is the "follower hard after" $a$. Let this successor be $b$. Then the assertion is that no other number $c$ has $b$ for its successor. Suppose there are two numbers, $a$ and $c$, both having $b$ for a successor. By Precept I, either $a$ follows $c$ or $c$ follows $a$. Suppose the first. Then since by hypothesis $b$ follows $c$, and $a$ follows $c$, but $b$ follows $a$, $a$ must lie between $b$ and $c$ so that $b$ is not the successor of $c$, contrary to supposition. But suppose $c$ follows $a$. Then by the same reasoning, $c$ lies between $a$ and $b$ and $b$ is not the successor of $a$, contrary to supposition. Hence by excluded middle, no two numbers have the same successor. Finally (2) follows from the fact that all members of the series are defined to be numbers. Since the Peano axioms are demonstrably adequate for arithmetic, it appears that Peirce's system — i.e. Precepts I and II and the "sparse sequence" — is also adequate.

Thus far, Peirce's system, like Peano's, gives only an implicit definition of its primitive terms and is quite consistent with a formalist in-

---

[13] Russell, *Introduction to Mathematical Philosophy*, pp. 5f.

terpretation. But Peirce actually regarded the pure number system as a special case of the ordinals. "Dedekind and others consider the pure abstract integers to be ordinal; and in my opinion they are not only right, but might extend the assertion to all real numbers." (4.633) Thus it is not just any endless simple sparse sequence which composes the pure number system but the ordinal sequence beginning with zero. Accordingly, we must examine Peirce's theory of ordinal number in some detail.

In order to define the ordinal numbers, Peirce introduces an operation which he calls "subjectal" or "hypostatic" abstraction.[14] This operation consists in converting a predicate of a subject into a subject, or, more exactly, instead of using a predicate, P, as a way of thinking about something, as when we say that "x is a P," we rather make P the subject of thought and predicate other characters of it, as when we say that "P is a color." (4.332; 4.235) With the help of this operation, Peirce then defines a "place." Given an endless, simple sparse sequence, and any member of that sequence, say x, there is another member of the sequence, say y, such that x follows hard after y. From this relation of "follows hard after" we can obtain the relational property of "following hard after" and we can say that x has the property of "following hard after y," or x is "the follower hard after y." By hypostatic abstraction we now convert this property into a "subject of thought," thus making "the follower hard after y" a definite, abstract entity; and we may now omit all reference to x and speak only of "the follower hard after y," since in this particular case x is the only such entity. We now repeat this process; that is, there is some member of the sequence, z, such that y follows hard after z, and we may at once convert y into "the follower hard after z," and so on. The expression "the follower hard after y" now becomes "the follower hard after the follower hard after z." This process may obviously be continued until we reach "0" which does not follow anything, but we may substitute for "0" the property "the follower of no member of the sequence." The result of this process, Peirce holds, is that from the original sequence composed of . . . z,y,x, . . . , we obtain a new sequence defined by the same relation of sequence as the original but which has for members hypostatized predicates, or "places," each of which designates unambiguous-

[14] Goudge, "Peirce's Theory of Abstraction," pp. 124f.

ly the position of an element in a linear sequence relative to a given element. Since all reference to the particular members of the original sequence has been eliminated, these predicates are applicable to any linear sequence which is endless, simple, and sparse (in modern terminology, well ordered). We can now introduce convenient symbols to designate these "places," and these symbols we will call "ordinal numbers." "So an *ordinal number* is an abstraction attached to a *place*, which in its turn is a hypostatic abstraction from a relative character of a unit of a *series*, itself an abstraction again." (5.534)

This theory may appear plausible at first sight, but a closer examination reveals difficulties. Let us designate the elements of the original sequence by . . . w,x,y,z . . . , and the relation "follows hard after" by F. Then "the follower hard after y" is F'y — the F of y. Our sequence then takes the form O, F'O, F'F'O, F'F'F'O, . . . Such expressions as "the F of y" are singular descriptive phrases — they apply only to a unique simple sparse sequence. Since the definition of the original sequence is such as to guarantee that no two elements are F's of the same y, no difficulty arises so long as we remain with the original sequence. But with this Peirce is not satisfied. He wishes his ordinals to denote place in any simple sparse sequence, not just in one. To do this, Peirce generalizes his sequence of singular descriptive functions into a sequence of plural descriptive functions applicable to members of all sequences. If we denote the class of simple sparse sequences by L, then the first member of the new sequence will be x̂ where

$$\hat{x}\,\{(a)((a \,\epsilon\, L) \cdot (x \,\epsilon\, a) \supset \sim (\exists y)(y \,\epsilon\, a.xFy))\},$$

i.e., the class of all members of any simple sparse sequence which follow no other member of those sequences. And this class Peirce calls "O". In similar manner we may define the second element as the class of all elements of simple sparse sequences which are F's of their first elements. This element Peirce calls "1". And similarly "2", "3", etc.

But here the difficulties become obvious, for O and 1 as here defined are not ordered by F. Indeed it is obvious that, if 1 is equivalent to the class of all things which are members of simple sparse sequences and F's of O, then 1 is not an F of O, since if it were 1 would be a member of itself. On the other hand, 1 is defined to be the F of O. Thus a paradox is created. The numbers cannot designate places in all simple sparse sequences and yet be themselves members of places in simple sparse sequences without designating themselves.[15]

Peirce's theory of ordinals gives us a sequence of classes instead of Cantor's classes of sequences. This fact is evident from the above discussion and from the fact that Peirce always refers to ordinals as designating places *in* a simple sparse sequence. (4.337) One result of this position is that if we regard the first five members of this sequence as a distinct subsequence, and the first ten members as another subsequence, then, although it follows that the tenth place is after the fifth place, nothing whatever follows concerning any relation between the two subsequences. The relation of sequence is defined only among members, not among classes or sequences of members.[16] In order to prove such a relation among the sequences, or among collections generally, something more than ordinal number is required, namely, the theory of multitude.

In order to develop Peirce's theory of multitudes, it is first necessary to define the concept of "collection" — a notion of which Peirce remarked, "I know no concept of logic more difficult to analyze than that of a collection." [17] Although his various analyses of it differ on some points, the following eight characteristics appear to be essential. First, "a collection is a single object distinct from its parts. A nation is not a man; nor is it all the men it contains, since they are many while it is one." [18] Second, a collection is an abstraction which depends for its being upon the existence of its members. Furthermore,

The ultimate parts, or units . . . even if they have some abstractness, are not so abstract as the collection. They have . . . their existence distinct from the collection, and are, at least, so far independent of each other, that any one may enter into or be excluded from a collection independently of any other or others. From the circumstance that a collection has only a being *in posse*, and is devoid of *hecceity*, or thisness, except as derived from its units, it

---

[15] In 4.635 Peirce develops the theory of climacote numbers along these same lines. The system is cyclic, but is easily rendered linear. Peirce there employs a concept of "step" rather than "place" — a "step" being defined as a substitution which brings the F'x to the position of x. Such an operation would be the function $\check{F}'$ (F'x) = x, repeated application giving $\check{F}'\check{F}'$ (F'F'x) = x, etc. The steps are then abstracted and made designata of ordinal numbers. Clearly, the same difficulties arise here as in the case outlined above.

[16] See, however, 4.332. This would seem to require that counting be an ordinal concept, which it is not on Peirce's theory of finite ordinals.

[17] "Map Colouring," p. 3.

[18] *Ibid.*

follows as a corollary that two collections, in order to be distinct must differ in some generally describable respect, while the distinct units may be alike in all such respects and only be distinguishable in their reactions, like two drops of water.[19]

Third, "every respect in which two distinct collections differ is of this sort, that some unit of the one is not a unit of the other." [20] Fourth, "Let there be any general description, applicable only to units of a collection, and whatever units of the collection there may be of that description form by themselves a collection. Even if the description be self-contradictory, it determines the null collection. Thus the idea of a collection carries with it that of a complete system of sub-collections." [21] Fifth, "a collection is an individual object, not in the least indeterminate, and . . . different collections may form the units of collections of collections." [22] Sixth, "in order that a collection should have any definiteness, it is necessary that its units should conform to certain conditions. Thus, the population of the United States differs from minute to minute, and is definite only on the assumption that the date is fixed. Such conditions can never be fully described in purely general terms." [23] Seventh, every aggregate of independent individuals is a collection, for there is always some property common to these and to no other individuals. (4.649) Eighth, "there is a collection corresponding to every common noun or general description." (4.171)

This definition contains an important inconsistency — namely, the second and eighth provisions are not wholly consistent. There are general descriptions which determine aggregates the members of which are not independent. According to two above, such aggregates are not collections; thus Peirce writes:

. . . we can say that the collection of all the letters of the alphabet is the collection of a, b, c, d, e, . . . x, y, z, as parts, or we can equally well say that the same collection consists of two parts, the collection of all the vowels and the collection of all the consonants. But we cannot say that it is a whole whose parts are the collection of vowels and a, b, c, d, e, . . . x, y, z, since the collection of the vowels is not independent of a, e, i, o, u.[24]

[19] *Ibid.*, pp. 3f.
[20] *Ibid.*, p. 4.
[21] *Ibid.*, p. 5.
[22] *Ibid.*
[23] *Ibid.*
[24] "Numeration," n.d., p. 14, IA3.

Furthermore, by provision two above, the members of a collection must be independent of the collection, for the members can exist independently of the collection, while the collection derives its existence from the members. Yet by eight, it would appear that even nonindependent aggregates constitute collections, since they are determined by general descriptions. Clearly, what is required here is some limitation of principle eight which would admit to collectionhood only aggregates which meet the independence requirement.

Peirce's second principle contains in essence the basis for a solution to Russell's paradox. The independence requirement prohibits a collection from being a member of itself, and the doctrine that a collection is always more abstract than its units, had it been rigorously applied, would have led to a type hierarchy similar to Russell's. But unfortunately Peirce's theory of abstraction levels seems to have been derived from the Scholastic division between first and second intention and it was not rigorously developed, as the contradictions in his theory of ordinals show. Even when Peirce finally came to recognize that such predicates as "collection of all possible objects" could not be permitted to determine collections on pain of contradiction,[25] he did not perceive the underlying principle and such rare qualifications of principle eight as he did make were introduced in a purely *ad hoc* fashion. As we have already seen, he never knew of Russell's paradox, and when he encountered difficulties in the theory of transfinite numbers he did not turn to type theory to solve them.

A further question which is posed by Peirce's definition of a collection is whether or not there is a null collection. Peirce firmly asserts that there is:

. . . when we say that there is a collection we merely mean that its units may have a relation to one object, common and peculiar to them. In this sense, we may certainly say that there is a collection embracing but a single unit. . . . Similarly there may be a relation in which nothing stands to something, and thus there is a collection of nothing. This collection has the mode of existence of a single collection, while its units are null. There is, of course, but one collection of nothing.[26]

Since however the being of the collection is derived from that of its

[25] "Theory of Collections," p. $\frac{1}{2}$, Peirce Papers, Houghton Library.
[26] "Map Colouring," p. 4.

members, it is not clear that this is wholly consistent. It would rather seem that on Peirce's theory a collection without members would not be a collection at all. But once again Peirce ignores his second principle and takes the existence of the null-collection as unquestionable.

Three relations among collections are of particular importance — those of equality, greater than, and less than. Following Bolzano [27] and Cantor,[28] Peirce defines these as follows:

To say that the collection of M's and the collection of N's are equal is to say:
There is a one-to-one relation, $c$, such that every M is $c$ to an N; and there is a one-to-one relation, $d$, such that every N is $d$ to an M.
To say that the collection of M's is less than the collection of N's is to say:
There is a one-to-one relation, $c$, such that every M is $c$ to an N; but whatever one-to-one relation $d$ may be, some N is not $d$ to any M.
To say that the collection of M's is greater than the collection of N's is to say:
Whatever one-to-one relation $c$ may be, some M is not $c$ to any N; but there is a one-to-one relation $d$ such that every N is $d$ to an M. [4.177]

The question at once arises whether or not every two collections must stand in one of these three relations — that is, whether or not it is possible that "whatever one-to-one relation $c$ may be, some M is not $c$ to any N and some N is not $c$'d by any M." (4.177) If such were the case there would be "incomparable" collections — collections which could not be compared as to size. Peirce denies such a possibility, and asserts that any two collections are comparable, i.e., one of the three relations always holds. (4.177ff)

Peirce notes that the three relations — equals, greater than, and less than — are all transitive and such that "if A is smaller than B, and B is equal to C, A is smaller than C; and if A is greater than B, and B is equal to C, A is greater than C." [29] He then defines "multitude": "The propositions . . . [the definitions above] constitute a linear order among collections not equal to one another. The place of a collection in this order may be termed its *multitude*. That is, of two equal collec-

[27] Bernard Bolzano, *Paradoxes of the Infinite*, trans. F. Prihonsky (London, 1950), pp. 95ff.
[28] Georg Cantor, *Contributions to the Founding of the Theory of Transfinite Numbers*, trans. P. E. B. Jourdain (New York, n.d.), pp. 86ff.
[29] "Map Colouring," p. 7. Peirce has, "if A is greater than B, and B is equal to C, A is equal to C." This is obviously a slip.

tions the *multitude* is *the same*, while of unequal collections the greater has the *greater multitude*." [30] The "multitude" of a collection is thus the "place" or "grade" of the collection in a linear sequence of collections ordered with respect to the relation "greater than." "Multitude" is the ordinal place of a collection in a sequence of collections. And *"Ordinals,* in general, are designations of *grades,* each grade being possibly occupied by what I will call *numerates,* or subjects of numeration. In the special case in which the numerates are *plurals,* the grades are *multitudes,* and their ordinals become cardinals . . . " [31] It should be remarked that multitude is a property of a collection — not of the members individually. The linear sequence, the grades of which are multitudes, is a sequence of collections, not of members of collections. Furthermore, it is not the multitude of a collection which makes it greater or less than another collection; rather it is the fact that the collection is greater or less than another collection that determines the relations of greater or less among the multitudes.

You will observe that . . . it was not members of a *multitude* that were put into the different parts of another *multitude,* but members of a *collection* which are attached to different singulars of a *collection.* Now while numbers *may* on occasion be, or represent, multitudes, they can never be collections, since collections are not *grades* of any kind, but are single things. [4.663]

The relations of one-to-one correspondence, upon which equality, greater, and less depend, are relations among collections. It is only when the sequence of collections has been established that grades are applicable.

Every place in a simple sparse sequence is named by an ordinal number. When the places are multitudes, the ordinals become cardinals. This does not mean, however, that multitudes and cardinals are identical. "A cardinal number, though confounded with multitude by Cantor, is in fact one of a series of vocables the prime purpose of which, quite unlike any other words, is to serve as an instrument in the performance of the experiment of counting . . . " (3.628) At first sight it might appear that counting must be an ordinal function, but according to Peirce it is so only to the extent that the cardinals are ordinal, i.e., as involving succession. On the other hand, counting involves the

[30] *Ibid.,* pp. 7f.
[31] Peirce to Judge Russell, September 18, 1908, p. 5.

cardinals essentially, for "the process of counting a collection is brought to an end exclusively by the exhaustion of the collection, to which thereafter the last numeral word used is applied as an adjective." (4.155) This adjectival number designates the multitude of the collection and is therefore a cardinal number.

But the last statement assumes a very important principle — namely, that the number which results from counting a collection is the same as the number designating the multitude of that collection, or, as we may say, as the multitude of the collection. And this principle has to be proved, for as we saw above the fact that the fifth place is before the tenth does not prove that the collection of numbers less than ten is greater than the collection of numbers less than five. In order to prove this, Peirce first defines the term "count." Let $c$ be a one-to-one relation. Then, "If every object, $s$, of a class is in any such relation being $c$'d with a number of a semi-infinite discrete simple system, and if further every number smaller than a number $c$'d by an $s$ is itself $c$'d by an $s$, then the numbers $c$'d by the $s$'s are said to count them, and the system of correspondence is called a count." (3.281) By this definition a count consists in a one-to-one correspondence between the members of a collection and some section of the sequence of cardinal numbers which begins with one and ends with $n$.[32] The numbers in this section of the sequence form a collection, and since there is a one-to-one correspondence between the members of this collection and the members of the collection, S, the two collections are equal and have the same multitude. Accordingly, the problem is equivalent to that of proving that the multitude of the collection of numbers greater than O and less than or equal to $n$ is equal to $n$.

The proof is by induction. Peirce first proves the equivalence for one. Letting "not-follows" be "as small as" Peirce argues:

Suppose that in any count the number of numbers as small as the minimum number, one, is found to be $n$. Then, by the definition of a count, every number as small as $n$ counts a number as small as one. But by the definition of one there is only one number as small as one. Hence, by definition of single correspondence, no other number than one counts one. Hence, by the definition of one, no other number than one counts any number as small as one.

---

[32] We exclude the number "o" so that "1" now fulfills the function of the first number.

Hence, by the definition of the count, one is, in every count, the number of numbers as small as one. [3.283]

We have now to show that if the equivalence holds for any number it holds for the successor of that number. Let the multitude of the collection of numbers which are as small as $n - 1$ be equivalent to $n - 1$. Then we have to show that the multitude of numbers as small as $n$ is equal to $n$ — i.e., if $A = \hat{x}$ ($x$ is a number, $x \leqq n - 1$) and $B = \hat{z}$ ($z$ is a number. $z \leqq n$) then $M(A) = n - 1 \blacksquare \supset \blacksquare M(B) = n$. Then consider the class $Y = A \cup \{n\}$. By the definition of "greater than," $Y > A$. Moreover, it is obvious that there is no class $W$ such that $Y > W > A$. Hence $Y$ is the next greatest collection after $A$, and must occupy the next grade of multitude which is $n$. But $Y = B$, for the members of $B$ are all the numbers less than $n$ and $n$ itself. Hence $M(B) = n$. Therefore, the multitude of numbers less than or equal to $x$ is equal to $x$, for all finite values of $x$. (3.287) It should be noted that this proof affords the sole connection between cardinality and multitude in Peirce's theory, and further that it is only through counting that the magnitude of two sequences can be compared.

The theory of counting is thus a part of the theory of collections, and specifically of the theory of multitudes. (4.163) So also is the so-called Fundamental Theorem of Arithmetic, which asserts "that a finite collection counts up to the same number in whatever order the individuals of it are counted." (4.163) Peirce gives a rather detailed proof of this theorem which I will not repeat here. (4.187n) Neither the theory of counting nor the Fundamental Theorem is assumed by the theory of ordinals which relates only to "place."

Thus far we have dealt only with Peirce's theory of the finite numbers. In the extension to the infinite, Peirce in general follows Cantor, but there are important differences between them. For Cantor, cardinal numbers are properties of sets or aggregates; ordinal numbers are properties of well-ordered sets. In particular, therefore, the well-ordered set of finite ordinal numbers has an ordinal which, being the number of an infinite set, is infinite and forms the limit of the finite ordinals. Cantor has given a very clear and precise explanation of this idea which is well worth quoting:

Finally I have still to explain to you in what sense I conceive the minimum of the transfinite as limit of the increasing finite. For this purpose we must consider that the concept of "limit" in the domain of finite numbers has two essential characteristics. For example, the number 1 is the limit of the numbers $z_\nu = 1 - 1/\nu$, where $\nu$ is a variable, finite, whole number, which increases above all finite limits. In the first place the difference $1 - z_\nu$ is a magnitude which becomes infinitely small; in the second place 1 is the least of all numbers which are greater than all magnitudes $z_\nu$. Each of these two properties characterizes the finite number 1 as limit of the variable magnitude $z_\nu$. Now if we wish to extend the concept of limit to transfinite limits as well, the second of the above characteristics is used; the first must here be allowed to drop because it has a meaning only for finite limits. Accordingly I call $\omega$ the limit of the increasing, finite, whole numbers $\nu$, because $\omega$ is the least of all numbers which are greater than all the finite numbers. But $\omega - \nu$ is always equal to $\omega$, and therefore we cannot say that the increasing numbers $\nu$ come as near as we wish to $\omega$; indeed any number $\nu$ however great is quite as far off from $\omega$ as the least finite number. Here we see especially clearly the very important fact that my least transfinite ordinal number $\omega$, and consequently all greater ordinal numbers, lie quite outside the endless series 1, 2, 3, and so on. Thus $\omega$ is *not* a maximum of the finite numbers, for there is no such thing.[33]

As far as finite aggregates are concerned, Cantor proved that every well-ordered set of the elements of a given aggregate has the same ordinal number, and this ordinal number corresponds uniquely to the cardinal number of the aggregate. But in regard to infinite aggregates Cantor showed that this is not the case. The ordinal numbers of a well-ordered sequence of elements of a given infinite aggregate will differ depending upon the order in which the elements of the aggregate stand in the sequence. Thus if we add the two sequences, $S = \{1,2,3, \ldots\}$ and $T = \{0\}$ whose ordinals are $\bar{S} = \omega$ and $\bar{T} = 1$, we have in the first case $T + S = \{0\} + \{1,2,3, \ldots\} = \{0,1,2,3, \ldots\}$, the ordinal of which is $\omega$, so that $1 + \omega = \omega$. But in the second case, $S + T = \{1,2,3, \ldots\} + \{0\} = \{1,2,3, \ldots 0\}$, the ordinal of which is greater than $\omega$ by virtue of the definition of "greater than" for sequences in terms of one to one correspondence preserving order. Hence $\bar{S} + \bar{T} = \omega + 1 > \omega$. We thus obtain a sequence of transfinite ordinals $\omega$, $\omega + 1$, $\omega + 2 \ldots$[34] And since there are an infinite number of ways of

---

[33] Cantor, *Transfinite Numbers*, p. 78. The meaninglessness of "$\omega - \nu$" is the result of the fact that transfinite numbers are not decreased by the subtraction of finite numbers.

[34] Fraenkel, *Set Theory*, p. 195. For a lucid exposition of Cantor set theory, the reader is referred to this work.

well-ordering an infinite aggregate, there will be a corresponding infinity of ordinal numbers. The cardinal number of an infinite aggregate, however, does not depend upon the order of the elements. Hence, corresponding to a given infinite aggregate there is only one cardinal number, but an infinity of ordinal numbers. Concerning this astounding result Cantor wrote: "The conception of number which, *in finito*, has only the background of enumeral (Anzahl),[35] splits, in a manner of speaking, when we raise ourselves to the infinite, into the two conceptions of *power* . . . and *enumeral* . . .; and, when I again descend to the finite, I see just as clearly and beautifully how these two conceptions again *unite* to form that of the finite integer." [36]

Peirce's theory of ordinal number differs from Cantor's in that for Peirce ordinals designate place in a sequence rather than the sequences themselves. Hence to reach the infinite, Peirce must generalize Cantor's notion of limit: "the finite system is a *teres totus atque rotundus*. Nothing can be added to it. But there is another kind of *nextness* which can be introduced without modifying any of the above definitions. Namely a grade may be 'next', — not to any one grade, but to an endless series of grades . . . Cantor denotes that which is 'next' to the whole series of finites by the ordinal $\omega$." [37] Thus $\omega$ represents the place "after" the endless sequence of finite ordinals. Furthermore Peirce follows Cantor in making transfinite addition noncommutative. Thus he writes, there are "two ways in which a unit may be added to an endless series [sequence], namely by incorporation into the series, or by immediately following the endless series . . . " (4.332) This leads to the result that $1 + \omega \neq \omega + 1$.

If we represent the places following $\omega$ by $\omega + v$, and we allow v to take all finite values, we obtain a new series $\omega + 1, \omega + 2 \ldots \omega + \omega = 2\omega$.

Peirce states:

Then comes $2\omega + 1 \ldots 2\omega + \omega = 3\omega$ and so on, until he [Cantor] has an endless series of endless series of ordinals. To say that there is a *next* grade to this seems to me a new extension of the idea of nextness, since *this* next is neither *next* to any grade nor *next* to any endless series of grades, but is only

---

[35] "Enumeral" means "ordinal," "power" may be taken here to mean "cardinal."
[36] Cantor, *Transfinite Numbers*, p. 52.
[37] Peirce to Judge Russell, September 18, 1908, p. 6.

next to an endless series of endless grades. Here therefore it seems to me clearly that we have a new kind of afterness . . . [38]

Here again a generalization of "after" is required which stands to the series $\omega + 1$ . . . $v\omega + v$ as $\omega$ stands to the series of finite ordinals. The new limit number is $\omega^2$. We then have $\omega^2 + 1, \omega^2 + 2$ . . . $\omega^3 + 1$ . . . $\omega^k + 1$ . . . $\omega^\omega$ and so on. And beyond these there lie yet further infinite series of ordinals $\omega^{\omega^{\omega^{\cdot^{\cdot^{\cdot}}}}}$ . . . $\omega^{\omega^{\cdot^{\cdot^{\cdot}}}}$ .[39] As Peirce notes the series can be extended even beyond ordinals for which we can write the symbols.[40] The series of transfinite ordinals is thus unending, compounding infinity upon infinity *ad infinitum*.

In dealing with the finite numbers, Peirce made multitudes and cardinal numbers special cases of the ordinals. The "multitude" of a collection was defined as the ordinal place which it has in the sequence of collections ordered by the relation "greater than." "Cardinal numbers" were defined as ordinals used in counting, and have the characteristic that when a collection has been counted by a segment of the sequence of cardinals, the final cardinal is both the cardinal number of the collection and equal to the multitude of the collection. Thus we have two ways of establishing the multitude of a collection — by determining its place in the sequence of collections of increasing size and by counting. That these two methods coincide is true only in the finite case: as soon as infinite numbers are reached the coincidence ends and Peirce's theory breaks down on several scores. First, if the multitudes are the successive ordinal places occupied by collections in the sequence of collections of increasing size, the successor to the collection occupying the $\omega$th place ought to occupy the $\omega + 1$-th place. Accordingly, to every member of the sequence $\omega, \omega + 1, \omega + 2, \ldots$ there ought to correspond a distinct multitude. But since the same collection can be so ordered as to be countable by the segment of ordinals terminating with $\omega$, or with $\omega + 1$, or with $\omega + 2$, or with any member of the sequence $\omega, \omega + 1, \ldots$ , this result is obviously inconvenient at best. Peirce tries to resolve this problem by the following strategy:

[38] *Ibid.*, p. 7.
[39] Fraenkel, *Set Theory*, pp. 289, 301f.
[40] Peirce to Judge Russell, September 18, 1908, p. 7.

Cantor simply speaks of $\omega^2$ without regarding himself as introducing any new conception; and his reason is that the *multitude* is unchanged. That is to say there is an order of counting according to which $\omega^2 = \omega$. But it seems to me the better way of expressing this would be to say that the multitude of infinites, or transfinites, as he calls them, depends on the order of the count, and that the minimum count of $\omega^2$ equals that of $\omega$.[41]

It is important to note that Peirce regards the *multitude* of the collection as varying with the order of the count. He then invokes the rule "that the multitude of a collection is not the last ordinal in this or that count of it, but is the earliest ordinal that can count it, the count varying according to the order of counting." [42] Thus a class of multitudes, as determined by the method of counting, corresponds to a single multitude, determined by place in the sequence of collections of increasing size, and the rule correlating multitude and ordinal place is revised to read: (1) the true multitude of a collection is given by the earliest ordinal that can count it, and (2) the next greater collection to a given collection does not necessarily occupy the next ordinal place, but occupies the place of the earliest ordinal that can count it.

Second, Peirce's concept of cardinal number involves a mixture of what in Cantor's theory are ordinal and cardinal ideas, and the differentiation between these two sorts of numbers which occurs when the infinite is reached divides Peirce's concept of cardinal into three incompatible notions. First, in the finite case, the cardinal of a collection is equal to the multitude of the collection of cardinal numbers (including o) less than the given cardinal. Peirce preserves this meaning of cardinal in the notion of "arithm." The "arithm" of a collection is the multitude of multitudes less than the multitude of that collection. (4.213) But this definition renders the notion of arithm useless in the infinite case because — for reasons to be explained below — Peirce held that the collection of all multitudes was only denumerable and therefore $\aleph_0$ is the only infinite arithm. (4.213) Second, in the finite case, the cardinal number of a collection always equals the multitude of that collection. But since the connection between cardinals and multitudes depends upon the multitude of cardinals $<$ n being equal to n, and since this theorem becomes ambiguous in the infinite case, as

[41] *Ibid.*, p. 7.
[42] *Ibid.*, p. 8.

the notion of arithm shows, the term "cardinal" also becomes ambiguous. Peirce sometimes restricts it to mean arithm (4.657), but at other times he uses it as a synonym for "multitude" (4.674), and accordingly the term really ceases to have any clear meaning. Third, the primary significance of "cardinal number" in the finite is that of vocables used in counting. In the infinite this meaning is wholly abandoned, and counting is made a purely ordinal function.[43] Thus Peirce's concept of "cardinal number" breaks down in the transition to the infinite and becomes almost useless.

Thirdly, and most important, Peirce's theory utterly fails to deal with simple sparse sequences rather than with their elements and so fails to distinguish clearly between cardinal and ordinal numbers. Since his ordinals are themselves merely places in a sequence, the only means Peirce has for comparing sequences is by counting. But as was noted above, the fact that the ordinal place 10 is after the ordinal place 5 does not, in Peirce's theory, establish anything about the relations between the sequences of five and ten members. Accordingly, it is never made clear precisely what is established by counting a sequence. For the number thus attached to the sequence is not properly a multitude because (1) multitude belongs properly to a collection rather than to a sequence, and (2) since a given collection can be ordered in many ways, sequences having different counts may be correlated with a single multitude. Nor is this number an ordinal, since ordinals are not properties of sequences but of places. The result is a confused situation in which Peirce attempts to class Cantor's ordinals and powers together under the term "multitude," and so comes to use the term ambiguously as referring to the magnitude of both sequences and collections.[44]

Just as there are transfinite ordinals, so there are also transfinite multitudes, and to the theory of these we must now turn. Peirce defines the finite multitudes in general in a rather unique but quite legitimate manner — namely, as the multitudes of collections to which the syllogism of transposed quantity applies. This syllogism was first introduced by De Morgan in 1847 (4.103), and may be illustrated by the following:

[43] As, e.g., in the passage last quoted above.
[44] Peirce to Judge Russell, September 18, 1908, p. 7.

Balzac, in the introduction of his *Physiologie du mariage*, remarks that every young Frenchman boasts of having seduced some French woman. Now, as a woman can only be seduced once, and there are no more French women than Frenchmen, it follows, if these boasts are true, that no French woman escapes seduction. If their number be finite, the reasoning holds. [6.114]

The transposition of quantity consists in the interchange of universal and existential quantifiers. The inference is legitimate just in case the population of France is finite. For if every S is a P, and there are just as many S's as P's, then if the number is finite, every P is an S. (3.288) If the number is infinite, however, the inference fails, for since infinite sets have proper subsets "equal" to themselves, there could still be P's not S's. In other words, the validity of the syllogism of transposed quantity rests upon the principle that the part is always "less" than the whole, and this principle holds only for sets which are finite. Peirce calls such sets "enumerable" to emphasize the fact that their enumeration can be completed. (4.182) [45]

The smallest infinite multitude Peirce calls the "denumerable" (4.188f), and following Cantor he symbolizes it by the sign $\aleph_0$ — aleph-null.[45a] The collection of the natural numbers is a typical example of such a collection. The defining criteria of a collection of this multitude are that the syllogism of transposed quantity does not apply but that reasoning by mathematical induction does. Since it is not true of such collections that the part is always "less" than the whole, the Fundamental Theorem of Arithmetic does not hold for them. (4.187)

For the generation of the higher multitudes, Peirce relies upon a theorem which is often called "Cantor's theorem" — namely, that $2^n > n$ for all cardinals n.[46] The importance of the theorem lies in the fact that if a collection has n members, then the number of subcollections contained in the collection (including the null-collection) is $2^n$. Accordingly, given any collection, k, of n members, the so-called power-collection of k, which has for members all the subcollections of k, has $2^n$ members and is greater than k. Hence it follows that every collec-

---

[45] In the following pages, I will use the terms "enumerable" and "denumerable" in Peirce's sense.

[45a] More exactly, Peirce uses various symbols for this multitude, and where he uses the letter aleph he does not attach the subscript 0, but to avoid otherwise inevitable confusion, I have added the subscript throughout.

[46] Stephen Cole Kleene, *Introduction to Metamathematics* (New York, 1952), p. 15.

tion is "less than" another collection — namely, its own power-collection.

The second grade of infinity, which Peirce calls the "primipostnumeral" (4.200), or the "first abnumeral" (4.200), multitude, is the multitude of the power-collection of a collection of denumerable multitude, and is accordingly symbolized by $2^{\aleph_0}$. The third grade is called the "secundopostnumeral" (4.215) and is symbolized by $2^{2^{\aleph_0}}$ ; the fourth the "tertiopostnumeral" (4.217) and is symbolized by $2^{2^{2^{\aleph_0}}}$ ; and so on. The method of generation can obviously be continued indefinitely, provided no contradiction arises.

From the constructions thus far given, it would seem that the sequence of multitudes and the sequence of ordinal numbers are both endless. This is equivalent to saying that there is no greatest ordinal and no greatest cardinal — a proposition which appears evident from the fact that $2^n > n$ for all values of n. But a paradox of considerable complexity here presents itself, for, Peirce argues, the proposition that there is no greatest multitude leads to an absurdity. Thus he writes:

Now suppose collections one of each postnumeral multitude, or indeed any denumerable collection of postnumerable multitudes, all unequal. As all of these are possible their aggregate is *ipso facto* possible. For aggregation is an existential relation, and the aggregate exists (in the only kind of existence we are talking of, existence in the world of noncontradictory ideas) by the very fact that its aggregant parts exist. But this aggregate is no longer a discrete multitude, for the formula $2^n > n$ which I have proved holds for all discrete collections cannot hold for this. In fact writing Exp. n for $2^n$, (Exp) $\aleph_0^{\aleph_0}$ is evidently so great that this formula ceases to hold and it represents a collection no longer discrete. [4.218]

A second and in some ways clearer statement is as follows:

Suppose we form a collection containing as parts, first, all the finite whole numbers, then all collections of finite whole numbers, then all collections of such collections, then all collections of these collections, and so on. As long as this series terminates, it forms a collection whose multitude is that of the collections of the last collections added, and a greater multitude exists. But nothing prevents the terms of this series being denumeral; for since there is a denumeral collection of finite whole numbers there can equally be a denumeral collection of these successive collections. In this case, there are no last collections added. Nor is there any such multitude, nor does the series form a collection. For if it did the collections of its ultimate parts would be these ultimate parts themselves, except for the finite whole numbers which would be wanting from among those last collections. Hence, the collections of its ultimate parts would be no more multitudinous than the ultimate parts themselves, which we have seen to be absurd.[47]

Let us for the moment disregard the question of discreteness and try to analyze the idea of this greatest collection. The argument depends upon the following theorem: "If M is a set of sets, and if to each member m of M there is another member m′ of M such that $\overline{\overline{m}} < \overline{\overline{m}}′$, then $\overline{\overline{m}} < \overline{S(M)}$ for every member m of M."[48] Now, Peirce argues, consider the collection K of collections $k_1$, $k_2$, $k_3$, . . . where the k's have the multitudes $\aleph_0$, $2^{\aleph_0}$, $2^{2^{\aleph_0}}$, . . . $2^{2^{2^{\aleph_0}}}$ . . . Taken in this order, each member of this collection has the multitude of the power collection of the preceding member. Hence by Cantor's theorem for any $k_x$ of K, there is a member $k_y$ such that the multitude of $k_x$ is less than the multitude of $k_y$. Therefore the sumcollection S(K) must have a multitude greater than that of any member $k_x$ of K. Thus, if we write the power-collection of k as Uk, then S(K) = $\overline{\overline{(k + Uk + UUk + UUUk + . . . )}}$ and $\overline{S(K)} > \overline{UUU}$ . . . Uk, no matter what member of the sequence k, Uk, UUk, . . . our UUU . . . Uk may be. But, Peirce argues, since the sequence k, Uk, UUk, . . . is endless, it is at least denumerable. Therefore the multitude of S(K), which is greater than that of any member of the collection K, must be at least equal to $2^{2^{2^{\aleph_0}}}$ where the sequence of 2's is denumerable. Peirce symbolizes this multitude by $2^{\aleph_0}$. Since the addition of a finite number of elements to a denumerable collection does not increase the multitude of the collection, it follows, according to Peirce, that $2^{\aleph_0} = 2^{2^{\aleph_0}}$ — i.e., the addition of another "2" cannot

---

[47] "Map Colouring," pp. 9f.

[48] Kleene, *Metamathematics*, p. 16. The symbols $\overline{m}$ and $\overline{\overline{m}}$ stand for the ordinal and cardinal numbers of the collection m. S(M) is the sumset of the set M — the set of members of members of M. Hence the members of S(M) are the members of all the m's.

increase the denumerable sequence represented by $2^{\aleph_0}$. But $2^{2^{\aleph_0}}$ is the multitude of the power-collection of the collection of multitude $2^{\aleph_0}$. It therefore follows that there is a collection, namely that whose multitude is $2^{\aleph_0}$, which is equal to its own power-collection. In other words, for a collection of multitude $2^{\aleph_0}$, Cantor's theorem is false, for $2^{2^{\aleph_0}} = 2^{\aleph_0}$ is equivalent to $2^n = n$. But since Cantor's theorem is proved true for all values of n, this is contradictory.

Despite its seeming plausibility, the proof is fallacious. The error arises from the failure clearly to distinguish $2^{\left(2^{\aleph_0}\right)}$ from $\left(2^2\right)^{\aleph_0}$. Symbols of the type $2^{2^{\aleph_0}}$ means the $2^{\aleph_0}$th power of 2, not the $\aleph_0$ power of $(2^2)$. For the latter quantity, by virtue of the rules for exponentiation for transfinite cardinals, is equal to $(2^2)^{\aleph_0} = (2^2)^{\cdot\aleph_0} = 2^{\aleph_0}.$[49] Hence the order of the exponents is not immaterial: the symbol $2^{2^{\cdot^{\cdot^{\cdot^{2^{\aleph_0}}}}}}$ really means

$$2^{\left(2^{\cdot^{\cdot^{\cdot^{\left(2^{\aleph_0}\right)}}}}\right)} \quad \text{not} \quad \left(2^2\right)^{\cdot^{\cdot^{\cdot^{2^{\aleph_0}}}}}$$

, although the difficulties of writing such a sign make the conventional omission of parentheses necessary. The addition of a further 2 may therefore occur in two different ways — either by incorporation into the sequence or by attachment after the sequence, corresponding to the ordinal additions $1 + \omega$ and $\omega + 1$. In the latter case, the 2 is added at the bottom of the series — graphically

$$\left(2^{2^{\cdot^{\cdot^{\cdot^{2^{2^{\aleph_0}}}}}}}\right)_\omega$$

— and does not therefore leave the value of the expression unchanged. Accordingly $2^{2^{\aleph_0}} > 2^{\aleph_0}$ and the paradox fails.[50]

---

[49] Fraenkel, *Set Theory*, p. 152.

[50] For this analysis of Peirce's paradox and of the error involved in it I am indebted to John Myhill.

But although Peirce has failed to produce a case in which $2^n = n$, it does not follow that no genuine case exists. In fact, there is such a paradox, called the paradox of the greatest cardinal, which was discovered by Cantor in 1899. The paradox is as follows: "Consider the set of all sets; call it M. By Cantor's theorem, $\overline{\overline{UM}} > \overline{\overline{M}}$. Also, since M is the set of all sets, and UM is a set of sets (namely, the set of the subsets of M), $UM \subset M$. Hence, . . . $\overline{\overline{UM}} \leqq \overline{\overline{M}}$; and so . . . not $\overline{\overline{UM}} > \overline{\overline{M}}$." [51] Even though Peirce failed to produce this paradox, the paradox he attempted to establish had some of the essential features of Cantor's paradox — namely, it is a case of $2^n = n$ and is based on the idea of a greatest cardinal. Accordingly, Peirce's solution to his own paradox, in so far as it involves only these ideas, will hold equally for Cantor's paradox, and is therefore of more than historical interest.

Peirce formulated his paradox of the greatest multitude in 1897 in a rather extended paper on "Multitude and Number." (4.170ff) Yet nowhere in this paper is mention made of Cantor's theory of ordinals or of the method of generating transfinite multitudes by number-classes, although these considerations are obviously relevant to his proof of the paradox. In fact, Peirce virtually ignores the theory of transfinite ordinals until after 1905 (4.331f) and does not really come to grips with it until 1908 and 1909.[52] It is tempting to seek an explanation of this fact in terms of the time at which he read various of Cantor's papers, but such an explanation will not do. The first papers of Cantor's which Peirce read were those in Volume II of *Acta Mathematica*, and one of these, "Fondements d'une théorie générale des ensembles," contains a very clear and precise explanation of the theory of ordinals, of number-classes, and of the alephs. Some other explanation must therefore be sought, but before turning to that task, it is first necessary to describe briefly the relevant portions of Cantor's theory.

It will be recalled that in Cantor's theory, the ordinal numbers $\omega$, $\omega + 1, \omega + 2, \ldots$ are ordinals of the well ordered sets of the same cardinality, $\aleph_0$. Let the collection of all such ordinals corresponding

---

[51] Kleene, *Metamathematics*, p. 36. The paradox is a special case of Russell's paradox and is eliminated by the theory of types or by set theory.

[52] See particularly the correspondence between Peirce and Judge Russell in Scientific Correspondence.

to a given cardinal — i.e., whose correspondent well ordered sets have a common cardinal — be called a "number-class." In the case of the finite numbers, the correspondence between cardinals and ordinals is one-to-one, and the concept of number-class is trivial. To avoid an initial infinity of such number-classes, therefore, let us call the class of finite ordinals the first number-class. The second number-class is the class containing $\omega, \omega + 1, \ldots$ all of which correspond to the cardinal $\aleph_0$. It is clear from the definition of these ordinals that they form a well ordered set. It can then be shown [53] that this set has a limit which is greater than any of its members; and this limit we call $\omega_1$. That is to say, the ordinal number of the well ordered set of ordinals of the second number-class is greater than any member of the second number-class. Furthermore, the cardinal of the well ordered set whose ordinal is $\omega_1$ is greater than $\aleph_0$ and is denoted by $\aleph_1$. Similarly, to the cardinal $\aleph_1$ there corresponds a third number-class, $\omega_1, \omega_1 + 1, \omega_1 + 2, \ldots$ The limit of the infinite set of ordinals of the third number-class is $\omega_2$ and the corresponding cardinal is $\aleph_2$. In general, the class of ordinals corresponding to a given cardinal $\aleph_a$, ordered according to the magnitude of the ordinals, has the cardinal $\aleph_{a+1}$, and the ordinal $\omega_{a+1}$.[54] Obviously this method may be continued to reach higher and higher numbers. In each case the cardinal corresponding to the initial ordinal of the new number-class, i.e., $\aleph_0$ to $\omega$, $\aleph_1$ to $\omega_1$, etc., is the cardinal of a well ordered set, and these cardinals Cantor calls the "alephs." [55]

Cantor's theory thus provides two distinct methods of generating transfinite cardinals: the method of power-sets depending upon the theorem $2^n > n$ for all values of n, and the method of number-classes. We so obtain two distinct series (sequences), $\aleph_0$, $2^{\aleph_0}$, $2^{2^{\aleph_0}} \ldots$ and $\aleph_0, \aleph_1, \aleph_2, \ldots$ The question therefore arises, how are these two series related? There are actually two distinct problems involved here: are the two series related at all? if so, how? The first question is the question of comparability: is it possible for there to be two sets, A and B, such that A is neither equal to B nor less than B nor greater than B? If such incomparable sets exist, the consequences for mathe-

[53] Fraenkel, *Set Theory*, pp. 281f, 299f.
[54] *Ibid.*, p. 302.
[55] *Ibid.*, pp. 298ff.

matics are extreme since the whole theory of the relations among cardinal numbers must be revised. But it is not possible to prove that all sets are comparable without an additional axiom; the most that can be done is to prove that all well ordered sets are comparable. It was for this reason that Cantor limited the term "aleph" to cardinals of well ordered sets. Indeed, Cantor wished to restrict the term "cardinal number" to well ordered sets as well, and to call cardinals generally by the term "powers." [56]

The consequences of admitting incomparable sets are so severe that Cantor and his successors sought to avoid them by introducing as a postulate the principle that every set can be well ordered. This principle is unprovable and must be taken to be one of the basic postulates of set theory.[57] It may be stated in many forms; usually it is called the axiom of choice [58] although other forms are possible — i.e., the multiplicative axiom of Russell.[59] But in any form its effect is the same: it prohibits incomparable sets. By so doing it guarantees that all cardinals are alephs, since every cardinal is now the cardinal of a well-ordered set. Accordingly, the members of the power series are alephs; what remains to be determined is what alephs they are. Despite almost desperate efforts, Cantor was never able to answer this problem — the most he could do was to conjecture that $2^{\aleph_0} = \aleph_1$. This conjecture is known as Cantor's continuum hypothesis. In a more general form, known as the general continuum hypothesis, the conjecture is that $2^{\aleph_v} = \aleph_{v+1}$. If the hypothesis is true, it correlates the power series and the alephs and so solves the problem of their relation. Yet in spite of some sixty years of intensive work by the foremost of mathematicians, including Cantor, Hilbert, Gödel, and many more, no one yet knows whether it is true or not.[60]

[56] *Ibid.*, p. 306.

[57] *Ibid.*, pp. 306–308.

[58] *Ibid.*, pp. 309f.

[59] Russell, *Introduction to Mathematical Philosophy*, pp. 117f.

[60] To date, the most important result obtained is that of Gödel, which proves that the conjectured equality cannot be disproven within set theory as it now stands. In other words, the hypothesis of equality is consistent with the axioms of set theory. From this result it follows that if the conjecture is disproved, then something is wrong with the axioms of set theory. And Gödel has observed that "against the numerous plausible propositions which imply the negation of the continuum hypothesis, not one plausible proposition is known which would imply the continuum hypothesis. Therefore one may on good reason suspect that the rôle of the continuum problem in set theory will be this, that it

Since Peirce does not tell us either the history of his own doctrine of ordinals or his reasons for not employing number-classes, any explanation of the evolution of his thought on this question must be somewhat conjectural. Nevertheless, I believe that the general line of development can be traced. It will be recalled from the discussion of the relation between ordinals and multitudes given earlier that in passing to the infinite Peirce was forced to revise his rule governing the relation as follows: the true multitude of a collection is given by the earliest ordinal which can count it, and the next greatest collection to a given collection does not necessarily occupy the next ordinal place, but occupies the place of the earliest ordinal which can count it. From this rule it follows that, if $2^{\aleph_0}$ is the multitude of the collection next greater than the collection of multitude $\aleph_0$, then the ordinal corresponding to $2^{\aleph_0}$, which we may define to be $\omega_1^*$, is the earliest ordinal which counts the collection of multitude $2^{\aleph_0}$. Our problem then is to determine which ordinal $\omega_1^*$ is. Since by definition $\omega_1^*$ is the earliest ordinal which counts any collection of multitude $2^{\aleph_0}$, the multitude of the set of ordinals less than $\omega_1^*$ must equal $2^{\aleph_0}$ by the definition of a count and of equality for sets. $\omega_1^*$ is therefore according to Peirce the place after the first $2^{\aleph_0}$ ordinal places, and the problem is to determine what collection of ordinal places beginning with o and taken in order of magnitude has the multitude $2^{\aleph_0}$. I suspect that Peirce reasoned as follows. Since $\bar{\omega} = \aleph_0$, $\omega_1^*$ is after $\omega$. Moreover transfinite numbers are not changed by the addition of or multiplication by finite numbers, so that $\omega_1^*$ is after the series $\omega + 1$, $\omega + 2 \ldots 2\omega, 2\omega + 1, \ldots 3\omega. \ldots$ The limit of this series is $\omega^2$, but $\bar{\omega}^2 = \aleph_0^2 = \aleph_0 \cdot \aleph_0 = \aleph_0$. The same is true for $\omega^3$, $\omega^4$, $\ldots$ up to $\omega^\omega$ but $\bar{\omega}^{\bar{\omega}} = \aleph_0^{\aleph_0} = 2^{\aleph_0}$. Therefore Peirce concluded $\omega^\omega = 2^\omega = \omega_1^*$. Here, however, Peirce has fallen into a serious error. He deals with ordinals as if they were cardinals. He failed to discover the difference between exponentiation for ordinals and for cardinals. Evidently he was misled by assuming that the same rule of correspondence exists between $\omega$ and $2^\omega$ which exists between $\aleph_0$ and $2^{\aleph_0}$, and he also falsely correlated $\omega^\omega$ with $\aleph_0^{\aleph_0}$. These errors are likely and

will finally lead to the discovery of new axioms which will make it possible to disprove Cantor's conjecture." Kurt Gödel, "What is Cantor's Continuum Problem?," *American Mathematical Monthly*, LIV, 524 (November 1947).

would be easy for a pioneer in the then new field.[61] But as a result of this confusion, I think Peirce was led into two further errors. First, he believed the initial numbers of the number-classes were $\omega$, $\omega^\omega$, $\omega^{\omega^\omega}$, . . . , all of which are actually members of the second number-class, and second, he concluded that the equivalences

$$\bar{\omega} = \aleph_0$$

$$\bar{\omega}^{\bar{\omega}} = \bar{2}^{\bar{\omega}} = 2^{\aleph_0}$$

$$\bar{\omega}^{\bar{\omega}^{\bar{\omega}}} = \bar{2}^{\bar{2}^{\bar{\omega}}} = 2^{2^{\aleph_0}}$$

guaranteed the relation between number-classes and power sets so that by definition the power sets "are really the alephs although differently defined." [62]

If in fact Peirce did fall into these errors, it would have been entirely natural for him to develop the theory of multitude without reference to number-classes, for their introduction would have been redundant. But he must also have believed that the series of ordinals $\omega$, $\omega^\omega$, $\omega^{\omega^\omega}$, . . . is the entire series of ordinals and that there are no further ordinals beyond it. For since these ordinals correspond to the multitudes $\aleph_0$, $2^{\aleph_0}$, $2^{2^{\aleph_0}}$, . . . and since there are no multitudes beyond this series, if there were ordinals beyond the series $\omega$, $\omega^\omega$, $\omega^{\omega^\omega}$, . . . there would be a collection of ordinals greater than any collection — i.e., Peirce's paradox of the greatest multitude would recur in full force. All that would be required, therefore, to bring Peirce's theory to grief would be some reason for believing that still greater ordinals existed. Just what brought Peirce to this conclusion we do not know but that he reached it by May 8, 1908, is strongly suggested by the following letter which he wrote on that date:

Nobody ever doubted (by nobody I mean nobody worth considering) the possibility of the aleph multitudes and I am the author of the first proof of the general proposition that there is a multitude greater than any given multitude. But what has been doubted and what I *think* Russell is right in what he *means* when he says that the question is one of logic not of mathematics, (and I have done a great deal of work upon it) is those $\omega$ multitudes (I mean the multitudes corresponding to $\omega$ numbers) [of] Cantor which surpass all

[61] Fraenkel, *Set Theory*, pp. 285f.
[62] C. S. Peirce to F. W. Frankland, May 8, 1908, p. 4, Scientific Correspondence.

the alephs, and of which the peculiarity is that two collections of such multitude can neither of them be related to the other so that if the one be called the collection of As and the other the collection of Bs, there is any relation in which every A stands to some B to which no other A is in that relation, nor the converse.[63]

It is quite clear that Peirce meant to exclude by this means only collections greater than the members of his denumerable series of comparable collections, but the result is to throw the whole theory into confusion. For clearly, to say a collection is greater than another is to say that the two are comparable; if they are incomparable neither can be said to be greater than the other. The admission of such collections thus throws the entire theory of transfinite sets into confusion, and accordingly it need no longer be true that the power series is a series of alephs.

What apparently drove Peirce to take so ill advised a step was the fact that if such collections are admitted to be comparable, his paradox recurs in full force. Therefore, he argued, there can be no such multitude, and since the collection exists, it must be incomparable. But to maintain that such collections of ordinals are incomparable is certainly not tenable, for they are by definition well-ordered collections and therefore they are comparable. The better solution would have been to abandon the limit on the number of multitudes of collections, but this Peirce believed undesirable.

By the fall of 1908, Peirce had recognized that the axiom of choice could not be so lightly denied, and that he must therefore face the recurrence of the contradiction. As he wrote to Judge Francis Russell:

Of course there will be a next to any endless series of numerates which is not next to any numerate, and there will be a next to an endless series of endless series of numerates which is neither next to an endless series of numerates each having next to another [sic], nor is next to any numerate, and there will be a next to an endless series of endless series of endless series of numerates and so on indefinitely. And then (what we can only express indirectly by a sign describing a sign,) the whole lot of numerates expressible by "series of series" etc. is supposed itself to have a next; though it is not evident that that does not land itself in an absurdity. This method Cantor supposes to be carried out endlessly; and he assumes (I can find no attempt

---

[63] *Ibid.*, pp. 1–3.

to prove it) that in this way his grades will attain every possible multitude. But that is an entirely illogical assumption. For I have proved that every multitude has a higher multitude, the plural of all plurals of M's being always greater than the plural of all M's. If Cantor has really proved, as he says he has that by his method, starting from $\omega$ he reaches $2^\omega$ (or as he expresses it, $\omega^\omega$, which is the same multitude) and $2^{2^\omega}$ and $2^{2^{2^\omega}}$ and so on indefinitely, then he certainly has ordinals that count a series greater than any collection. But his multitudes being themselves a collection, and not skipping but always advancing to the next, it is impossible they should count a series more multitudinous than themselves; so that there must be an error somewhere. It may be the fallacy lies in not observing that the multitude of a collection is not the last ordinal in this or that count of it, but is the earliest ordinal that can count it, the count varying according to the order of counting. Or it may be owing to his not having proved that none of his descriptions of ordinals involve any absurdity. Schönflies agrees with me that Cantor has not proved all he thinks he has.[64]

One sees here both the identification of $2^\omega$ with $\omega^\omega$ and the fact that it is evidently the limit of the series $\omega$, $\omega^\omega$, $\omega^{\omega^\omega}$, . . . which is the trouble maker. The passage also shows Peirce's ambiguous use of the term "multitude" to refer to both series and collections, and his adherence to the thesis that series are compared only by counting. Yet by July of 1908, Peirce had already stumbled upon a clue to one of his errors. In a fragment written in July of 1908(8.G–1908), he wrote:

The positive integers form the most obviously denumeral system. . . . So does a Cantorian collection [65] in which the endless series of all positive integers is immediately followed by $\omega_1$, and this by $\omega_1 + 1$, this by $\omega_1 + 2$, and so on endlessly . . . in short, any system in which every member can be described so as to distinguish it from every other by a finite number of characters joined together in a finite number of ways, is a denumeral system. . . . Consequently whatever can be arranged in a block of any finite number of dimensions can be arranged in a linear succession. Thus it becomes evident that any collection of objects, every one of which can be distinguished from all others by a finite collection of marks joined in a finite number of ways can be no greater than the denumeral multitude. (The bearing of this upon Cantor's $\omega^\omega$ is not very clear to my mind.) [4.639]

[64] Peirce to Judge Russell, September 18, 1908, pp. 7f.
[65] Peirce calls a collection "Cantorian" if it is well ordered.

The passage strongly suggests that Peirce was starting to question the status of $\omega^\omega$. Once Peirce had rid himself of the error concerning the initial numbers of the number-classes, his difficulties were at least partly resolved, for he could now take the series $\omega$, $\omega_1$, $\omega_2$, . . . as correlated to his series of multitudes. In fact this is done explicitly in a paper of 1909.

There is no $\omega$-abnumerable collection; which is a corollary drawn by me from my proof that $2^x$ is always greater than x. There is no multitude greater than the finitely-abnumerable multitudes. Consequently, the total multitude of possible multitudes is denumeral. The *objects* of *any* abnumerable collection are in greater multitude than all multitudes. The reason, of course, is that the addition of a unit to an infinite collection never increases its multitudes. But that new unit will always carry a new ordinal number. If therefore, we extend the term "cardinal number" so as to make it apply to infinite collections, a multitude of ordinal numbers will be possible exceeding that of all possible cardinal numbers in any infinitely great ratio you please, without having begun to exhaust the ordinals in the least. [4.674]

The concept of number-class here achieves at least partial clarity. It will be noted that in this passage Peirce uses "cardinal number" as equivalent to multitude, while counting is made purely an ordinal function. His contention is that since the total series of multitudes is only doubly denumerable, while all abnumerable collections contain more than a denumerable number of members, it follows that every abnumerable collection has more members than the collection of all multitudes. Though puzzling at first, this situation is the legitimate outcome of Peirce's curious ordinal theory. In the series of ordinals

$$1,2,3, \ . \ . \ . \ \omega,\omega+1,\omega+2, \ . \ . \ . \ \omega_1,\omega_1+1, \ . \ . \ . \ \omega_2, \ . \ . \ . \qquad (1)$$

only certain ordinals determine multitudes — namely

$$1,2,3, \ . \ . \ . \ \omega, \ . \ . \ . \ \omega_1, \ . \ . \ . \ \omega_2, \ . \ . \ . \qquad (2)$$

for it is the earliest ordinal that counts a collection which gives its multitude. What Peirce still assumes is that the set of terms of the series (2) is only denumerable. But since each ordinal of (2) counts a collection, then, by the definition of a count as a one-to-one correspondence, the set of the subseries of the series (1) of $\omega$'s less than $\omega_n$, for $n > 0$, is more than denumerable. Thus any abnumerable collection has more members than there are multitudes. So far there is no problem. But the crucial question for Peirce is, whether the collection constituting the set of the terms of the series (1) is not greater than any member of his denumerable series of abnumerable collections. Had Peirce followed Cantor's theory of number-classes strictly he would of course have had to admit this but the conclusion does not follow from his own theory. For Peirce's ordinals refer to places in a series, not to series themselves: accordingly the series (1) does not have an ordinal, nor does it necessarily have any limit which could serve as the initial number for a greater aleph. This is why the Burali-Forti paradox [66] does not arise for Peirce; there is no ordinal of the series of ordinals since ordinals are not properties of series. Peirce is not therefore committed to holding that there are ordinals beyond the elements of the series (1), nor does there appear to be any way in which it can be proven on Peirce's theory that the multitude of ordinals is super-abnumerable. Thus Peirce escapes the problems raised by the number-classes and so he is not forced to abandon the limit on the series of multitudes.

There are objections which can be raised to this interpretation of Peirce's ordinal theory. For example, in 1909 Peirce asserted that the greatest unsolved problem in set theory was the proof of the axiom of choice (4.675). But if the interpretation given above were true, every collection would be countable by the ordinals, and since the series of ordinals is well-ordered, it would follow that every collection is well-ordered. Again, in 1909, Peirce wrote, "Yet so far as I know . . . it has never been exactly proved that there are no multitudes between two successive abnumerable multitudes." (4.656) But Cantor had already shown that there are no intermediaries between the successive alephs,[67] so if all multitudes are alephs, the proof had been given. More important, however, the assumption that the power series is the aleph series is equivalent to the acceptance of the general continuum hypothesis. But the question of whether or not there are

---

[66] The paradox of the greatest ordinal was discovered by Cesare Burali-Forti in 1897 and is usually called by his name. Russell states the paradox as follows: "It can be shown that every well-ordered series has an ordinal number, that the series of ordinals up to and including any given ordinal exceeds the given ordinal by one, and (on certain very natural assumptions) that the series of all ordinals (in order of magnitude) is well-ordered. It follows that the series of all ordinals has an ordinal number, $\Omega$ say. But in that case the series of ordinals including $\Omega$ has the ordinal number $\Omega + 1$, which must be greater than $\Omega$. Hence $\Omega$ is not the ordinal number of all ordinals." (Whitehead and Russell, *Principia*, I, pp. 60f.)

[67] Cantor, *Transfinite Numbers*, pp. 59f, 206.

intermediate multitudes is a special form of the same hypothesis, and if Peirce had already accepted the general principle there would be no reason to question it in particular cases. Nevertheless, these difficulties do not seem to me to be fatal. I suspect that his concern over the axiom of choice relates specifically to the problem of potential aggregates where counting is impossible.[68] In respect to the continuum hypothesis, despite Peirce's identification of the aleph series with the power-class series, it is not at all clear to me how one would prove on his theory that there are no multitudes between successive abnumerable multitudes. In fact, it would seem to me that the differences between Peirce's theory and Cantor's would make it impossible to show this.

Yet the question still remains, why should Peirce's handling of the ordinals have differed so radically from Cantor's? The answer lies, I believe, in the fundamentally different attitudes which the two men held toward the nature and function of the ordinals. Whereas in Cantor's work, the cardinal numbers are given priority as being logically simpler than the ordinals, Peirce held precisely the opposite position. For him the concept of ordinal number is prior to and more general than that of cardinal number or multitude: "ordinals are the general, multitudes the special." [69] Strictly speaking, the sole function of Peirce's ordinals is to express relative position in a simple sparse sequence (4.337). The ordinals themselves simply name "places" which are relative characters determining classes of members of such sequences. Thus the ordinals, as classes, are more general than their members, among which are the collections to which multitudes are attributed. Actually, however, Peirce's definition makes the ordinals members of themselves since they are ordered by the same relation of simple sparse sequence, and this fact introduces a curious duality into his theory. The ordinals not only "express" relative place, they illustrate it, and in fact Peirce seems to have regarded them as the type or exemplar of the order in which they stand. Thus he writes: "But the highest and last lesson which the numbers whisper in our ear is that of the supremacy of the forms of relation for which their tawdry outside is the mere shell of the casket." (4.681) The result

[68] See below, pp. 278f.
[69] Peirce to Judge Russell, September 18, 1908, p. 5.

of this doctrine is curious, for it seems as if Peirce were seeking a definition very like that which was developed by Frege and Russell in which the ordinals are the typical members of equivalence classes.[70] The fact that Peirce did not develop his theory in this way is to be attributed, I think, to three basic differences between his point of view and theirs. First, in arguing that the ordinals are prior to the multitudes, Peirce holds that whereas the doctrine of multitude involves the use of one-to-one correspondences as well as a relation of sequence, the theory of ordinals involves only the latter. On this ground he holds that ordinals are logically simpler than multitudes (4.337) and therefore constitute the prior doctrine. But obviously the development of the Cantor-Russell ordinals is impossible without the use of one-to-one correspondences. Second, Peirce attempted to distinguish between a serial relation and a series. Let us first be clear as to the true relation between these two concepts. Russell has put the matter concisely:

A *series* is the same thing as a serial relation. It might have been thought that a series should be the *field* of a serial relation, not the serial relation itself. But this would be an error. For example, 1,2,3; 1,3,2; 2,3,1; 2,1,3; 3,1,2; 3,2,1 are six different series which all have the same field. If the field *were* the series, there could only be one series with a given field. What distinguishes the above six series is simply the different ordering relations in the six cases. Given the ordering relation, the field and the order are both determinate. Thus the ordering relation may be taken to *be* the series, but the field cannot be so taken.[71]

But Peirce regarded his ordinals as exemplifying the pure serial relation which is instanced in all series. That is, he seems to have thought that the pure ordinal places express the relation in a simple sparse sequence in abstraction from any particular members — i.e., as a sequence of "places" for members into which particulars could be put to form a sequence.[72] Any particular sequence then constitutes an ordering of a given collection as field by assigning each member of the collection to a place. Thus the series is, so to speak, an intermediary between the

---

[70] Russell, *Introduction to Mathematical Philosophy*, pp. 56f.

[71] *Ibid.*, p. 34.

[72] "But *ordinals*, in general, are designations of *grades*, each grade being possibly occupied by what I will call *numerates*, or subjects of numeration." Peirce to Judge Russell, September 18, 1908, p. 5.

serial relation and the field. Finally, underlying this division of series and serial relations is Peirce's belief that magnitude cannot be attributed to a relation itself. Since on the Cantor-Russell theory, the series is the serial relation, the ordinal numbers are really relation numbers.[73] But for reasons which will be made clear in Chapter XIV,[74] Peirce believed that all pure relations are continuous, and therefore, if they have any multitude at all, it is the multitude of the continuum. Hence Peirce could not accept Cantor's theory since from his point of view it confounded the relation of ordinals and multitudes, confused series and serial relations, and falsely attributed magnitude to relations themselves.

It is one of the obvious results of this situation that Peirce's theory of series is ambiguous. The series constitutes for him an application of the serial relation to a collection constituting the field of the relation. The result is that the series is treated as a kind of quasi collection. As a series its members have positions designated by ordinals, but as a collection it has a multitude which is determined by the use of the one-to-one correspondence constituting a count. The number assigned to the sequence by the count is not an ordinal number, for ordinals do not apply to sequences and do not involve the use of one-to-one correspondences, nor is it an ordinary multitude. Yet since counting is a one-to-one correspondence the resulting number belongs in some sense among the multitudes, and we therefore find Peirce using the term "multitude" ambiguously for both series and collections.

Assuming that Peirce's proof of his paradox is correct (although it is not) he has shown that there is a greatest collection and that there is no greatest collection. To resolve this contradiction several courses were open to him. He could have denied the existence of any transfinite collections; or he could have developed his theory of abstraction levels into a theory of types similar to Russell's; or he could have denied that the greatest collection is the same kind of collection as the lesser ones by, for example, distinguishing between sets and classes. The last approach is the one which Peirce took, but in a rather unique form.

To describe this development, it is first necessary to define what

[73] Russell, *Introduction to Mathematical Philosophy*, pp. 56f.
[74] See below, pp. 317ff.

Peirce meant by the term "discrete." Something is discrete if and only if it possesses a unique designation. (4.172) Any entity which has a designation possessed by no other entity of the universe is discrete, and no entity not possessing such a designation is discrete. Accordingly, Peirce holds that three sorts of entities may be discrete: *haecceities*, entities possessing nonrelative qualities per se, and entities in one-to-one correspondence with entities already discrete. (3.568) Let us analyze these in order.

*Haecceity* is a *term* derived from Scotus and used by Peirce to designate the peculiar nature of existential things. The *haecceity* of something consists of its *thisness* — its brute insistency on being this particular thing here and now. (1.405; 3.434) As this statement suggests, Peirce does not regard terms such as "this," "that," "here," "now," or terms serving as spatiotemporal coordinates as qualities; rather they are regarded as indexes or indicators having a purely denotative role. (3.434) If this doctrine be granted, it follows that the Identity of Indiscernibles does not hold for *haecceities*; two things may have identical properties yet be distinct in their spatiotemporal properties. (4.198) Accordingly, Peirce holds that a *haecceity* can never possess a quality per se — a quality in the possession of which its individuality consists — for if it did it would have to be identical with anything also possessing that property, even if this other thing had different spatiotemporal coordinates.

On the other hand, Peirce does regard collections as possessing qualities per se — namely, their defining properties. (3.537n1; 4.390; 4.649) The statement is imprecise since taken strictly it would imply that every class is a member of itself whereas what Peirce meant was simply that every class had a defining property which is unique. Since discreteness depends upon unique designation, it would be better to say that every class can be named by an expression involving its defining property — namely, "the class of all x's such that $\phi x$." This statement would be true in Peirce's theory since every class has a defining property and every property defines a class. (4.171; 4.649)

*Haecceities* and collections, and entities in one-to-one correspondence with *haecceities* and collections, are discrete. The importance of this distinction becomes apparent in relation to Peirce's theory of primal order. A finite collection may be composed of *haecceities* or of collections — an infinite one cannot be composed entirely of *haeccei-ties*. For, "no arrangement of an enumerable collection has any different properties from any other arrangement; for the units are or may be in all respects precisely alike, that is, have the same *general* characters, although they differ individually, each having its proper designation." (4.198) In this respect there is a striking difference between enumerable and denumerable collections, for:

Every [denumerable] collection has a *primal* arrangement, according to its *generating relation*. There is one unit, at least, which arbitrarily belongs to the collection just as every unit of an enumerable collection belongs to that collection. But after that one unit, or some enumerable collection of units, has been arbitrarily posited as belonging to the collection, the rest belong to it by virtue of the general rule that there is in the primal arrangement one unit of the collection next after each unit of the collection. Those last units cannot be all individually designated, although any one of them may be individually designated . . . this primal arrangement is an arrangement according to a general rule, and its statement constitutes, therefore, general differences between the units of the denumerable collection . . . any unit whatever of a denumerable collection may be individually designated, as well as all those which precede it in the primal arrangement. And these can be all exactly alike in their general qualities. Yet there must always be a latter part of the collection which is not individually designated but is only generally described. In this part we recognize an element of the ideal being as opposed to the brute and surd existence of the individual. [4.198]

A collection of *haecceities* must therefore be finite; but an infinite collection may still be composed of discrete entities although not all of them can be *haecceities*. The element of ideality does not vitiate this, for although all of the members cannot be individually designated, any member can be. (4.178; 4.211)

The admission of this ideal element does not prevent the comparison of collections or operations upon them. Thus Peirce argues:

. . . it is not necessary actually to construct the correspondence. It suffices to suppose that a certain number of units of the two collections having been brought into such a relation (and, in fact, they always are in such relations), then the general rules of the genesis of the two collections necessitate the falling of all the other individuals into their places in the correspondence. [4.178]

Hence the presence of the ideal element does not affect the relations among collections.

Peirce then gives the following theorem concerning discreteness.

. . . if a collection is not too great to be discrete, that is, to have all its units individually distinct, neither is the collection of sets of units that can be generally formed from that collection too great to be discrete.

For we may suppose the units of the smaller collection to be independent characters, and the larger collection to consist of individuals possessing the different possible combinations of those characters. Then, any two units of the larger collection will be distinguished by the different combinations of characters they possess, and so being distinguished from one another they must be distinct individuals. [4.180]

Thus every member of the denumerable series of transfinite collections is a discrete collection, since each after the first is the power collection of its predecessor. The element of ideality increases as we ascend the series, for the portion of the collection which is not completely enumerable constantly increases. Thus of the primipostnumeral Peirce remarks that "in the primipostnumeral multitude the same phenomenon is much more marked. It is impossible to designate individually all the units in any part of a primipostnumeral multitude." (4.211) Yet since any given unit can be designated, he holds that "notwithstanding a certain incipient cohesiveness between its units, it it a discrete collection . . . " (4.211) All the collections in the abnumerable series of collections are thus discrete. (4.217) But the limit of this series is not discrete. For if it were, there would be a yet greater discrete collection — namely, its power collection; but as Peirce believed he had shown, no such collection could exist. The paradox of the greatest multitude is therefore resolved by denying that the greatest collection is a collection of discrete members. And since this collection has no discrete members, it cannot have a power collection, nor can it be a sumcollection. The series $k + Uk + UUk + \ldots$ has no sum in the strict sense, but it does have a limit which is, according to Peirce, the linear continuum. "Since then there is a multiplicity or multiplicities greater than any discrete multitude, we have to examine continuous multiplicities . . . although it is true that a line is nothing but a collection of points of a particular mode of multiplicity, yet in it the individual identities of the units are completely merged, so that not a single one of them can be identified . . . " (4.219) This doctrine rests on two basic assumptions; that there are collections of possibilities, and that these collections have linear order. In respect to the first, Peirce asserts:

Remembering that the word "potential" means *indeterminate yet capable of determination in any special case,* there may be a *potential* aggregate of all the possibilities that are consistent with certain general conditions; and this may be such that given any collection of distinct individuals whatsoever, out of that potential aggregate there may be actualized a more multitudinous collection than the given collection. Thus the potential aggregate is, with the strictest exactitude, greater in multitude than any possible multitude of individuals. But being a potential aggregate only, it does not contain any individual at all. It only contains general conditions which *permit* the determination of individuals. [6.185]

Linear continua are thus the collections of all the possibilities consistent with the general laws which serve to define them. They contain no actualities, for Peirce holds, "It thus appears that true continuity is logically absolutely repugnant to the individual designation or even approximate individual designation of its units, except at points where the character of the continuity is itself not continuous." (4.220) But that all potential collections are of the simple sparse type is an assertion for which Peirce was never able to find a satisfactory proof. Since he identified simple sparse ordering with well ordering (4.675), this proposition is equivalent to the axiom of choice. Peirce recognized perfectly the basic character of this principle and regarded its proof as the most pressing problem of set theory. (3.538–549)

In addition to the quantitative definition of continuity given above, Peirce has also given us a qualitative definition in terms of what he called "Kanticity." Something is Kantistic according to Peirce if and only if "every part has itself parts of the same kind." (3.569; 6.168) This definition is not equivalent to infinite divisibility, although Peirce confounded the two in his first formulation of Kanticity (6.120f) — rather it is a denial that ultimate parts exist. For every such part must itself be capable of division, so that no ultimate parts are ever attained. Thus Peirce remarks: "It seems necessary to say that a continuum, where it *is* continuous and unbroken, contains no definite parts; that its parts are created in the act of defining them and the precise definition of them breaks the continuity." (6.168) Thus, understanding that by "part" is here meant definite and therefore actual part, the qualitative definition in terms of Kanticity and the quantitative definition in terms of multitude come to the same thing.

Cantor held, as do analysis and coordinate geometry, that the power of the n-dimensional continuum must be the same as the power of the set of real numbers. Peirce's theory of the continuum is a denial of this assumption: the multiplicity of the continuum according to him is infinitely greater than $2^{\aleph_0}$. But how is such an assertion to be proven? Continuum is a concept of geometry; the collection or set is a concept of the theory of sets and is generally regarded as a logical or arithmetic concept. To say that a given collection is a continuum implies in some form a unification of arithmetic and geometry.

From the very beginning of history, the division between arithmetic and geometry has been the fundamental division in the house of mathematics. It has never been bridged. But in the theory of abstract sets we have attained the nearest approach to a unification of these fields that has been, or is likely to be achieved. Through set theory the fundamental notion of arithmetic — the notion of number — has received for the first time a precise and adequate definition. Indeed, as Cantor, Frege, Russell, Whitehead, and their successors have shown, the whole of arithmetic can be deduced from logic, of which set theory is a fundamental part. On the other hand, the theory of sets is the foundation of modern topology, and as we have already seen, topology is the most general form of current geometry.[75] Thus Fraenkel remarks:

The theory of sets forms a mathematical branch which unites in itself an arithmetical-discontinuous attitude (preferred as the starting point in modern mathematics) and the feature of continuity predominating in geometry and analysis, which in Greek mathematics was widely accepted as the primitive basis . . . In a certain sense set theory may thus be considered as the fundament of mathematics in general.[76]

But the unification is, and must remain, incomplete. The relation of topology to set theory is the same as the relation of metric geometry to projective, or of projective geometry to topology. Set theory is presupposed by modern topology, but modern topology cannot be logically deduced from abstract set theory. The "points" which are assumed as primitive in topology appear simply as elements, or members, of sets

[75] Lefshetz, *Topology*, p. 3.
[76] Fraenkel, *Set Theory*, p. 330.

in abstract set theory, and are undistinguished from any other such elements. Sets of points, to which are added properties which allow us to define relative positions of points in the set, are called "spaces"; "the added properties or relations, and properties or relations definable from them, we can call *geometric*." [77] Such spaces may be metric, if relative position is established by introducing a distance function, or they may be nonmetric, in which case the positions are usually defined by "neighborhoods." [78] Special sets of points, which are definable in terms of the geometric properties, are called geometric figures, complexes, or configurations.[79] But these complexes, and spaces themselves, are not logically reducible to the theory of abstract sets alone: the geometric properties are essential and these must be added to set theory to give us topology.[80]

The set theoretic formulation of topology is a work of very recent date, and belongs to the present century.[81] But the possibility of using set theory to unify arithmetic and geometry was recognized by Cantor, for, according to Felix Klein:

. . . Cantor would (as he himself told me in 1903 at the meeting of the natural scientists in Cassel) achieve, in the theory of assemblages [sets], "the genuine fusion of arithmetic and geometry." Thus the theory of integers, on one hand, as well as the theory of different point continua, on the other, and much more, would form a homogeneous group of equally important chapters in a general theory of assemblages.[82]

It will be recalled from the preceding discussion that topology as it existed before 1900 was chiefly combinatorial topology — the study of spatial configurations or complexes. In order to place this form of topology upon a set theoretic foundation it was necessary to find a method of defining the primitive concepts of combinatorial topology — which included "line" and "surface" — in terms of "point" and "set."

[77] Raymond Wilder, *Introduction to the Foundations of Mathematics* (New York, 1952), p. 179.

[78] *Ibid.*, p. 178.

[79] *Ibid.*, p. 179.

[80] *Ibid.*

[81] Nicolas Bourbaki, *Topologie Générale* (Paris, 1951), 125–129. Raymond Wilder, *Topology of Manifolds*, American Mathematical Society Colloquium Publications (New York, 1949), XXXII, 10–16.

[82] Felix Klein, *Elementary Mathematics from an Advanced Standpoint: Arithmetic — Algebra — Analysis* (New York), p. 266.

And the primary difficulty in achieving this lies in defining the property of continuity, which is possessed by geometric lines and surfaces, in terms of noncontinuous, discrete entities such as points. Intuitively it seems impossible that this should be done, for continuity and discreteness appear to be mutually exclusive terms; yet it was one of Cantor's outstanding achievements to have accomplished just this seemingly "impossible" task. The method he used was to demonstrate that a collection of entities having the multitude of the set of real numbers, and over which certain order relations are defined, possesses every property of the continuum, and may accordingly, for all purposes, be treated as the continuum.[83] And in particular, where the entities in question are "points of a real line" the continuum is the geometrical continuum. Upon the basis of this principle, it is then possible to define all geometrical entities in terms of sets of points of various kinds, and even space itself becomes a particular kind of set.[84]

Peirce's denial that the multiplicity of the continuum is equal to that of any discrete multitude whatever is thus a direct denial of Cantor's theory. If Peirce is to sustain his position, he must therefore show two things: (1) that the continuum as he defines it has all the properties which the mathematical continuum must have, and (2) that his definition is superior to any other, particularly to Cantor's. In respect to the first of these requirements, it is obvious that the chief difficulties are presented by the calculus and analytic geometry, for on Peirce's theory the limit of a convergent series of intervals on the geometric line will be an interval rather than a point. Peirce's theory thus implies, as it was meant to imply, the reality of infinitesimals. (3.569f) In fact, this doctrine follows directly from the property of Kanticity, since every part of a line must be a line interval capable of division. Accordingly all positions on a plane are not uniquely paired to number couples of Cartesian coordinates: rather these coordinates define a network covering the plane, the points of intersection of which comprise only a small part of the positions on the plane itself. But so far as the operations of analytic geometry or the calculus are concerned, no significant differences result from Peirce's theory. Equations may still define figures, it being assumed that passage from one point to another of the

---

[83] Bertrand Russell, *The Principles of Mathematics* (New York, 1950), pp. 276–303.
[84] Wilder, *Topology*, pp. 2f, 12–15.

coordinate network involves passage through all intermediaries. In the calculus, infinitesimals had long been used, and the difficulties which arise from them are not difficulties in operation but in conceptual clarity. Thus Peirce's definition of continuity can be used in mathematics: the real question is whether or not there is any reason to adopt it. Accordingly, Peirce must show that his definition is superior to Cantor's.

Against Cantor's theory of continuity Peirce employed two arguments: first, he held that it does not provide an adequate basis for topology, and therefore is not a satisfactory reconstruction of the continuum concept; second, he held that its use leads to contradiction. Let us examine these arguments in order. The first depends upon the Listing theorem and makes explicit a principle which Listing took for granted — namely, that every topological continuum either contains its limits or returns to itself. This may be illustrated as follows. Let the line o–1 be cut at the points x and y. Furthermore, let x and y be both irrational points, and let y be assigned as the least member of the segment c and x as the greatest member of the segment a. Now examine the census value of the line o – 1. Taken by parts we have:

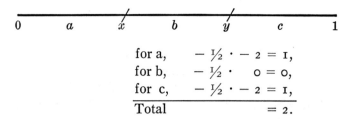

$$\text{for } a, \quad -\tfrac{1}{2} \cdot -2 = 1,$$
$$\text{for } b, \quad -\tfrac{1}{2} \cdot \quad 0 = 0,$$
$$\text{for } c, \quad -\tfrac{1}{2} \cdot -2 = 1,$$
$$\text{Total} \qquad\qquad = 2.$$

But, Peirce would argue, consider the census value of the following complex.

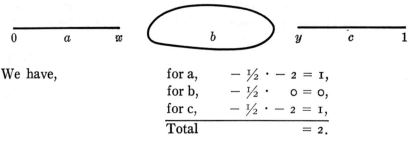

We have,
$$\text{for } a, \quad -\tfrac{1}{2} \cdot -2 = 1,$$
$$\text{for } b, \quad -\tfrac{1}{2} \cdot \quad 0 = 0,$$
$$\text{for } c, \quad -\tfrac{1}{2} \cdot -2 = 1,$$
$$\text{Total} \qquad\qquad = 2.$$

Hence a line with such a double cut is equivalent to two lines and a cycle, which is absurd. For cutting a line can never render the line cyclic, since it has the effect either of dialysis or of increasing the chorisis, and in either case the total cyclosis is diminished. Hence since such a cut is possible on a linear point set continuous in the sense of Dedekind and Cantor, such a set is not a geometrical continuum.

It is clear, then, that Peirce is committed to the position that there can be no line segment without end points. Thus he writes:

. . . if there were only one point for each distance from a fixed point among the distances of which the doctrine of limits takes cognizance, then the terminal point of a line might logically be removed, since without falling into any contradiction we speak quite often of all real quantities less than a given value, — $\pi$. . . . Suppose, then, that a line were to extend from the origin of measurement to a distance of $\pi$ units of length inclusive; and let its terminal point at just that distance from the origin be removed. That terminal, or limiting, point being removed, *there would remain no last point*, the line would no longer have any end. This, however, becomes absurd; — not merely impossible, but absurd, — as soon as it is assumed that the line is truly continuous.[85]

Since it is obvious that if we can conceive a line with end points, we can also conceive a line with those end points eliminated, it seems at first that Peirce has fallen into an obvious error. For to hold that when the end point is eliminated, there is still an end point would appear to mean that each point has a point next to it, and this is clearly untrue of any dense, not to speak of continuous, set. But Peirce's argument is not so naive. For if a line is continuous in his sense, it is not a point set at all — in fact, the only two points in such a continuum would be the end points. There is no point next to these end points for the points are breaches of continuity and if there were next adjoining points the line would not be continuous. But if an end point is removed, then, since the line does terminate, there is a break in the continuum, and by definition such a break is a point. Peirce's doctrine is thus not contradictory, and only appears to be so when it is assumed that the linear continuum is a point set.

Peirce's second argument against Cantor's definition rests upon the relation between magnitude notions and continua generally. This argu-

---

[85] "Topical Geometry," pp. 5f.

ment actually takes two forms, depending upon which of Cantor's two definitions of continuity is involved. Cantor's first definition requires two properties of a series which is continuous — it must be "perfect" and "cohesive." By "cohesive" Cantor meant, "We call $T$ a cohesive collection of points, if for any two points $t$ and $t'$ of $T$, for a number $\epsilon$ given in advance and as small as we please, there are always, in several ways, a finite number of points $t_1, t_2 \ldots t_\nu$, belonging to T, such that the distances $tt_1, t_1t_2, t_2t_3 \ldots t_\nu t'$ are all less than $\epsilon$." [86] But as Peirce remarks of this definition, "In the first place, it turns upon metrical considerations; while the distinction between a continuous and a discontinuous series is manifestly non-metrical." (6.121) Clearly, Peirce is right in this objection, for if continuity could not be defined except by distance, then nonmetrical geometries, including topology and projective geometry, would be impossible. Cantor himself subsequently recognized the justice of such criticisms and his later definition of continuity involves no reference to distance.

Nevertheless in the later definition Cantor does maintain that the continuum is a point set of the power $2^{\aleph_0}$, and although this proposition involves no metrical concepts, it does involve concepts of magnitude. Peirce's argument against the second definition is therefore not that it is metrical, but that the attribution of any magnitude notions to the continuum leads to contradiction. And to prove this he points to the famous paradox of Achilles and the tortoise. Achilles and the tortoise run a race. Let the line segment represent the path they cover. Achilles

$P_4 \quad P_3 \qquad P_2 \qquad\qquad P_1$

begins at the right-hand end of the line; the tortoise is given a head start and so begins at $P_1$. Let us assume that Achilles runs twice as fast as the tortoise. Nevertheless the tortoise will always be ahead of Achilles. For when Achilles has reached $P_1$, the tortoise will be at $P_2$; when Achilles is at $P_2$, the tortoise will be at $P_3$; when Achilles is at $P_3$, the tortoise will be at $P_4$; etc. But the tortoise is always ahead of Achilles, and since the number of segments $P_nP_{n+1}$ is infinite, Achilles will never catch him.[87]

Zeno produced a number of paradoxes similar to this one, all of

[86] Russell, *Principles*, p. 288.
[87] Fraenkel, *Set Theory*, p. 11.

which rely on the same basic idea — the completion of an infinite series in a finite time. The fundamental fallacy involved here, according to Peirce, is the assumption that Achilles must pass through any determinant series of segments at all. As he points out in discussing a similar paradox: "We must not allow ourselves to be drawn by the word 'endless' into the fallacy of Achilles and the tortoise. Although, so long as $r$ has not yet reached the value 3, another year will still leave it less than 3, yet if years do not *constitute* the flow of time, but only *measure* that flow, this in no wise prevents $r$ from increasing in the flow of time beyond 3 . . . " (1.276) This argument is based upon the dictum of Riemann, "that in a discrete manifoldness, the ground of its metric relations is given in the notion of it, while in a continuous manifoldness, this ground must come from outside." [88] To say that Achilles' position at any time is determinate is to say that a measure schema is introduced and that his position is defined in terms of this metric. Since the metric is a system of discrete values, it introduces the fiction that there are discrete points on the line which correspond to its value. But this is, according to Peirce, purely a fiction: the number and relations of "points" are relative to a metric and vary for different choices of the metric. The continuum itself is wholly independent of the metric and of all notions of magnitude. Hence Zeno's paradoxes arise from the confusion of measurement with thing measured. The fact that Achilles' path can be measured in this way relative to a given metric does not mean that it has this character relative to any metric or that the path itself has this character. But if on the other hand it is maintained that the continuum is composed of discrete elements, whether they are segments or points, then the paradox holds. For in that case the basis of the metric is given in the notion of the set of such elements, and Achilles must actually complete the infinite series, which is absurd.

Peirce accordingly holds that to define the geometrical continuum as a collection of discrete points must inevitably lead to contradiction. Hence he holds that the continuum must contain no discrete points at all, except for such as constitute a breach of continuity. Such a discontinuity is always in the form of a topical singularity — a place of lower dimensionality than the whole from which the number of beginning generations is less than from a neighboring place. In the case of

[88] Riemann, "Hypotheses," p. 37.

one-dimensional continua, such a singularity must be a point. Hence to say a line is "cut" or broken is the same as to say it contains a singularity. This is the basis for the argument against the Dedekind cut, for the line segment *b* is held to be an open line yet to involve no terminating singularity. But this, by the Listing theorem, is impossible. Accordingly, Peirce believed that he had shown that Cantor's theory of the continuum was inadequate and self-contradictory while his own fulfilled all the requirements necessary.

Peirce's theory of the transfinite sets, is, to say the least, unique. It leads from finite collections which are absolutely discrete through the denumerable series of abnumerable collections of decreasing discreteness to the wholly nondiscrete linear continuum of pure possibility. The theory thus combines elements of the logistic theory with principles of a decidedly intuitionistic caste.[89] Compare for example Peirce's definition of an infinite collection by its generating relation quoted above with the following definition of a set given by Brouwer.

---

[89] Mathematical intuitionism is a theory of the nature of mathematics which, in its modern form, dates from Kronecker, and has been given its most powerful statement by L. E. J. Brouwer. Following Kant, Brouwer accepts time as a "form of intuition" universally valid for all empirical experience. Time affords us the intuition of an undivided continuum. Brouwer then postulates an operation which he calls "two-oneness," and which consists in separating the undivided continuum into a single element and an undivided remainder, repeating the process to obtain another element, and combining the two elements to form a single one. (Hermann Weyl, *Philosophy of Mathematics and Natural Science*, Princeton, 1949, p. 63.) Repetition of this intuitive process is sufficient to yield all finite numbers, but no matter how far the repetition is carried the undivided remainder remains and is "open towards infinity." (*Ibid.*, p. 37.) Accordingly, the intuitionists object to any theory which treats the infinite as "closed" — as e.g., capable of being treated as a definite, completed whole. They regard the infinite as an undifferentiated continuum of possibility into which we can advance only by finite steps. They therefore require that every number be "constructible" — that it be possible to create the number by the process of successive additions of one. Hence to say that a given number "exists" means, for the intuitionist, that there is a definite method of constructing the number. It follows from this that an existence statement which is not accompanied by a method of construction is meaningless, for unless the number is either shown to be constructible or shown not to exist there is no way of deciding the truth or falsity of the statement. This position requires abandoning the law of excluded middle as applied to nonfinite sets. And this in turn requires a reformulation of logic so as to make the law of excluded middle unprovable. This is usually done by defining the operators "not", "and", "or", and "if-then" independently and in such a way that none of them is definable in terms of the others.

Acceptance of the intuitionist position entails rejection of a large part of the theory of transfinite numbers, since numbers greater than aleph-null are nonconstructible. (For accounts of intuitionism see Weyl, *Philosophy of Mathematics;* Kleene, *Metamathematics*, pp. 46–53; Wilder, *Introduction*, pp. 230–249.)

A *set* is a *law*, on the basis of which if an arbitrary natural number is repeatedly chosen, then each of these choices either generates a definite symbol array with or without termination of the process, or brings about stoppage of the process and rejection of its result; for every $n > 1$ following a non-terminating and non-stopped sequence of $n - 1$ choices, at least one natural number can be given which, if it is chosen as the $n$th natural number, does not bring about stoppage of the process. Every sequence of symbol arrays generated in this manner by an unlimited sequence of choices (which is then generally not presentable in finished form) is called an *element of the set*. The common origin of the elements of a set $M$ we shall usually designate briefly as *the set of M*.[90]

For Brouwer a set is thus a law according to which the elements of the set may be constructed. It is not a finished totality, nor need any particular element of it be a finished totality; nonterminating decimals, for example, may be elements of a set but they are determined only to the extent to which they are constructed.[91] This definition certainly is very similar to that given by Peirce. Nevertheless, Peirce is not an intuitionist. For although Peirce employs intuitionistic distinctions between enumerated, enumerable, and nonenumerable collections, the conclusions which he draws from them are entirely opposed to intuitionism. The difference lies in the attitude toward possibility. Peirce never hesitates to deal with possibilities as forming collections and to extend the operations of classical logic — including the law of excluded middle — to such collections. (6.185f) In fact, it was by invoking collections of possibilities that Peirce believed the paradoxes of set theory could be avoided. No position could be more openly opposed to intuitionism. For the intuitionists regard this use of the possible as responsible for the paradoxes of set theory. Thus in rejecting Russell's analysis of the paradoxes, Weyl writes: "The deepest root of the trouble lies elsewhere: a field of possibilities open into infinity has been mistaken for a closed realm of things existing in themselves. As Brouwer pointed out, this is a fallacy, the Fall and Original Sin of set-theory, even if no paradoxes result from it." [92]

Peirce's theory thus stands between those of the intuitionists and the logistic school. Whereas the latter regard elements as a pre-exist-

---

[90] Wilder, *Introduction*, pp. 233f.
[91] *Ibid.*, p. 234.
[92] Weyl, *Philosophy of Mathematics*, p. 234.

ing totality, and the former deny the existence of any elements not constructible, Peirce is willing to admit a pre-existing totality of possibilities but recognizes only a small part of these as actually existent. In spirit, however, Peirce has more in common with the logistic school than with intuitionism. For the heart of the intuitionist position is its empiricist demand that mathematics limit itself to the range of objects it can construct. With such a position Peirce had no sympathy; he accepts unhesitatingly sets and elements which are not constructible in the intuitionist sense. Although Peirce sometimes speaks of the mathematician as "creating" the objects with which he deals, he did not mean this in Brouwer's sense of "construct" but in the sense in which all ideal entities are products of the mind. Peirce was no more willing than Hilbert to abandon the "paradise created by Cantor," [93] paradoxes or no paradoxes.

[93] David Hilbert, quoted in Fraenkel, *Set Theory*, p. 331.

# PART FOUR

# XIV

## *The Later Years*

On December 22 of 1883, Daniel Gilman received the following brief note from Simon Newcomb:

I felt and probably expressed some uneasiness in the course of our conversation the other evening, lest I might have been the occasion of doing injustice to persons whose only wrong had been lack of prudence. I have therefore taken occasion to inquire diligently of my informant, and am by him assured that everything I had said was fully justified. Furthermore, he deemed it part of the obligation of friendship to make known to you the exact state of the case, and would avail himself of the first opportunity to do so.[1]

Almost at once Gilman and the Executive Committee met to consider certain "information" concerning Mr. Peirce. By early January, the committee had made its decision. On January 26 the department was reorganized and Peirce's position was abolished, without however naming him specifically. But the correspondence between Gilman and the Executive Committee makes it perfectly clear that the purpose of the reorganization was to eliminate Peirce.[2]

Why was Peirce fired? No one knows. But since he was on a one-year appointment and the Executive Committee could easily have allowed his appointment to lapse in June, it is obvious that the situation must have been quite serious to require such immediate and drastic action. Moreover, the course of action adopted by the Executive Committee was curiously indirect. After his dismissal Peirce wrote the trustees a scathing twenty-two page letter charging that he had been treated "treacherously and unjustly." There was not a little justice to Peirce's charge. He was not told the real reason for his dismissal. And as he said:

[1] Fisch and Cope, "Peirce at Hopkins," p. 360n103.
[2] Daniel Coit Gilman, fragment of a report to the trustees, November 15, 1884; Gilman Papers.

The resolution of the Trustees was artfully framed to injure me as much as possible.

If it had named me, I suppose it would have failed to pass the board, for I hope you or somebody would have suggested that I be allowed to resign.

But it passed because it was expressed in general terms and extended to all the instructors in the department.

Now all the others have been taken back, the disguise is thrown aside and I am spoken of as dismissed personally by the Trustees.[3]

Furthermore, on the basis of Gilman's assurances early that fall that he was in good standing with the university, Peirce had contracted for a house for two years and had to sustain about a thousand dollars loss in order to free himself of it — a claim which was recognized by the trustees who paid him a thousand dollars compensation. The actions of the trustees had been motivated by the desire to remove Peirce with the least possible publicity, either for him or themselves. As Gilman stated in a report to the trustees, "I am sorry that the desire to treat Mr. Peirce with consideration and equity and to attract as little attention as possible to his release from office, should appear to him in such a different light." Yet the procedure used by the university authorities could be interpreted as indicating incompetence on Peirce's part and it was not therefore entirely just.

Peirce's dismissal had important consequences for both his personal career and his philosophy. Although he had many friends in influential academic positions and a brother who was dean of Harvard College, Peirce never again held an academic position. What had appeared to be an extremely promising university career was thus brought to an abrupt end when he was only forty-five years of age and still in his prime. During the next few years he wrote little and spent most of his time working for the Coast Survey. His temper, which had never been good, now had free rein and he railed against his superiors on the survey, accusing them of unfair discrimination against him. In 1887, having inherited a little money, he retired to Milford, Pennsylvania, and in 1891 he left the survey for good.

From 1887 on, Peirce lived in almost total isolation. Although he kept up a large correspondence and followed the journals at least sporadically, he was not in direct contact with the men who were doing

[3] C. S. Peirce to G. W. Brown, October 1884, pp. 13f, Gilman Papers.

new and exciting work even in his own fields. Many of the difficulties in Peirce's later philosophy could have been avoided if he had known the new developments in logic, mathematics, physics, and other fields. But although Peirce often had the books and journals which contained these new developments, he was too engrossed in his own often erroneous ideas to be bothered with them. Had he been a member of an academic community, that kind of isolation at least would have been impossible, for his students and colleagues would have forced him to keep abreast of the new work. Such was the cost, to Peirce and to American philosophy, of his discharge from Johns Hopkins.

During the remainder of his life, Peirce lived with his second wife at Milford. The ever-loyal James helped to arrange occasional lectures for him, and in 1892 and 1903 he lectured before the Lowell Institute in Boston. James was also responsible for arranging the seven lectures on pragmatism which Peirce delivered at Harvard in 1903 and the two lectures on scientific method which he gave before the Harvard Philosophy Club in 1907. Nevertheless, Peirce's only steady income was from his writings and from the reviews which he wrote for the *Nation* and other periodicals. As the years went by, his financial position steadily declined, partly through his own bad management and partly through progressively diminishing income from his inheritance. Although J. M. Baldwin employed him in 1901 to write most of the articles on logic for the *Dictionary of Philosophy and Psychology*, by 1906 his situation had become so desperate that he was reduced to living on a small fund which James had raised for him by appeals to former students and old friends. He was in virtual penury when he died of cancer in 1914, "a frustrated, isolated man, still working on his logic, without a publisher, with scarcely a disciple, unknown to the public at large." [4]

In the late 1880's, Peirce began to write again, and during the twenty years from 1890 to 1910 he labored with undiminished intellectual vigor at the philosophical system which he called "synechism." This system was never completed, and the twelve-volume elaboration of it which he planned never approached completion. (8.G. c.1893) Indeed, with the tools he had at his command, it seems clear that the system could not have been completed. Nevertheless, Peirce's

[4] Weiss, "Peirce," p. 403.

synechism was the fruit of his entire life's work and the summation of all he had hoped to achieve.

In the following chapters, we shall be concerned with the details of this final system; what needs to be made clear here are Peirce's reasons for constructing it. In preceding chapters, evidence has been presented which should be sufficient to show that, although Peirce was never a theologian, his writings do involve a heavy religious commitment. This is no less true of his first essays in philosophy than of his final writings, despite the fact that the nature of his religious ideas changed considerably during his life. But Peirce was also a scientist, and when the Darwinian controversy erupted in 1859 he found himself caught between two fires. It therefore became one of his chief aims to construct a philosophy which would effect a reconciliation between religion and science and permit scientific men to believe once more — as his father and Agassiz had believed — that science is the study of God's works. It is, I believe, Peirce's desire to achieve this goal which explains the spell which the architectonic concept of philosophy cast over his mind.

The desire to prove that science cannot conflict with religious belief was also one of the primary aims of Kant. In the Critical philosophy, this is accomplished by proving that scientific knowledge is limited to phenomena whereas our religious and moral beliefs pertain to things-in-themselves. In the course of this argument, the theory of architectonics plays an important role, for it is only through this theory that Kant is able to demonstrate theorems concerning the whole of our empirical knowledge. Thus, if it were not for the relation between the categories and the forms of judgment, there would be no way of proving that the list of categories is complete. Whatever its faults, then, the architectonic theory is in essence a way of circumscribing the totality of knowledge so that general theorems can be proven concerning this totality.

The architectonic plays a role in Peirce's philosophy similar to that which it plays in Kant's. Since Peirce denies any division between knowledge of phenomena and knowledge of things-in-themselves, it is clear that if he is to prove religion and science compatible, it must be by showing that no knowledge of any kind can conflict with our religious beliefs. In order to do this, Peirce holds that religion is chiefly a question of sentiment — of the heart (6.493), and that while philosophy may go so far as to hypothesize the existence of God, it cannot go beyond this point. But this requires that Peirce too must be able to circumscribe the scope of empirical and philosophical inquiry in such a way that he can prove general theorems true of this totality, and it is the architectonic which makes this possible. Thus Peirce claims that in his philosophy "a massive foundation has been laid for a philosophy which shall not take for its first axiom a principle utterly irreconcilable with all spiritual truth . . . " (8.G.1893-1895)

The philosophy of continuity is peculiar in leading unequivocally to Christian sentiments. But there it stops. This metaphysics is only an appendix to physics; it has nothing positive to say in regard to religion. It does, however, lead to this, that religion can rest only on positive observed facts, and that such facts may prove a sufficient support for it. As it must rest upon positive facts, so it must itself have a positive content. A series of plays upon words will not answer for a religion. This philosophy shows that there is no philosophical objection to the positive dogmas of Christianity; but the question as to their truth lies out of its province. [8.G.c.1893-1895]

The attempt to create such a philosophy is not unique to Peirce; many men in the age of Darwin faced a similar problem and sought a similar solution. But what is unique to Peirce is the method by which he sought to achieve it. In seeking to develop a fully articulated philosophic system based upon a rigorous logical and mathematical foundation, Peirce chose a road which only Whitehead has since followed. For both men understood that in an age of science, the right to believe cannot be won by ignoring science, still less by combatting science, but only by a path which "lies through the thorniest mazes of a science as dry as mathematics." (8.38) Such was the road that Peirce took.

# XV

# *The Revision of the Categories*

I N Part Two, I have argued that Peirce's work of the 1870's constitutes a revision of his earlier system in the light of the new
logic of relations. But there are several serious objections to this interpretation which require consideration. If this interpretation were
true, one would expect Peirce to have applied himself first to an exhaustive study of the theory of relations, then to a revision of the
categories in the light of the new logic, and lastly to a revision of the
theory of cognition. Yet this is not the order in which he actually proceeded. Between 1870, when his first paper on relations appeared (3.
45–149), and 1880, when the "Algebra of Logic" was published (3.
154–251), Peirce wrote very little on relations — indeed, his contributions to logic in this period are very meager. (8.G.1870–1880)
Moreover, although some tentative attempts at a revision of the categories were made in the late 1870's — e.g. the correlation of Thirdness
with continuity — no thoroughgoing revision was made until 1885.
What Peirce did undertake in the 1870's was only the revision of the
theory of cognition. It would seem therefore that Peirce did not follow the architectonic plan, and that the preceding interpretation is
false.

That in general Peirce did follow the architectonic plan is supported
by so much evidence that it seems to me unquestionable. Why then did
he depart from it in this specific case? The answer lies I believe in the
facts of Peirce's biography. It must be kept in mind that in the early
1870's Peirce was working both for the Harvard Observatory and for
the United States Coast and Geodetic Survey,[1] and he cannot have had
much time free for philosophy. Moreover, it was at just this time that
the Metaphysical Club became operative, and Peirce played a leading

---

[1] Fisch and Cope, "Peirce at Hopkins," pp. 277–279. This study is the general source
for biographical material in this chapter.

part in the discussions of this group. I suspect that his attention was drawn to the theory of inquiry because this question was of interest to the whole club, whereas pure logic and the theory of the categories were not. Actually, the whole of the theory of inquiry was formulated by 1873 and was heavily indebted to the discussions of the club, as Peirce himself has testified.[2] But in 1873 or 1874 the Metaphysical Club ceased to meet, and from then on Peirce became so heavily involved in scientific work that he had little if any time for philosophy. From 1875 on he was repeatedly in Europe on government business. Moreover, it was in this period that his marital problems became serious, leading to a separation from his wife in 1875 and to divorce in 1883. Indeed, from the little we know of Peirce's life in the late seventies, it seems very unlikely that he did any philosophic work at all. His only important publications in these years were the six articles for the *Popular Science Monthly*,[3] and these, although they are among his most famous papers, simply codify the work he had done between 1870 and 1873 rather than break new ground. It is even possible that Peirce might have abandoned philosophy altogether at this time had not William James' letter to Gilman brought him the appointment at Johns Hopkins University in 1879.

Although Peirce held only a part-time position at Hopkins and continued to work for the Coast Survey on the side, nevertheless he found the Hopkins environment highly stimulating and the years he spent there were highly productive. Brought at last into daily contact with men such as Sylvester, Story, O. H. Mitchell, and Thomas Craig, Peirce returned at once to the logic of relations and began the long delayed exploration of the territory he had discovered ten years before. During the next four years, he published steadily on this subject as well as on the theory of probable inference and on purely mathematical subjects (8.G.1880–1884), and he succeeded in communicating his enthusiasm to his students. The collection of papers written by Peirce and his students, *Studies in Logic*, which Johns Hopkins published in 1883 was certainly the most important single volume on logic written in America in the nineteenth century.

Once the new logic was in order Peirce would probably have turned

---

[2] Peirce, "Pragmatism Made Easy," pp. 4–6.
[3] 2.619–644; 2.645–668; 2.669–693; 5.358–387; 5.388–410; 6.395–427.

to a revision of the categories in any case. But the immediate cause of his doing so in 1885 was the discovery by O. H. Mitchell and himself of the theory of quantification.[4] In its implications for the categories, this discovery is second only to that of the logic of relations. For just as the logic of relations suggested to Peirce the correlation between continuity and Thirdness, so it was the discovery of quantification which led to the final revision of Secondness.

It will be recalled that in the "New List," Peirce, like Kant, had based the possibility of a list of categories upon the fact that the manifold of sense must be brought to the unity of a proposition. But for Peirce, unlike Kant, the significance of the proposition lies simply in the fact that it illustrates the sign relation. It is this tripartite sign relation which is the fundamental synthetic relation, and it is only because all synthesis involves this relation that any synthesis may be used to derive the categories — that the propositional synthesis may stand for all others. The categories of the "New List" are the concepts of connection required to make possible this sign relation and may be viewed as an explication of its nature. But at the same time, Peirce's concept of the sign relation is heavily indebted to the traditional subject-predicate theory of the proposition. Thus, the subject of the proposition denotes the object of the sign, the copula expresses being or the possibility of determination of the subject, and the predicate makes this determination. In 1867 Peirce regarded this interpretation as true for all complete sign situations: so in an argument the premisses designate a state of fact which, taken as subject, is determined by the conclusion as predicate. (1.545–559)

The theory of the "New List" had to be abandoned when Peirce's logic required him to abandon the subject-predicate theory of the proposition, and this occurred in 1870 when he discovered the logic of relations. It is essential to the argument of the "New List" that the three kinds of relations should be intermediaries at different levels of abstraction between Being and Substance, for otherwise neither the necessity nor the completeness of the categories can be proven. But the theory of relations shows that the three kinds of relations are equally abstract and that each may serve as a proper predicate. To say that a

---

[4] O. H. Mitchell, "On a New Algebra of Logic," *Studies in Logic*, pp. 72–106; 3.351–354; 3.393 ff.

monadic predicate is joined to its object by a triadic relation therefore solves nothing, for we must then ask, what joins the triadic relation to its subjects, and so on. Thus the logic of relations undercuts the whole concept of the "New List."

The theory of quantification further undermined the "New List" by raising fresh problems concerning the nature of the object. In a paper of 1885 (3.359–403), Peirce makes this connection between quantification and Secondness quite explicit. He first analyzes propositional constituents into two classes of signs which he calls "tokens" and "indices." By a "token" Peirce means in this paper (but not in some others) a symbol, or a sign related to its object only in virtue of a mental association or habit. (3.360) An "index" is then described as follows: "The index asserts nothing; it only says 'There'! . . . Demonstrative and relative pronouns are nearly pure indices, because they denote things without describing them . . . " (3.361) Peirce then shows why indices are necessary.

But tokens alone do not state what is the subject of discourse; and this can, in fact, not be described in general terms; it can only be indicated. The actual world cannot be distinguished from a world of imagination by any description. Hence the need of pronoun and indices, and the more complicated the subject the greater the need of them. The introduction of indices into the algebra of logic is the greatest merit of Mr. Mitchell's system. He writes $F_1$ to mean that the proposition $F$ is true of every object in the universe, and $F_u$ to mean that the same is true of some object. This distinction can only be made in some such way as this. [3.363]

To express the propositions $F_1$ and $F_u$ Peirce introduced the notations Π iFi and Σ iFi respectively which became the standard symbolism of the Boole-Schröder algebra. These are equivalent to the modern forms (x)Fx and (Ex)Fx respectively.

The theory of the index which is here introduced marks a decided break with Peirce's earlier theory. It is true of course that the term "index" was used as early as 1867 to refer to signs "whose relation to their objects consists in a correspondence in fact . . . " (1.558) But there is the important difference between the index of the "New List" and the index of quantification. The index "It" of the "New List" is a concept — namely, the concept of *"the present, in general"* (1.547) — and it does not refer directly to an individual since Peirce then held individuality to be ideal. As I have argued above, this theory, although historically derived from Kant's appendix to the Transcendental Dialectic, is logically the result of the fact that the logics which Peirce employed contained no concept of the individual.[5] The use of the term "index" to mean a sign which refers not to a concept but to an individual directly does not appear until 1885 and its introduction is due to Mitchell's theory.[6] It is at this point that the notion of individuality becomes important for Peirce.

Peirce attributed his new theory of individuality to new developments in logic, but that there is anything in the theory of quantification itself which requires such a theory of individuality is doubtful, the more so since no other modern writer has found it necessary to follow Peirce's lead. In fact, there is nothing in the logic of quantification itself which requires Peirce to abandon his previous theory of the proposition. For as we have seen in discussing the "New List," Peirce's early analysis of propositions makes use of the Scholastic theory of supposition according to which a proposition such as "all S is P" is regarded as affirming "P" of whatever objects x there may be of which "S" is affirmed. Thus the propositional analysis of the theory of supposition is in line with that of quantification, although it is less explicit, and the introduction of quantifiers and variables could very well be viewed as simply a completion and extension of the earlier position. But in the case of propositions of the form "this is red" the adequacy of the earlier theory is less evident. Such a proposition is of the form $\phi a$ where $a$ is an individual and would clearly seem to be incompatible with the analysis of the "New List." So far as I can see, there are only two alternatives open to Peirce in this case. He must either adopt the view that "this is red" does require a pure individual, or he must interpret "this" as a bound variable which serves to link the extension of

---

[5] See above, pp. 131–137.

[6] "He [Royce] seems to think that the real subject of a proposition can be denoted by a general term of the proposition; that is, that precisely what it is that you are talking about can be distinguished from other things by giving a general description of it. Kant already showed, in a celebrated passage of his cataclysmic work, that this is not so; and recent studies in formal logic* [*Peirce's footnote: *Mitchell* in Logical Studies by members of the Johns Hopkins University and *Peirce* in the American Journal of Mathematics, vol. vii] have put it in a clearer light. We now find that, besides general terms, two other kinds of signs are perfectly indispensable in all reasoning. One of these kinds is the *index*." (8.41) See also 3.363.

"red" to the extension of some preceding term. That is, he must regard "this is red" as an incomplete sign which is only interpretable when joined to a prior sign of the same sort, and which asserts redness of the objects in the extensional domain of that prior sign. It is obvious that this latter approach leads to an infinite regress, for every atomic sentence would have to be so interpreted and we should never reach any first sentence which would tell us what we are talking about. Yet this is precisely the alternative taken by Peirce in the "New List" and the 1868 papers on cognition, and he had lived happily with this *regressus ad infinitum* for eighteen years. Why then did he suddenly abandon it in 1885?

In keeping with his architectonic hypothesis, Peirce attributed his revision of the categories to his logic. But I think there are other and more important reasons for this revision. As we have seen in some detail in Chapter VII, Peirce's theory of reality had run into serious difficulties in the late 1870's. This theory of reality is a direct result of the categorical theory of the "New List" and the cognitive theory of the 1868 papers. By denying the existence of first impressions of sense, Peirce had completely sundered the real from perception, so that direct acquaintance with reality cannot be gained by going to the source of our cognitions. The only alternative left therefore was to locate the real at the end of the series of cognitions by defining reality as that which is thought in the final opinion to which inquiry will lead. But Peirce then found himself unable to prove that in fact inquiry will ever lead to any final result and accordingly unable to prove that there is any reality. As a result, Peirce's position degenerates into an extreme form of subjectivism in which we are lost in a phantasmagoric maze of our own concepts. For one who called himself a realist, such a development was intolerable.

Just when Peirce decided that his early theory of reality had to be abandoned we do not know, but it was sometime between 1880 (3.161) and 1890. In the last of the *Monist* papers, Peirce remarked:

Dr. Carus holds that from my social theory of reality . . . the existence of something inevitable is to be inferred. I confess I never anticipated that anybody would urge that. I thought just the reverse might be objected, namely, that all absoluteness was removed from reality by that theory; and it was many years ago that, in my "Theory of Probable Inference," [2.694–754] I admitted the obvious justice, as it seemed to me, of that objection. We cannot be quite sure that the community ever will settle down to an unalterable conclusion upon any given question. [6.610]

The paper referred to does not contain any such statement, but the remark indicates that Peirce had come to this conclusion sometime in the 1880's. Further evidence of his decision can be found in the revisions which he made in the 1877–1878 papers on inquiry when they were rewritten in 1893 as a part of the "Grand Logic." The effect of many of these revisions is to eliminate the assertion that the final opinion will be attained and to replace it by the much milder statement that in order to make certain that inquiry will be pursued it is necessary to hope that the ultimate agreement will come (5.407) — i.e., to change the doctrine from a constitutive to a regulative principle of knowledge. It is true that even after 1890, Peirce does sometimes state the theory of the final opinion in its earlier form but I think these statements are elliptical; his considered doctrine seems to be that the coming of the ultimate agreement is a regulative principle only. (1.405; 2.113; 3.432; 4.61)

If the doctrine that the ultimate agreement will come is abandoned, or transformed into the mere hope that agreement may come, what becomes of the theory of reality? We have already seen that Peirce's theory of reality contains several definitions of reality, not all of which are synonymous. The first definition is that which will be thought in the opinion ultimately agreed upon, and this is the one now given up. The second is that which is independent of what may be thought by you, me, or any limited group — i.e., any group less than the community itself. I have urged above the quite obvious criticism of this definition that it takes for granted the reality of the community and therefore assumes as a premiss what is probably the most difficult part of the whole theory to prove — the reality of other minds. But Peirce's reason for assuming the existence of the community is that if there is to be an infinite process of inquiry there must be an infinite inquirer, and this cannot be a single man. Accordingly, the agreement of observers may be regarded as another aspect of the agreement of different observations, whether made by the same man or not, and so of a coherence theory which holds the real to be that which is thought in the opinion which reduces our experience to coherence. All three of these positions are to be found in

Peirce. With the relinquishing of the demand for an eternal investigator, we may now regard the real as depending upon the coherence of observations. The existence of real objects cannot therefore be asserted a priori, for until observation ends we can never know that what brings present experience to unity will continue to do so, but it can be affirmed as a likely postulate well supported by present evidence.

It is clear that this revision of the definition of the real requires a substantial revision of both the theory of the categories and the theory of cognition. If the real is that which gives coherence to experience, then in order to escape from pure conceptualism it is necessary that that to which coherence is given should involve something other than purely conceptual elements. Yet Peirce's cognitive theory of 1868 makes this virtually impossible for no matter how far we retrace our steps in cognition we never reach anything but concepts. The truth is that Peirce is here between the devil and the deep blue sea. On the one hand, he must have some kind of sensory elements if he is to escape conceptualism. But on the other, this imperative drives him back toward first impressions of sense which he regarded as leading inevitably to Humean scepticism. The 1885 revision of the categories was, I believe, an attempt to find a way out of this dilemma — an attempt which actually took Peirce back to a position more like Kant's than his early one.

Peirce introduced his revised list of categories in 1885 in a paper entitled "One, Two, Three: Fundamental Categories of Thought and of Nature." [7] Instead of deriving the categories from the analysis of the sign relation as he had done in the "New List" Peirce presents them directly as three sorts of logical relations — monadic, dyadic, and triadic. This procedure has the advantage of generality, for all possible logical relations including the sign relation are asserted to belong to one of these three classes. Accordingly, every predicate of a proposition is classified by the schema, so that the categories hold good for all possible cognitions.

The classification of relations by the number of correlates they involve is strictly a matter of formal logic and has no particular con-

---

[7] Parts of this paper are to be found in 1.369–372, 1.376–378. Brief comments on the revised list and on its connection with the theory of signs are to be found in two other papers of 1885 — "On the Algebra of Logic: A Contribution to the Philosophy of Notation" (3.359–403M) and the "Review of Royce." (8.39–54)

nection with empirical knowledge. Remaining on this purely formal level, the next question is what sorts of relations belong to each class. Monadic relatives include absolute terms, or ordinary nonrelative predicates. (1.370) Dyadic relations Peirce classifies as genuine or degenerate, depending upon whether the relative properties derived from the relation would be possessed by those subjects even if the other correlate of the relation were to be eliminated — i.e., irrespective of the relation. (1.365) Thus the relation "as blue as" gives the relative property "blue" which either subject would have independently of the other. But the relation "brother of" yields a relative property which would not be possessed irrespective of the existence of the other correlate. (1.358;1.365) It will be objected that the relation "x is similar to y" would on this reading be a genuine dyad, contrary to Peirce's intent, but I think that here Peirce would hold that the relation is incompletely stated until the respect in which similarity obtains is introduced. In that case, the relation would become a comparative like "as blue as." Triads may be handled similarly. Doubly degenerate triads would be those in which the subjects retain their relative properties independently of the other correlates. Singly degenerate triads would be those in which the dyadic relations among pairs of members would continue to obtain in the absence of any third. For example, the sign relation involves a dyadic relation between sign and object. If this relation would continue to exist independently of the third member of the relation then the relation is degenerate. A genuine triad is a relation in which neither the relative characters of the correlates nor the dyadic relations among pairs of correlates would exist if any of the correlates were eliminated. (1.366f; 1.370–372)

It should be clear from what has been said that Peirce regarded genuine dyadic and triadic relations as irreducible. The justification for this in the case of dyadic relations is easy to see. Every dyadic relation can be construed as a class of ordered pairs, and the pairs can then be defined as a union of unit classes.[8] But in this definition the relation of membership between class and element is assumed so that a dyadic relation must be taken as primitive in any case. But Peirce also holds that triadic relations are irreducible on the ground

---

[8] Willard V. Quine, *Mathematical Logic* (Cambridge, Mass., 1951), pp. 198ff.

that all genuine triadic relations are combinatorial and that all combinatorial relations are triadic. He thus rejects the doctrine of modern logic that a triadic relation can be reduced to dyads — i.e., that $R(xyz) = df\ R(\iota x,y;z)$ where $y;z = df(\iota y \smile \iota(\iota y \smile \iota z))$.[9] From Peirce's point of view this mode of analysis assumes that all triadic relations are degenerate and may be regarded as a relation between an element and a dyadic relation independent of that element. But in what Peirce calls a genuine triadic relation, the relation which holds between any two of the elements would not exist without the third. His favorite example of such a genuine triad is the sign relation. For the relation between sign and object is made by the third or interpretant; the relation between the interpretant and the object is made by the sign which brings its interpretant into that relation; and the relation between the sign and the interpretant exists only through the object which is the common value in the extensional domain. (1.480; 6.32) When Peirce used linear figures to represent relations, he always diagramed the genuine triad as $\lambda$. (4.309f; 4.445) The line figure is the same as that which he used to represent implication, $\prec$ (3.375f), and his use of it here is to indicate that each correlate implies the dyadic relation between the other correlates so that the loss of any correlate would dissolve the relation.

It is the fact that all combinatorial relations are triadic (1.515) which permits Peirce to demonstrate both the irreducibility and the completeness of his categories. They are irreducible because such a reduction could only consist in analyzing them into elements and a combinatorial relation. But since that relation would be itself triadic, no reduction is effected. The list moreover is complete, because once the notions of combination and of elements are available, any higher relation — tetradic, quintic, etc. — can be built up out of combinations of triads. Accordingly, the list contains all the elementary relation forms and only these. (1.363)

Since signhood is a particularly important logical relation, Peirce devoted special attention to its analysis. As one might expect, signhood has three forms. If the relation is doubly degenerate, the sign is an icon: the characters which it derives from the relation it would possess in any case, and so would its object. If the relation is singly degenerate,

[9] *Ibid.*, pp. 198–201.

the sign is an index: it has a real relation to its object independent of any third. If the relation is genuine, the sign is a symbol. (2.247f) All words are symbols, so in the analysis of linguistic signs there are no pure indices or icons. Nevertheless, we may extend these terms to cover linguistic signs provided it is clear that this extension is somewhat metaphorical. Even though there would be no relation between sign and object without the interpretant, a linguistic sign may be called an icon if it is interpreted as expressing a monadic character; an index if it is interpreted as being in a genuine dyadic relation to its object; and a symbol if it is interpreted as standing in a genuine triadic relation to its object. (3.359f)

So far, Peirce's development of the categories is purely formal and involves nothing more than a purely logical classification of relations and the application of this classification to a particular logical relation — that of signhood. In order to give empirical content to these logical schemata, the data of experience are required. From purely logical considerations alone, we can know a priori that whatever relations we experience will fit one of these three classes. But whether our experience contains such elements, and if so what their nature will be, can only be known a posteriori. Peirce had now come to accept Kant's teaching that while the logical form of knowledge can be known a priori, its content must come through sensory experience. The categories of the revised list therefore present a double aspect: in their formal aspect they have to do only with the logical classification of relations while in their material aspect they deal directly with the classification of experience. (1.452)

The revised concept of Firstness is in its formal aspect simply that of a monadic or nonrelative term and is therefore quite compatible with the Firstness of the "New List." But in its material aspect, there are marked differences. In the "New List," Firstness was presented as the most abstract of the categories, and is in fact the embodiment of a pure abstraction. All qualities are Firsts, but the emphasis in the "New List" is on quality as conception — as referring to abstraction. This is partly owing to the fact that Peirce then regarded the proposition as joining an abstract property to a thing, and partly to his desire to stress the conceptual, nonintuitional nature of quality. He did not therefore concern himself with quality as pure sensation — it is quality as predicate determining a class that he is concerned with. But in the 1885 formulation, the emphasis is reversed, and it is precisely the sensory aspect which now comes to the fore. Indeed, pure Firstness in this later, sensory sense does not occur in the "New List" at all. Thus in 1890 Peirce wrote: "The idea of the absolutely first must be entirely separated from all conception of or reference to anything else" (1.357); while in the "New List" the First is that which refers to a ground, and it is the reference to the ground which makes it a First. "The first must therefore be present and immediate . . ." (1.357) But in the "New List" it is the mediate character of quality which is emphasized: "the present in general" is substance. "It precedes all synthesis and all differentiation; it has no unity and no parts" (1.357); yet in the "New List" quality is what brings unity to the manifold. "It cannot be articulately thought: assert it, and it has already lost its characteristic innocence; for assertion always implies a denial of something else" (1.357); yet in the "New List" quality is asserted hypothetically of substance and this assertion makes the judgment which reduces the manifold. "What the world was to Adam on the day he opened his eyes to it, before he had drawn any distinctions, or had become conscious of his own existence — that is first, present, immediate, fresh, new, initiative, original, spontaneous, free, vivid, conscious, and evanescent." (1.357) What Peirce is describing here is obviously something very different from the embodied abstraction of the "New List."

A First is not the same as what is usually called a percept. A percept is an image which has a structure and which combines a number of sense qualities. A pure First, on the other hand, is simple and devoid of structure. But every percept has a First which is the single impression created by the total ensemble of its elements. (1.425) Moreover, if a single sense quality of a percept is prescinded from all the rest and is considered by itself, such a quality is a First. (1.303) A First, then, is a simple, unanalyzable, and independent sensation which is immediately perceived — indeed, its most prominent trait is its lack of mediacy.

Peirce repeatedly speaks of Firsts as "irrational." By such statements he seems to have meant two things. In the first place, pure sense quality is not definable by concepts alone; to be known it must be experienced. In this sense, it is a given of experience which cannot be analyzed or explained and so is not of a "rational" — i.e., conceptual — nature. (5.49) Secondly, Peirce asserts that the suchness of quality is *sui generis* and inexplicable. (1.420; 1.357; 2.85) Again, the point is the contrast between concept and sense quality. Even if our senses were wholly different than they are, so that our sense qualities were quite unlike those we now experience, still as long as we have sense qualities of some kind, and as long as a regular connection obtains between those qualities and their stimuli, our concepts of the world would be unaltered. If we could not perceive color, we should not conceive trees as green and brown, yet our concept of what a tree is, of its nature, composition, and growth would not be changed. It is true that our conceptions of sense qualities would be altered, but not significantly; instead of associating red with a given wave length we should now associate blue, or green, or yellow, with that wave length, but so long as the association was invariable this would no more affect our knowledge than would the substitution of one term for an equivalent. Indeed, sensations are like arbitrary names which our physiological nature gives to certain stimuli — any other name would do just as well.[10] It is this arbitrariness, this lack of derivability from antecedent reasons, which Peirce means to stress in calling Firsts irrational. (2.85; 5.49)

It should be clear from the above that in a strict sense a pure First viewed in its material aspect is not a concept. (1.424) When Peirce talks of red as a First, it is not the concept of red that he means but the particular sensation or feeling which I have when I look at a red thing. The concept of red is an abstract entity predicable of many things; the sensation of red is a peculiar tinge of emotion or feeling. A concept is eminently a rational sort of entity; a feeling is eminently irrational. Since Peirce regards consciousness as being identical with feeling (5. 492; 7.540f), it is really the state of mind or "modification of consciousness" produced by seeing a red thing which is the First. Such a feeling may be a thought-sign of which the concept "red" is the meaning, but it cannot be the concept itself.

But it is one of the most ubiquitous sources of confusion in Peirce's writing that in respect to the status of concepts the material and formal aspects of the categories do not agree. Formally considered, concepts

[10] This is of course Peirce's theory of constitutional nominal hypotheses. See above, pp. 7of.

are monadic predicates; it would therefore appear that they must be Firsts. Yet materially considered concepts are not Firsts but Thirds. The result is at best lack of clarity and at worst downright inconsistency, as in the classification of mathematical objects such as numbers as Firsts. (4.161) [11] Nor can this confusion really be avoided. It is a presupposition of Peirce's formal classification of relations that no relation is at once monadic and triadic. Yet it is precisely the point of pragmatism to show that in respect to concepts this presupposition is false.

Peirce's revision of the category of Secondness was no less radical than his revision of Firstness. In the "New List," Secondness included the concepts of denotation and of the object, but the object itself was never immediately known. Thus, as we have noted, a sentence such as "this is red" is regarded as an incomplete sign in which "this" refers to an object in the extensional domain of the preceding sign, but the object is only specified as one of those for which that preceding sign stands. With the introduction of quantification, Peirce abandoned this theory and interpreted "this" as a sign having the power to designate an existent individual object directly. But how is such a designation possible? If objects are known only through their properties, so that the Identity of Indiscernibles holds true of them, then a sentence of the form "this is red" is always ambiguous, for what thing is this? It can only be the thing possessing such and such properties, for there are no other sorts of things. But then the sentence "this is red" is an incomplete sign, and we do not know what we are talking about until the object is specified. If, on the other hand, we wish to regard "this is red" as an informative sentence, then we must postulate some characteristic of objects in virtue of which they are namable by the nonqualitative term "this," and it is precisely the purpose of the new theory of Secondness to provide such a characteristic — namely, "thisness." Accordingly, it is "thisness" — the characteristic of being designatable unambiguously by "this" — which Peirce now makes his principle of individuation. (3.434; 3.460)

Peirce did not employ the term *haecceity* as an equivalent for "this-

---

[11] It might seem that Peirce's definition of a proposition as involving an icon predicated of an index illustrates this confusion, since it is obvious here that it is a universal rather than a sense quality which is predicated. But that "icon" is really a rhematic symbol and is only a First in a metaphorical sense. (2.261f)

ness" until 1890 (1.405), but there is little doubt that the concept of *haecceity* influenced his formulation in 1885. Peirce had been a student of Scotus since the early 1860's; he was thoroughly acquainted with Scotus' theory of individuation and the parallels between it and his own theory of 1885 are so obvious that they can hardly be accidental. The simplest explanation is that when the theory of quantification and the difficulties in his theory of the real convinced Peirce that a positive nonqualitative principle of individuation was necessary he immediately recognized the Scotian doctrine as supplying precisely the sought-for solution and adopted it for his own.

*Haecceity* is more than just a semiotic device — it is pre-eminently a kind of experience. This experience is probably best rendered as shock. Peirce describes it as involving "resistance," "brute reaction," "compulsion," "interruption," "intrusion," etc. — all of which seems to be aspects of a single experience of shock. (1.334–336; 1.431) Accordingly, *haecceity* is irrational in the sense that it cannot be conceptually defined; it can only be known by ostension — by "hefting its insistency." (6.318)

The possession of *haecceity* is what gives existence to the object. (6.318) Peirce here follows Scotus precisely in making the principle of individuation carry the burden of the existence quantifier, and he thereby resolves the difficulty that only individuals can exist. (3.613) It follows, of course, that existence is not a predicate, and that in Peircean logic the existence quantifier is taken as basic and the universal quantifier is defined in terms of it.[12] And, curiously enough, this theory also has the effect of bringing Peirce back to the Kantian position that existence can never be given in concepts but only in intuition. (A50–52 B74–76)

The possession of *haecceity* therefore confers upon its object both individuality and existence. But it does not necessarily confer externality. (1.376) Peirce usually gives three tests for externality: (1) direct inward effort to suppress the apparition, (2) appeal to other observers, (3) tests by physical concomitants and effects. (6.334) Thus the externality of an object is inferred, not perceived, whereas *haecceity* is perceived, not inferred. (1.376) Nor is the experience of *haecceity* proof of reality. Realities may be internal or external. A hallucination

---

[12] 4.404. The unenclosed dot is equivalent to "(Ex)".

refers to nothing real; yet the fact that the hallucination occurred is a real fact. Similarly, there can be hallucinations of *haecceities* just as there can be hallucinations of anything else. There are thus real *haecceities*, but reality does not consist in *haecceity*. (5.503; 6.349)

Since *haecceity* is a nonqualitative experience, the question immediately arises whether *haecceities* can occur without being conjoined with qualities. It is obvious that there is no logical reason why this should not happen — *haecceity* does not imply quality nor conversely. But such a state of affairs, though interesting, would be inconvenient; if objects are to serve as loci for clusters of qualities, a world full of delinquent *haecceities* is best done without. Both Scotus and Peirce reject such a possibility by conceiving *haecceity* as the final or last determination of an already determined nature. (1.456f) [13] In Peirce's view the *haecceity* is the limit of an endless series of determinations. (1.456f) The same effect is achieved by Peirce's explicit assertion that all *haecceities* are subject to the laws of excluded middle and non-contradiction. (3.613) Again, the definition of *haecceity* does not imply subjection to these laws nor the converse, but if these laws do apply then every *haecceity* would have qualitative determinations.

There is however a paradox here which is of considerable interest. In the 1860's Peirce denied the existence of individuals on the ground that no real object can satisfy these laws. Any object which exists at all, Peirce then argued, exists for some time. But in any interval of time, no matter how small, there is some change. Such change must involve a passage from Fx to $\sim$ Fx, for some property F relative or absolute — otherwise there would be no change. Therefore, for any state of an object x, Fx and $\sim$ Fx. (3.93n1) The crux of this argument lies of course in the question of whether or not there are indivisible states of an object — i.e., instantaneous states. In the 1860's Peirce held that there were not, and the argument was based upon the impossibility of distinguishing such a state by general properties — i.e., on the fact that such a state would be individual and Peirce then had no concept of independent individuals. Accordingly, the introduction of *haecceity* ought to resolve the problem by supplying such a concept — the instantaneous state should now be specifiable by indices. And indeed the problem would be solved if it were not for one unfortunate

[13] Boehner, "Scotus," p. 104.

fact, namely, that by Peirce's theory no qualities can exist in an instant.[14] Therefore, even if *haecceities* have instantaneous states, they can have no qualities during those states.

It is obvious that this difficulty results from Peirce's determination not to admit first impressions of sense and his attempt to differentiate qualities from impressions by making the former endure through an interval while the latter are instantaneous. So long as temporal status is used to effect this distinction, therefore, the paradox is a genuine one, and Peirce must either admit first impressions or render his definition of *haecceities* vacuous.[15] The first alternative Peirce steadfastly refused to adopt (6.492), but the second was no more inviting. It was not until the formation of the normative theory of inquiry after the turn of the century that he found a satisfactory solution to this dilemma. For in the normative theory, the distinction between first impressions and qualities is redefined in terms of conscious control rather than time, and Peirce is then able to admit instantaneous qualities while still denying first impressions. (1.343; 2.85)

I have already suggested that Peirce's revision of the categories was an attempt to escape from the subjectivism in which the collapse of his theory of reality left him. In one sense, the theory of *haecceity* is a curious and inspired answer to this problem, for it brings Peirce back into contact with something which can be taken as a starting point in cognition and it does this without falling prey to the dangers of the Identity of Indiscernibles. That is to say, Berkeley's annihilation of matter is achieved by abstracting and subjectifying every property of matter. When this has been done, there then remains no matter whatever, since the matter is known only through the properties. But if each thing qua thing possesses *haecceity* then the abstraction of properties is not sufficient to destroy its identity; the *haecceity* remains, and since it is not a property it cannot be abstracted. Wherever there is *haecceity* there is individuality and thinghood, and experience is therefore not resolvable into a series of eternal states or qualities — it contains elements of another nonconceptual variety.

*Haecceity* is the material aspect of Secondness — it is an experience

---

[14] See above, pp. 70f, 118f.

[15] If there were no instantaneous qualities, the laws of excluded middle and of non-contradiction would hold vacuously of *haecceities*.

rather than a concept and is indefinable. But in so far as this experience is a reaction, it does involve a genuine dyadic relation and therefore is wholly consistent with the formal aspect of Secondness. Not all genuine dyads, however, involve *haecceity*; "entailment" between concepts would appear to be a genuine dyad yet concepts have no *haecceity*. And the degenerate form of Secondness is really a comparative relation among qualities. Nevertheless, the formal and material aspects of Secondness do correspond relatively well — better certainly than in the case of Firstness, and somewhat better than in the case of Thirdness.

Formally viewed, Thirdness is simply the category of triadic relations. But as we have already seen there are two particular kinds of triadic relations upon which Peirce lays special emphasis — combinatorial relations and sign relations. Whether the latter should be regarded as falling under the formal or the material aspect of Thirdness is rather a moot point and depends upon the breadth allowed to the term "material." When Peirce declared Firstness and Secondness to be irrational, he in effect identified rationality with Thirdness (1.345f; 1.405f; 5.49), and he does regard rationality or intelligibility as in some sense experienced. Accordingly, we may regard those aspects of signhood requisite for this experience as the material aspect of Thirdness. This does involve using "experience" in a wider sense than usual, but it is obvious that this must be done in any case if Thirdness is to have any material aspect. (cf. 1.475f)

The intelligibility of a sign depends upon its having a meaning, and meaning is wholly an affair of Thirdness. But Thirdness enters into the meaning situation in several ways which must be clearly distinguished. The third correlate of the sign relation is the interpretant. Since the interpretant sign is asserted to translate the primary sign, it is at first glance quite natural to assume that the interpretant sign is the meaning, and numerous statements can be found in Peirce's writing which appear to bear this out.[16] Nevertheless, this interpretation is incorrect; the interpretant sign is never the meaning of another sign. The interpretant sign is defined as a second sign which is determined by the primary sign to refer to the same object to which the primary sign refers and which translates the meaning of the primary sign.

---

[16] George Gentry, "Habit and the Logical Interpretant," in Wiener and Young, *Studies*, pp. 75–92.

(1.339; 1.553; 2.303) The meaning of the interpretant is therefore the same as, or a more developed form of, the meaning of the primary sign. (1.339; 2.228) But this is to say that the two signs have the same meaning, not that one is the meaning of the other. Thus in the early period Peirce defines the meaning of a sign as "the respect in which signs which translate each other are conceived to agree." [17] Here, as in the "New List," he is thinking of meaning as the abstract quality or ground which is the first reference of a sign. The fact that every sign has an interpretant sign is not owing to the fact that the interpretant is the meaning, but to the fact that it is the interpretant which joins the sign to its meaning. (1.339) The relation of a sign to its meaning exists only because the sign is interpreted as having that meaning by an interpretant sign. (1.339) It follows that there must be an infinite series of interpretant signs, but this does not mean that the series of interpretants constitutes the meaning of the sign, although it is a necessary condition of the sign's having meaning. The meaning itself lies outside this series: in the early theory it is the abstraction constituting the unconscious idea, and in the later theory it is habit.

In his brilliant study of Peirce's philosophy, Justus Buchler has given an explication of Peirce's theory of meaning which is in many ways admirable. Buchler divides the pragmatic criterion into two parts, one relating to concepts and the other to sentences. The former he states as follows:

A predicate is a meaningful predicate if (and only if) it is definable in terms of a type of sensible result following a type of operation upon that of which it is predicated. And any statement that contains a meaningful predicate is nothing less than a kind of *rule*. For the statement to which it is equivalent asserts that when a definite operation is performed, a definite sensible result follows. This is nothing but a rule or formula or "precept" for gaining "perceptual acquaintance." [18]

Now in the language of the theory of inquiry of the 1870's, such a rule is clearly a possible habit, for if believed, and so acted upon, it would be a general rule governing conduct. The meaning of a concept therefore lies in the set of conceivable habits in which it is involved. This is why, strictly speaking, all concepts are Thirds.

[17] "Notes for Lectures on Logic to be given First Term 1870–1871," p. 1, IB2 Box 10.
[18] Buchler, *Peirce's Empiricism*, pp. 114f.

In extending the criterion to sentences, Buchler writes as follows:

> The proposition which gives the meaning of another . . . is a formula, stating that *whenever* certain operations are performed certain results follow, and these are definite operations and definite results. . . . The meaning is thus given in a "conditional" proposition . . . Peirce intends to say that the conditional translation which gives the meaning is a *prescription* for attaining definite experimental results. . . . As the meaning of a given statement we require another statement that is general. . . . It will be, in effect, a *formula for the entire class of confirmable consequences* of a statement . . . [19]

Buchler regards this formula itself as the meaning,[20] whereas I think the correct reading is that what the formula expresses is the meaning. The conditionals are formulations of the habits which the adoption of the given statement as a belief would imply. The full meaning is thus the total set of habits implied by the given statement.

The view that the meaning is a habit finds explicit statement in one of Peirce's late papers entitled "A Survey of Pragmatism." Thus Peirce:

> The real and living logical conclusion *is* that habit; the verbal formulation merely expresses it. I do not deny that a concept, proposition, or argument may be a logical interpretant. I only insist that it cannot be the final logical interpretant, for the reason that it is itself a sign of that very kind that has itself a logical interpretant. The habit alone, which though it may be a sign in some other way, is not a sign in that way in which that sign of which it is the logical interpretant is the sign. . . . The deliberately formed, self-analyzing habit — self-analyzing because formed by the aid of analysis of the exercises that nourished it — is the living definition, the veritable and final logical interpretant. Consequently, the most perfect account of a concept that words can convey will consist in a description of the habit which that concept is calculated to produce. But how otherwise can a habit be described than by a description of the kind of action to which it gives rise, with the specification of the conditions and of the motive? [5.491]

Even this statement is less precise than one would like, but Peirce does clearly separate the meaning from the particular interpretant signs and define it as the habit. The meaning thus is not a linguistic entity but a peculiar sort of psychological rule which Peirce regards as irreducible. These habits themselves are not signs in the same way that

[19] *Ibid.*, pp. 118f.
[20] *Ibid.*, pp. 112–120, 153–160.

linguistic signs are, for clearly the pragmatic definition of meaning would be redundant if applied to them. But Peirce does not say that habits are not signs in any sense; indeed, we shall see below that there is a sense in which they are signs.

The interpretation which I have given here differs considerably from that of Buchler and Gentry,[21] both of whom regard Peirce's earlier (pre-1906) theory as identifying the interpretant sign with the meaning. But as I have already argued, the interpretant sign cannot be the meaning. It is certainly true that Peirce's own statements on this matter are very loose and that he does give the term "interpretant" a very wide application: witness the above quoted passage. Nevertheless, I think it is clear that in the "New List" the interpretant sign is not the meaning but only serves to translate the abstraction which is the meaning. Similarly, the whole point of pragmatism is the identification of meaning and habit. For if the purpose of inquiry and thought is to attain stable beliefs, and if beliefs are simply habits of action, then what is expressed by the statement which is believed must be what habit it is that is held. And how would making our ideas clear help us reach stable habits if not by discovering to us what habits our ideas involve? Thus in the original paper of 1878, Peirce wrote, "To develop its meaning, we have, therefore, simply to determine what habits it produces, for what a thing means is simply what habits it involves." (5.400) It is true that by applying the pragmatic maxim we translate sentences into conditional sentences. But what those conditionals express is the habit. For as Peirce remarks above, "how otherwise can a habit be described than by a description of the kind of action to which it gives rise, with the specification of the conditions and of the motive?" (5.491)

The fact that meaning is a habit or law explains why it is that Peirce regards every instance of a law as a sign. For quite literally whatever is subject to law is a sign of the law to which it is subject and which forms its meaning. As he later wrote to William James:

The third element of the phenomenon is that we perceive it to be intelligible, that is, to be subject to law, or capable of being represented by a general sign or symbol. . . . The essential thing is that it is capable of being represented. Whatever is capable of being represented is itself of a represen-

---

[21] Gentry, "Habit and Logical Interpretant," pp. 75ff.

tative nature. The idea of representation involves infinity, since a representation is not really such unless it be interpreted in another representation.[22]

Whatever is subject to law is capable of representation by a sign of which that law is the meaning, and whatever is subject to law is itself a sign of the law to which it is subject. It is in this sense that Thirdness is at once the category of law and of rationality or intelligibility. In so far as we experience laws we experience rationality itself; and in so far as the intelligibility of phenomena can be said to be experienced, we experience laws.

The transferring of meaning from category the First to category the Third is one of the most important consequences of the discovery of the logic of relations. But there is an equally important respect in which the logic of relations had a decisive effect on the category of Thirdness — namely, in relating Thirdness to continuity. This relation is first asserted in the 1870's, and was to become one of the most basic themes of Peirce's thought. Yet it is by no means obvious why continuity should be peculiarly related to Thirdness or to the logic of relations. Part of the answer lies, I believe, in the peculiar interpretation which Peirce gave to one of the consequences of the logic of relations. One of his clearest statements of this is as follows:

. . . the grammarians usually limit the term [subject] to the subject nominative, while I term anything named in the assertion a Subject, and although I do not always express myself so accurately, I regard everything to which the assertion relates and to which reference can be removed from the predicate, although what is referred to be a quality, relation, state of things, etc., as a Subject. Thus one assertion may have any number of Subjects. Thus, in the assertion "Some roses are red," i.e. possess the color redness, the color redness is one of the Subjects; but I do not make "possession" a Subject, as if the assertion were "Some roses are in the relation of possession to redness," because this would not remove relation from the predicate, since the words "are in" are here equivalent to "are subjects of," that is, are related to the relation of possession of redness. For to be in relation to X, and to be in relation to a relation to X, mean the same thing. If therefore I were to put "relation" into the subject at all, I ought in consistency to put it in infinitely many times, and indeed, this would not be sufficient. It is like a continuous line: no matter what one cuts off from it a line remains. So I do not attempt to regard "A is B" as meaning "A is identical with something that is B." I call "is in the

---

[22] Perry, *James*, II, 429.

relation to" and "is identical with" Continuous Relations, and I leave such [relations] in the predicate.[23]

From this seemingly trivial fact, I believe that Peirce drew two of the most important principles of his entire philosophic system — indeed, two of the chief principles upon which synechism is based. In the first place, he drew the conclusion that relations constitute continuous connections among their correlates. (6.143) The criterion here employed is that of Kanticity — i.e., the relation is divisible only into parts of the same nature as the whole. Should Peirce's metaphysical realism lead him to hold that there are quasi-Platonic entities of a relational variety, therefore, it is clear that these entities will have to be continua. Thus the way is opened for a new ontology in which what there is would be continua. But in the second place, suppose two objects, x and y, to be brought into the relation R. In order for this to occur they must first be brought into the relation R′ which joins them to R, and hence into the relation R″ which joins them to R′, and so on.[24] In other words, relations cannot be created except as specifications of already existing relations. And since relations constitute continuous connections among things, new relations are only possible as specifica-

---

[23] "Logic. Chapter 1. Common Ground," October 28–31, 1908, pp. 13–15, IB2 Box 9.

[24] "When we have analyzed a proposition so as to throw into the subject everything that can be removed from the predicate, all that it remains for the predicate to represent is the form of connection between the different subjects as expressed in the propositional *form*. What I mean by 'everything that can be removed from the predicate' is best explained by giving an example of something not so removable. But first take something removable. 'Cain kills Abel.' Here the predicate appears as '―― kills ――.' But we can remove killing from the predicate and make the latter '―― stands in the relation ―― to ――.' Suppose we attempt to remove more from the predicate and put the last into the form '―― exercizes the function of relate of the relation ―― to ――,' and then putting 'the function of relate to the relation' into another subject leave as predicate '―― exercizes ―― in respect to ―― to ――.' But this 'exercizes' expresses 'exercizes the function.' Nay more, it expresses 'exercizes the function of relate,' so that we find that though we may put this into a separate subject, it continues in the predicate just the same. Stating this in another form, to say that 'A is in the relation R to B' is to say that A is in a certain relation to R. Let us separate this out thus: 'A is in the relation R¹ (where R¹ is the relation of a relate to the relation of which it is the relate), to R to B.' But A is here said to be in a certain relation to the relation R¹. So that we can express the same fact by saying 'A is in the relation R¹ to the relation R¹ to the relation R to B,' and so on *ad infinitum*. A predicate which can thus be analyzed into parts all homogeneous with the whole I call a *continuous predicate*. It is very important in logical analysis, because a continuous predicate obviously cannot be a *compound* except of continuous predicates, and thus when we have carried analysis so far as to leave only a continuous predicate, we have carried it to its ultimate elements." (Peirce, *Letters to Lady Welby*, pp. 24f; cf. Russell, *Principles of Mathematics*, pp. 99f.)

tions of antecedently existing continuous connections. Should it turn out that the universe evolves, therefore, that evolution must proceed from more general to less general continua through a process of successive differentiation. And if such is the nature of the universe, the mathematics of continua should enable us to describe its general features and predict its course. This is in essence the program of synechism. To what degree it was achieved we shall see hereafter.

The revision of the categories which Peirce produced in 1885 was to remain substantially unchanged until his death. As I have argued above, there were two major reasons for this revision: the discovery of quantification and the desire to escape from the problems involved in the theory of reality. But the revised theory itself raises problems which required further modifications of Peirce's system. The division between formal and material aspects of the categories, while leading back to a more reasonable empiricism, is not wholly consistent with Peirce's theory of cognition. The sense qualities which comprise the material aspect of Firstness have an alarming similarity to the simple ideas of Locke and the impressions of Hume, and so raise again the problem of first impressions of sense. Similarly, Peirce's perennial problem of the relation between the discrete and the continuous recurs once more in the question of whether or not *haecceities* are really determinate. But more than this, the admission of three irreducible kinds of experience raises the question as to what realities lie behind these experiences. Is it simply an ultimate and inscrutable fact that there are three sorts of experience, or does this riddle admit of an intelligible solution?

Before turning to these problems, however, a final word is in order concerning the names of the categories. In earlier chapters I have described the origin of Peirce's categories and the formulation of them given in the "New List." It is obvious that the revision of 1885 led to very substantial changes in the definitions of these categories. Indeed, these changes are sufficiently great so that Peirce ought to have adopted new names for them to prevent confusion with his earlier papers. It is a striking example of Peirce's method of work that this is precisely what he did not do. He evidently thought of these revisions as merely a correcting and developing of his system within the overall architectonic plan: the plan itself, including the terminology, remains unchanged. And nowhere in Peirce's writing is there any explicit statement which would indicate that beneath this shell of changeless terminology major alterations have been made. The result is a confusion which one who regarded himself as an expert on the ethics of terminology ought to have spared his readers. (2.219ff) [25]

[25] So far as I am aware, only one of Peirce's commentators, David Savan, has recognized the extent to which the early and late theories of the categories differ. See David Savan, "On the Origins of Peirce's Phenomenology," in Wiener and Young, *Studies*, pp. 185–194. Peirce might try to justify his retention of his early terminology on the ground that the categories are altered only materially, not formally. But although this is partially true, Peirce did not conceive the categories as having separate formal and material aspects until 1885 so there is a marked change in any case.

# XVI

# *Cosmology*

I T was probably in 1890 that Peirce began the composition of a paper which he entitled "A Guess at the Riddle." (1.354–416) The riddle referred to is the riddle of the sphinx in Emerson's poem of the same name: [1] it is the ultimate nature of the universe. Peirce never published this paper; instead he expanded it into a series of five articles which appeared during the next year or so in the *Monist*. These papers are "The Architecture of Theories" (6.7–34), "The Doctrine of Necessity Examined" (6.35–65), "The Law of Mind" (6.102–163), "Man's Glassy Essence" (6.238–271), and "Evolutionary Love." (6.287–317) There is also a sixth paper (6.588–618) which is a reply to criticisms of the other five by Paul Carus, the editor of the *Monist*, but although this sixth paper furnishes some important clarifications of points in the other papers, it was not a part of the original design.

In the opening paragraphs of "A Guess at the Riddle," Peirce sketched the plan which the work was to follow. There were to have been nine chapters or sections. Of section 1, Peirce writes, "Section 1. One, Two, Three. Already Written." (1.354) This refers to the 1885 paper "One, Two, Three: Fundamental Categories of Thought and of Nature," which we discussed in the last chapter, and in which the reformulation of the categories is presented. Section 2 was to deal with logic and semiotic.

Section 2. The triad in reasoning. Not touched. It is to be made as follows. 1. Three kinds of signs; as best shown in my last paper in the Am. Jour. Math. 2. Term, proposition, and argument, mentioned in my paper on a new list of categories. 3. Three kinds of argument, deduction, induction, hypothesis, as shown in my paper in *Studies in Logic*. Also three figures of syllogism, as shown there and in my paper on the Classification of Arguments. 4. Three kinds of terms, absolute, relative, and conjugative, as shown in my first paper on Logic of Relatives. [1.354]

[1] Ralph Waldo Emerson, "The Sphinx," *Poems* (Boston, 1889), pp. 9–13.

321

Peirce then describes various other trichotomies of logic: affirmative, negative, and intermediate, universal, particular, and enumerative, and even suggests developing a logic of plural values. (1.354) One can see here how Peirce planned to reintegrate his system on the basis of the revised categories. The first section was to be an exposition of the revised list. The opening part of section 2 was to be drawn from the 1885 paper on the Algebra of Logic which we have discussed above as one of the first presentations of the revised list. Then the various trichotomies of signs were to be reworked to bring them into line with the new categories. Peirce then goes on to describe the following sections.

Section 3. The triad in metaphysics. This chapter, one of the best, is to treat of the theory of cognition.
Section 4. The triad in psychology. The greater part is written.
Section 5. The triad in physiology. The greater part is written.
Section 6. The triad in biology. This is to show the true nature of the Darwinian hypothesis.
Section 7. The triad in physics. The germinal section. 1. The necessity of a natural history of the laws of nature, so that we may get some notion of what to expect. 2. The logical postulate for explanation forbids the assumption of any absolute. That is, it calls for the introduction of Thirdness. Metaphysics is an imitation of geometry; and mathematicians having declared against axioms,[2] the metaphysical axioms are destined to fall too. 4. Absolute chance. 5. The universality of the principle of habit. 6. The whole theory stated. 7. Consequences.
Section 8. The triad in sociology. . . . That the consciousness is a sort of public spirit among the nerve-cells. Man as a community of cells; compound animals and composite plants; society; nature. Feeling implied in Firstness.
Section 9. The triad in theology. Faith requires us to be materialists without flinching. [1.354]

It is clear from this outline that the ideas of the *Monist* series were largely developed by 1890. Sections 4 and 5, which were the only two besides section 1 that were substantially complete at this time, became the third and fourth *Monist* papers. Section 6 was never developed as an independent paper, but its content is to be found in the first and fifth papers particularly. Section 9 finds its best expression in the fifth, although like sections 3 and 7, elements of it are to be found through-

---

[2] What Peirce means here is that the axioms of pure geometry are postulates rather than self-evident or absolute truths. (1.401)

out. Section 8 is the only one of which virtually nothing was explicitly developed.

The sudden appearance of this cosmological doctrine in 1890, following five years of very slight philosophical activity (8.G.1885–1889), may at first appear to argue a fundamental alteration in Peirce's position. But I think this conclusion is not called for. It is clear from the above outline that the cosmological papers of the *Monist* series are a further extension of the architectonic design. And this extension is in part due to the revision of the categories which we discussed in the preceding chapter. For any explanation of why we have the three and only three kinds of experience which we do would involve an account of the realities which produce these experiences, and so would be an account of the constitution of the universe which would solve the riddle of Emerson's sphinx. Moreover, the theory of inquiry of the 1870's had by 1890 led to problems which are answerable, if at all, only by cosmology.

The theory of inquiry which Peirce formulated in the 1870's involves an implicit adoption of the theory of evolution. We have noted above that in the 1860's Peirce was not particularly favorable toward evolution.[3] This was probably the result of the friendship between his family and Agassiz, and of his own studies under Agassiz.[4] But by the 1870's even Agassiz's students had deserted their master and the acceptance of the doctrine was virtually universal among scientific men,[5] although controversy still raged in lay circles. Wright, James, and the members of the Metaphysical Club were already evolutionists[6] and Peirce could not well avoid adopting the theory in some form. Indeed, as noted above, one virtue of Bain's theory is that it brings the production of belief into line with similar processes in animals by giving a more or less physiological interpretation to the process, and this is even more strongly the case in Peirce's formulation of it. The process of knowing now becomes an aspect of the interaction of organism and environment. Inquiry arises when some action pattern is frustrated, or when an unfamiliar object is encountered in the environment in regard

[3] Wiener, *Evolution*, p. 77.
[4] *Ibid.*, pp. 78f.
[5] Richard Hofstadter, *Social Darwinism in American Thought* (Philadelphia, 1945), pp. 4f.
[6] Wiener, *Evolution*, pp. 31f, 99f, 130f, 152f, 174f.

to which there is no established pattern of action. The frustration, or disruption, of the established pattern produces an irritation (called doubt) which continues until a new pattern of action is established. Thus the motivation for inquiry is shown to be the removal of an irritant — an activity which has obvious adjustive value for the organism. Belief, or the established habit of action, is accompanied by a feeling of serenity and is a state sought for its own pleasure as well as for relief of anxiety. In fact, beliefs differ only in slight degree from the instincts of the animals, the primary differences being that whereas the animal instinct is invariable, beliefs or habits can be disrupted and modified to make a better adjustment possible. That this process of modification should cause a stimulation of feeling called consciousness is almost accidental.[7]

Such a theory is clearly in line with evolutionary principles, and indeed, the superiority of an organism which can modify its habits in new situations may be used to explain the survival of the organism on grounds of natural selection. In this respect, Peirce's theory is not dissimilar to those of evolutionists such as Sumner[8] and Ward.[9] But the same line of reasoning may be pursued further, for it is clear that the greater the efficiency of the organism in finding satisfactory habits of action the more favored the organism will be. Thus it is natural to expect that over a sufficient period of time natural selection will favor any organism which happens to be particularly adapted to guessing correctly what habits will best fit the existing situation. This line of thought Peirce developed in his "Theory of Probable Inference" in 1883 when he wrote: "Nature is a far vaster and less clearly arranged repertory of facts than a census report; and if men had not come to it with special aptitudes for guessing right, it may well be doubted whether in the ten or twenty thousand years that they may have existed their greatest mind would have attained the amount of knowledge which is actually possessed by the lowest idiot." (2.753) Peirce, like all students of scientific method, was particularly struck by the marvelous ability of the human mind to guess correctly. Considering the possible infinity of false hypotheses which might be proposed for

---

[7] See below, p. 346.
[8] Cf. William Graham Sumner, *Folkways* (New York, 1940), chap. if.
[9] Cf. Lester Ward, *The Psychic Factors of Civilization* (Boston, 1901).

any question, the accuracy of our guesses argues some special adaptation of the mind to nature. It is not that such an adaptation is needed to support the validity of ampliative reasoning, for such reasoning is valid apart from any particular constitution of the universe (2.749), but rather that the validity of ampliative inference does not explain the rapidity with which we reach the correct solutions. (6.414–418) But this accuracy of our guesses could be explained by postulating such an adaptation, and such a postulate is quite consistent with the evolutionary speculation current in that day.

This line of reasoning led Peirce, as it led many others in this period, to place a high valuation on the so-called "instinctive," or "common sense," judgments of the untutored mind. For common sense, being conceived as a sort of intermediary between instinct and higher reason, was presumed to contain judgments developed by the race through centuries of experience, and transmitted by the inheritance of acquired characteristics. (That such characters could be transmitted through heredity was then believed by many, including, at times, even Darwin himself.) [10] Peirce was less naive in this regard than some of his contemporaries, for he did insist that these common sense beliefs be criticized before they were accepted. Granted an innate tendency toward the correct understanding of nature, that tendency would manifest itself in the fact that a slightly larger proportion of guesses would turn out to be right than would happen by chance, but since the odds against any given guess being correct by pure chance would be almost infinite, even a probability of 1/100 would constitute a very large innate adaptation. Yet a probability of 1/100 is not a good betting stake, and before any common sense belief is adopted as true it ought therefore to be subjected to rigorous testing. (5.173; 7.220) Peirce's doctrine of "critical common sensism" is thus not a naive reliance on the value of ignorance, but rather an argument that beliefs which have been accepted for long periods of time and which have become as it were intuitive for us probably have a higher probability of being true than have parvenu doctrines, although neither has the probability of a tested scientific theory. (5.173; 5.522)

The doubt-belief theory of inquiry and the doctrine of critical common sensism are both parts of a more general but implicit theory

---

[10] Loren Eiseley, *Darwin's Century* (New York, 1958), pp. 209–221.

concerning the relation of man and nature. Accordingly questions of the evolution and behavior of both man and nature are involved. In this theory, man is regarded as an organism seeking satisfactions, one of which is belief. Inquiry and reasoning therefore exist only as means to this end, and are fortunately reinforced by an innate proclivity which aids them in attaining their goal. But it is clear that on such a theory a significant change in the nature of either man or the environment can alter the desirability and utility of belief or the effectiveness of our ways of seeking it. Accordingly the doubt-belief theory, in imbedding the theory of inquiry in a psychobiological context, has actually made the entire process of inquiry relative to a particular evolutionary adaptation of the permanence of which we have no guarantee. (5.28) And it is quite conceivable that evolution could take a course which would make our current adaptation positively dysfunctional. It therefore becomes a matter of considerable importance to science and philosophy alike to determine what the future course of evolution — human and environmental — will be. That is to say, we need a cosmological theory which will tell us what sorts of laws, if any, we may expect nature to follow in the future and in areas as yet little explored, and we need a method for finding methods so that we may be certain of being able to deal with such situations as may arise. (6.10 –13) Thus I think it is not surprising that in the early 1890's Peirce's mind should have turned to just these problems, which achieve their classic statement in the famous series of articles in the *Monist* of 1891–1893.

The first article of the *Monist* series is entitled "The Architecture of Theories" and appeared in January of 1891. As one would expect, this is an introductory statement of the reasons for the development of the cosmology and of the methods to be pursued in its construction. Using his critical common sensism as a premiss, Peirce argued that the mind is naturally adapted to the comprehension of nature and that this adaptation is what had led us to our present knowledge of nature. Thus he remarks, "A modern physicist on examining Galileo's works is surprised to find how little experiment had to do with the establishment of the foundations of mechanics. His principal appeal is to common sense and *il lume naturale*. He always assumes that the true theory will be found to be a simple and natural one." (6.10) The intuitive character of this true theory is due, Peirce holds, to the fact that the mind was formed under the direct action of these laws, and so they seem simple to us. That is, mankind evolved in an environment where objects acted under the guidance of these laws and so where an intuitive grasp of them had survival value. But physics has now pushed beyond that portion of the world which has operated selectively upon us. As research penetrates into the world of molecular and atomic phenomena, the ideas of the common sense world may no longer be applicable. "The further physical studies depart from phenomena which have directly influenced the growth of the mind, the less we can expect to find the laws which govern them 'simple,' that is, composed of a few conceptions natural to our minds." (6.10) Accordingly *il lume naturale* will cease to be a reliable guide to the discovery of nature's laws, and the philosopher of science must face the problem of whether any substitute can be found which will act to guide our guesses as to nature's secrets. Such a substitute is possible, Peirce holds, in the form of an evolutionary cosmology.

To find out much more about molecules and atoms we must search out a natural history of laws of nature which may fulfill that function which the presumption in favor of simple laws fulfilled in the early days of dynamics, by showing us what kind of laws we have to expect and by answering such questions as this: Can we, with reasonable prospect of not wasting time, try the supposition that atoms attract one another inversely as the seventh power of their distances, or can we not? To suppose universal laws of nature capable of being apprehended by the mind and yet having no reason for their special forms, but standing inexplicable and irrational, is hardly a justifiable position. Uniformities are precisely the sort of facts that need to be accounted for. . . . Law is *par excellence* the thing that wants a reason. [6.12]

To appreciate the significance of Peirce's argument, one must bear in mind what the situation was in the physical sciences in the early 1890's. The reign of Newtonian mechanics was rapidly drawing to a close, and many of the fundamental difficulties were already known which within fifteen years would lead to the complete revision of physical theory. The Michelson-Morley experiment was already four years old,[11] and with it the demonstration that there was something fundamentally wrong with our theories of the ether. The crisis thus in-

---

[11] William Dampier, *A History of Science* (New York, 1949), p. 401.

troduced into physics was among the most serious in the history of science, involving a conflict between the two sets of equations which scientists regarded as expressing the most fundamental laws of nature — Newton's laws and Maxwell's equations.[12] At the same time, problems had also arisen in the area of atomic physics which indicated that the classical laws of mechanics might not be applicable in this domain, and indeed some scientists had even been led to assert that no explanation of these phenomena was possible at all.[13] The solution of these problems came almost simultaneously in both macro- and microphysics with the work of Einstein and Planck in and about 1905, and in both cases it is true that the new theories did involve fundamental departure from what can be called the realm of common sense ideas. In fact, Peirce saw the actual situation with remarkable clearness, although his explanation of it leaves a great deal to be desired. In attributing the naturalness of Newtonian explanations to an innate proclivity of the human mind Peirce shows an ignorance of the culture concept not unusual in his day. The intuitiveness of Newton's laws is the result of cultural conditioning — they were not intuitive to Aristotle — and *il lume naturale* notwithstanding, Galileo's insight that the natural state of a terrestrial body could be uniform rectilinear motion was perhaps the most important intellectual feat in the history of Europe.[14] Nevertheless, in seeing that the contradictions fast proliferating within physics would require for their solution the adoption of radically new ideas, Peirce showed both an extraordinary awareness of the fundamental character of these difficulties and a brilliant intuition as to the nature of the solutions required.

If the further progress of physics will lead farther and farther away from the realm of common sense experience, any theory which might help us to foresee the direction in which the correct solutions might lie would be of great value. Such a theory, Peirce held, would be a natural history of the laws of nature. "Now the only possible way of accounting for the laws of nature and for uniformity in general is to suppose them results of evolution." (6.13) That is, a theory of the evolution of the

---

[12] A. D'Abro, *The Evolution of Scientific Thought from Newton to Einstein* (New York, 1950), chap. 11–12.

[13] Emil Du Bois-Reymond, "The Limits of Our Knowledge of Nature," *Popular Science Monthly*, V, 17–32 (May 1874).

[14] H. Butterfield, *The Origins of Modern Science* (New York, 1956), pp. 2f.

universe itself is required — a general theory of cosmology which will tell us how the universe came to be as it is and what it is likely to become.

The projection of general evolutionary cosmologies was not a new undertaking in this period. Herbert Spencer,[15] and John Fiske,[16] and Frank Abbot,[17] to mention only a few obvious examples, had already tried their hands at such a task. But such theories were so largely fanciful and so clearly nonscientific that scientists themselves remained highly skeptical. It was Peirce's endeavor to build a cosmological theory which would be broad enough to afford a view of the probable course of future events yet specific enough to be scientifically acceptable. To do this there were certain requirements which the theory had to meet.

The first such requirement was that the system had to be constructed architectonically.

> That systems ought to be constructed architectonically has been preached since Kant, but I do not think the full import of the maxim has by any means been apprehended. What I would recommend is that every person who wishes to form an opinion concerning fundamental problems should first of all make a complete survey of human knowledge, should take note of all the valuable ideas in each branch of science, should observe in just what respect each has been successful and where it has failed, in order that, in the light of the thorough acquaintance so attained of the available materials for a philosophical theory and of the nature and strength of each, he may proceed to the study of what the problem of philosophy consists in, and of the proper way of solving it. [6.9]

It is clear that this passage involves a generalization of Kant's idea of architectonic. Kant had asserted a relation between logic and metaphysics; Peirce here suggests a relation between the special sciences in general and philosophy as a whole. As the subsequent argument of this paper, and of "A Guess at the Riddle," makes clear, the fundamental ideas of the special sciences turn out to be classifiable by the categories, so that what is really being argued is something with which Kant would have fully agreed, namely, that the categories are the basis of all special knowledge. But I think it is not too much to see in this passage

---

[15] Herbert Spencer, *First Principles* (New York, 1862).

[16] John Fiske, *Outlines of Cosmic Philosophy Based on the Doctrine of Evolution*, 2 vols. (Boston, 1874).

[17] Francis Ellingwood Abbot, *Scientific Theism* (Boston, 1885).

329

the origins of an endeavor upon which Peirce was to be increasingly occupied during the next twenty years, the classification of the sciences. The architectonic theory itself is a kind of classification of science in terms of presupposition although it happens to involve only logic and metaphysics. But since Kant regarded his categories as presuppositions of all synthetic knowledge, there is no reason not to carry the classification through to include all the sciences and this is precisely what Peirce did. What is missing in the papers of 1891 is the clear hierarchical order — Peirce is content to let all the special sciences stand on one level so long as it is clear that they all involve the more fundamental ideas of the categories. In later years, the relations among particular sciences were to be worked out in great detail.

But the important question is why Peirce should have been interested in doing this. After all, Kant never bothered to do so. If the categories are true of all thought, they are true of the special sciences by definition — why bother to prove in detail what is obvious a priori? Peirce's answer to this question is very unclear in the *Monist* papers, and indeed it does not become clear until 1902. But the answer is actually twofold. In the first place, the aim of the architectonic, as of the classification, is to prove certain general theorems concerning all of human knowledge. But this means not only all present human knowledge, but all possible human knowledge, for Peirce is proposing to predict nothing less than the direction in which future discovery must go. To do this Peirce must be able to prove that there is an order in human knowledge such that if theorems are established as true for some primary segments of our knowledge then they are necessarily true for all others. It must therefore be shown (1) that such a dependence among our fields of knowledge does exist, and (2) that certain theorems are true of the primary fields. Neither part of this endeavor was well developed in the *Monist* papers and the classification of the sciences is ill-defined — as Peirce wrote in "A Guess at the Riddle," "The argument of this book has been developed in the mind of the author, substantially as it is presented, as a following out of the three conceptions, in a sort of game of 'follow-my-leader' from one field of thought into another." (1.364) Nevertheless, it is clear that the categories are regarded as the basis of the whole endeavor, and these of course are derived from logic. But secondly, it is one of the most significant results of the doubt-belief theory that the legitimacy of the architectonic principle itself is called into question. For if inquiry is relative to a particular state of evolution, then logic is itself merely a means to the attaining of an end which may not be desirable in a further evolutionary stage. To found a cosmology upon categories derived from a logic which that cosmology shows to be of temporary value only is not likely to advance the cause of knowledge. Thus I believe Peirce's increasing concern with the question of the classification of the sciences after 1890 reflects his growing recognition that logic does not afford so solid a basis for knowledge as Kant and he had believed. And this is confirmed by the fact that his final classification of the sciences differs from its predecessors in separating the theory of the categories from logic.[18]

There are two further requirements which Peirce laid upon his theory. First, it must explain. That is to say, it will not do to take for granted the results of the whole inquiry at the start by postulating that laws have been from everlasting to everlasting, for such a procedure would merely restate the facts to be explained without really explaining them. (6.171; 6.12; 6.60) The theory must therefore actually explain the origin and development of the natural order including the laws of nature. But second, if the theory is to be in any sense a scientific theory, it must lead to conclusions which are capable of verification. Some result must follow which is actually capable of test, and which will differentiate the theory from the rival theories which Peirce attacks. Unless this could be done, Peirce felt that his theory must be set down as a failure. (1.410; 6.62)

In the second paper of the *Monist* series, Peirce turned to the consideration of some of the alternative theories which had been presented to account for the present state of the universe. Such a critique was really well-nigh inescapable: in the 1890's Peirce could hardly advance his own theory without at least passing reference to Spencer and the necessitarians who had been so active in this sort of speculation. Peirce is particularly interested here in refuting both the necessitarians and the mechanists, but the emphasis falls on the doctrine of necessity — i.e., of complete determinism — since this is a basic premiss of both schools.

Against the doctrine of necessity Peirce advances three arguments:

[18] See below, pp. 366f.

331

first, it is not a priori certain; second, it is not required by science; third, it does not fit the facts. The first argument is proven by historical example. It is not true that this doctrine has always been believed by rational men, as is obvious from the fact that Aristotle himself condemned it. There is therefore nothing in the nature of the mind or reason which requires such a belief. (6.36) The iron hold which it had upon the minds of the nineteenth century was chiefly due to the belief that it was demonstrated by science, and to this argument Peirce now turns.

The thesis that determinism is a postulate of science is, Peirce holds, based simply upon a false notion of scientific reasoning. The validity of scientific reasoning rests upon the validity of induction and hypothesis — that is, upon the validity of ampliative inference. But the validity of such inference depends upon no particular assumptions about the constitution of nature, necessitarian or other. Peirce then proceeds to show that induction is a form of statistical inference and that its validity depends only upon random sampling and predesignation — substantially the argument of his paper of 1878. Therefore, he concludes, no necessitarian postulate is required to validate science. (6.39–42)

But finally, cannot the necessitarian position be proven empirically by the observation of nature? Peirce's answer is that it cannot. "For the essence of the necessitarian position is that certain continuous quantities have certain exact values. Now, how can observation determine the value of such a quantity with a probable error absolutely *nil?*" (6.44) From the fact that observation always does involve some element of error, Peirce then drew the famous conclusion that there is absolute chance in the universe.

Those observations which are generally adduced in favor of mechanical causation simply prove that there is an element of regularity in nature, and have no bearing whatever upon the question of whether such regularity is exact and universal or not. Nay, in regard to this *exactitude*, all observation is directly *opposed* to it; and the most that can be said is that a good deal of this observation can be explained away. Try to verify any law of nature, and you will find that the more precise your observations, the more certain they will be to show irregular departures from the law. We are accustomed to ascribe these, and I do not say wrongly, to errors of observation; yet we cannot usually account for such errors in any antecedently probable way. Trace their causes back far enough and you will be forced to admit they are always due to arbitrary determination, or chance. [6.46]

Thus was born Peirce's famous theory of tychism, or absolute chance. Although the doctrine was not formulated until the late eighties or early nineties, its origins can be traced back to some of Peirce's earlier writings. It was probably the question of the validity of induction which first led Peirce to stress the disorderliness of the universe. Thus, in his paper "Grounds of Validity of the Laws of Logic" in 1868, Peirce remarked in answer to the question, how is induction possible, "The usual reply is that nature is everywhere regular; as things have been, so they will be; as one part of nature is, so is every other. But this explanation will not do. Nature is not regular. No disorder would be less orderly than the existing arrangement." (5.342) Again in 1878 in his paper on "The Order of Nature," Peirce reiterated his denial of complete order. There is some order in the universe, he admits, "But whether the world makes an exact poem or not, is another question. When we look up at the heavens at night, we readily perceive that the stars are not simply splashed onto the celestial vault; but there does not seem to be any precise system in their arrangement either." (6. 399) Yet Peirce did not at this point generalize this observation into the theory of tychism. The earliest statement I have found which does seem to be clearly a statement of the tychistic theory occurs in 1887 when Peirce used the variety of nature as an argument against the mechanical philosophy. "The endless variety in the world has not been created by law. It is not of the nature of uniformity to originate variation, nor of law to beget circumstance. When we gaze upon the multifariousness of nature we are looking straight into the face of a living spontaneity. A day's ramble in the country ought to bring that home to us." (6.553) The doctrine then reappears fully formulated in "A Guess at the Riddle" in 1890 (1.402ff), and was given its public introduction in the second *Monist* paper in 1891. (6.47f)

By the term "absolute chance" Peirce means the existence of real indeterminacy as opposed to an indeterminacy arising merely from our ignorance. (6.57f) The latter kind of indeterminacy was well known and fully accepted in nineteenth-century science: it underlies, for example, the kinetic theory of gases, where although the position, direction, and velocity of every molecule are theoretically determinate at every instant, the difficulties, amounting to impossibility, of calculation make it necessary to deal with them statistically. Peirce's theory differs from the classical one precisely in that for Peirce the position, direction, and velocity are not even theoretically determinate at every instant — they are objectively indeterminate.

Peirce advanced five reasons for believing in the objective existence of absolute chance. First, he argued that the facts of growth and increasing complexity in nature cannot be explained by mechanical forces and therefore require the postulation of "some agency by which the complexity and diversity of things can be increased . . ." (6.58) Peirce is here contrasting reversible with irreversible processes, and particularly with those irreversible processes such as growth and evolution which lead from a simple to a more complex state of organization. Since all mechanical processes are reversible, his argument is that these irreversible processes must be explained on other than mechanical grounds. (6.14) Second, Peirce also says that the sheer variety of nature cannot be explained by the laws of mechanics. By "variety" Peirce means the number of independent quantities in nature. The operation of an exact law always leaves this number unchanged, so if laws are exact the variety of nature cannot have increased through evolution but must be assumed to have existed in the primordial state.[19] The problem then is why this diversity should have existed in the beginning, and from the nature of the case there can be no answer at all to such a question, the initial state being simply an ultimate given. Peirce also posits diversity in the beginning as an ultimate fact, but he does so by positing an agent — absolute chance — which would produce this diversity continuously in time. Thus, he argues, "I account for all the variety and diversity of the universe, in the only sense in which the really *sui generis* and new can be said to be accounted for." (6.59) Third, if a cosmology is to explain the evolution of law, it is clear that that evolution must proceed from something not law to something which is law — otherwise there would be no evolution. But if a uniformity is to develop from something not a uniformity, then it must develop from some state of indeterminacy such as chance. (6.60) Fourth, the necessitarian theory makes the freedom of the will an

[19] Peirce, Commonplace Book, August 29, 1908, IB2 Box 6.

illusion, for every state and act of the organism must be strictly deter-mined. But Peirce argues that this is contrary to experience, and that there is no empirical evidence to support it. (6.61) Finally, Peirce states that from this hypothesis he has drawn consequences which can be empirically verified. (6.62) In this paper Peirce does not state what these consequences are, but it is clearly an important question concern-ing both the legitimacy of his whole undertaking and the good faith in which it was made whether in fact there are such consequences and whether Peirce actually made any attempt to put them to the test. To those questions, which are not answered in the *Monist* series, we shall return below.

Having stated his general aim, discussed and, as he believed, re-futed the necessitarian position, and introduced his own theory of tychism, Peirce now returned to the main argument of the cosmology. Clearly the process by which the cosmos evolves will depend upon the constitution of the cosmos itself, and here there are only three alter-native hypotheses: either the entire cosmos, including the mind, is material, or it is mental, or it is composed of both sorts of elements. (6.24) The latter hypothesis is condemned by Ockham's razor, at least until the other two have been tried. (6.24) Accordingly, the question lies between materialism and idealism, and the only way to decide it is to develop each hypothesis and to see how nearly each can be made to account for the known facts. To this task the third and fourth of the *Monist* papers are dedicated: "The Law of Mind," which appeared in July of 1891, undertakes the development of the idealistic theory, and "Man's Glassy Essence," which appeared in the next volume, develops the materialistic theory.

The paper on "The Law of Mind" marks the first public appearance of Peirce's synechism. In the introduction to the article, Peirce refers to his paper of 1868 on "Some Consequences of Four Incapacities" (5.264–317) as constituting an earlier and rudimentary statement of this position, and, as will be clear from the contents of this paper, this is partly true. But the concept of continuity used in 1891 is more advanced than that used in 1868, and the conclusions are far more sweeping, although they point in the same directions.

The law of mind, as Peirce states it, is "that ideas tend to spread continuously and to affect certain others which stand to them in a peculiar relation of affectibility. In this spreading they lose intensity, and especially the power of affecting others, but gain generality and become welded with other ideas." (6.104) The remainder of the paper is devoted to an elucidation of the meaning of this statement: namely, to the definition of continuity, to the proof of the continuity of mental phenomena, and to the analysis of the relations among ideas. The first problem of the paper is therefore the definition of continuity. Peirce was later to refer to this section of the paper as "my blundering treatment of Continuity" (6.174), and in fact it is just that. He had not yet come to see the grounds for the differences between himself and Cantor, and in this paper he cites the authority of Cantor in support of his argument for the reality of infinitesimals! (6.113) Moreover, he adopts Cantor's theory that the real numbers are in one-to-one correspondence with the points on a line (6.118) and so fails to make his case for potentiality clearly. These defects, however, were corrected in the later theory of continuity, so that there is no need to stress their presence here.

Granting, then, Peirce's mathematical theory of continuity, what grounds can be alleged for believing that mental phenomena are continuous? The argument which Peirce presents is similar to that which he had used in 1868 — if they are not continuous it is impossible to explain how anyone can have any memory.

> How can a past idea be present? Can it be present vicariously? To a certain extent, perhaps, but not merely so; for then the question would arise how the past idea can be related to its vicarious representation. The relation, being between ideas, can only exist in some consciousness: now that past idea was in no consciousness but that past consciousness that alone contained it; and that did not embrace the vicarious idea. [6.107]

Is it then possible for the past idea to be present at all? Peirce argues that it is, but only through the theory of infinitesimals. "How can a past idea be present? Not vicariously. Then, only by direct perception. In other words, to be present, it must be *ipso facto* present. That is, it cannot be wholly past; it can only be going, infinitesimally past, less past than any assignable past date. We are thus brought to the conclusion that the present is connected with the past by a series of real infinitesimal steps." (6.109) According to Peirce, this conclusion requires us to be immediately conscious of an infinitesimal interval as an interval having a beginning, middle, and end. Upon this interval there then follows another whose beginning is the middle of the first. Remembering that Peirce used the term "instant" to mean a point in time and "moment" to mean an infinitesimal interval (6.111), his argument is as follows:

In an infinitesimal interval we directly perceive the temporal sequence of its beginning, middle, and end — not, of course, in the way of recognition, for recognition is only of the past, but in the way of immediate feeling. Now upon this interval follows another, whose beginning is the middle of the former, and whose middle is the end of the former. Here, we have an immediate perception of the temporal sequence of its beginning, middle, and end, or say of the second, third, and fourth instants. From these two immediate perceptions, we gain a mediate, or inferential, perception of the relation of all four instants. This mediate perception is objectively, or as to the object represented, spread over the four instants; but subjectively, or as itself the subject of duration, it is completely embraced in the second moment. . . . If it is objected that, upon the theory proposed, we must have more than a mediate perception of the succession of the four instants, I grant it; for the sum of the two infinitesimal intervals is itself infinitesimal, so that it is immediately perceived. It is immediately perceived in the whole interval, but only mediately perceived in the last two-thirds of the interval. Now, let there be an indefinite succession of these inferential acts of comparative perception, and it is plain that the last moment will contain objectively the whole series. Let there be, not merely an indefinite succession, but a continuous flow of inference through a finite time, and the result will be a mediate objective consciousness of the whole time in the last moment. In this last moment, the whole series will be recognized, or known as known before, except only the last moment, which of course will be absolutely unrecognizable to itself. [6.111]

This is a rather nice blend of Peirce's old and new theories of cognition. One has here the continuous series of cognitions, but without any explicit statement as to how the series originates, individual thoughts which are realized in infinitesimal intervals, and a continuous connection among thoughts which enables any two to be compared and which makes memory possible. One has also a synthesis of recognition in which a series of sensations is summed and known as standing for a common object. But one has also an immediate perception of the interval itself which is not inferred and which serves as a datum from which mediate inferences are drawn. Here again Peirce is very close to the admission of first impressions of sense or direct intuition in some form. This is one of the most significant differences between the cognitive theory of the *Monist* series and the papers of 1868.

Having established to his satisfaction the temporal continuity of mental phenomena, Peirce now turns to the law of their behavior. This portion of the paper is among the least clear of all Peirce's writings but the ideas involved are basic to his philosophy and it is therefore essential to see just what he was trying to do. In trying to devise a general formula of mental action, Peirce is attempting what might be called a rational reconstruction of the doctrine of association which had played so important a part in British empiricism since Hume. It was Hume's position that perception gives us sense impressions from which our simple ideas are copied and that from these simple ideas we derive both complex and general ideas through the agency of association.[20] This doctrine had been further developed by Hartley [21] and had become so standard a part of the psychological theory of Peirce's time that any theory he presented concerning the action of the mind would have had to deal with it. The wisest course was therefore to meet the question head on.

In considering Peirce's argument there is a terminological problem which must be constantly kept in mind. The doctrine of association concerns relations among "ideas," which to the British empiricists meant "simple ideas" or sense qualities. But the term "idea" in Peirce's writing is highly ambiguous. Since he denies the existence of first impressions of sense, there can be no ideas copied from those impressions. Indeed, we have no knowable sense data at all but only inferences from data of which we are not conscious. (7.465) To what degree these "ideas" are general is therefore unclear from the beginning and, since I believe Peirce was at this time uncertain of his own stand on first impressions, he does not clarify the matter. In the "Law of Mind" he calls an "idea" "an event in an individual consciousness" (6.105) and one may deduce from his argument on memory that it is an event occupying only an infinitesimal interval. Where examples of "ideas" are given they always turn out to be Firsts such as "blue" (7.392) or "red" (6.136) and I think it is legitimate to regard the discussion as

[20] Hume, *Treatise*, pp. 10–13, 17–25.
[21] Harald Höffding, *A History of Modern Philosophy* (New York, 1955), I, 446–449.

relating chiefly to the association of Firsts conceived as very nearly simple ideas.

An idea or First is capable of two alternative descriptions. Epistemologically, it is an idea of a sense quality; psychologically, it is a feeling or state of consciousness at a particular moment. Either description is legitimate, depending upon one's intent: the idea of red is a feeling, and it is about the sense quality of redness; but it is not an idea about a feeling, and it is not itself red. Peirce switches from one mode of description to the other with such abruptness that it is often difficult to tell which he is using unless one keeps this duality continually in mind.

Peirce's treatment of the law of association by contiguity is entirely conventional. Given any two objects, $a$ and $b$, if they are repeatedly found to be contiguous in time or space then the ideas $f(a)$ and $f(b)$ will be so associated that the occurrences of the one will bring the other to mind. This is exactly the principle of the associationists and involves no departure from the traditional formulation. (7.391; 7.451f) But in respect to association by resemblance, Peirce adds a distinctive note. Association by resemblance is usually regarded either as a special case of association by contiguity in which it is the association which makes the ideas appear similar, or else as an autonomous principle whereby ideas which resemble each other are associated. But Peirce holds that association by resemblance is not reducible to association by contiguity, yet that ideas resemble one another because they are associated. The argument rests upon his belief that Firsts are whatever they are irrespective of anything else. A First considered in itself is not like anything else, and in themselves no two Firsts have any more in common than any other two things.

The idea of yesterday and that of today are two ideas; they have nothing in common, unless it be that the mind naturally throws them together. Some beginner may object that they both have a *blueness* in them; but I reply that blueness is nothing but the idea of these sensations and of others I have had, thrown together and indistinctly thought at once. Blueness is the idea of the *class*. It is absurd to say that different things which cannot be compared are alike, except in the sense that they act alike. Now, two ideas are compared only in the idea of a class, lot, or set to which they belong; and they act alike only in so far as they have one and the same relation to that connecting idea. Resemblance, then, is a mode of association by the inward nature of ideas and of mind. [7.392]

The class concept of blue is a general idea which forms a connection among sensations, but the general idea does not produce those associations — rather it is an idea of the sensations which the mind groups together. It is the fact that the mind connects these ideas which makes them similar — not their similarity which leads the mind to connect them. (7.392; 7.498)

What lies behind Peirce's theory of resemblance is doubtless in part Hume's insistence on the ultimate character of the laws of association,[22] but I think there is also another factor of greater importance. For let us recall Peirce's thesis that the mind is by natural selection adapted to the understanding of nature, and so to the forming of correct hypotheses. If this is true, in what way can this adaptation operate? Clearly not through association by contiguity, unless what is meant is that our senses permit us to perceive only certain objects, and even then it is difficult to see how such selectivity would aid us since the association of those objects depends upon factual coincidences beyond our control. But in the case of association by resemblance, such an adaptation could operate very easily. A hypothetic inference is an inference of the form

S is P' & P'' & P'''
M is P' & P'' & P'''
S is M

The truth of the conclusion depends upon the degree to which the joint possession of these predicates by S and M indicates a real connection — i.e., on whether or not we have attended to the significant aspects of S and M. An innate adaptation to the understanding of nature which would aid us in framing true hypotheses might therefore be found in an innate disposition to classify certain attributes or effects of objects as similar. The similarity exists because they are classed together, and they are classed together because they indicate important relations among objects. Ultimately, the explanation for such association lies in the structure of the brain where evolution and natural selection have produced this disposition. (7.498) Thus I believe Peirce's theory of

---

[22] Norman Kemp Smith, *The Philosophy of David Hume* (London, 1949), pp. 240f.

association constitutes an ingenious attempt to provide a basis for his theory of knowledge.

But even if this explanation of the epistemological nature of association is correct, it remains to explain its psychological nature. Psychologically viewed, ideas are feelings, and what Peirce has now to show is how the entities which are the ideas are connected in consciousness. In keeping with his view that relations are possible only where continuous connections exist, he has therefore to show that there is continuity among feelings and to explain what the nature of that continuity is. Peirce describes three sorts of continuity applicable to ideas, but the three kinds are widely different. There is in the first place temporal continuity, as he has shown in the argument from memory. This sort of continuity is both objective and subjective: not only is the object of the idea continuous temporally but the idea itself is continuous in time. (6.107–111) Secondly, Peirce argues for what he calls "intensive" continuity of ideas. (6.132) "Intensity" here may be used in either a subjective or an objective sense. "A high color, a loud sound, a burn have, *per se*, high objective intensity." (7.396) "Subjective" intensity means the degree of influence on the sense involved or the intensity of awareness — substantially what Kant meant in speaking of "intensive magnitudes." (A166 B208) It is the latter kind of intensity which is referred to in the "Law of Mind." (6.132) In general, Peirce holds that ideas are subjectively intense if they are objectively intense (7.398) but this subjective intensity rapidly decays when the stimulus is removed.

Thirdly, Peirce claims that ideas have "extensive" continuity. To illustrate what he means, he cites the example of the behavior of a gob of protoplasm under excitation. When the gob is irritated at a given point, the excitation is observed to spread continuously through the substance. "Whatever there is in the whole phenomena to make us think there is feeling in such a mass of protoplasm — *feeling*, but plainly no *personality* — goes logically to show that that feeling has a subjective, or substantial, spatial extension, as the excited state has." (6.133) This argument has nothing to do with the object of the feeling-idea which may or may not be spatially extended; what Peirce is maintaining is that the feeling-idea, viewed as itself an object, is extended in space, so that for example there may be a continuity of feeling among all the parts of the mind. Moreover, Peirce holds that in the continuous spreading of the feeling through the protoplasm, the excitation is observed to follow certain paths, which paths he holds to be associations of feeling-ideas. (6.254; 6.259–270)

Perhaps Peirce's clearest description of association is as follows. An idea, $A$, is brought into the mind. This idea calls up other ideas so that a compound idea $AB$ is formed in the mind. $A$ then drops out and $B$ remains. (7.393–417) In this process, what is $AB$? It is not simply the conjunction of $A$ and $B$; rather it is a single idea in which $A$ and $B$ are "thought at once." (7.392; 7.407) As Peirce describes it, the merger of $A$ into $AB$ decreases the intensity of the constituents, and the greater the number of ideas that are blended into this compound, the less the intensity and distinctness of any one. At the same time, the more ideas are included in the compound, the more ideas the compound can recall to consciousness. (7.398; 7.436) Presumably then the development of this compound idea is accompanied by a spatial spreading of the excitation within the mind in which paths of connection become prominent, which paths constitute the chains of association. Thus general ideas are literally continua of feeling. "I think we can only hold that wherever ideas come together they tend to weld into general ideas; and wherever they are generally connected, general ideas govern the connection; and these general ideas are living feelings spread out." (6.143) But such general ideas connecting general ideas are habits or laws, which psychologically viewed, are also feeling continua.

> The first character of a general idea so resulting is that it is a living feeling. A continuum of this feeling, infinitesimal in duration, but still embracing innumerable parts, and also, though infinitesimal, entirely unlimited, is immediately present. And in its absence of boundedness a vague possibility of more than is present is directly felt.
>
> Second, in the presence of this continuity of feeling, nominalistic maxims appear futile. There is no doubt about one idea affecting another, when we can directly perceive the one gradually modified and shaping itself into the other. [6.138f]

The continuum connecting the general ideas $\phi$ and $\psi$ is thus not only a rule of sequence but an active agent through which one idea in the mind affects another.

From the standpoint of logic, the analogue to the psychological relation of affection is predication. "We can now see what the affection of one idea by another consists in. It is that the affected idea is attached as a logical predicate to the affecting idea as subject. So when a feeling emerges into immediate consciousness, it always appears as a modification of a more or less general object already in the mind." (6.142) The three forms of inference now become the logical representations of the psychological processes of association. Hypothetic reasoning is the process whereby sensations become welded together to form a general idea. Induction is equated to the process of habit formation whereby a number of sensations followed by one reaction are combined into a general idea followed by that reaction. And deduction is the process by which the rule or habit is actualized in conduct. (6.144–146) "That is the way the hind legs of a frog, separated from the rest of the body, reason, when you pinch them." (6.144)

It is obvious that Peirce's theory of association involves a host of stratification problems and that these are the direct outcome of his concept of continuity. Thus on Peirce's analysis the general idea of a triangle would have to consist of a melange of all triangles somehow "thought at once" — a construction which abandons the far superior interpretation in terms of propositional functions and variables.[23] Indeed, the very idea of the continuum as that every part of which is similar to the whole so obliterates the distinctions between class and member, individual and general, concrete and abstract that it is impossible to make the notion precise without running into contradiction. These difficulties are most evident whenever Peirce turns to psychological questions. His attempt to correlate logical, epistemological, and psychological processes of association therefore fails to hold up because the psychological processes remain shrouded in vagueness. And this fact is the more unfortunate since his cosmology assigns so crucial a role to just these psychological processes.

But Peirce's theory does at least lead to an interesting analysis of the concept of personality. The phenomena of multiple personality had already made it clear that the definition of a person is not synonymous with that of a human being.

[23] Lewis, *Survey*, pp. 93–94. Compare Peirce's descriptions of association in 7.392–393, 7.407–408, 7.410, 7.435. His "forms" or "skeletons" in 7.426f do not remove the confusion, even if they are regarded as propositional functions. The concept of the variable is still muddled.

But that which these cases make quite manifest is that personality is some kind of coördination or connection of ideas. Not much to say, this, perhaps. Yet when we consider that, according to the principle which we are tracing out, a connection between ideas is itself a general idea, and that a general idea is a living feeling, it is plain that we have at least taken an appreciable step toward the understanding of personality. This personality, like any general idea, is not a thing to be apprehended in an instant. It has to be lived in time; nor can any finite time embrace it in all its fullness. Yet in each infinitesimal interval it is present and living, though specially colored by the immediate feelings of that moment. [6.155]

Every integrated system of habits is therefore a person, for these habits form a continuum of feeling, and since consciousness is only an aspect of feeling, it will be present in any such continuum. Thus Peirce was led not only to reaffirm his conclusion of 1868 that every person is a symbol involving a general idea (5.313–317; 6.270), but to draw the further conclusion that "every general idea has the unified living feeling of a person." (6.270)

The law of mind is thus a general formula of mental action which is intended to include the two principles of association as special cases. The emphasis is upon the psychological aspect of the process rather than the epistemological. Actually, the law is not a law in any rigorous sense: "The truth is, the mind is not subject to 'law' in the same rigid sense that matter is. It only experiences gentle forces which merely render it more likely to act in a given way than it otherwise would be. There always remains a certain amount of arbitrary spontaneity in its action, without which it would be dead." (6.148) But it does provide a description of mental processes which can be compared to the description of physical processes given by physics.

In order to settle the question between idealism and materialism Peirce must show either that mental phenomena are explainable by physical laws or that physical phenomena are explainable by mental laws. Having now established what the law of mind is, he is prepared to undertake this task. In the fourth paper of the series, "Man's Glassy Essence," Peirce therefore examines the question of whether or not it is possible to construct a theory from the known principles of physics which will account for mental phenomena. To do this, Peirce takes protoplasm as being mind in its lowest form. (6.238f) The strategy here is obvious. Since Peirce's theory is an evolutionary one, he is committed to the continuity of higher and lower organisms. To draw a division between mind and nonmind within the organic realm is difficult and arbitrary and the attempt to make such a division could leave him open to charges of stacking the deck in his own favor. Moreover, if he can show that the behavior of protoplasm is not explicable on physical principles, it will scarcely be contended that that of the higher organisms is more so.

Peirce's molecular theory of protoplasm need not be examined at length. It assumes as a starting point a planetary model of the molecule which in the case of protoplasm is conceived as very complex and unstable. Peirce explains the liquefaction of the slime under excitation in terms of the ejection of submolecules from their orbits. These free particles collide with and disrupt other molecules, thus producing a chain reaction which explains the spreading of the disturbance in a continuous fashion. The solidification of the slime after the excitation has ceased is then explained as the result of the recapture of the free submolecules by the larger ones. (6.246–263) With this theory Peirce holds that it is possible to explain every property of protoplasm except one.

But what is to be said of the property of feeling? If consciousness belongs to all protoplasm, by what mechanical constitution is this to be accounted for? The slime is nothing but a chemical compound. There is no inherent impossibility in its being formed synthetically in the laboratory, out of its chemical elements; and if it were so made, it would present all the characters of natural protoplasm. No doubt, then, it would feel. To hesitate to admit this would be puerile and ultra-puerile. By what element of the molecular arrangement, then, would that feeling be caused? This question cannot be evaded or pooh-poohed. Protoplasm certainly does feel; and unless we are to accept a weak dualism, the property must be shown to arise from some peculiarity of the mechanical system. Yet the attempt to deduce it from the three laws of mechanics, applied to never so ingenious a mechanical contrivance, would obviously be futile. It can never be explained, unless we admit that physical events are but degraded or undeveloped forms of psychical events. [6.264]

Here, then, is Peirce's basic argument for objective idealism. Whatever theory of mental phenomena is to be adopted must account for the presence of feeling: the mechanical theory cannot account for feeling; therefore the mechanical theory cannot account for mental phenomena.

The argument illustrates all too well the iron hold of Newtonian mechanics upon the minds of physicists at the end of the nineteenth century. There is throughout an implicit assumption that the fundamental laws of the physical world are Newton's laws, that any nonpsychical explanation is ultimately reducible to the laws of mechanics, and therefore that to show that something is not derivable from those laws is to show that it can never be explained by physics. This point of view is in no sense unique to Peirce — it was part of the scientific climate of opinion of that day.[24] What its ubiquitousness does indicate is how great an act of imagination was required to produce the theory of relativity.

If it be granted that mind is inexplicable by mechanics, it still remains to be shown that the law of mind can explain mechanical phenomena. But if matter is conceived to be a form of mind in which habit has become so fixed as to be virtually invariable, then the exactness and regularity of mechanical processes may be explained as differing only in degree from the mild and erratic tendencies which govern mental action. Indeed, we may regard habits as varying continuously in their degree of exactitude from utter invariability to utter chaos. The laws of mechanics will then be near one end of the continuum and the laws of the mind near the other. (6.264) And since according to the law of mind there is an inverse relation between the vivacity of feeling and the rigidity of habit (6.264), and since vividness of feeling is positively correlated with consciousness (6.264f), the degree of consciousness will be highest in those forms of mind least ruled by habit and least in those most ruled by habit. We should therefore expect that where mind is hidebound with habit there will be virtually no evidence of consciousness — that is, it will appear to us as dead, although, being mind, it will still possess a dull sort of feeling. (6.268) The opposite of regularity is indeterminacy. When feeling is particularly vivid, therefore, this indeterminacy will be at its height, and will manifest itself in a positive tendency toward random variation which might well be called spontaneity. Any phenomena in which this spontaneity is prominent will be observed to act in ways which appear to us wholly fortuitous or chancelike. Thus the presence of absolute chance in the universe is a necessary corollary to this theory of objective idealism. (6.264–267)

Of his three psychological categories, Peirce devotes the least an-

[24] Du Bois-Raymond, "Limits of our Knowledge," pp. 17–32.

alysis to the will, yet in some ways this is the most interesting part of his psychology. His theory is much indebted to Scotus' argument concerning the freedom of God's will. Unlike Thomas, Scotus held that for the will of God to be free, it cannot be wholly determined by reason. God's will never contravenes his reason, but his reason does not wholly determine the action of his will. There remains an area of arbitrariness within which the will is free to act or not. Peirce adopts a similar approach in holding that acts of volition are brute compulsions which, although they may conform to law, are not determined to occur by the law. Thus reason may resolve upon a course of action which it would be well to follow, but wishing is not doing and until there is some determination of the will the resolve remains a dream. (1.380) For Scotus, acts of creation are particularly good examples of the action of God's will. Whatever is created will have an intelligible nature, but the nature does not confer existence — that is conferred by fiat of the will in the form of *haecceity*. Peirce adopts this idea of making *haecceity* the objective counterpart of will. Objective mind, being mind, has all three categories of mental phenomena, and hence manifests volition. These acts of will appear to us in *haecceities* or experienced reactions which, because objective mind is habitbound, are entirely regular and consistent. (1.410–416; 6.189–209; 8.41)

Thus all mind presents a double aspect, depending upon the way in which it is viewed. Peirce usually contrasts these as the inside and the outside of the phenomenon (6.268f) — a peculiarly unfortunate choice of terms since on his theory of psychology psychic phenomena are as much inferences from observation as are those of mechanics. It would be better to say that the same phenomenon can be described in two languages — one, that of psychology in which the key terms are feeling, will, and habit, and the other, that of physics in which the key terms are chance, *haecceity*, and law. What the postulate of objective idealism does is to identify the corresponding members of these triads, and to tell us that the first is the more fundamental of the two. By so doing, it explains both what chance, *haecceity*, and law are and also how they can affect us. For since ideas can only be affected by other ideas which are in continuous connection with them (6.158), it is clear that our sensations must emanate from mind continuously connected with our own.

347

The principle with which I set out requires me to maintain that these feelings are communicated to the nerves by continuity, so that there must be something like them in the excitants themselves. If this seems extravagant, it is to be remembered that it is the sole possible way of reaching any explanation of sensation, which otherwise must be pronounced a general fact, absolutely inexplicable and ultimate. Now absolute inexplicability is a hypothesis which sound logic refuses under any circumstances to justify. [6.158]

Thus objective idealism serves as an explanation not only of what is and how it is but of how we can know it. The real world is the world of mind, and real objects are simply portions of mind which have assumed a particular form. And the proof of this fact, Peirce maintains, is that it explains why we experience what we do in the way we do. For since the three categories of phenomena yield all the phenomena there are, once we have produced a consistent theory explaining their nature, origin, and behavior, we have done all that metaphysics requires.[25] And having now, as he believed, established the ontological nature of the universe, Peirce turned in the last of the five *Monist* articles, "Evolutionary Love," to the question of its origins, and particularly to the question of the origin of the laws which govern its behavior.

There are two ways of accounting for the present laws of nature: one is to hold that they have been operative from the beginning and the other is that they have evolved from something other than law. The first course Peirce rejects on the ground that the existence of law is pre-eminently that which requires explanation, and that to assert that it is an ultimate fact affords none. (6.12; 6.60) Moreover, to assert that the present laws of nature have always operated requires positing a variety of kinds of laws, some reversible, some irreversible, some absolute, some statistical tendencies, with no apparent reason for such differences except that it has always been so. But if the second course is adopted, then clearly Peirce must argue that chance begets order — that law has developed out of nonlaw, uniformity from randomness. This is in effect the burden of the law of mind, which, given Peirce's equations of chance and feeling, *haecceity* and will, and law and habit, describes the development of law from chance. The resulting theory must therefore take somewhat the following form. It is necessary to postulate the existence in the beginning of a kind of soul-stuff or mind-

---

[25] Peirce, Commonplace Book, August 28, 1908.

stuff which would be a continuum of pure feeling. The behavior of this pure feeling would be utterly irregular: there would be unlimited and arbitrary variation. "This feeling, sporting here and there in pure arbitrariness, would have started the germ of a generalizing tendency. Its other sportings would be evanescent, but this would have a growing virtue. Thus, the tendency to habit would be started; and from this, with the other principles of evolution, all the regularities of the universe would be evolved." (6.33) That is to say, the tendency to take habits is itself a result of the quite fortuitous variations of the primeval chaos of feeling, but this particular sport, being a tendency for a sport to repeat, would tend to perpetuate itself, since every sport which did repeat would only further strengthen the tendency. Thus there would be an evolution from Firstness (feeling) through Secondness (actual occurrences which are repeated) to Thirds (laws).

Such a process of cosmic evolution would obviously lead from a less to a more orderly world. But this alone does not tell much of the future. For there are various forms by which such an evolution might proceed, and it is not even certain that the entire process might not reverse by a chance weakening of the tendency to take habits. Accordingly, it is necessary to specify in more detail precisely how this process operates. Peirce considers three alternative theories. The first of these, which he equates with the Darwinian theory, leaves the entire process to the operation of chance alone. In this theory the sole agent of proliferation is fortuitous variation in the strictest Darwinian sense. (6.296f) The second theory makes mechanical necessity to be the basis of all development, so that virtually the whole process is predetermined by the laws of mechanics and the original state description. (6.298) The third theory is that of Lamarck. Between this theory and the law of mind Peirce sees a close connection particularly as regards the inheritance of acquired characteristics.

Such a transmission of acquired characters is of the general nature of habit-taking, and this is the representative and derivative within the physiological domain of the law of mind. . . . The Lamarckians further suppose that, although some of the modifications of form so transmitted were originally due to mechanical causes, yet the chief factors of their first production were the straining of endeavor and the overgrowth superinduced by exercise, together with the opposite actions. Now, endeavor, since it is directed toward an end,

349

is essentially psychical, even though it be sometimes unconscious; and the growth due to exercise, as I argued in my last paper, follows a law of a character quite contrary to that of mechanics. [6.299]

The fact that the Lamarckian theory is "essentially psychical" means that it fits Peirce's idealistic ontology better than the other theories, and Peirce therefore adopts it as the most reasonable account of evolution. (6.300) But what makes it psychic is the fact that the process is directed toward an end. For individual creatures that end is survival in a given environment, but for the universal mind itself there can be no struggle for survival and some further purpose must therefore be sought which directs the whole process of evolution.

The search for an ultimate goal of evolution leads Peirce to the consideration of the religious problem. Up to this time Peirce had avoided dealing directly with questions of theology. That there is a religious interest and commitment behind much of his thought is, I believe, clear from many points which have been discussed above. But in his philosophic work he had avoided religion in the belief that knowledge of God was beyond the scope of reason. Moreover, the years of bitter controversy which had raged between scientist and theologian all through Peirce's adult life can have given him little relish for theological argument. But now he felt that his theory committed him to dealing in some fashion with certain parts of the religious question.

In the first paragraph of the paper, Peirce refers to the writings of Henry James the elder as affording the true answer to the problem of evil. (6.287) On this problem and the problem of creation there is a striking parallel between Peirce's doctrines and those of the elder James, and in view of Peirce's repeated and explicit references to James' writings on these matters (6.287; 6.507; 8.263) it seems a justifiable conclusion that his own theories owed something to James'. According to James, God is literally the stuff of life. Therefore James holds that he cannot create life, for this would be to create Himself — He can only communicate life by embodying Himself in some other form. Creation, therefore, is incarnation.[26] Such a theory would very quickly run into pantheism unless the creature so made became utterly distinct from the creator — that is, acquired a separate individual identity of his own. And this can only happen by there being a radical

[26] Henry James, *Substance and Shadow* (Boston, 1863), p. 433.

differentiation amounting to opposition between creature and creator. The creature only knows itself as a separate thing by contrast against the creator. He says:

The sole possible basis of identity for the creature, the only conceivable ground for attributing distinctive character or selfhood to him, lies in his being in himself a direct contrast to the creator: empty where He is full, impotent where He is omnipotent, ignorant where He is omniscient, evil where He is good. Did he not possess this formal constitutional identity, were he not by nature the characteristic well-defined opposite of all Divine perfection, he could not possibly be a proper object of the creative Love: since the very distinction of that Love, regarded as infinite or pure of all infirmity, is that it is utterly void of self-love, having no respect to any worthiness in its object but what grows out of the object's utter want. It is no doubt very tolerable finite or creaturely love to love one's own in another, to love another for his conformity to oneself: but nothing can be in more flagrant contrast with the creative Love, all whose tenderness *ex vi termini* must be reserved only for what intrinsically is most bitterly hostile and negative to itself.[27]

Evil is therefore necessary, for it is the differentia which sets the creature apart from the creator and makes it possible for God to love his creations. James out-Calvins Calvin in this ringing denunciation of anything resembling self-love, even on the part of God. The argument is essentially that evil is necessary in order to preserve God from the sin of self-love. Creation therefore originates that which is hostile to God, evil actually being the principle of individuation, and then the "creative Love" brings the creature back into a harmony with the creator through redemption.[28]

The elder James was more of a Calvinist than Peirce, and his ferocious demand for the utter depravity of the creature finds no real parallel in Peirce's writings. For Peirce the differentiation from the universal mind is accomplished by ignorance and error — not by sin (5.234f); and the opposition between creator and creature need not amount to quite so polar a contradiction. But Peirce does follow James in holding that individuality is a state which is, if not sinful, yet deplorable. (6.290–294) And rank individualism amounting to downright selfishness is condemned in Peirce's paper with a fervor which shows that a New England upbringing is not without its effects even upon a

---

[27] *Ibid.*, p. 442.
[28] *Ibid.*, p. 443.

philosopher. Peirce sharply attacks the hedonistic theory that men seek only their own pleasure, and particularly the classical economic theory which makes the maximization of individual profit the key to the social welfare. And writing of the nineteenth century, Peirce states:

> Here, then, is the issue. The gospel of Christ says that progress comes from every individual merging his individuality in sympathy with his neighbors. On the other side, the conviction of the nineteenth century is that progress takes place by virtue of every individual's striving for himself with all his might and trampling his neighbor under foot whenever he gets a chance to do so. This may accurately be called the Gospel of Greed. [6.294]

But if the selfhood which is the inevitable fate of man is an evil, what is to be done to escape from it? According to James, there is a process of redemption in which the alienated man is called back into harmony with the creator.[29] This position is iterated by Peirce: "The movement of love is circular, at one and the same impulse projecting creations into independency and drawing them into harmony." (6.288) But Peirce then readapts James' theory to suit himself and his own notions of what constitutes creation.

> Everybody can see that the statement of St. John ("God is Love") is the formula of an evolutionary philosophy, which teaches that growth comes only from love, from I will not say self-*sacrifice*, but from the ardent impulse to fulfill another's highest impulse. Suppose, for example, that I have an idea that interests me. It is my creation. It is my creature; for as I have shown in last July's *Monist*, it is a little person. I love it; and I will sink myself in perfecting it. It is not by dealing out cold justice to the circle of my ideas that I can make them grow, but by cherishing and tending them as I would the flowers in my garden. The philosophy we draw from John's gospel is that this is the way mind develops; and as for the cosmos, only so far as it yet is mind, and so has life, is it capable of further evolution. Love, recognizing germs of loveliness in the hateful, gradually warms it into life, and makes it lovely. That is the sort of evolution which every careful student of my essay "The Law of Mind" must see that *synechism* calls for. [6.289]

The aim, end, and *raison d'être* of evolution therefore is the development of an idea through "cherishing love" or agapé. "The agapastic development of thought should, if it exists, be distinguished by its purposive character, this purpose being the development of an idea."

[29] *Ibid.*

(6.315) But as we have already seen, this description precisely fits the Lamarckian form of evolution. Accordingly here, as in the 1870's, the ultimate goal turns out to be the realization of the idea, which is accomplished literally by the living of the idea — i.e., by its being made the governing principle of action and thought. Such a ruling idea is in fact what constitutes the personality of the individual. But since two persons are simply two general ideas, whenever these are brought into a teleological connection and close communication, a supraindividual personality is formed. (6.155f; 6.271) Just as there can be more than one personality in a body, so there can be more than one body in a personality. Group personality is therefore entirely possible, and such phenomena as *esprit de corps*, group cohesion, and simultaneous discovery in science are cited by Peirce as proof of its existence. (6.271; 6.307; 6.315–317) Indeed, since the whole universe is but mind, the evolution of the cosmos itself is in fact the evolution of an all embracing community of mind, or communal personality, of which each particular person is a part. This is that community of investigators of which Peirce has so often spoken. To carry this out fully one may say that each man (i.e., individual person) is a part of the total personality in development, or, put another way, that to each man is entrusted the development of a particular part of the total personality. The harmonious function of all the individual parts will have the effect of merging them all into a harmonious person, as distinct from the continuous but "unpersonalized" feeling from which the evolution proceeds. In a quite literal sense, then, each man has a part to play in the development of the universal mind. But it is of the essence to realize that this part is freely played: it is by voluntarily striving after the realization of the end that the development is made. (1.615)

But in this paper, Peirce fails to explain what leads the individual to abjure his individuality and seek the good of the whole. Having already damned hedonism, Peirce cannot resort to any principle of pleasure; what he actually does is to introduce what is implicitly an aesthetic standard. Thus he writes:

The agapastic development of thought is the adoption of certain mental tendencies, not altogether heedlessly, as in tychasm, nor quite blindly by the mere force of circumstances or of logic, as in anancasm, but by an immediate attraction for the idea itself, whose nature is divined before the mind possesses it, by the power of sympathy, that is, by virtue of the continuity of mind . . . [6.307]

It is therefore the attractiveness of the idea which is what leads the individual to devote himself to its development, but Peirce does not explain how the idea is divined, nor in what that attractiveness consists. Yet he does suggest that the judgment of sentiment may play an important part. Declaring himself a sentimentalist, he writes: "But what after all is sentimentalism? It is an *ism*, a doctrine, namely, the doctrine that great respect should be paid to the natural judgments of the sensible heart." (6.292) This suggests, although it does not assert, that there is a relation between these two methods — that sentiment (i.e., feeling) is related to aesthetics and both to religious perception. Neither of these ideas is developed, but if it is true that God is a person too and continuously related to us, so that there is in some sense a direct perception of the divine — and as Peirce himself pointed out, synechism requires such a conclusion (6.162) — then some theory of religious perception has got to be forthcoming.

# XVII

# *The Last Revision, 1896–1914*

THE doubt-belief theory of inquiry of the 1870's may be regarded as an attempt to imbed the earlier theory of the 1860's in an evolutionary context. But the result of this procedure, as Peirce subsequently came to see, is that in a certain sense logic itself is made to depend upon psychology. Looking back on the papers of the seventies after twenty-five years, Peirce wrote:

> But how do we know that belief is nothing but the deliberate preparedness to act according to the formula believed?
>
> My original article carried this back to a psychological principle. The conception of truth, according to me, was developed out of an original impulse to act consistently, to have a definite intention. But in the first place, this was not very clearly made out, and in the second place, I do not think it satisfactory to reduce such fundamental things to facts of psychology. For man could alter his nature, or his environment would alter it if he did not voluntarily do so, if the impulse were not what was advantageous or fitting. Why has evolution made man's mind to be so constructed? That is the question we must nowadays ask, and all attempts to ground the fundamentals of logic on psychology are seen to be essentially shallow. [5.28]

The reduction of logic to psychology which the doubt-belief theory involves has the effect of making the value of logic relative to a particular phase of development and so undercuts the entire architectonic theory. Confronted by so unwelcome a development, Peirce found himself with only three possible alternatives: to abandon the architectonic theory, to revise it by founding the theory of the categories upon some other basis than logic, or to prove that the end of man will forever be the fixation of belief. The first alternative Peirce rejected, for it involved the surrender of what he seems to have regarded as the true purpose of philosophy. It was just this hope of creating an all embracing system which would serve as the framework for all future discovery and knowledge which seems to have motivated Peirce's work. But the other two alternatives he did accept, and as I have noted above they account for much of his work during the 1890's. Both "A Guess at the Riddle" and the "Architecture of Theories" are explicitly concerned with the question of the architectonic. In 1896 Peirce returned to this subject in an extended paper on the "Logic of Mathematics" (1.417–520), in which he endeavored to develop a more detailed classification based on the categories. And in that same year he began a tentative classification of science based on the principles of August Comte. (3.428) His interest in the problem persisted until in 1902 he finally produced the elaborate system of classification which he retained until his death, and in which for the first time in any of his writings the theory of the categories is separated from logic. (1.203–283)

The third alternative finds its expression in the cosmology. If our proclivity to seek settled belief is a mere adaptive result of evolution, then the question which must be asked is, "Why has evolution made man's mind to be so constructed?" (5.28), and will this proclivity be found to be nonadaptive in the future? These questions can be answered only by a theory of cosmic evolution in which the relation between the mind and nature is explored, and such a theory Peirce's cosmology seeks to provide. According to this theory, the universe is itself mind, and therefore the processes of nature cannot be radically different from those of our own minds. The logical patterns of hypothesis, induction, and deduction which we employ to fix belief turn out to be the same as those which the universe employs to create order. (2.713; 6.189f) Thus in the long run there cannot be a disparity between the human mind and nature, for both are parts of the evolving universal mind.

But the cosmological solution is not as satisfying as might at first appear. For the mode of evolution described by the cosmology is not really consistent with the doubt-belief theory of inquiry even though both lead to the fixation of belief. The desire to realize and develop ideas which is the driving force behind agapastic evolution is largely due to the attractiveness of the ideas themselves (6.307), and this mode of evolution is held to be true both of the individual and the universal minds. But in the doubt-belief theory the motive for fixing belief is the escape from doubt; judged by the standards of 1893 this is close to development by anancasm, or mechanical necessity, for the development is initiated not by the idea as final cause but by the irritation of doubt as efficient cause. (6.305) In so far as there is purpose in the doubt-belief theory it is either negative — the removal of irritation — or hedonistic — the pleasure of belief — as contrasted to the quasi-aesthetic purpose of agapasm. And even if the doubt-belief theory were maintained in regard to human individuals, it cannot be held true of mind in general, for it is scarcely plausible to say that the evolution of the laws of nature results from the desire of the universal mind to escape from doubt. Thus although the cosmology seems to solve Peirce's problems concerning the relativity of logic, in fact it raises yet more serious problems, for it involves a theory of inquiry very different from that of the 1870's.

As the nineteenth century drew to a close, therefore, Peirce's philosophical suitcase was bulging with unsolved problems. His theory of cognition was badly in need of repair, particularly as concerned the status of sense impressions. The problem of the relation of *haecceity* to continuity was as yet unresolved. The legitimacy of the architectonic theory was in question and with it the basis of the categories. His theory of inquiry was not wholly compatible with his cosmology, and the ultimate goal of the cosmic process needed clarification. Peirce was surely aware of these difficulties. Yet in the years immediately following the completion of the *Monist* series, he was not able to solve them, and although he continued to work away at them no major advances came until after the turn of the century. Doubtless part of the explanation for this lack of productivity is to be found in the personal misfortunes which now rained about him.[1] Part, too, must be laid to his engagement in other philosophical activities such as the completion of the "Grand Logic" in 1893 (8.G.1893), the discovery of the system of logical graphs in 1896 (4.394ff), the Cambridge lectures in 1898 (8.G. 1898), and the articles for Baldwin's *Dictionary*. (8.G.1901) But I think there is also another reason. During these years Peirce must have been working steadily on the mathematics of continuity. Believing as he did that continuity was the key to the treasures of philosophy, his obvious course of action would be to perfect the mathematical theory and then to turn to its philosophical interpretation. I suspect that this was in fact Peirce's plan of study in the 1890's. The mathematics was

[1] See above, p. 293.

worked out between 1891, when he published his singularly inept treatment of continuity in the "Law of Mind" (6.112–126), and 1897, when the paper on "Multitude and Number" was written. (4.170–226) And in the last years of the century we know that the problem of the "logic of continuity" was much in his mind. (8.G.1898; 6.185–237) Meanwhile, he let the other problems accumulate.

What brought Peirce back to these problems, and that quite suddenly and unexpectedly, was James' public announcement of pragmatism. I do not think that the significance of this event for Peirce has really been understood. It is of course true that Peirce originated pragmatism and that he published the famous pragmatic maxim in 1878 in the second paper of the *Popular Science Monthly* series. But as I have noted before, in neither the famous maxim nor the famous paper does the word "pragmatism" occur, nor did Peirce ever use this term in print before James' California lecture.[2] For Peirce, "pragmatism" was simply one aspect of the doubt-belief theory of inquiry, and it was not a sufficiently important aspect to justify the use of a separate name. Moreover, by the late 1890's, as I have tried to suggest, Peirce was not so devoted to the doubt-belief theory as he had once been, and he was already working on a new theory which would be less psychological and less positivistic. Then suddenly James published, and Peirce found himself famous as the inventor of "pragmatism."

Peirce was now in an intolerable intellectual position. When James delivered his California address in 1898, Peirce was the forgotten man of American philosophy, and he was in desperate financial straits.[3] The ever loyal James had once again come to his rescue in an hour of dire need, and had given him a chance not just for fame but for money which that fame could bring through articles and lectures. For financial and personal reasons, therefore, Peirce could not disown the doctrine; nor could he honestly embrace it without qualification. And as controversy — and therefore interest — gathered about the doctrine, and as James, and subsequently Dewey and Schiller, made their interpretation of it more explicit, Peirce was more and more compelled to dissociate himself from the school, to stress the differences between his doctrines and theirs — even going so far as to invent a new name,

[2] See above, p. 156.
[3] See above, p. 293.

"pragmaticism," for his own doctrine (5.414) — and yet to use the notoriety which he had acquired as the inventor of pragmatism to publicize the aspects of his work which he considered important and to try to make enough money to keep the wolf a little longer from the door.[4]

The sudden, almost spectacular, reformulation of Peirce's philosophy which occurred in 1901–02 cannot be laid wholly at James' door. As I have tried to show, many of the problems underlying it were on Peirce's mind before 1898 and would doubtless have reached solution in due time. What James did do was force the issue. Peirce was compelled to decide where he stood not only on pragmatism itself but on a wide range of associated questions. The results were a sweeping revision of the architectonic, the introduction of phenomenology and normative science, an extension of the theology, and a complete revision of the theory of cognition.

The theory of normative science was the result of a long process of development which goes back to the cognitive theory of 1868. In those early years, Peirce had held that all thinking follows the forms of logic, and had even gone so far as to attempt a proof that there are no mental processes not describable as an inference of some sort.[5] Logic thus became virtually a description of how the mind operates. We reason as we breathe — involuntarily, and whether these inferences are recognized as such is immaterial. But with the development of the doubt-belief theory in the 1870's, the use of logic comes to be regarded as one among several possible means for attaining a goal, and since there are alternative means it is no longer possible to hold that the mind is inescapably logical. The decision to be logical now becomes a conscious choice, made on the basis of reflection and the critical study of available methods. Peirce does not bother to make the obvious point in the 1870's that this is only possible for processes subject to self-control, and therefore of which we are conscious. But he does make this point very clearly in 1893.

What seems to have led Peirce to clarify his position in 1893 was, first, his own work with Jastrow on small differences of sensation, and,

---

[4] Cf., e.g., the Lowell Lectures of 1903 and other late writings on pragmatism. 8.G.1903ff.
[5] See above, pp. 114f.

secondly, James' *Principles of Psychology*.[6] Working at Hopkins in the early eighties, Peirce and Jastrow had succeeded in proving that sensory stimuli too slight to be recognized consciously nevertheless influence judgment. (7.21–35) This result served to emphasize the importance of unconscious mental processes in the formation of belief, and so to point out that conscious inference is not an adequate explanation of knowledge. The publication of James' *Principles of Psychology* in 1890 added fresh support to this view by its emphasis on the mind as a natural phenomenon to be explained within the framework of natural law. In 1891 Peirce wrote a review of James' work in which he considered particularly the question, "Is Perception Unconscious Inference?," and vigorously defended the thesis that it is. The distinction between "conscious" and "unconscious" inference, Peirce argues, is that between inferences recognized as being inferences and inferences not so recognized. He then seeks to show that perception, and association in general, are inferential and do conform to the forms of valid ampliative reasoning. (8.64f) Thus Peirce holds that all unconscious mental processes conform to the patterns of logic. But in 1893 he added to this assertion the further claim that such processes, being unconscious, cannot be criticized.

> Such inferences are beyond the jurisdiction of criticism. It is the part of psychology to explain their processes as it can; but, as long as they are out of the focal plane of consciousness, they are out of our control; and to call them good or bad were idle. The ordinary business of life is, however, best conducted without too much self-criticism . . .
> Quite otherwise is it with the actions which carry out our grander purposes. Here all must be voluntary, thoroughly conscious, based on critical reflection. Logic is wanted here, to pull inferences to pieces, to show whether they be sound or not, to advise how they may be strengthened, to consider by what methods they ought to proceed. [7.448f]

Thus by 1893 the identification of unconscious inference with the involuntary psychological processes of association, and of conscious inference with the deliberate, critical, voluntary, self-controlled application of logic to the correction of our methods of reasoning was complete. From here it would appear to be only a step to the recognition that logic is a normative science. Yet it was almost nine years before Peirce

---

[6] William James, *The Principles of Psychology*, 2 vols. (New York, 1890).

took this step, and it might well have been longer had it not been for James. For James not only forced Peirce to review his own theory of knowledge — I suspect it was also James' doctrine that the truth is a species of the good [7] which suggested to Peirce the idea of the dependence of logic on ethics. Certainly, the priority here belongs to James: as late as 1898 Peirce regarded ethics as a practical discipline of no philosophic consequence. (1.666–669) But for William James, the theory of normative science might very well have remained unborn, and Peirce might never have resolved the question of the ends of reasoning.

The problem of the ends of reasoning can be stated in various ways, and receives different answers depending upon how it is stated. It may be asked for example what the end of reasoning *is*. This is presumably an empirical question, and falls within the province of the special sciences, particularly psychology and social psychology. But since these sciences presuppose logic, the validity of the inquiry will depend upon whether or not the reasoning involved is good and these sciences cannot set the standard of goodness itself. It may also be asked what the end of reasoning must be? But then the question is, must be for what? To attain a given end? But again, what end? What is required here is an answer to the question of what the end of reasoning ought to be, and this involves the question of what ends in general ought to be adopted. This inquiry, however, is clearly ethical. In so far, then, as logic is to be regarded as a normative science, it must depend upon the science of norms and therefore upon ethics. (1.611f; 2.198)

But Peirce soon came to see that ethics itself is composed of two parts — one, the science of how to regulate conduct in accordance with our ultimate ends, and, two, the science which defines those ultimate ends. These ultimate ends, since they are to be sought for their own sakes, cannot be means to anything, but must be desirable in and of themselves. This fact led Peirce to say that the science of the ultimately good, or the *summum bonum*, must be aesthetics. (1.191; 1.612f; 2. 199)

Several reasons can be cited for Peirce's decision on this question. In the first place, the ever present architectonic is here seen again, for there must be three normative sciences if there are any, and since logic

[7] Perry, *James*, II, 450–456; James, *Pragmatism*, pp. 75f.

deals with thought, ethics with action or will, another is needed to deal with pure feeling or quality, and aesthetics fits this description. Moreover, since the *summum bonum* is that which is attractive in itself, apart from anything else, it must clearly be a First. (1.612f; 5.110–114; 5.129) The schema falls in neatly therefore with the categorical pattern. (5.129) Secondly, the definition of the true as a species of the good raises particular difficulties for Peirce. All the pragmatists agreed that the true was in some sense the "satisfactory"; but what is the "satisfactory"? (5.552)

Is the Satisfactory meant to be whatever excites a certain peculiar feeling of satisfaction? In that case, the doctrine is simply hedonism in so far as it affects the field of cognition. For when hedonists talk of "pleasure," they do not mean what is so-called in ordinary speech, but what excites a feeling of satisfaction.

But to say that an action or the result of an action is Satisfactory is simply to say that it is congruous to the aim of that action. Consequently, the aim must be determined before it can be determined, either in thought or in fact, to be satisfactory. An action that had no other aim than to be congruous to its aim would have no aim at all, and would not be a deliberate action. [5.559f]

Yet as Peirce went on to remark, "It is, however, no doubt true that men act, especially in the action of inquiry, *as if* their sole purpose were to produce a certain state of feeling, in the sense that when that state of feeling is attained, there is no further effort. It was upon that proposition that I originally based pragmaticism . . ." (5.563) Since Peirce regarded hedonism almost as a form of bestiality he had no desire to see his own doctrine in such company. Yet short of rejecting the whole normative concept, the only alternatives lay in defining the good in terms which have nothing to do with individual feeling, or in showing that that feeling is something more than individual gratification. The first alternative however is difficult if one is to hold, as clearly Peirce must, that those who pursue inquiry do seek what they ought to seek. The second alternative is therefore the most promising, and the choice of the beautiful is a fairly obvious one. Even if it were not automatically suggested by the juxtaposition of the true and the good, it is a goal the attainment of which gives a "satisfaction," but a "satisfaction" traditionally regarded as more noble than other forms of gratification. (5.111)

Peirce's theory of aesthetics is not very fully developed, but he does make clear what it is that constitutes the beautiful for him. It might be thought at first that Peirce's theory would virtually preclude intelligent aesthetic distinctions, since Firsts are what they are independent of all else, and it is with Firsts that we are here concerned. Nevertheless, there are different kinds of Firstness: there are, for example, pure Firsts, Firstnesses of Secondness, pure and degenerate, and Firstnesses of Thirdness of all grades. That which seems to constitute the acme of beauty for Peirce is the Firstness of genuine Thirdness carried to the furthest extreme — that is to say, it is the quality arising from order, and the more developed the order the greater the beauty. The First itself, of course, remains a simple quality, but it is occasioned by the symmetrical order of the involved aggregate. And the more complex and symmetrical that order, the higher the quality ranks on the scale of beauty. Now that order will be the result of laws or habits — Thirds which control the arrangement of the aggregate of Seconds. Accordingly, the maximum beauty is the Firstness of a system of Seconds in which the development of Thirdness has proceeded to the highest conceivable degree. (5.111–113)

It is clear from the cosmology that the creation of the state of maximum beauty is the objective toward which the universe is evolving. Out of the original chaos of chance-feeling, Seconds are actualized which, through habit taking, become ordered under laws. And as the cosmic evolution proceeds, both the number and exactitude of these laws tend always to increase while at the same time they come to form a more and more perfect system.[8] Viewed from the inside — i.e., in psychological terms — this process leads to the creation of a single all embracing personality out of the primordial chaos of unorganized feeling. And since rationality consists for Peirce in the rule of feeling and action by general principles, this process may also be called the evolution of rationality made concrete by being embodied in action, or, in brief, of concrete reasonableness. (1.615)

It should now be evident in what sense pragmaticism consists in subserving the growth of concrete reasonableness. The original pragmatic maxim made the meaning of a concept to consist in all the habits in which its object is involved. But clearly the meaning of a concept

---

[8] Peirce, Commonplace Book, August 29, 1908.

viewed as a means to attaining concrete reasonableness will consist precisely in the habit or pattern of rational action which its accept-ance would involve, so the two definitions come to one. (5.3f; 5.433) Moreover, the doubt-belief theory itself becomes merely an imperfect statement of the fact that the goal of thought is the creation of rational order. The motive for seeking this goal, however, is no longer merely negative, it is the inherent aesthetic attraction of that order. And every man has it in his power to aid the divine plan by making his own life and conduct the embodiment of rationality. "Under this conception, the ideal of conduct will be to execute our little function in the opera-tion of the creation by giving a hand toward rendering the world more reasonable whenever, as the slang is, it is 'up to us' to do so." (1.615)

What remains to be shown, however, is why the end which will be attained coincides with what ought to be attained. To assert that such is the case is to assert that evolution is a moral process. "Almost every-body will now agree that the ultimate good lies in the evolutionary process in some way." (5.4) But the only final explanation of this fact lies in the relation which Peirce postulates between the universe as a whole and God. It is clear that Peirce regards the evolving universe as being itself a person of an extended sort. Is the universe then God? I think not, both because Peirce avoids any such pantheistic statement, and because the solution of the problem of evil which Peirce says he derived from Henry James, Sr., forbids it. (6.287) God can only love the world and man on condition of their being different from Himself. But James held that the "soul-stuff" of the universe is literally the sub-stance of God incarnated in another form. Does Peirce then accept this doctrine? I think he does, and for two reasons. First, Peirce asserts that in the original chaos nothing existed but the *Ens Neces-sarium*, which is God. Now this comes to asserting that the original feeling was a part of God.[9] Second, Peirce believed that his synechism required him to maintain that we are in continuous connection — and therefore direct communication — with God. (6.162) But this would be possible only through a continuous connection in feeling, so that feel-ing must be a part of God. Moreover, Peirce asserts a peculiarly close relation among feeling, aesthetics, and God. In the "Neglected Argu-ment for the Reality of God" (6.452–493), or the "N.A." as he calls

[9] *Ibid.*, August 28, 1908.

it, Peirce advances three distinct arguments in support of God's reality. The first of these he calls the "Humble Argument," and it is as follows. The investigator must bring himself into a state of "musement" — an activity which involves no serious purpose but merely the pure play of the mind. It is an attitude of wide-eyed and idle wonder at the world about. "The particular occupation I mean . . . may take either the form of aesthetic contemplation, or that of distant castle-building . . . or that of considering some wonder in one of the Universes, or some connection between two of the three, with speculation concerning its cause. It is this last kind — I will call it 'Musement' on the whole — that I particularly recommend, because it will in time flower into the N.A." (6.458) Musement is thus a form of free speculation on the nature and origin of the world about us. Peirce holds it to be inevitable that such speculation will suggest the idea of God as creator and governor of the universe, and that once suggested the idea will prove irresistibly attractive. Indeed, the investigator "will come to be stirred to the depths of his nature by the beauty of the idea and by its august practicality, even to the point of earnestly loving and adoring his strictly hypothetical God . . ." (6.467) The argument is not as uncritical as might at first appear, for the third of the three arguments consists of a critical evaluation of the "humble argument" which shows the hypothesis of God's reality to be not only a legitimate hypothesis but a quasi-instinctual common sense belief. (6.468f) [10] This is a natural judgment of the "sensible heart."( 6.493) But why is the hypothesis of God's reality so natural to us? "The second of the nest [of arguments] is the argument which seems to me to have been 'neglected' by writers upon natural theology, consisting in showing that the humble argument is the natural fruit of free meditation, since every heart will be ravished by the beauty and adorability of the Idea, when it is so pursued." (6.487) In other words, what justifies us in adopting this hypothesis, which is admittedly so vague as to admit of no precise test and which therefore a truly rigorous critical common-sensism would reject, is the immediate aesthetic attraction of the idea itself. On the basis of Peirce's aesthetic, this attraction consists in the order which the hypothesis gives both as an intellectual explanation of the origin of the universe,

[10] For an excellent analysis of this paper of Peirce's, see John Smith, "Religion and Theology in Peirce," in Wiener and Young, *Studies*, pp. 251–270.

and as an Ideal of conduct. (6.465) So seen, the universe itself would be a symbol of God. (5.119) I think this is what Peirce meant when he said habits were not signs in the ordinary sense: they do not have logical interpretants but the universe of habits is a developing icon of God's purpose whose ultimate aim is the revelation of his glory. (5.119)

The development of the theory of normative science is a part of the new and quite elaborate classification of the sciences which Peirce produced in 1902. He first divided all sciences into two branches — practical, meaning technological skills, and theoretical. The theoretical sciences are divided into sciences of review, which occupy themselves with digests and reviews of the results of other sciences, and sciences of discovery. The latter branch is then subdivided into three parts. First comes mathematics, which is presupposed by all other sciences of discovery. Peirce subdivided mathematics into three branches: mathematics of logic, mathematics of discrete series, and mathematics of continua and pseudocontinua. Second among the sciences of discovery is philosophy, or "coenoscopy." (1.241) The distinctive characteristic of this science is asserted to be that it deals with matters of fact, but uses only such observations as occur in everyday experience and require no special instruments or procedures. The three branches of philosophy are phenomenology, normative science, and metaphysics, in that order, each presupposing its predecessor, and all presupposing mathematics. The divisions of normative science are as we know aesthetics, ethics, and logic; for metaphysics Peirce lists ontology, religious metaphysics, and physical metaphysics. The third branch of the sciences of discovery, coming after and presupposing mathematics and philosophy, is Ideoscopy, or the specialized sciences which involve specialized procedures and observations. These Peirce further divided into physical and psychical, and then into more detailed subclasses. (1.193–202)

There are several features of this classification which are of interest. It is of course obvious that the introduction of the theory of normative science requires a revision of the architectonic theory. Since logic is only one of the normative sciences, and since the divisions of the normative sciences are themselves obviously based on the categories, it is clear that Peirce can no longer rest his theory of the categories on logic. Peirce's solution to this problem is the introduction of a new science which he called "phenomenology" or "phaneroscopy," and which stands between mathematics and the normative sciences. The sole function of this new science is to provide the basis for the categories. (1.280)

Although Peirce calls this science "phenomenology," this term is not here used in its customary sense. The subject matter of this science is not limited to what is actually presented as phenomena: rather it includes all that can possibly be an object of thought, whether it is actually perceived or not. Accordingly, any conceivable thing is an element of the phaneron: the difference between the perceived and conceived, or the external and internal, is not a difference relevant to the phaneron, for those distinctions are distinctions made by inference, whereas the problem of the phenomenology is the analysis of whatever is before the mind in any sense, regardless of its externality. (2.197; 2.84) Indeed, this science is so purely observational that it scarcely involves reasoning at all. It consists strictly in the observation and classification of whatever seems to be before the mind at any given time (2.197), and the discovery of the characters, if any, which are universally present in all such phenomena. (1.286; 2.84) The propositions of phenomenology are thus virtually indubitable, for the only proof that something is before the mind is simply that it seems to be there. (1.288; 2.197)

As actually practiced, Peirce's phenomenology differs in no respect from the doctrine of the categories as he had presented it since 1885. The characters universally present in the phaneron are of course Firstness, Secondness, and Thirdness, and the descriptions of these categories simply repeat what he had already said about them in their material aspects. But what is of more interest is that Peirce actually preserves in the phenomenology the formal aspects of the categories as well. Thus in 1905 Peirce opens his discussion of phenomenology with a consideration of the forms of relation and shows, a priori, that there can be three and but three such relational forms. Thus he writes: "We find then *a priori* that there are three categories of undecomposable elements to be expected in the phaneron: those which are simply positive totals, those which involve dependence but not combination, those which involve combination. Now let us turn to the phaneron and see what we find in fact." (1.299) Now it is obvious that these a priori elements are not observed in the phaneron, and that they cannot be derived from logic; how then do we come to have them?

What Peirce has done here is to divide his logic into two parts and to classify formal logic as a part of mathematics — namely, as the mathematics of logic. In 1902 — the same year that the classification of the sciences appeared and that the phenomenology was introduced — Peirce wrote a paper entitled "The Simplest Mathematics" in which he gives a formal development of the algebra of logic, including relations (4.245–323), as a part of mathematics. Since, then, phenomenology presupposes mathematics, it is possible for Peirce to utilize the formal properties of relations as a basis for the classification of the elements of the phaneron without circularity.[11]

It is impossible to regard Peirce's phenomenological treatment of the categories as anything more than a quite unsuccessful sleight of hand. Even if his attempt to identify formal logic with mathematics is accepted, the most that results from it is that there is an algebra isomorphic to the logical system of relations. Now this algebra could certainly be used to classify the elements of the phaneron, if those elements should happen to exhibit characteristics which would admit of such a classification, and it is the purpose of the phenomenology to show that in fact such a classification can be made. But what the phenomenology does not show is why it should be made. There are certainly other ways of classifying the elements of the phaneron which are equally simple and exhaustive, and no reason is given as to why the classification by relations is to be preferred. It is obvious that Peirce does not regard the categories as simply the most convenient available system of classes,[12] but his method of classifying the sciences has now made it impossible for him to prove that his categories are either necessary or particularly important. For as Kant had shown long before, it is the fact that cognition must have a certain logical form which enables us to argue that whatever is necessarily true of anything which can be known in such a cognition is true of all we can know. The significance of Peirce's categories consists in the fact that every cognition involves

---

[11] Manley H. Thompson, *The Pragmatic Philosophy of C. S. Peirce* (Chicago, 1953), pp. 156–162.

[12] Peirce states (1.284) that there are alternative sets of categories, but in none of his writings are these ever developed, nor does he ever really question the superiority of his own set.

predication, and all predicates are of one of these classes. But this is not a doctrine of mathematics: it results from the application of the mathematics of logic to the theory of cognition, which is a part of logic — presumably of speculative grammar. (1.191) If the basis for the categories is not demonstrable until we reach speculative grammar, then the whole argument is circular, for speculative grammar itself presupposes the categories of phenomenology. Peirce's classification of the sciences, therefore, does not succeed in providing an adequate alternative to the Kantian architectonic and the theory of the categories remains purely contingent.

Regardless of whether the categories are based on logic or on phenomenology the description of them in their material aspect undergoes no significant change from 1885 until Peirce's death. But this description is markedly different from the pre-1885 description and this fact raises problems in the theory of cognition. For as we have noted above, Peirce describes Firsts in terms which make them virtually identical with the simple ideas of British empirical philosophy, and Seconds are presented as directly experienced rather than inferred. During the 1890's Peirce seems to have wavered on these questions, and no decision was forthcoming until 1902. Again, I suspect that it was the revival of pragmatism which was the immediate occasion for this clarification, although it seems clear that eventually it would have had to come in any case.

In 1902 Peirce introduced, I believe for the first time, the theory of the percept and the perceptual judgment. (2.27) [13] The percept is not identical with the data of sensation. The pure sense data — what Peirce used to call the matter of receptivity — consists of neural stimuli. These data are never directly known; their existence is a postulate of physiology rather than a fact of consciousness. What is known is the percept which is a construct resulting from these data. (2.141) The percept is a nonlinguistic entity; it is a picture, image, or impression which is somehow constructed from the nerve excitations. (5.115) But so far as the conscious mind can tell, the percept is the "first" impression we have and it must therefore be taken to be the evidence of our senses. (5.115f)

---

[13] The theory is a much developed form of the early theory of constitutional nominal hypotheses.

The theory of the percept and sense data is based largely on physiology and psychology. It is a hypothesis to explain how, in terms of perceptual psychology, nerve stimulations are translated into sensory images. Little enough is known about this today, less was known in Peirce's time; and his own theory goes only so far as to maintain that the percept is in some way a construct which the mind creates, by processes not yet understood, out of the stimuli supplied by the nerves. (2.141) This explanation of course begs the question, but it is a legitimate question-begging since the problem is one of empirical science, and it would be stupid to be more precise than the facts warrant.

The percept is not identical with the sense data, but neither is it a proposition. In fact it is very like Kant's synthesis in intuition. It is true that in the early nineties Peirce denied this doctrine of Kant's, stating that what perception gives us is a confused mass which we then analyze and make distinct. (1.384) But since the percept itself is constructed from sense data, the difference is one of degree. Kant regarded the process by which the synthesis of intuition is made as susceptible of philosophic analysis whereas Peirce regards it as completely beyond the reach of consciousness. What Peirce means then is that we are not conscious of a synthesis behind the percept, although psychology tells us that such a synthesis occurred. (2.141)

The bringing of the percept to clarity is accomplished by a perceptual judgment. Such a judgment is a proposition asserting what the content of the percept is, or was. It is, if you like, the proposition which brings the manifold to unity. Such a proposition, however, is not analytic, although it is an explication of the percept; rather it is a hypothesis explaining what the percept is. That is to say, the percept is not a proposition; it is the extralinguistic referent of the proposition — the percept is the reality. (5.568) The perceptual judgment is the statement as to what that reality is — a judgment as to the nature of the percept. Accordingly, the process of judging the nature of the percept is abductive — it is the making of an explanatory hypothesis. (5.182f) But this hypothesis is peculiar in that it is indubitable; under no circumstances can it be proven false. If I now judge that what is before me is red, there are two possible interpretations of the judgment I affirm: (1) "this is red" and (2) "I judge that this is red." That (2) is true is obvious; in fact I do judge this whether I am right or wrong. But (1) must also be true, for it could only be shown to be false by comparing it with another contradictory judgment of the same object — say "this is blue." But since two judgments cannot be made simultaneously, the contradiction is only apparent: the two judgments relate to different percepts and both are true. (5.115)

It seems to me that on this question Peirce has made an error. Goodman has suggested that a perceptual judgment such as "this is red" can be disproven if we can also affirm of the same patch both (3) "this is blue" and (4) "this patch has not changed color." [14] Since on Peirce's theory of cognition, perception is continuous through an interval of time and we are immediately conscious throughout the interval, it seems clear that change of color could actually be perceived, and therefore that (4) can be regarded as a perceptual judgment rather than as a mediate inference. Only if perception were instantaneous so that change of color must be inferred by comparison of distinct judgments would the theory of the indubitable perceptual judgments be tenable.

We have then three sorts of elements in perception: sense data, percepts, and perceptual judgments. The process by which percepts result from sense data is unknown; that by which perceptual judgments result from percepts is abduction; but in both cases the process itself is automatic and not subject to self-control. We may experience the percept, but we cannot really think of it without thinking of it in some proposition or other — that is, without thinking that it is so and so. And this statement that it is so and so is a perceptual judgment. Accordingly Peirce holds that the lower limit of controlled thought is the perceptual judgment. (5.115f)

Recalling that logic is the science of the reference of symbols to their objects, the significance of this assertion of Peirce's is clear. What he is saying is that questions regarding the truth of perceptual judgments are pseudoquestions, because they can have no possible answer. Epistemological doubts, therefore, are useless for there is no way of getting behind the perceptual judgment to find out whether or not it is true. It can no more be criticized than the growth of the hair can be criticized. (5.130) For criticism is only meaningful where self-control is possible. (7.448f; 7.457) It is here that the influence of the norma-

[14] Nelson Goodman, "Sense and Certainty," *Philosophic Review*, LXI, 160–167 (April 1952).

tive theory can be seen. By dividing the processes of the mind into involuntary inferences which cannot be controlled, and voluntary inferences which can be controlled, Peirce is able to harmonize the conflicting elements of his cognitive theory. In respect to the involuntary inference, the argument of 1868 still applies: there is no first sense datum because no such datum can be specified, and the percept must be regarded as constructed or "inferred" although by processes not subject to control. Nevertheless the percept is not a copy of the sense data, nor is it a copy of an external reality. Because it is beyond control and criticism, the percept must be accepted without question as being both real and the given of experience. And because perceptual judgments are indubitable, their testimony as to what the percept is must be accepted as authentic. Thus the perceptual judgment is the first premiss of voluntary inference. (2.27; 5.181)

. . . consider the judgment that one event C *appears to be* subsequent to another event A. Certainly, I may have inferred this; because I may have remarked that C was subsequent to a third event B which was itself subsequent to A. But then these premisses are judgments of the same description. It does not seem possible that I can have performed an infinite series of acts of criticism each of which must require a distinct effort. The case is quite different from that of Achilles and the tortoise because Achilles does not require to make an infinite series of distinct efforts. It therefore appears that I must have made some judgment that one event *appeared to be* subsequent to another without that judgment having been inferred from any premiss [i.e.] without any *controlled* and *criticized* action of reasoning. If this be so, it is a perceptual judgment in the only sense that the logician can recognize. [5.157]

This passage was written in 1903 — thirty-five years after the papers of 1868 in which Peirce had defended precisely the opposite point of view. The normative theory permits him to retain his older doctrine in regard to unconscious inference, while at the same time holding perceptual judgments to be the first premisses of our knowledge. It is this strategy which allows him to hold that the categories are immediately perceived — i.e., given in the perceptual judgment — without assuming first impressions of sense. The perceptual judgments thus become the real basis of our empirical knowledge, for they form the evidence statements against which our theories are to be tested and to which our constructs of real objects must give coherence. (5.116)

Having thus revised the basis of his theory of cognition, Peirce attempted to prove that we directly perceive Firsts, Seconds, and Thirds. That Firsts, or qualities of sense, are directly perceived, is generally agreed by most philosophers and need not be argued. That this is true of Seconds, however, is another matter. What is actually perceived in the case of Secondness is, Peirce held, shock or resistance or surprise. (5.45) Most will admit that something of this general character is perceived but the critical question is whether this sense of shock is not a quality of sense also. Peirce argued that it is not. For, he said, examine the perceptual facts in a case of surprise. At one moment:

Your mind was filled [with] an imaginary object that was expected. At the moment when it was expected the vividness of the representation is exalted, and suddenly, when it should come, something quite different comes instead. I ask you whether at that instant of surprise there is not a double consciousness, on the one hand of an Ego, which is simply the expected idea suddenly broken off, on the other hand of the Non-Ego, which is the strange intruder, in his abrupt entrance. [5.53]

If this account of the perceptual facts be accepted, then this experience involves a direct perception of a relation and therefore is not simply a sense quality.[15] The same argument obviously applies to other experimental equivalents of *haecceity* such as resistance, shock, intrusion, and so on. In every case a direct "upagainstness" is involved which Peirce regards as requiring at least two correlates.

But the most important philosophic question involved in the perception of the categories is that of the perception of Thirdness. Peirce maintains that we have direct perception of Thirdness and his argument for this is as follows: "A proposition may have any number of subjects but can have but one predicate which is invariably general. . . . Consequently, it is now clear that if there be any perceptual judgment, or proposition directly expressive of and resulting from the quality of a present percept, or sense-image, that judgment must involve generality in its predicate." (5.151)

To demonstrate this assertion Peirce relies not only upon this analysis of the proposition itself but upon the further statement, "If

[15] Peirce adds a second argument based on the principle that "when a man is surprised he knows that he is surprised." (5.57) The argument however is not strong and contradicts his own theory that individual existence is inferred from error.

a perceptual judgment involves any general elements, as it certainly does, the presumption is that a universal proposition can be necessarily deduced from it." (5.156) Let us take these two claims in order.

Peirce's argument from the generality of the predicate is based upon an analysis of the proposition into a rhema, or propositional function $\phi x$, which is the predicate, and a subject or subjects which constitute the values of the variable. In saying that the predicate is necessarily general, Peirce means that it may apply to any number of possible objects: a man is not necessarily this man or that man. The subject on the other hand is individual, being in fact a *haecceity*. Thus the proposition does apply a general predicate to an individual or individuals. And if the proposition is a perceptual judgment, and therefore an indubitably true description of a percept, it follows that the percept must have been as the judgment represents it to have been — that is, must have possessed a general character. (5.151–158; 5.183f) The only objections to this conclusion would seem to be that (1) the analysis of the proposition is erroneous, or (2) that the percept was of a different character than it is represented to be. But (1) is refuted by the theory of signs (2.309f), and (2) by the theory of cognition which shows that the verdict of the perceptual judgment as to the character of the percept cannot be questioned. Thus Peirce remarks that the man who holds generality to be perceived "will hold, with firmest of grasps, to the recognition that logical criticism is limited to what we can control." (5.212)

Peirce supports his second argument — that a universal proposition can be deduced from the perceptual judgment — by citing the example of the perceptual judgment "a follows b." That this is a perceptual judgment Peirce argues in an above quoted passage [16] from the fact that if it is inferred it must be inferred from a judgment of the same form, and since there cannot be an infinite series of deliberate inferences, some judgment of the form "a follows b" is a perceptual judgment. But from "a follows b" one may derive "(z) z follows a then z follows b" which is a universal proposition. This inference is certainly valid, so the only objections which can be raised to Peirce's argument are that (1) "a follows b" is not a perceptual judgment, or (2) the inference of a universal statement does not prove that the

---

[16] See above, p. 370.

given statement contains generality. As to the first objection, since we do in fact know statements which assert that "a follows b," the argument would have to be that what we perceive is not the relation "follows" but a particular instance of it. But if the perceptual judgment merely signifies that in this percept a thing, *a*, and a thing, *b*, have a special suchness, *follows*, rather than being the objects *a* and *b* under the general *follows*, then in the first place the predicate would not be general which is contrary to the thesis Peirce has already established above, and in the second place the perceptual judgment ought to be wholly determinate and to show no marks of interpretation. But as Peirce notes, "The fact is that it is not necessary to go beyond ordinary observations of common life to find a variety of widely different ways in which perception is interpretative." (5.184) Among these Peirce cites the obvious case of optical illusions in which the interpretation of the figure has every appearance of being given in perception. (5.183) Thus the perceptual judgment is an abduction which explains the percept by classing it as one of a general kind. And since the normative theory prevents our going behind the perceptual judgment, that general must be taken as perceived.

In regard to the second objection, however, Peirce's argument does not seem so strong. For the inference of the universal is actually from two premises, the perceptual judgment and the universal statement "$(x)(y)(z)xFy.yFz \supset xFz$", and it can certainly be argued that all the universality of the conclusion comes from the major premiss rather than the minor. Moreover, there is a further difficulty in Peirce's argument, for as he states his thesis the inference of the universal proposition depends simply on the generality of the predicate. In the case of "follows," however, it depends upon the relation having certain formal properties such as transitivity which are not possessed by other relations such as "lover of." Yet on his principles "lover of" must be general too and therefore must also yield a universal. The kind of universal proposition that Peirce actually seems to require would be one which is a purely formal consequence of the fact that the predicate is true of more than one object — i.e., a statement such as

(I)    $(x)(y)(z)yLx.zLx \supset y,z \in D'L$.[17]

From "aLb" then it would follow that "$(z)zLb \supset a,z \in D'L$". Here

---

[17] Whitehead and Russell, *Principia*, theorem 33.01.

the major premiss is in effect a definitional statement concerning the domain of $L$ and may be regarded as a direct consequence of the generality of $L$ itself. The inference of the universal, therefore, while of course it involves the major premiss (I), would thus be in effect an explication of "aLb". Peirce's position would therefore come to this — that we perceive relations, that analysis shows these relations to be predicable about more than one correlate, and that from this fact about the relation together with the original perceptual judgment we can derive a universal proposition. Thus the second argument is dependent upon the first — that the predicate is general — and does not add independent support to it.

Why is Peirce so anxious to prove that Thirdness is perceived? In 1903 he spelled out the significance of the perception of Thirdness in some detail. There are, he holds, three possible positions which can be taken in regard to Thirdness: first, that it is not admissible at all, being neither perceived nor verifiable; second, that it is not directly perceived but is verifiable; and third, that it is given in perception. The first alternative is rejected out of hand, on the ground that it makes all prediction impossible and is therefore absurd. (5.210) But the second position is extremely interesting, for I believe it reflects Peirce's judgment on his own earlier views. His statement of it is as follows:

> The man who takes the second position will hold thirdness to be an addition which the operation of abduction introduces over and above what its premisses in any way contain, and further that this element, though not perceived in experiment, is justified *by* experiment. Then his conception of reality must be such as completely to sunder the real from perception; and the puzzle for him will be why perception should be allowed such authority in regard to what is real.
>
> I do not think that man can consistently hold that there is room in time for an event between any two events separate in time. But even if he could, he would (if he could grasp the reasons) be forced to acknowledge that the contents of time consist of separate, independent, unchanging states, and nothing else. There would not be even a determinate order of sequence among these states. He might insist that one order of sequence was more readily grasped by us; but nothing more. Every man is fully satisfied that there is such a thing as truth, or he would not ask any question. *That* truth consists in a conformity to something *independent of his thinking it to be so*, or of any man's opinion on that subject. But for the man who holds this second opinion, the only reality, there could be, would be conformity to the ultimate result of

inquiry. But there would not be any course of inquiry possible except in the sense that it would be easier for him to interpret the phenomenon; and ultimately he would be forced to say that there was no reality at all except that he now at this instant finds a certain way of thinking easier than any other. But that violates the very idea of reality and truth. [5.211]

That Peirce did sunder the real and the perceived about as thoroughly as possible and that he did regard reality as conformity to the ultimate result of inquiry we have seen already in regard to his earlier work. Why then does he reject this view? The argument depends upon the theory of multitudes which he developed in the late 1890's. If Thirdness is not in perception, what is? Clearly, Secondness and Firstness. Now Secondness is not general, and in itself could not lead to any inference of generality. Firsts in themselves are eternal states — that is what Peirce means in saying that perception for this man would consist of eternal changeless states. Consider then the collection of all such changeless states. The collection of all those states which are perceived by the given man is at most finite; therefore there is no defined order given in the collection itself. That is to say, it is only in the case of infinite series that there are relative characters which define the order uniquely — for the finite series, there is no character of the members per se which determines their place in the order. Hence, although order could be introduced by hypothesis, there would be no perceived fact or character which could be taken as determining the correct order, or as distinguishing one order from another. The order then would rest upon mere convenience. Therefore there could not be a true "course" of experience — that is, a determined sequence converging to a limit, there would be no ultimate upshot of inquiry, and the real would be merely that which is most convenient. Thus this position leads to its own defeat and turns into subjectivism. So much Peirce had learned from the affair with the diamond.

The third position — that Thirdness is directly perceived — is Peirce's own. For he holds that unless generality is given in perception, it can never be known at all. Thus for him perception and reality are reunited, but, thanks to the normative theory, without subjectivism. So Peirce can hold that *"nihil est in intellectu quod non prius fuerit in sensu"* (5.181), for what is *in sensu* now includes Thirdness, and this is all that Peirce requires. "The elements of every concept enter into logical thought at the gate of perception and make their exit at the gate of purposive action; and whatever cannot show its passports at both those two gates is to be arrested as unauthorized by reason." (5.212) Thus the categories may be shown to be given in perception, and as such to form the elementary concepts out of which all else is to be constructed. The purposes of action are given by normative science, and come ultimately to the realization of the *summum bonum*. And pragmaticism now becomes the method of uniting these two by translating concepts into rules governing percepts and action so that conduct may be made more and more the embodiment of rationality.

# XVIII

# *Synechism*

PEIRCE's metaphysics is a difficult subject to deal with because of its heterogeneous character and it is therefore essential at the outset to determine just what he thought this subject embraced. Metaphysics as a whole he defined as the third branch of coenoscopy, following and depending upon mathematics, phenomenology, and normative science. (1.185–186) Accordingly, metaphysics is a positive science, only differing from the special sciences in that it relies upon ordinary daily experience to supply its observational basis. (1.241) Since metaphysics presupposes phenomenology, it presupposes as well the theory of the categories, at least in so far as they constitute a classification of phenomena. On the other hand, the question of what realities, if any, the categories represent is a question of metaphysics and not of phenomenology. In the outline classification of the sciences, Peirce describes metaphysics as follows: "Metaphysics may be divided into, i, General Metaphysics, or Ontology; ii, Psychical, or Religious, Metaphysics, concerned chiefly with the questions of 1, God, 2, Freedom, 3, Immortality; and iii, Physical Metaphysics, which discusses the real nature of time, space, laws of nature, matter, etc." (1.192) It is questionable how deeply pondered this division really is; the inclusion of the Kantian formula is gratuitous since Peirce gives little or no attention to freedom and immortality,[1] and the cosmology, to which he did devote great attention, is not mentioned. Nevertheless, if we accept the three major classes as constituting a meaningful division, we may range under them most of the specific problems which Peirce seems to have regarded as falling within the domain of metaphysics. Under ontology we have, first, the question of the nature of reality, and the modes of being of real things. Second, there is the problem of the truth of the ontological postulate of objective idealism. Third, the

---

[1] See Gallie, *Peirce and Pragmatism*, pp. 209f; also 6.518f; 6.556.

existence of God is in part an ontological problem, as is the mind-body problem and the cosmology. And fourth, there is the question of the status of universals which, in Peirce's formulation, is the issue of synechism. Under psychic or religious metaphysics one must obviously include all questions concerning God. The cosmology also falls under this heading, both because of its religious nature and because, by the postulate of objective idealism, the universe is Ideal. The mind-body problem and questions concerning the nature of feeling and consciousness similarly fall here. Finally, under physical metaphysics Peirce includes all questions of the nature of time, space, matter, and natural law — in short, the questions of the nature of physical reality. (6.6) This list is by no means exhaustive, but it may be taken as affording a general outline of what Peirce thought constituted the subject matter of metaphysics. In the present chapter, I wish to examine such of these questions as we have not touched on before. In particular, I wish to deal with the problems of time, space, matter, and natural law, with the modes of being, the relation between mind and body, and finally with the question of synechism.

The basic elements of Peirce's theory of space and time are to be found in the writings of the *Monist* series, but some of the most important arguments of the doctrine could not be fully formulated until the completion of the theory of continuity in the years 1896–97. The pre-1896 theory is therefore less adequate than the later theory but the fundamental ideas of both are identical and the only change is in the concept of continuity. It will therefore be most convenient to deal with the theory of space and time in its post-1896 form and so to assume from the beginning that space cannot be an aggregate of actual points.

In view of Peirce's philosophical background it is not surprising that his theory of space and time should be heavily indebted to Kant. Like his master, he holds that space and time are forms characterizing respectively the outer and the inner worlds. (4.157) This definition, of course, echoes Kant's distinction between inner and outer sense.[2] But as usual, Peirce gives to this Kantian doctrine a realistic interpretation. If these forms are true of all we can know, then they are real.

[2] The argument is very different from Kant's however, since the forms are derived from the contents of the worlds. 1.492ff.

That is to say, if there is no thing-in-itself, nothing but the phenomena and the constructs which explain the phenomena, then whatever phenomenal existence there is is in time and space, and there can be nothing outside of time and space unless we should find it necessary to postulate the existence of such an entity to explain some element of the perceived phenomena. Space and time are therefore real but general entities the existence of which must be postulated to bring coherence to our experience. (1.489–513; 6.82)

But although space is a form of the outward world, it does not constitute a test of externality. What is represented to be external is represented to be in space, and what is represented as being in space is represented as external. This does not mean, however, that either representation is true — that question must be settled by other tests. It is not to account for externality that space is invoked. Rather that which is explained by the hypothesis that we are in space is a peculiarity of our experience — namely, the existence of multiple subjects of a property. We find by experience that properties are not proper names — that there is more than one thing to which these properties apply. Moreover, no matter how far we determine properties there is still more than one thing to which they apply. Thus e.g., two drops of water are precisely alike in all their properties (excluding for the moment temporal and spatial location) yet they differ from one another in *haecceity*. In order to explain how this can be, it is necessary to introduce some manner of being which admits the coexistence of two things which have identical properties, and space is this manner of existing. The assumption that objects are in space permits there to be innumerable objects with identical properties, yet different spatial coordinates. (1.501f; 3.613; 6.82)

This definition at once makes it clear why space and existence are so closely related for it is only in respect to things which may have all properties identical yet remain distinct that the postulate of space is necessary — that is, in respect to *haecceities*. Classes, which have intelligible essences but no *haecceity*, are subject to the Identity of Indiscernibles,[3] and so need not be represented as being in space, although of course they can be so represented for convenience if we wish. Space therefore intrinsically involves dyadic relations, since indeed it is a

---

[3] Peirce, "Map Colouring," pp. 3f.

postulate required to account for the existence of *haecceities*. (6.82)

It follows from this general position that some space must be real. But what is to be the nature of that space? The most important property of space is that it forms a Peircean continuum. (1.319; 6.82) For the proof of this fact Peirce need only cite his solution to the paradoxes of Zeno. Whatever space we postulate must contain point masses, which are *haecceities*, and since it is an empirical fact that these point-masses undergo motion, the space we postulate must be such that motion is possible. But as we have seen already, Peirce held that to conceive space as composed of a point set of any variety is to fall head-long into the difficulties of Achilles and the tortoise. The escape from this difficulty he held to lie in his own theory of the continuum, and therefore he held that real space must be conceived to be such a continuum.

Like all Newtonians, Peirce held that space and time are absolute entities. His reasoning follows Newton's precisely — it is the absolute character of velocity of rotation which is taken as the decisive evidence. (5.496; 7.486–488) While Peirce recognized that Newton's solution to the problem was not the only possible one, it is obvious that he regarded it as the only sensible one. Thus in 1898 he reviewed briefly Mach's argument for the relativity of motion and dismissed it as scarcely worth attention. (7.485–487) It must be noted in Peirce's defense, however, that virtually all scientific men of that day shared his view. The absolute character of space and time was one of the pillars on which nineteenth-century physical science rested; its denial was impossible without a revision of that science as drastic as that which Einstein effected.

Granting then that space is absolute and a real Peircean continuum, the question of the specific nature of this continuum and of the measure relations possible within it remains to be dealt with. As was pointed out in Chapter XI, Peirce was greatly influenced on these questions by the writings of Bernhard Riemann. He interpreted Riemann as holding that the differentiation of the less from the more general geometries was accompanied by the introduction of "matters of fact" or existence postulates of the proper kinds. This does not involve a confusion of pure and applied geometry — on that distinction Peirce was perfectly clear. (3.557) But it does mean that Peirce conceived pure mathematics in a rather curious way. Since mathematics is the practice of necessary reasoning, any deductive system — including Newtonian mechanics — is mathematics, and it is pure mathematics so long as we do not inquire into its empirical truth. When we do so inquire, the existence postulates of the mathematical theory are transformed into physical existence postulates which must be empirically tested. Thus to say projective geometry is empirically true of real space meant for Peirce that there is a real point at infinity; and to say that real space has metric properties is to say that Cayley's Absolute exists. And since Newtonian space does in fact have real metric properties, Peirce was brought to the conclusion that in fact Cayley's Absolute exists in real space (6.82).

Peirce's interpretation of the nature of applied geometry serves to clarify two further matters. Peirce believed that all straight lines in real space are self-returning. This position is of course derived from the fact that in projective space, all infinitely extended lines are conceived to meet in an ideal point at infinity and so to be self-returning. When the metric is introduced, the points at infinity are identified with the points of intersection of lines with the point-pair Absolute. There is thus no need to postulate infinitely extended open lines, and this fact enables Peirce to maintain his topological argument that every element which is not limited by a singularity of some sort is self-returning — i.e., there are no non – self-returning elements which do not contain their own limits. The importance of this assertion we have already noted in Peirce's argument against Cantor's definition of continuity.

If Cayley's Absolute is a reality, it follows that real space is a metric space. But the question remains as to what that metric is. Peirce was well aware that in his day the actual metric of space could not be determined with accuracy, but he nevertheless indulged in conjectures as to its probable nature. He seems to have cherished a particular liking for a hyperbolic metric and, utilizing his astronomical training, he attempted to demonstrate that space was hyperbolic.

The physical geometry of celestial triangles needs examination, in order to ascertain whether the constant of space may not have a sensible magnitude. I have undertaken such an examination. I began by forming a list of all possible methods of determining this quantity by means of the following observations: 1st, the parallaxes of stars; 2nd, the numbers of stars of each parallax;

3rd, the proper motions of stars; 4th the numbers of stars of different proper motions; 5th the spectroscopic determinations of the motions of stars in the line of sight; 6th the magnitudes of stars; 7th, the numbers of stars of each magnitude . . . I applied several methods: they seemed to indicate a hyperbolic space with a constant far from insignificant. [8.93n2]

It is easy to see why Peirce was not disposed to regard space as elliptic; for reasons to be discussed below he was anxious to show that space is infinitely extended. But his reasons for preferring hyperbolic to Euclidean space appear to be analogical rather than logical. Although Peirce never envisaged time as the fourth dimension (1.273; 6.575), nevertheless it seems to have been the desire to model time upon a one-dimensional continuum in hyperbolic space which governed his preference. Since time and space are for Peirce independent entities, there would appear to be no reason but analogy for also requiring space to be hyperbolic.

I have pointed out above that space is regarded by Peirce as the form which permits the existence of a number of subjects having identical properties. This of course assumes that the spatial coordinates are not qualities or properties, since if they were, two things differing in spatial location would differ in properties. The basis for this denial of the qualitative nature of spatial coordinates is simply the continuity of space. For if spatial coordinates were qualities, then, being distinct from each other, they would be discrete. There would therefore be a collection of them which would also be discrete. And that collection would have to have the multiplicity of the continuum. But this is contradictory, since no discrete collection can have the multiplicity of the continuum. Therefore, according to Peirce, the spatial coordinates cannot be qualitative, and therefore those things which occupy discrete spatial positions cannot be such that their being depends upon possession of an intelligible essence — i.e., they must be *haecceities*. And this argument of course applies with equal force to temporal coordinates.

Peirce's theory of time is very similar to his theory of space. We have seen that the hypothesis of space explains how there can be things which have the same properties yet are distinct — how there can be many subjects of one property. Symmetry requires, therefore, that time should explain how there can be many properties of one subject. (1.492

–495; 1.501) That something should be both p and not-p at once is impossible, but that it can be first p and then not-p is quite possible. That Philip is both drunk and sober requires that there be a decent interval between the two inspections. (1.494) Accordingly, the hypothesis of time is required to explain how a single thing may possess contradictory properties. Thus that which never changes — which has always the same properties and no others — is not in time.

In his writings before 1885 Peirce had vigorously defended the thesis that neither time nor space is directly perceived. He regarded Berkeley's argument in the *New Theory of Vision* as proving that the third dimension must be inferred rather than perceived, and he sought to extend this conclusion to the other dimensions. (6.416) An examination of the retina shows that it is not a surface but is rather composed of needle-like nerves only the points of which are sensitive to light.

Now, of these points, certainly the excitation of no one singly can produce the perception of a surface, and consequently not the aggregate of all the sensations can amount to this. But certain relations subsist between the excitations of different nerve-points, and these constitute the premises upon which the hypothesis of space is founded, and from which it is inferred. That space is not immediately perceived is now universally admitted; and a mediate cognition is what is called an inference, and is subject to the criticism of logic. . . . The same thing is equally true of time. That time is not directly perceived is evident, since no lapse of time is present, and we only perceive what is present. [6.416]

Peirce's later theory contradicts two of the basic premises of this passage: in the "Law of Mind" Peirce held that we are directly conscious of an interval rather than merely of an instant (6.110f), and in the normative theory of inquiry he held that logical criticism cannot apply to unconscious inferences. (7.451–457) Having rejected the premises, he also rejected the conclusion: in the later theory time and space are regarded as directly perceived. This is not explicitly stated in regard to space, but it is clear that on the percept-perceptual-judgment theory space must be taken as given in the percept. In the case of time, however, Peirce does explicitly state his position.

Abridge our theory as we may and must, there is one detail which it will not do to omit. That is the use which is made of the psychological doctrine of the "time span." That singularly accurate observer, Thomas Reid . . . seems to have been the first distinctly to recognize that we have something very like a direct perception of duration or, at least, of motion; and he drew the needful distinction between the lapse of time during the act of perception and the lapse of time represented in the percept . . . the best modern psychologists . . . recognize that our image of the last six to twelve seconds past is almost or quite of the nature of a percept, while the remoter past and the future are represented in a more mediated way. One opinion which has been put forward and which seems, at any rate, to be tenable and to harmonize with the modern logico-mathematical conceptions, is that our image of the flow of events receives, in a strictly continuous time, strictly continual accessions on the side of the future, while fading in a gradual manner on the side of the past, and that thus the absolutely immediate present is gradually transformed by an immediately given change into a continuum of the reality of which we are thus assured. The argument is that in this way, and apparently in this way only, our having the idea of a true continuum can be accounted for. [8.123n20]

This comes to saying (1) temporal flow is perceived, and (2) if it were not perceived, we could have no idea of continuity. Yet these arguments are not convincing. Peirce admits that time is a form of change, and that without change there is no time. (6.132) It would seem then that what is actually perceived is a change of state and that time is actually inferred either from the fact of contradictory properties in objects or from a feeling of extension of the object or process involved. (1.492–495; 6.110f) In either case, time can be regarded as perceived only by a refusal — amounting to willfulness — to go behind the abductive perceptual judgment. (7.535) One notes here again the significance of Peirce's statement: "The man who takes the third position [that we directly perceive Thirdness] . . . will hold, with firmest of grasps, to the recognition that logical criticism is limited to what we can control." (5.212)

What led Peirce to take this position that time is perceived was the need to show that we perceive something which is a true Peircean continuum. In line with the argument that Thirdness is perceived, and that nothing is in intellect which is not first in sense (5.181), Peirce must show that there is an observational basis for his concept of continuity. Moreover, as we shall see below, it is only by arguing that time is continuous that Peirce is able to prove that there are real continua. The doctrine that time is perceived thus results not from any necessity in the theory of time itself but from extrinsic considerations related to the general metaphysic.

In so far as time is a pure continuum, it has neither direction nor metric, and if these characteristics are to be introduced, then, as in the case of space, they must be due to the contents of time. The fact that time does have a direction and flows always from past to future Peirce ascribes to the law of mind. It will be recalled that that law involves the relation of affectibility among ideas. This relation is asymmetrical, transitive, and irreflexive; accordingly, it defines a serial order among ideas such that for any two ideas *A* and *B*, either *A* is affectible by *B* or *B* is affectible by *A* or neither is affectible by the other. Using this relation, it is then possible to define the order of ideas in time as follows:

    1) if A is affectible by B, then A is later than B

    2) if A is not affectible by B and B is not affectible by A, then A and B are simultaneous.

Thus the direction of causality among ideas is the basis for temporal direction. (6.127–131)

By the ontological postulate of objective idealism, all matter is really mind, and therefore a definition of temporal order by the order of mental process also fixes the direction of time for the physical world. The fact that time does possess such direction is actually one of the chief supports for Peirce's ontology, for since all mechanical processes are reversible, there is no uniquely defined causal direction in mechanics. (6.554; 6.68ff) It will be objected — and rightly — that this begs the question, since there are nonmechanical physical processes which do have a direction — for example, those involving entropy. But again one must recall that Peirce believed all nonpsychic phenomena to be reducible in principle to Newton's laws, so that the force of this objection would have escaped him. Peirce would argue then that the fact time has direction shows that at bottom all processes are psychic. Curiously, Peirce's argument implies that if somehow the direction of time were to be reversed, even strictly mechanical processes would turn out to be irreversible. For instead of the system running indefinitely in reverse, the laws of mechanics would themselves become increasingly inexact and would eventually vanish into chaos.[4]

---

[4] Against Peirce's reduction of temporal direction to causality there is an obvious objection: such a reduction makes all statements of causal relation between past and future analytic. Yet it is clear from Peirce's discussions of the relation between past and

The metrical properties of time Peirce also ascribes to the contents of the continuum rather than to the continuum itself. One means of establishing such metric relations is offered by the first law of motion which correlates the temporal and spatial intervals traversed by a body moving in the absence of force. (6.82) If either a temporal or a spatial metric is determinate, therefore, it may be used to determine the other. Actually, of course, there are any number of such means which can be, and in fact are, used to determine the metric of time.

There is however one aspect of Peirce's theory of time which appears to involve an unavoidable contradiction. Since pure time is continuous, it follows from Peirce's principle that every continuum either contains its own limit or is self-returning, that time must be cyclic. And Peirce himself explicitly drew just this conclusion on several occasions. (1.274; 1.498; 6.210) But if time is cyclic, two problems arise at once: (1) did time exist before the creation of the universe as depicted in Peirce's cosmology, and (2) if so, does this not require that the entire cosmological process is cyclic? In answer to the second question, Peirce considered various alternatives which he describes by modeling time on a one-dimensional continuum in metric space. If the space is elliptic, then the cycle is finite and all motion is simply repetitive. If the space is parabolic, the starting point and ending point are identical and therefore the cosmic evolution will return to the state from which it began. If the space is hyperbolic, however, "Reason marches from premises to conclusion; nature has ideal end different from its origin." (6.582) Evidently what Peirce means here is that if the two points at infinity are regarded as the starting and ending points of evolution, then the process does not return to its original state. Clearly, Peirce preferred the later alternative as more consistent with his cosmology. (8.317)

But this leads us back to the first question: if time is cyclic and the starting and ending points of the cosmic evolution do not coincide, then there are stretches of time with no events. Yet Peirce explicitly asserts that time cannot exist without something to undergo change. (6.132) And further, how can time have been created as a product of cosmic evolution if that evolutionary process is itself contained in time? Peirce

future that he did not regard such statements as analytic. The only conclusion possible would appear to be that Peirce simply did not think of this objection.

tells us explicitly that time itself evolved from the original chaos (1. 412; 6.200; 6.214) and that time cannot exist without something to undergo change. (6.132) Yet he also asserts that time can exist without events (1.498), and that evolution is contained within the cycle of time. (6.210) These statements cannot be made consistent.[5]

Peirce's theories of space and time are somewhat bizarre, yet on the whole they represent an attempt to develop a theory which would be consistent with the most modern mathematical theory and with Newtonian physics. For since Peirce was himself a scientist, he recognized perfectly that if his theory was to be acceptable at all it must be consistent with the physics of his time. In fact, Peirce was much more aware of this necessity than has generally been recognized, and his theory of Secondness is designed specifically to meet it. The world as it is known to Newtonian physics consists entirely of mass-points undergoing translations in absolute space and time under the laws of mechanics. In fact, besides space and time the only representative of reality in the Newtonian system is the mass-point. All bodies are conceived either as points or as aggregates of such points.[6] Within this system duality plays an extraordinary role: all forces act between pairs of points only, and in the direction of a right line joining these points. Thus all the forces in the Newtonian world constitute dyadic relations among point-masses. Moreover, the only fundamental dynamic property which is assigned to the points is mass, and this property is defined implicitly by the equations

$$F = ma$$

and
$$F = g \frac{m' \cdot m''}{d^2}$$

By the first equation, mass may be regarded as the power of inertia of a point — i.e., as the resistance to change of state of the point. By the second, mass may be taken to be the ground of the forces of attraction between two points. And since by the second law of motion every action

[5] See, however, 8.317. It is conceivable that what Peirce meant is that although pure time itself is cyclic, antedates the universe, and can exist without events, the temporal metric which permits us to speak of one event as preceding another only comes into being when events are created. If this is Peirce's meaning, in his expressions of it he achieved an obscurity which he seldom equaled elsewhere.

[6] Albert Einstein, "Clerk Maxwell's Influence on the Evolution of the Idea of Physical Reality," in *Essays in Science* (New York, 1934), p. 41.

has an equal and opposite reaction, these points will also be the subjects of such reactions in so far as they exist at all.[7] Thus the fundamental properties of the mass-point turn out to be remarkably similar to those of *haecceity*: resistance to change of state, reaction when acted upon, absolute determination in space and time, and subjection to dyadic relations. Peirce's category of Secondness is something more than the dying gasp of an outworn Scholasticism. In the nature of existence as described by Newtonian mechanics there is a great deal which corresponds very well with this category.

But why not simply adopt mass as the characteristic property of existents? The answer lies in the fact that Peirce was an idealist. By translating mass into other terms, it is perfectly possible to eliminate all assumptions concerning the existence of matter in favor of immaterial points which are centers of forces. Such a theory was in fact developed by the Jesuit Boscovich who in 1758 published a treatise entitled *Theoria Philosophiae Naturalis redacta ad unicam legem virium in Natura existentium*,[8] in which he argued that matter is nothing but an aggregate of immaterial points which are centers of inertia and of forces of attraction and repulsion. This theory, which still had able defenders in the nineteenth century, Peirce adopted as his own and held until the late 1890's. (6.242; 6.82) And this was one reason why Peirce was so willing to build atomic models of mind: since Boscovichian atoms are immaterial his idealism is in no way compromised.

Around the turn of the century, however, Peirce abandoned the Boscovichian theory of the atom in favor of the theory that atoms are vortices in an incompressible ether. The physics of this theory need not concern us. It was one of the many attempts made at the end of the century to construct a mechanical model of the ether. The theory aroused great interest at the time, owing partly to the crisis in physics over the problem of the ether, partly to the great promise of the theory, and partly to the fact that its inventor was Sir William Thomson, Lord Kelvin, who was generally regarded by his contemporaries as England's greatest physicist.[9] From a metaphysical point of view, Peirce found the vortex theory preferable to the theory of Boscovichian atoms. For

[7] John Theodore Merz, *A History of European Thought in the Nineteenth Century* (London, 1923), vol. I, chap. IV.
[8] *Ibid.*, pp. 357f.
[9] *Ibid.*, II, 57–66.

although vortex atoms retain all the mechanical properties of Bosco-vichian atoms, they have the great advantage of being motions in an underlying continuum and this fact makes the theory far more com-patible with synechism and with an ontology which holds that all that is is mind. In fact Peirce describes in a rather extended passage how his theory of cosmic evolution could be modeled in terms of vortices.

. . . universes of soul and of matter were not distinct there being throughout space (not necessarily restricted to three dimensions) a sort of fluid under no very definite laws, which was somewhat conscious but without distinction into separate personalities — a sort of *soul-stuff*. I will suppose that, in the absence of laws, this fluid had various motions in different parts. These motions, from the empirical point of view . . . would have appeared to be without any law, and therefore to be absolutely fortuitous and arbitrary; while from a higher point of view, they could only be regarded as effects of direct creative energy. The fluid, originally homogeneous, in consequence of these various motions, mixed with a capricious (i.e., creative) viscosity set up vortices. These increased in number as time went on, until these vortices became the atoms of a secondary fluid, — just as vortices are atoms of a fluid in the vortex-theory of atoms. In this fluid, in which the viscosity, or internal fric-tion, was somewhat greater, new vortices were set up, just as, according to the vortex-atom theory, there are vortices in rapidly and variously moving water, while water itself consists of a collection of vortices in an underlying fluid. I will suppose that in this second fluid, governed by habits altogether independ-ent of consciousness, there was a secondary consciousness far less intense than in the underlying fluid. I will suppose that this second fluid came to have such a multitude of vortices that they constituted a third fluid. And I will suppose that this process went on until there were an endless (or nearly endless) series of fluids each composed of vortices of the next underlying fluid. All this is easy to conceive. In the final [illegible word] composite, fluids, Feeling would have almost disappeared, and they would be regulated by former habits. For the formation of habit always lowers the intensity, i.e. vivacity of Feeling. Finally the last of these fluids, or rather the totality of its vortices, is what we recognize as matter.[10]

Such a theory is of course highly speculative, but then, so was the vortex theory of the atom itself. Nevertheless, this passage shows that Peirce did attempt to make his theory consistent with the best thinking of his day in physics and to keep even his speculative cosmology in line with some kind of model of physical reality.[11]

[10] C. S. Peirce to Cassius Keyser, n.d., pp. 19–21, Scientific Correspondence.
[11] It is ironic that Peirce seems never to have known of the work of Einstein and

Peirce also used the theory of the series of ethers as a basis for explaining the relation of mind and body. Since matter is the totality of the vortices of the last fluid in the series, we may conceive any impulse transmitted to the material body as setting up vibrations or waves which will move with the velocity of sound.[12] Owing to the viscosity of matter, however, part of this motion would be converted into heat, which is a motion of the vortex atoms themselves. That heat he supposes transmitted to the last ether itself, creating a motion of its atoms which are vortices in the next to last ether, and so on.

Peirce supposes the velocity of transmission to increase from ether to ether by the proportion of the velocity of sound to that of light (the fastest waves in the luminiferous ether). Hence an endless series of ethers could be gone through almost instantaneously. Beyond that first infinite series of ethers, which Peirce supposes to be all so habit-bound as to be under the sway of mechanics, he postulates a second series which is beginningless and which represents the soul-ethers in which teleological causation is dominant. The impulse having passed through these two series $P_1$, $P_2$, $P_3$, . . . , . . . , $T_3$, $T_2$, $T_1$ arrives finally at the ether constituting the fully conscious mind. Naturally the process is reversible so that the action is reciprocal. (8.122n19; 7.370–372)

The object of this theory of connection is to reconcile the mechanical causation of physics with the teleological causation of mind, by showing that matter and mind can affect each other without doing so directly. Since in fact matter is mind, the connection is between different phases of the same substance, so that it is not at first apparent why Peirce thinks the series must be doubly infinite. The reason is

---

never to have appreciated fully that of Maxwell. See, however, Carolyn Eisele, "Charles S. Peirce, Nineteenth Century Man of Science," *Scripta Mathematica*, XXIV, 305–324 (1959). For as Einstein has noted, "Before Clerk Maxwell people conceived of physical reality — in so far as it is supposed to represent events in nature — as material points, whose changes consist exclusively of motions, which are subject to partial differential equations. After Maxwell they conceived of physical reality as represented by continuous fields, not mechanically explicable, which are subject to partial differential equations. This change in the conception of reality is the most profound and fruitful one that has come to physics since Newton . . ." (Einstein, "Maxwell," p. 44.) Had Peirce recognized this change, he would certainly have seen in it a confirmation of synechism, and the theory of synechism might itself have been developed along other and more fruitful lines.

[12] Peirce says that the impulse will set up sound waves, but it is probable that he used sound waves only as representing the waves of maximum velocity in air.

suggested in a letter to Royce in 1902: "That self-control, selfconsciousness, involve endless series is clear." (8.122n19) Evidently what Peirce meant is that each rational act presupposes some prior rational act:

If the dog is to be let out, the door must be opened; if the door is to be opened, I must open it. But if I am to open it, I must go to it; if I am to go to it, I must walk; if I am to walk, I must stand; if I am to stand, I must rise; if I am to rise, I had better put down my pen; and there consciousness becomes dim. But there must be an infinite series of such ratiocinations if the mind only acts rationally. [7.371]

Obviously, these acts cannot all be conscious, so the early part of the beginningless series must lie in the realm of unconscious action. If therefore a definite physical event involving matter initiates the process which leads to the door being opened, there must be two series, one without end and the other without beginning.

There is however one difficulty with this theory. According to the cosmology, the order of evolution must be from more to less general continua, or from more conscious to less conscious soul-ethers. But if cosmic evolution has passed through $*\omega + \omega$ stages, then some of those stages must have been infinitesimally brief. Yet it is not at all clear that Peirce's theory of the ether series would permit the formation of enough vortices to constitute a new ether in an infinitesimal interval. Peirce made no mention of this difficulty, but since he never elaborated his mind-body theory systematically this is hardly surprising. Indeed, what we have of his theory is only a sketch of his position, the full development of which was to have been a part of the great metaphysics that was never written.

Secondness is designed to correspond to the notion of physical existence; Firstness corresponds to sensation and Thirdness to law. This division of all there is into three orders goes back to the beginning of Peirce's philosophical writing. Even in the early papers, he speaks of the categories as "worlds" or "universes" each occupied by a different sort of entity.[13] Thus the categories are more than simply classes of phenomena: they are fundamental ontological divisions, as the *Monist* papers made clear. (cf. 1.409; 6.32) Yet until 1896 Peirce does not appear to have conceptualized these differences as differences

[13] See above, pp. 36, 89f.

393

in mode of being. What finally led him to do so is explained in a letter which he wrote to William James in March of 1897. "The other was your remark that the question is, Is possibility a mode of being? Good. Precisely so. . . . I reached this truth by studying the question of possible grades of multitude, where I found myself arrested until I could form a whole logic of possibility . . ." [14] Thus it was the conclusions concerning multitude and the continuum which led Peirce to expand the categories into modes of being. This extension is not implicit in the categories, nor is it necessary to convert them from phenomenal to ontological divisions since they were that already. The necessity arises entirely from the proof that continua must contain unactualized possibilities.

Traditionally the three modes of being are possibility, actuality, and necessity, and it was natural that Peirce should have tried to correlate his categories with the classic triad. (6.342) The correlation, however, leaves much to be desired. There is no problem in matching Secondness with actuality, but Firstness and Thirdness do not correspond easily with possibility and necessity. Peirce had already spoken of Firsts as possibilities in earlier papers, but only in a rather special sense. (1. 422–424; 2.250f) Namely, to call "__φ" a possibility means that it is an unasserted predicate: if the index is supplied the predicate is asserted of an existent object, but until this is done it remains a description of a possible object merely. Thus any First is a description of a possible object. But if this is all that is meant, it is obvious that there are two kinds of possibility — relational and nonrelational — so that possibility is not confined to Firstness but must be reintroduced in the other categories as well. In respect to Thirdness and necessity the lack of correlation is even more obvious. Peirce seeks to justify his position by arguing that just as the logical verb reappears in metaphysics as quality, and the individual subject as a thing, "so the logical reason, or premiss, reappears in metaphysics as a reason, an *ens* having a *reality*, consisting in a ruling both of the outward and the inward world, as its mode of being." (1.515) But the analogy is poor: it confounds the necessity of the logical deduction from a premiss with the necessity of the premiss itself. If the law is true and the antecedent conditions are realized, the occurrence of the consequent is "necessary" in at least

[14] Perry, *James*, II, 223.

one sense of the term. But the law itself is contingent, and so is the result. This is the "necessity" of ordinary logic, not that of modal logic, and no proposition is derivable in ordinary logic which is necessary in the modal sense.[15]

It was typical of Peirce's architectonic mind that having resolved upon a division of modes of being he should have made it triadic and should have tried to relate it to the traditional divisions. But his division is not the traditional one and it makes much better sense to regard the whole theory as having little connection with the traditional problems of modality. What Peirce is really concerned with is the determination of the kind of being applicable to the three sorts of metaphysical entities he had already posited. The investigation was undertaken at the point when he found that at least one of these entities did involve possibilities which are not even actualizable in principle, and he was therefore forced to examine the question as to what sort of being such an entity might have.

The discovery of the new concept of the continuum in 1896 was an event of the greatest philosophical importance for Peirce. It will be recalled that in the 1870's Peirce's theory of reality had come to grief on just the problem of unactualized possibilities. Lacking a division of modes of being, Peirce had then adopted the principle that whatever is possible must become actual and he had therefore found himself unable to deal with possibilities which do not become actual. For the theory of reality as then formulated, this failure was tantamount to a reduction to subjectivism, as his disastrous affair with the diamond showed. To extricate himself from this impasse was by no means easy for, as Moore has pointed out, Peirce needed a property of almost magical characteristics.[16] Namely, he required a property characterizing unactualized possibilities which would be itself actual so that it could be observed. Yet incredibly enough Peirce found such a property in 1896 in continuity. For by his definition of the continuum — and it must be borne in mind that he regarded his definition as the only one which avoided the paradoxes of set theory — any true continuum must contain potentialities which are not only not now actualized but

[15] It is not intended to deny that some propositions of ordinary logic become necessary if modal operators are introduced but only that they do not become necessary until such operators are introduced.

[16] Moore, "Metaphysics and Pragmatism," pp. 183–191.

which are greater in multitude than any set of events which can ever be actualized. Whatever is continuous therefore involves real possibility and is accordingly of a general nature. This is what Peirce meant when he said that synechism was the new Scholastic realism. (6.163)

But this line of argument can be carried even further. On Peirce's theory not only all continua but all infinite sets involve possibility. For as we have seen there can be no set of *haecceities* which is more than finite, since *haecceities* cannot possess properties per se while some members of any infinite class must possess properties per se. Therefore the nominalist position as Peirce defines it is actually a finitist position, and the problem of demonstrating that nominalism is a doctrine which no intelligent man can hold reduces to that of showing the consequences of denying the existence of infinity.

I do not think we can ever have a logical right to infer, even as probable, the existence of anything entirely contrary in its nature to all that we can experience or imagine. But a nominalist must do this. For he must say that all future events are the total of all that will have happened and therefore that the future is not endless; and therefore, that there will be an event not followed by an event. This *may* be, inconceivable as it is; but the nominalist must say that it *will* be, else he will make the future to be endless, that is, to have a mode of being consisting in the truth of a general law. For every future event will have been completed, but the endless future will not have been completed. There are many other turns that may be given to this argument; and the conclusion of it is that it is only the general which we can understand. [8.208]

Peirce's argument is that no concept involving infinity, and no process of reasoning involving infinity — such as the calculus — can be consistently employed by a nominalist. If this argument be granted, then it is clear that a nominalist will have a very difficult time in dealing with mathematics or with science, particularly if it should turn out to be the case that real space is infinite. And it is worth pointing out that although Peirce's arguments as to why one who believes in the real infinite is a realist have not been accepted, nevertheless a consistent nominalist must be a finitist in mathematics. For no way has yet been found to construct transfinite numbers without utilizing abstract objects such as sets or classes, and such objects nominalists do not accept.[17]

[17] Willard Quine, *From a Logical Point of View* (Cambridge, Mass., 1953), pp. 128f. Modern nominalists would admit that their position implies finitism only if the universe is finite.

General concepts and laws come under the heading of Thirds, and it is Thirds particularly that are related to continua. Not only are all laws intensively continuous — they are also extensively continuous. Peirce states:

. . . every general concept is, in reference to its individuals, strictly a continuum. This (though asserted by Kant and others) did not appear quite evident as long as the doctrine of generals was restricted to non-relative terms. But in the light of the logic of relatives, the general is seen to be precisely the continuous. Therefore, the doctrine of the reality of continuity is simply that doctrine the scholastics called realism . . .[18]

That is, if all realities are continuous, so that a range of real possibility exists beyond all that can be actual, then to assert a concept or law of all possible things is to assert it of those possibilities as well as of those things which are actual. It was on this basis that Peirce returned to, and revised, his position regarding the diamond.

I myself went too far in the direction of nominalism when I said that it was a mere question of the convenience of speech whether we say that a diamond is hard when it is not pressed upon, or whether we say that it is soft until it is pressed upon. I *now* say that experiment will prove that the diamond is hard, as a positive fact. That is, it is a real fact that it *would* resist pressure, which amounts to extreme scholastic realism. I deny that pragmaticism as originally defined by me made the intellectual purport of symbols to consist in our conduct. On the contrary, I was most careful to say that it consists in our *concept* of what our conduct *would* be upon *conceivable* occasions. [8. 208]

. . . it is plain that no possible collection of single occasions of conduct can be, or adequately represent *all* conceivable occasions. For there is no collection of individuals of any general description which we could not conceive to receive the addition of other individuals of the same description aggregated to it. The generality of the possible, the only true generality, is distributive, not collective. [5.532]

There is however one very serious contradiction which is at once apparent. Synechism holds that all that is is continuous, yet *haecceities*, according to the theory of the modes of being, are the very opposite of

---

[18] "Advertisement for 'How to Reason'," p. 11, IB2 Box 1. "Corresponding to *generality* in *nonrelative* logic is *continuity* in *relative* logic, and the development of the principle of continuity in the light of that logical view and the adoption of it as the central principle of metaphysics is an indication of what I mean by synechism." (C. S. Peirce to F. C. S. Schiller, May 12, 1905, p. 3, Scientific Correspondence.)

the general. The difficulty cannot be escaped by positing the three realms of being as separate universes. Synechism applies to everything there is including the universes. Besides such a theory of wholly separate universes is forbidden by Peirce's cosmology which shows that all that is is mind, including *haecceities* as well. Rather the resolution must be sought by looking more closely at Peirce's concept of *haecceity*. Perhaps his clearest statement of this doctrine is as follows:

> According to this definition, that which alone immediately presents itself as an individual is a reaction against the will. But everything whose identity consists in a continuity of reactions will be a single logical individual. Thus any portion of space, so far as it can be regarded as reacting, is for logic a single individual; its spatial extension is no objection. With this definition there is no difficulty about the truth that whatever exists is individual, since existence (not reality) and individuality are essentially the same thing; and whatever fulfills the present definition equally fulfills . . . the principles of contradiction and excluded middle . . . [3.613]

What we actually experience as individual is the shock of reaction, not the entity. That entity, like all entities, is a construct which serves two basic functions. Like the Boscovichian atom, it is a center of forces or reactions and may therefore be used to represent the point-masses of physics. At the same time it serves as a carrier for inhering qualities, which, by so inhering, become actualized. This thing may be, and ontologically it must be, immaterial, whether it is defined as a point or a vortex. But its existence is dependent solely upon its dynamic functions — not upon its inhering qualities. From this it follows (1) that all qualities of *haecceities* are accidents (1.458), (2) that the Identity of Indiscernibles is false (3.613), and (3) that the identity of the *haecceity* lies in its dynamic functions. (3.434; 3.460; 6.340)

If the self-identity of *haecceity* lies in its dynamic functions, then since identity is continuous in time one of four possibilities must be true. (1) The identity might consist in a "continuity of reactions." (3.613) But this contradicts either the definition of reaction as instantaneous or of continuity — there cannot be a continuum of instantaneous events. (2) The identity might consist in the spatiotemporal continuity of the center of the reactions. But space would then be involved in the definition of *haecceity*, whereas space is defined as a form for *haecceities*. (3) Identity might be defined as a special form of continuity appropriate only to *haecceities*. Actually there is evidence that Peirce seriously considered this alternative, for he speaks of dyadic identity as a relation which has meaning only when applied to *haecceities* (1.446; 1.461; 4.561), he gives identity a special status as a relation among *haecceities* in the Existential Graphs (4.448), and he singles out identity as a special form of continuous relation.[19] Yet there are strong objections to this view. For Peirce also states that triple identity is not reducible to dyadic identity (4.561), and the argument concerning the special status of identity as a continuous relation is unclear. Peirce holds that this relation is continuous because, in the formula $x = y$, any number of correlates can be interposed between $x$ and $y$. But this is true of every symmetric and transitive relation — e.g., "of the same hue as" among colors — and therefore is not peculiar either to this relation or to relations among *haecceities*. Accordingly, if Peirce does regard identity as a special sort of continuity for *haecceities*, the case is certainly not clearly made. (4) The identity may consist in the regularity of reactions. (1.411) In this latter case, however, the identity consists in a law, and the fact that the law is general means that the *haecceity* is likewise general. This actually appears to be the most reasonable position. It does not reduce Secondness to Thirdness, since the reactions themselves remain irreducibly Seconds (3.613; 4. 157), nor does it compromise the principle that existence consists in reactions. (3.613; 6.330) And *haecceities* still remain subject to excluded middle and noncontradiction at any one instant, since an instant is a point of temporal discontinuity.

Synechism is the doctrine that all that is is continuous. In order to prove this proposition Peirce employs an argument of three steps, the first of which is that time is a true (Peircean) continuum. That this is so Peirce holds to be a fact of direct perception as we have seen above.[20] Yet although the direct perception of temporal continuity is necessary to explain how we have the idea of continuity and to furnish an observational basis for asserting continuity of time, it is obvious that Peirce cannot, by direct perception, distinguish a true continuum from a pseudocontinuum (Cantorian continuum). Such a distinction can only be made by reason upon an analysis of the content of the per-

[19] See above, pp. 317f.
[20] See above, p. 386.

ception. That time is truly continuous is proven for Peirce both by the argument from memory noted above (6.110f), and by arguments of the same sort as Zeno's. (1.276) Namely, if time were not truly continuous, any sort of motion or change in time would be impossible, since an infinite series of discrete steps would have to be completed during the process. (1.276) If these arguments are granted, then Peirce can show that there is at least one thing — namely time — which is continuous.

The next step in the argument is to show that more than one thing is continuous and to do this Peirce invokes a regulative principle: "The reality of continuity once admitted, the next question is what are we to regard as continuous and what as discontinuous? . . . to say that anything is continuous is to leave possibilities open which are closed by asserting that it is discontinuous. Accordingly a regulative principle of logic requires us to hold each thing as continuous until it is proved discontinuous." [21] This argument rests upon two premises: first, that we should always adopt the hypothesis which admits the greatest number of possibilities, and, second, that the hypothesis that things are continuous offers more possibilities than the contrary hypothesis. The latter principle is demonstrated by the fact that the multiplicity of possibilities in the continuum infinitely exceeds any discrete multitude. Hence, for example, to say that all colors form a continuum is to admit the possibility of "more" colors than are possible if there is only a discrete multitude of distinct colors. Therefore, Peirce argues, one should always assume that something is continuous until there is reason for believing otherwise.

The final step of the argument is now obvious. "But absolute discontinuity cannot be proved to be real, nor can any good reason for believing it real be alleged. We thus reach the conclusion that as a regulative principle, at least, ultimate continuity ought to be presumed everywhere." [22] The crucial word is "absolute." As we have seen in discussing the Listing theorem, a continuum, for example a surface, can be limited by a continuum, for example a line, and therefore the fact that a continuum is interrupted does not suffice to demonstrate that the thing which interrupts it is itself noncontinuous. To demonstrate that, it would have to be shown that the entity in question was absolutely

---

[21] "How to Reason," pp. 10f.
[22] *Ibid.*, p. 11.

discrete — determinate in every respect. But every entity either endures through some interval of time or it does not. If it does, then, since time is continuous, the entity has temporal continuity and must therefore involve possibilities of determination which remain unactualized. If it does not, then I think Peirce would hold that such an entity could never become an object of knowledge. A percept of such an object, if there could be such a percept, could only represent it as an instantaneous flash, unrepeated and wholly unique. Of such an object, nothing could be known and the assumption of its reality would therefore be unwarrantable since nothing would be explained by it. Accordingly, Peirce holds that we must assume all things to be continuous until reason be found for the contrary assumption, and that no such reason can ever be found.

Since all things are continuous, it follows that in particular those things which constitute the extensions of universals are continuous. Peirce's synechism is thus a much more extreme form of realism than the moderate position of Scotus, to whose school he sometimes claimed to belong. The Scotian position is that universals are real because there are real things in the world corresponding to those universals. Those real things, however, are singular, and the common nature which appears as universal in the mind, appears in the external object as singular.[23] But as Peirce remarks, "Even Duns Scotus is too nominalistic when he says that universals are contracted to the mode of individuality in singulars, meaning, as he does, by singulars, ordinary existing things." (8.208) Peirce's position is that universals are real because there are real continua which correspond to them, and these continua are themselves of a general nature. Although Peirce is not a Platonist, since continua are not Platonic archetypes, his position is as extreme a realism as Plato's, since for both the referent of the universal is a real general entity.

Even more than the reality of the traditional universals, Peirce insisted upon the reality and physical efficacy of laws. That laws correspond to real continua is easily shown from Peirce's position, for, as Boole had long before noted,[24] any universal proposition is interpretable as referring to the temporal occasions upon which it is true. Thus

[23] See above, pp. 126ff.
[24] Boole, *Laws*, pp. 164ff.

"(x) $\phi$x" means "$\phi$x always" or "at all times $\phi$x", and "all times" form a continuum. But that laws are physically efficient can, I think, only be understood by regarding them as habits of an organic universe which exert a felt compulsion. (5.431) [25] Anyone who has ever had to break a deeply ingrained habit such as smoking knows very well from personal experience that some form of genuine compulsion is involved in habit.

The fact that all physical laws determine a temporal continuum means that they are equal in respect to the multiplicity of instances to which they apply. But Peirce does not appear to have regarded all continua as being of equal multiplicity. His position on this point is not wholly clear: in one passage he states that the number of points on a surface is equal to the number of points on a line (6.118) [26] — in another he states that it is the square of the number of points on the line. (4.226) These two statements are not necessarily contradictory since the number might be one whose square was equal to itself, but the fact that Peirce does regard a continuum as more general the more dimensions it has strongly suggests the latter view. (6.132) Actually, since Peirce held that the continuum is not a point set and therefore its magnitude cannot be given in the concept of it, such a question does not, strictly speaking, admit of an answer. But dimensionality is a topological characteristic of pure continua which can be given a numerical statement, even though the continuum itself is taken to be a pure continuum of possibility, and it certainly seems evident on a common sense basis that an n-dimensional continuum must contain "more" possibilities than an n-1 dimensional continuum. It would thus be exceedingly easy to regard the infinite series of continua of increasing dimensionality as a series of multiplicities coming after the series of multitudes. This would seem to be the clear implication of the closing paragraph of the 1897 paper on multitudes; "The multiplicity of points upon a surface must be admitted, as it seems to me, to be the square of that of the points of a line, and so with higher dimensions. The multitude of dimensions may be of any discrete multitude." (4. 226) After all, the fact that the cardinal number of the set of points

---

[25] Gallie, *Peirce and Pragmatism*, p. 202.

[26] It should, however, be borne in mind that Peirce later rejected his statement of continuity in this paper.

in an n-dimensional space is equal to that of the set of points on a line is so far from obvious that Cantor himself remarked of his own proof of this theorem, "Je le vois, mais je ne le crois pas." [27]

The belief that multiplicity increases with increasing dimensionality is of great importance in understanding the consequences which Peirce drew from synechism regarding the course of metaphysical evolution. For together with the principle that relations are only possible as determinations of antecedent continua, it means that evolution must proceed from continua of higher dimensionality to continua of lower dimensionality. The initial continuum must therefore be of maximum dimensionality, and every specialization of it will constitute a topical singularity of lower dimensionality. That is to say, let the original continuum be conceived as an n-dimensional continuum so that n variables are required to fix the position of a point. Now let any determinate relation be developed such that the values of one of the n variables are expressible as a function of the remaining $n - 1$. For example:

$$x_n = F(x_1 \ldots x_{n-1}).$$

Geometrically what is determined by this equation is a continuum of n-1 dimensions imbedded in an n-dimensional continuum. From the standpoint of the containing continuum the equation defines an arbitrary discontinuity or singularity which would be a Second. At the same time, from the standpoint of the contained continuum, the equation defines a law or regularity since for the elements which it contains certain possibilities of variation are elimininated. Of course in pure continua, metrical considerations are eliminated, so that "position" is meaningless. Nevertheless, the singularity formula

$$(g^s - g^p) \cdot (d^p - d^s) = S$$

has virtually the same meaning as the above equation for the topical singularity constituting the law would admit of less possibilities of variation (beginning generations) than the containing continuum and so would constitute a regularity within it. [28] Thus successive differentiations of the original continuum would lead to more and more determinate systems, each constituting a singularity in the preceding system. Thus Peirce writes: "As metaphysics teaches that there is a succes-

---

[27] Fraenkel, *Set Theory*, p. 139.
[28] See above, p. 207.

sion of realities of higher and higher order, each a generalization of the last, and each the limit of a reality of the next higher order, so space presents points, lines, surfaces, and solids, each generated by the motion of a place of lower dimensionality and the limit of a place of next higher dimensionality." (1.501)

Peirce's descriptions of the process of cosmic evolution are brief, vague, and somewhat metaphorical, but it is nevertheless clear that they are psychological models of the above theory. Thus for example in 1898 Peirce described the cosmic process as follows:

> Let the clean blackboard be a sort of diagram of the original vague potentiality. . . . I draw a chalk line on the board. This discontinuity is one of those brute acts by which alone the original vagueness could have made a step toward definiteness. There is a certain element of continuity in this line. Where did this continuity come from? It is nothing but the original continuity of the blackboard which makes everything upon it continuous. [6.203]

It will be noted that the line, although itself continuous, is a brute reaction relative to the containing continuum. Such relative Seconds will occur in the original continuum in a sporadic and random fashion, but without forming any consistent pattern or regularity. Hence no lasting differentiation can occur until some development occurs which permits these Seconds to repeat and endure. Such a development would be furnished by the birth of a tendency to form habits. "This habit is a generalizing tendency, and as such a generalization, and as such a general, and as such a continuum of continuity. It must have its origin in the original continuity which is inherent in potentiality. Continuity, as generality, is inherent in potentiality, which is essentially general." (6.204) Thus the law of habit is likewise a particular determination of the original continuum, which arises, like all determinations, as a singularity in the greater continuum. But this particular sport, being a tendency for sports to repeat, will perpetuate itself.

> Once the line will stay a little after it is marked, another line may be drawn beside it. Very soon our eye persuades us there is a *new* line, the envelope of those others. This rather prettily illustrates the logical process which we may suppose takes place in things, in which the generalizing tendency builds up new habits from chance occurrences. The new curve, although it is new in its distinctive character, yet derives its continuity from the continuity of the blackboard itself. [6.206]

This process is essentially a form of ampliative inference, and illustrates Peirce's thesis that the universe creates order by the use of the same logical processes which we employ to discover that order. Generalizations are thus built up from particulars by abduction and induction, these generalizations being themselves singularities in the containing continuum. By a continual repetition of this process, it is clear that more and more determinate systems would be created, each of which would then serve as a containing continuum for another and still more determinate system.

The model upon which Peirce based his metaphysics quite obviously is the topology of Listing. And this is in fact what one would expect, for his work in mathematics had led him to the conclusion that topology is the mathematics of pure continua. If there is any formal system therefore which ought to provide the key to the synechistic world, it is synectics or topology. Yet Peirce's topology was precisely the rock upon which his system foundered. Mathematically speaking, the Listing theorem is a low level theorem of very little power. Yet it was the only theorem of topology which Peirce had. Again and again in the later papers Peirce writes, "How are we to establish a method of reasoning about continuity in philosophy?" [29] "I find that when a continuum is met with, it does not suffice for the purposes [of] objective logic to say that the objects are continuous, it is necessary to examine the special nature of the continuum minutely. Its dimensionality must be ascertained, its Listing numbers, its singularities." [30] But when this has been done, what then? The topology which Peirce possessed was hopelessly inadequate to the demands he made upon it; the topology Peirce needed was still a thing of the future, and when it was discovered it was to be developed on principles diametrically opposed to his.[31] The only thing he could do in such a situation was to give the widest possible application to the few theorems he did have, even when it meant extending them almost by analogy.

In a late paper entitled "Continuity the Master Key," Peirce recounts something of the history of his own struggle with the concept of the continuum. Having been brought up in a mathematician's house-

[29] "The Logic of Continuity," p. 1.
[30] "Considerations for Eight Lectures," p. 2.
[31] Cf. pp. 194f, 280f. It was precisely Cantor's theory of continuity which made possible the set theoretic reconstruction of topology.

hold, he states, "It is no wonder that I was led at the very outset to think that one great desideratum in all theorizing was to make fuller use of the principle of continuity." [32] He then describes how with Cantor's help he finally attained an adequate definition of continuity and how, after considerable difficulty, he came to the certainty that there are real continua.

> Hitherto the uses of the principle of continuity have been quite restricted. Commonly it has been used only in a negative way. . . .
>
> For me, on the contrary, upon the first assault of the enemy, when pressed for the explanation of any fact, I lock myself up in my castle of impregnable logic and squirt out melted continuity upon the heads of my besiegers below.
>
> I do not merely use it subjectively as a way of looking at things, but objectively put it forward to account for all interaction between mind and body, mind and mind, body and body.
>
> This is a damned easy way of explaining things, my critics will say (I mean the really *noumenal* ones will say this) but how is this to be verified by observations? Good, I applaud this objection; and if I do not answer it satisfactorily set me down as a failure if not a humbug.[33]

But Peirce did not and could not answer this objection. He was convinced that in the concept of the continuum he had found the "master key" to philosophy. His set-theoretic proofs seemed to demonstrate that in his theory of continuity he had not only the precise mathematical definition of generality, but the basis for an irrefutable argument against nominalism. He firmly believed that he was on the right road toward establishing a philosophic system which would be a new synthesis of religion and science upon a thoroughly realistic foundation. As Peirce envisaged it, this system was to have been a great architectonic structure embracing all present knowledge and serving as a guide to future discovery. Its foundation was to have been mathematics and formal logic which would supply a priori the possible formal categories of thought, while the content of these categories would come from phenomenology. Upon this base would be built the normative theory of inquiry, which would supply the aim and methods of investigation for all areas of knowledge. Then should have come the metaphysics. The proof that everything is continuous would establish his realism while the principle of objective idealism would bring mental

[32] "Logic of Events. Continuity the Master Key," p. 1, IB3.
[33] *Ibid.*, p. 4.

and physical phenomena into a single ideal system. It should then have been possible, through the mathematics of continua, to determine the general outlines of not only the present but the future cosmos in sufficient detail so that all the future discoveries of special sciences would appear as the furnishing of a house already built. As Peirce wrote:

The undertaking which this volume inaugurates is to make a philosophy like that of Aristotle, that is to say, to outline a theory so comprehensive that, for a long time to come, the entire work of human reason, in philosophy of every school and kind, in mathematics, in psychology, in physical science, in history, in sociology, and in whatever other department there may be, shall appear as the filling up of its details. [1.1]

Such was the system Peirce dreamed of building, but the grand design was never realized.

As one reads through the thousands of pages of manuscript which are all that remain from Peirce's life's labor, one cannot escape the feeling that these are the ruins of a once great structure. Every paragraph and every doctrine seem to be fragmentary parts of some larger whole. As Morris Cohen has remarked: "In his [Peirce's] early papers, in the *Journal of Speculative Philosophy*, and in his later papers, in the *Monist*, we get indeed glimpses of a vast philosophic system on which he was working with an unusual wealth of material and apparatus." [34] But this is an illusion — Peirce's illusion: the grand design was never fulfilled. The reason is that Peirce was never able to find a way to utilize the continuum concept effectively. The magnificent synthesis which the theory of continuity seemed to promise somehow always eluded him, and the shining vision of the great system always remained a castle in the air.

[34] "Charles S. Peirce and a Tentative Bibliography of His Published Writings," *Journal of Philosophy, Psychology and Scientific Methods*, XIII, 727 (December 21, 1916).

# APPENDIX

# Preliminary Drafts of the "New List of Categories"[1]

## Draft 1.

## Chapter I.

The highest conception of all is that of being, that is, what is implied in the copula of a proposition. This conception is not given in the impressions of sense, but it is the final stroke which binds the elements of the judgment into unity. Its function is to unite the predicate to the subject; it is, therefore, immediately justified by the fact that a predicate cannot be brought into the understanding as such without it.

Being is a conception entirely without content. Character is the ground of being; whatever is, is by being somehow. A ground or reason is a predicate which enables us to draw an inference; therefore all character is ground. Ground then is the last prescindible conception with content. *Ground* itself is not given in the impressions of sense, but is the result of generalization. Now generalization is of related things; so that the function of the conception of a ground or character is to unite relate and correlate; it is justified therefore by the fact that without it reference to a correlate is unintelligible. I hold that that which immediately justifies an abstraction is the next highest element of cognition. Accordingly, next to possession of a character or reference to a ground comes reference to a correlate. This reference to a correlate is itself not given in the sensation, but requires an act of comparison, that is a determining of the imagination of one term by that of another. One term is united to the imagination by the reference of it to its correlate. The function, therefore, of the reference to a correlate is to perform the junction; and it is justified by the fact that the reference to the determinable image is only intelligible by saying that A refers to B as its correlate. Now the reference to a determinable image though not intelligible in the sensation (for sense does not understand) is yet just what constitutes sensation. This therefore completes the chain of elementary conceptions.

## Draft 2.

## Logic. Chapter I.

No study seems so trivial as that of formal logic, not only at first sight but until after long research. It is far too indeterminate to be of much use in actual reasoning, and it is too simple to interest like mathematics by involutions and

---

[1] The four manuscripts here reproduced are from IB2 Box 8. Starred numbers in square brackets indicate manuscript page numbers.

resolutions of forms. It has, however, a deep significance, one which was perceived most clearly by Aristotle and Kant and the recognition of which gave their two philosophies such preeminent vitality. It is the circumstance that the commonest and most indispensable conceptions are nothing but objectifications of logical forms. The categories of Kant are derived from the logical analysis of judgments, and those of Aristotle (framed before the accurate separation of syntax and logic) are derived from a half-logical half-grammatical analysis of propositions. Now upon the table [of] categories philosophy is erected, — not merely metaphysic but the philosophy of religion, of morals, of law, and of every science. To form a table of the categories is, therefore, the great end of logic.

Kant first formed a table of the various logical divisions of judgment, and then deduced his categories directly from these. For example, corresponding to a categorical form of judgment is the relation of substance and accident, and corresponding to the hypothetical form is the relation of cause and effect. The correspondences between the functions of judgment and the categories are obvious and certain. So far the method is perfect. Its defect is that it affords no warrant for the correctness of the preliminary table, and does not display that direct reference to the unity of consistency which alone gives validity to the categories.

Partly in order to remedy this defect, Hegel produced his logic. He begins at the unity of being and runs through the categories guided by the homogeneousness of their internal relationships, and ends with the functions of judgment. He brought to the task such a surpassing genius for this kind of thought, that [by] the result of his labor, this inverted method must be finally judged. Now his procedure does not seem to give determinate solutions; but the results seem to be arbitrary; for whereas he has finally arrived at the same divisions of the judgment as were made by Kant and currently received at Hegel's day, the more recent researches of logic have essentially modified these and have shown them to be wrong.

The method which ought to be adopted is one which derives the categories from the functions of judgment but which has its starting-point in pure being. The first step of such a process may be described beforehand. Sensation presents a manifold and this manifold must be conjoined under the unity of consistency. Now to combine the manifold of the immediately present, in general, requires the introduction of a conception not given, precisely as the manifold of optical phenomena can only be reduced to harmony by the foreign conception of a luminiferous ether. But perhaps this introduced conception in order to be combined [*2] with the immediately present requires the introduction of another conception. And so on, until the conception of being, which *is* the unity of consistency, can be directly applied. If, therefore, we begin with the conception of being and ask what it is that it conjoins to that which is present, we shall have the first conception under it. Then if we ask what *this* conception conjoins to that which is present we shall have the second conception. And we can proceed in this way until we finally arrive at the conception which directly combines together the immediately present, in general. This procedure seems to be absolutely determinative and to give no room for anything arbitrary. Now let us put it in practice.

The final unity of consistency is given by the conception of being, which is the force of the copula of a proposition. It is a conception without content, that is, to say that A is, is to say nothing of it. On this account its introduction requires no justification but its own possibility. Its function is to combine the subject presented with the predicate, and it is therefore possible whenever there is a predicate. Predicating, therefore, or abstracting from reference to a mind possession of character is the first conception with content. Character is the ground of being; whatever is, is by being *somehow*; at least, so we must conceive the matter. Character is then always a ground, and as ground is also always a character; the two terms are coextensive. Reference to a ground i.e. possession of a character is not a conception given in the impressions of sense but is the result of generalization. Now, generalization is from related things; so that the immediate function of reference to a ground is to unite relate and correlate, and hence its introduction is justified by the fact that without it reference to a correlate is unintelligible. Accordingly, reference to a correlate is the second conception with content. This conception is itself not given in sensation, but is the result of comparison. Now comparison is the determination of a representation by the medium of that which is present, in contradistinction to its determination simply by that which is present. For example, I put A into relation to B, when in contemplating A, I as it were see B through it. The representation determined by the medium of A, may be called its *correspondent*. Then the immediate function of reference to a correlate is to conjoin that which is presented with its correspondent, and the introduction of the former conception is justified by the fact that only by it is the latter made representable. Accordingly reference to a correspondent is the third conception with content. This conception is itself not in what is immediately present in its elements. But it is directly applied to the immediately present in general; for the bringing of the elementary sensations together into a notion of the immediately present in general, requires the introduction of the conception that this general represents its particulars, and in the conception of representation that of image determined as correspondent is contained.

We have, then, a uniform chain of conceptions stretching from [*3] pure being to the intuition in general. Now the three links composing this chain, namely, reference to a ground, to a correlate, and to a correspondent afford the elements for a complete system of logic.

Abstraction or Precision is of two kinds; by obscuration and by position. Thus, *two* may be prescinded from *units* by neglecting to make distinct the fact that it is always even in conception composed of units. On the other hand an elastic incompressible medium may be considered abstractly of any phenomena of light or heat, by neglecting to take account of the circumstances which alone could give rise to such a conception. Neither kind of precision is at all the same as *partition* or separation by the imagination. The distinction between imagining and conceiving is part of the very alphabet of philosophy. To imagine is [to] reproduce in the mind elementary sensible intuitions and to take them up in some order so as to make an image. To conceive is to collect under a supposition, to make a hypothesis, and therefore cannot dispense with the use of words. Thus, we comprehend phenomena of polarization by the conception of a perfectly elastic incompressible solid. No one can imagine such a solid, because nothing like it is met with in experience except surfaces. But we can conceive it very well inasmuch as we can consistently state its deduced properties. Now, it is clear from what has been said, that the reference to a ground may be prescinded by position from the reference to a correlate, and the latter in the same way from reference to a correspondent. Whereas, the reference to a correspondent cannot be prescinded by position from reference to correlate, nor this from reference to a ground. This fact, affords the basis for a division of *attributes* into three kinds. First, such as contain only reference to a ground; or simple *Qualities*. Second, such as contain references to a ground and a correlate necessarily connected together; or real *Relations*. Third, such as involve references to a ground, a correlate, and a correspondent, necessarily connected together; or *Representations*.

Relations on account of their double reference will be separable again into two kinds; and relations [2] on account of their triple reference, will be separable into three kinds. To begin with relations.

## Draft 3.

The first conception of all is that of substance or that which *is*.

Whatever is is of some kind; were it not of some sort there would be no necessity for supposing it to be. This conception, therefore, of Internal Mark or Quality (which is the same, objectified) — is the generalization of that which receives its physical explanation by the hypothesis that it is, though it is a generalization which can only be made in the light of the theory of *substance*. It is therefore a new law; namely, that whatever is must have a *ground* or general essence. This ground, to which being such and such, is reference to, when prescinded from this reference is pure form or Idea.

Of whatever kind anything is, it is in comparison with something else; Quality is only the outside of substance and implies therefore something without. This notion which appears as Relation or Act — according as it is viewed subjectively or objectively, is the second generalization which that of Quality enables us to make. What is must not only have a *ground* but also and therefore, an *object*. This *object*, regarded abstractly, is matter.

In whatever relation anything is, it is for some purpose effect or actuality, if nobody should make a comparison the comparison would not be made. This notion of representation or purpose — according as it is taken as logical or real — is a third generalization which succeeds to that of Relativity. What is, has a *ground*, since it has also an *object*, has in the third place a *subject*. This *subject*, which must not be supposed to be a mind though it may be a human representation, and which is only that which is determined by the representation to agree with it in its reference to the object on that ground, — this subject is an abstraction which the philosophers have left too much out of account.

There is no fourth generalization which can be made in this line.

Each of these three general conceptions reference to the ground, reference to the object, and reference to the subject, has three phases the Grammatical, Logical, and Real or as I prefer to say the Rhetorical. The grammatical phase comes first. The first element of grammar is the noun or rather the pronoun, *This*; then the reference of this to the ground is the application of the verb; the reference to the object is the suffering object; and the reference to the subject is the personal object. Grammarians enumerate two other completing objects viz. — the genitive and factitive. But a genitive object is only a suffering object which is considered particularly in its reaction; while the factitive object is philosophically a part of

---

[2] Obviously this should be "representations."

4 1 4

the verb for if I make a man a barbarian (or barbarize him) what particular barbarian I make him is only the barbarian which *that* man would be. Application of the verb, of the suffering object; and of the personal object; appear in logic as three kinds of marks; 1st the internal mark or the character of a term considered in itself; second the relation to a particular term; and third representation as a character of a term. The internal mark, Relation, and representation; in their transcendental (or rhetorical) transformation, appear as quality, event, and purposeful act.

But the purport of the above generalizations is that whatever is has a ground and then an object, and then a subject. That every noun has a verb applicable is obvious. But every verb does not appear to have a suf . . . [Manuscript breaks off here.]

## Draft 4.

## INTRODUCTION

### §1 Impressions.

*Intuition* is a term, which by the consent of philosophers stands for *immediate cognition*; but what *immediate cognition* stands for is not quite so well settled. In its most approved sense, however, it means any mental representation which does not represent its object by representing another conscious representation of the latter; in other words, it is that knowledge between which and the thing no other representation in consciousness, intervenes. Unfortunately, this definition turns on the word *consciousness*, a sadly equivocal expression, itself. Still, the widest acceptation of this term, to include the presentative character of all that is within us, is to be preferred both on the ground of usage and because it is the only way we have of expressing that most important conception. Thus interpreted, *immediate cognition* is the same as what is otherwise termed an ultimate fact; that is, a premiss not itself a conclusion, an empirical constituent of Knowledge not itself containing non-empirical parts, in short, an *impression*.

Whether there be any such ultimate premisses is a difficult question. It amounts, however, merely to this; whether the boundary of consciousness is in consciousness or out of it. In which ever way it be decided, the employment of a word to denote that boundary is legitimate.

No one can know what an Impression is like, in itself; for a recognized difference [*2] between two impressions would be a difference between them *as compared*, that is as mediately known, and not between them *in themselves*. An impression in itself is an uncomprehended impression, and hence, an undifferentiated sensation, like the feeling of our heart's motion. Colour is sometimes given as an example of an impression. It is a bad one; because the simplest colour is almost as complicated as a piece of music. Colour depends upon the *relations* between different parts of the impression; and, therefore, the differences between colours are differences between harmonies; and to see this difference we must have the elementary impressions whose relation makes the harmony. So that colour is not an impression, but an inference.

Whatever part impressions play in our Knowledge, they need to [be] reduced by the understanding to the unity of consistency and therefore to be combined, and that not by chaotic aggregation but in a determinate form. This form or way of combining impressions is an element of cognition not given in the impressions combined, but added to them in order to reduce them to the requisite unity. It is, therefore, a *hypothetically* adjoined element; for a hypothesis is something assumed in order to reduce an otherwise incomprehensible *datum* to unity. This element of cognition is termed *conception*.

We have, then, first an infinite manifold of points of impression upon the circumference of consciousness. Second, these are embraced into different groups by conceptions and these conceptions by others until one conception is universal and embraces all. Third, if this conception [*3] has any manifoldness, it is itself subjected to another; and so on until Fourthly, all are subjected to the unity of consistency or *I think* which is the centre of consciousness.

[Note. §2 should come after §4.] [2]

## §2. Precision, Discrimination, and Dissociation.

Precision and abstraction are two terms for the same process; and are now limited not merely to separation by the mind, but even to a particular kind of mental separation, namely, that by *attention* to one point and *neglect* of another. That which is attended to is said to be *prescinded*; and that which is neglected is said to be *abstracted from*. The definition should be strictly adhered to, however narrowly it may limit the application of the terms. Attention is a definite conception — or *supposition* of one element of consciousness, without any positive *supposition* of the other.

*Abstraction*, therefore, supposes a greater distinction between its members than *discrimination* which is the mere recognition of the difference between the presence or absence of an element of cognition; but it supposes less distinction than *dissociation* which is the consciousness of one thing without the necessary simultaneous consciousness of the other. Thus, I can discriminate, red from blue, space from colour, and colour from space; but not red from colour. I can prescind, red from blue, and space from colour (as [*4] is manifest from the fact that I actually believe that there is an uncolored space between my face and the page) but I cannot prescind colour from space, nor red from colour. I can dissociate red from blue, but I cannot dissociate space from colour, colour from space, nor red from colour. In the following table *O* shows what I can hold and X what I cannot hold.

|  | by discrim: | by precision: | by dissoc: |
|---|---|---|---|
| blue without red: | *O* | *O* | *O* |
| space without colour: | *O* | *O* | X |
| colour without space: | *O* | X | X |
| red without colour: | X | X | X |

If A can be discriminated or dissociated from B, B can also be separated from A, in the same way. But precision is not thus reciprocal; but on the contrary it is frequently the case that though A cannot be prescinded from B, B can be prescinded

[2] Peirce's note on the manuscript at this point.

from A. This circumstance is easily accounted for. Elementary conceptions only arise upon the occasion of experience; that is they are produced for the first time according to a general law the condition of which is the existence of certain impressions. Now if a conception does not reduce the impressions which it accompanies to unity, it would be a mere arbitrary addition to the latter, for there is no other condition for the production of a conception except that it shall make impressions comprehensible. Now if the impressions [*5] could be definitely conceived without the conception, the conception would not reduce them to unity. But attention is definite conception; therefore impressions (or more immediate conceptions) cannot be attended to, to the neglect of an elementary conception which reduces them to unity. On the other hand, when such a conception has once been obtained, there is no reason in general why the premisses which have occasioned it should not be neglected, and therefore the explaining conception may abstract from the more immediate ones and from the impressions.

## §3. Substance.

Impression in general or as such, is itself by virtue of its generality not an impression but a conception. An impression does not so much as conceive itself to be an impression. It is an undifferentiated feeling whose vagueness is feebly shadowed forth by that sense of dyspepsia which tinges a man's sentiments with melancholy without being directly noticed. Any reflection upon an impression, since it is a step toward bringing it to the unity of consistency, is a conception. To say, therefore, that this or that is an ultimate fact or even that it is present or is a fact, begins to go beyond the immediate fact itself and to be a hypothesis. Hence the predicate of such a statement, or *what is present in general*, is a hypothetic conception; that is, it cannot be applied to a subject without hypothesis. [*6] The hypothetic character of that predicate, however, consists merely in the impression's being viewed subjectively or reflected upon as being present. Now this reflection does nothing more than enable us to differentiate [*interlineated*: discriminate] the character of the fact from the fact itself; and therefore to say that "A is immediately present" is merely to say that A can have attached to it a predicate, real or verbal. But as this predicate is left entirely indeterminate, what has been said of A is an empty form. It has, therefore, the form of hypothesis without its matter; it is the starting-goal of all hypothetic thought. This conception of the immediately present as such, since it implies merely that A is the subject of a proposition, but not the predicate (since predicates are mediate cognitions) is properly indicated by the term *substance*.

## §4: Being.

When we can make a proposition, we *understand* the subject of it so far as the predicate indicates. Thus, when we say "man is intelligent," we have an understanding of *man* in respect to his mind. It is undoubtedly very confused in this instance, but the fact that it can only be made more distinct by predicating still more of man, shows that the unity to which the understanding reduces impressions is the unity of a proposition. This unity consists in the connection of the predicate with the subject; and introduces the conception of *being*, or that which is implied

in the copula. The copula has two meanings, *actually is* and *would be*, as in the two
[*7] expressions "There *is* no griffin" and "A griffin *is* an winged quadruped." But
as both these propositions afford understanding of their subjects, the meanings of
the copulas should be comprehended under *being*.

*Being* introduces nothing into the thought; for "A griffin is or would be" means
nothing. Hence, this conception is not materially hypothetical. It is rather the end
of all hypothesis — the accomplishment of that unity for which hypotheses are
instituted. If we say, "The ink is black," the ink is the *substance*, from which its
blackness has not been differentiated; and the *is* while it leaves the substance just
as it was seen, explains its confusedness by the application of blackness to it, as a
hypothetical predicate.

Though *being* does not affect the subject, it implies an indefinite determina-
bility of the predicate. For, if one could know the copula and predicate of the
proposition, — as ". . . is a tailed-man," he would know that the predicate
applied to something supposeable, at least. Accordingly, we have propositions
whose subjects are entirely indefinite as "There is a beautiful ellipse," where the
subject is *something* merely. But we have no propositions whose predicate is
entirely indeterminate for it would be quite senseless to say "A has the common
characters of all things," since there is no such character. Hence, to say that
*quality* has being or finds being, means something; but to say that *substance* had
being is absurd for it must cease [*8] to be substance before being or non-being,
in the present sense, are applicable to it.

The substance and being are the two poles of thought. Substance is the beginning, being the *end* of all conception. Substance is inapplicable to a predicate, *being*
is equally so to a subject.

## §5 Method of Searching for the Categories.

Every conception is introduced for the purpose of bringing the manifold to
unity; and in the case of an elementary conception this function is a condition of
the possibility of the conception's arising. A universal conception is one which is
applicable to every aggregate of impressions. The end of such a conception is either
to unite the manifold of substance in general or to conjoin to the latter some conception necessary to its being brought to unity.

These facts afford the basis for the mode of discovering all the conceptions
which reduce the manifold substance to the unity of being. For if we begin with
being and ask what it conjoins to substance, the answer will be easily obtained by observing the occasion of the introduction of being. Then the application to substance
of this conception, which being joins to it, is the immediate justification and condition of the introduction of being, and is, therefore, the first conception in order
in passing from being to substance. Now we may treat this conception in the same
way in which we have treated being. That is, we may ask 1st what is the occasion
of the introduction of this conception 2nd What conception besides substance is
required in such a state of cognition, which is joined [*9] to substance by the
given conception. Then this second conception is the next conception in order in
passing from being to substance. And we may repeat this process until we get to a
conception which does not unite anything to substance but only brings the manifold of substance itself together and, this will be the last conception.

These conceptions between *being* and *substance* are termed accidents; and the universal conceptions are termed *categories*.

Categories
$$\begin{cases} \text{Being} \\ \text{Accidents} \\ \text{Substance} \end{cases} \qquad \begin{cases} \text{Quality} \\ \text{Relation} \\ \text{Representation} \end{cases}$$

It should be noticed that throughout this process of finding the categories as well as throughout the book, *introspection* is never resorted to. Nothing is assumed respecting what is thought which cannot be securely inferred from admissions which the thinker will make concerning external facts.

## §6 The Ground.

The conception of *being* arises upon the formation of a proposition. A proposition, besides a term to express the substance, always has another to express the quality of that substance; and the function of the conception of being is to unite the quality to the substance. Quality, therefore, is the first conception in order in passing from being to substance.

Quality, at first sight, like every other elementary conception, seems [*10] given in the impression. Such results of introspection are untrustworthy.

A proposition asserts the applicability of a mediate conception to a more immediate one, — asserts, that is, that the former affords a means of reducing the latter to unity. Since this is *asserted*, the more mediate conception is clearly regarded independently of this circumstance, for otherwise the two conceptions would not be distinguished, but one would be thought through the other, without this latter being an object of thought, at all. The mediate conception, then, in order to be *asserted* to be applied to the other must be considered first without regard to this circumstance, and taken immediately. But, taken immediately it transcends what is given [in] the more immediate conception, and its applicability to the latter becomes hypothetical. Take, for example, the proposition "Ink is black." Here, the conception *ink* is the more immediate, that of *black* the more mediate, which to be predicated of the former must be discriminated from it and considered *in itself*, not as applied to an object but simply as embodying a quality, *blackness*. Now this *blackness*, is a pure *species* or abstraction, and its application is entirely hypothetical.

In the words of a philosopher of the 12th century "cum dicitur 'Socrates est rationalis' hic est sensus 'Socrates est unus de subjectis huic formae quae est rationalitas'." *Embodying rationality* defines *rational*. De Generibus et speciebus. p. 528.

We mean the same thing when we say "the ink is black" as when we say "there is blackness in the ink;" *embodying blackness* defines *black*. The proof is that these conceptions are applied indifferently to precisely the same facts. If, therefore, they were different; the one which was first applied would fulfill every [*11] function of the other; so that one of them would be superfluous. But now a superfluous elementary conception is impossible; for a superfluous conception would be an arbitrary fiction, whereas elementary conceptions arise only upon the requirements of experience. Moreover, the conception of a *pure abstraction* is indispensable, because we cannot comprehend an agreement of two things except as an agreement in some *respect*, and this respect is such a pure abstraction as *blackness*.

The pure abstraction reference to which constitutes a *quality* may be called a *ground*, of the character of the substance which has the quality. Reference to a ground, then, is the first accident. It cannot be prescinded from *being*, but being can be prescinded from it.

## §7 The Correlate.

All students of philosophy know that we become aware of any quality only through the relation of its subject of inhesion to something else; and it is an equally familiar fact that no relation can have place without a quality or reference to a *ground*. The occasion of the introduction of reference to a ground, therefore, is generalization or contrast.

In generalization and contrast, the primary substance has annexed to it a correlate. Reference to a correlate, then, is the next conception in order after reference to a ground. This conception is so easy to seize that no elucidation of it is needed. It cannot [*12] be prescinded from reference to a ground, although this latter can be prescinded from it.

## §8. The Interpretant.

Reference to a correlate is clearly justified and made possible solely by comparison. Let us inquire, then, in what comparison consists. Suppose we wish to compare | and ⊤; we shall imagine one of these letters to be turned over upon the line on which it is written as an axis; we shall then imagine that it is laid upon the other letter and that it is transparent so that we can see that the two coincide. In this way, we shall form a new image which mediates between the two letters, in as much as it represents one when turned over to be an exact likeness of the other. Suppose, we think of a murderer as being in relation to a murdered person; in this case we conceive the act of the murder, and in this conception it is represented that corresponding to every murderer (as well as to every murder) there is a murdered person; and thus we resort again to a mediating representation which represents the relate as standing for a correlate with which the mediating representation is itself in relation. Suppose, we look out the word *homme* in a French dictionary; we shall find opposite to it the word *man*, which, so placed, represents *homme* as representing the same two-legged creature which *man* itself represents. In a similar way, it will be found that every comparison requires, besides the related thing, the ground and the correlate, also a *mediating representation which represents the relate to be a representation of the same correlate* [*13] *which this mediating representation itself represents*. Such a mediating representation, I call an *interpretant*, because it fulfills the office of an interpreter who says that a foreigner says the same thing which he himself says.

Every reference to a correlate, then, unites to the substance a reference to an interpretant; which is, therefore, the next conception in the order we have adopted.

It must not be supposed that in giving a definition of interpretant, we admit at all that reference to an interpretant is a compounded conception. This definition is only a verbal one; for the conception of representation which it introduces itself contains that of reference to an interpretant. Reference to an interpretant, is simply, the *addressing* of an impression to a conception. To *address* or *appeal to*, is an act we, in fact, suppose everything to perform, whether we attend to the circumstance or not. It is unanalysable, I think; though it may be expressed more perspicuously by a periphrasis, as above.

It may perhaps be objected, that since an interpretant is necessarily a correlate, reference to an interpretant is merely a particular determination of the conception of reference to a correlate, and should not be coordinated with the latter. But an interpretant is not referred to as establishing a relation to a correlate, in so far as it is a correlate; it is not therefore *quatenus ipsum* a correlate. [*14] Reference to an interpretant is rendered possible and justified by that which renders possible and justifies comparison. But this is clearly the diversity of impressions. It is plain, that if we had but one impression, this impression would not require to be reduced to unity, and would, therefore, not need to be thought of as referred to an interpretant and the conception of reference to an interpretant would not arise. But the moment there are several impressions, that is a manifoldness of impressions, we have a feeling of complication or confusedness, which leads us to differentiate this impression from that, and they require to be brought to unity. Now they are not brought to unity until we conceive them together as being *ours*, that is, until we refer them to a conception as their interpretant. Thus the reference to an interpretant arises upon the holding together of diverse impressions, and therefore it does not join a conception to the substance, as the other two references do, but unites directly the manifold of the substance, itself. It is therefore the last conception in order in passing from *being* to *substance*.

## §9 Formal Objects.

We have found between the unity of being and the manifold of substance, three universal and necessary (*de omni*) conceptions; namely

Reference to a ground
Reference to a correlate
Reference to an interpretant

[*15] A ground is that pure abstraction, the embodiment of which makes a quality. A correlate is a second substance with which the first is in comparison. An interpretant, is a representation which represents that that which is referred to it is a representation of the same object, which it does itself represent.

These three conceptions are all we require to erect the edifice of logic. Why they should be three is unknown; although a reason can be given for every other logical division. But this number may indicate an anthropological fact.

In the section on precision, it was shown that more immediate conceptions cannot be prescinded from elementary conceptions which explain them; while there is no such impossibility of prescinding the more mediate from the less mediate. Hence, as the order in which we have taken the three references proceeds from the more mediate to the less mediate, it follows that no reference to an interpretant can abstract from reference to a correlate; nor any reference to a correlate from reference to a ground; whereas reference to a ground may be of such a kind that it can be prescinded from reference to a correlate; and reference to a correlate may be such that it can be prescinded from reference to an interpretant. Thus the three references give three prescindible objects, namely,

[*16] 1. Single reference to a ground,

      2. Double reference to ground and correlate,

      3. Triple reference to ground, correlate, and interpretant.

These may be termed Quality, Relation, and Representation and the objects to which they belong as characters, may be called Quale, Relate, and Representamen.

The quale, the relate, and the representamen may be termed formal objects because the prescinded conceptions of them contain no reference to variously determinable impressions.

# §10. Subdivisions of Formal Objects.

# Index of Names

423

# Index of Subjects